THE STUDY OF SOCIAL PROBLEMS

The Study of Social Problems

SEVEN PERSPECTIVES

FIFTH EDITION

Edited by
Earl Rubington
and
Martin S. Weinberg

New York/Oxford
OXFORD UNIVERSITY PRESS
1995

Oxford University Press

Oxford   New York   Toronto
Delhi   Bombay   Calcutta   Madras   Karachi
Kuala Lumpur   Singapore   Hong Kong   Tokyo
Nairobi   Dar es Salaam   Cape Town
Melbourne   Auckland   Madrid

and associated companies in
Berlin   Ibadan

Published by Oxford University Press, Inc.
200 Madison Avenue, New York NY 10016

Library of Congress Cataloging-in-Publication Data

The study of social problems : seven perspectives / [compiled by] Earl
Rubington and Martin S. Weinberg.—5th ed.
p.   cm.   Includes bibliographical references.
ISBN 0-19-508367-9
1. Social problems.   2. Sociology—United States.
I. Rubington, Earl.   II. Weinberg, Martin S.
HN17.5.S837   1995
361.1—dc20   94-29381

9 8 7 6 5 4 3 2 1

Printed in the United States on
Acid-free paper

Dedicated to
Rose L. Rubington
and to the memory of
Herman H. Rubington,
Edith L. Weinberg,
and Fred C. Weinberg

PREFACE

Sociologists have long felt a need for a book that places social problems in a sociological perspective. In addition, instructors of social problems courses have been looking for sociological explanations for, rather than mere descriptions of, various social problems. We planned the first edition of *The Study of Social Problems* to give instructors the backdrop, perspectives, and explanations they sought. In that edition, we examined the five major theoretical sociological perspectives on social problems: Social Pathology, Social Disorganization, Value Conflict, Deviant Behavior, and Labeling. For each perspective, an introductory essay dealt with the people and the works that had fashioned it, the circumstances and stage of American sociology during which it arose, and its essential characteristics. Reprinted readings that exemplified the perspective followed each introductory essay, along with a critique of the perspective. Each chapter ended with questions for discussion and an annotated reference list for further study and exploration. This was the framework with which we hoped to provide a brief but comprehensive survey of social problems theory.

The second and third editions, which took into account some of the criticisms from students and instructors regarding the complexity of some of the introductory essays and reprinted readings, were made clearer and more readable. Sue Kiefer Hammersmith played a major role in editing the introductions so that undergraduates could understand them more readily.

In the fourth edition, we added an increasingly popular sixth perspective, the Critical Perspective. In so doing, we acknowledged the fertility of a variety of holistic perspectives on culture and society that draw from the tradition established by Karl Marx more than a hundred years ago. We thank David Zaret for his helpful comments on a draft of this chapter.

In this edition, the fifth, we have added a seventh perspective, Social Constructionism. This perspective, a synthesis of some earlier ones, has captured the imagination of a whole network of sociologists who study social problems. We thank Joseph Schneider for his help in developing this chapter and William Pridemore for his administrative assistance.

The Study of Social Problems has always been intended for instructors who want to lay a sound theoretical foundation for their courses in social problems. We hope that this new edition will continue to be helpful in this enterprise.

Boston   E.R.
Bloomington   M.S.W.
July 1994

CONTENTS

III. THE PROSPECTS

9. A Sociological Review of the Perspectives, 355

The Seven Perspectives: A Rapid Review, Applicability, The Dual Mandate and Sociological Perspectives, Questions for Discussion, Selected References

I / THE PROBLEM

1 / SOCIAL PROBLEMS AND SOCIOLOGY

The morning paper reports a variety of social problems: war, pollution, traffic jams, and crimes. It also reports a decrease in automobile sales, rising prices, violence in high schools, an increase in drug use and cigarette smoking, and so on. After reading the news, readers find themselves upset about some of these reports, and, wanting to do something about them, they have mixed feelings about other news stories and are neutral or indifferent to many of the stories. On occasion, readers even experience secret or open delight at the misfortunes of others. The variety and inconsistency of these responses point to the complexities that surround the idea of social problems.

In addition, those who analyze social problems often differ among themselves. Some analysts say that modern society produces more social problems than do simpler societies; others disagree. Some say that modern society produces more problems than solutions, but others argue that the real difficulty lies in the overproduction of so-called solutions.

Trying to make sense of all this can easily result in confusion. Yet people continue to study social problems in an effort to understand how they occur and how they can be controlled. And more often than not the people studying social problems have been sociologists.

Sociologists have dominated the study of social problems for two reasons. First, sociology developed about a century ago, just when industrialization and urbanization seemed to be shaking the foundations of traditional society. At that time, there was a special interest in the problems people saw resulting from industrialization and urbanization, and sociologists, sharing this interest, took up the study of social problems as a relevant and challenging topic.

Second, sociology as a discipline lends itself especially well to the study of social problems. Sociology deals with social relations, those situations in which two or more people adapt their conduct to each other's. Most social problems arise in the course of, or as a result of, social relations. Few other disciplines in the late nineteenth century dealt with matters of this kind. Thus, partly by choice and partly by default, sociology arose to deal simultaneously with social problems and with social relations.

In this book, we look at how American sociologists have organized the study of social problems. We focus on the ideas and assumptions that have guided, and continue to guide, that study, and we examine the different perspectives on social problems that sociologists have developed. First, however, we examine just what sociologists mean by the term "social problem," how they came to study social problems, and how sociologists have differed in their treatment of social problems from time to time.

THE DEFINITION OF A SOCIAL PROBLEM

Some of the conditions we consider to be social problems were not so considered in earlier times. And some of the things our grandparents saw as social problems are accepted without question today. Some of the conditions we now ignore will undoubtedly come to be seen as social problems in the future. And there are probably some things that, regardless of their troublesome nature, never have been and never will be considered to be social problems.

What, then, makes a social problem? Sociologists usually consider a social problem to be *an alleged situation that is incompatible with the values of a significant number of people who agree that action is needed to alter the situation.* Let us consider this definition more closely.

An Alleged Situation.   This means that the situation is said to exist. People talk about it, and it may receive coverage on radio, on TV, and in the press. The allegation, however, need not actually be true. For example, a fear commonly expressed by white homeowners has been that desegregation of their neighborhoods would decrease the property values of their homes. Yet often the opposite is actually the case. There has been substantial demand for middle-class housing among blacks, and blacks have systematically been overcharged for such housing. As a result, after an initial period of panic selling by white homeowners, the same homes often sell for more after desegregation than before.[1]

Incompatible with Values.[2]   A situation is defined by people as a social problem in terms of certain values they hold. For example, pollution is considered to be a problem in light of the values people place on health and on preserving the natural environment. Traffic jams are considered to

1. See, for example, the description of blockbusting in Leonard Downie, Jr., *Mortgage on America* (New York: Praeger, 1974), pp. 14–22.

2. Note that many sociologists now emphasize "interests" rather than values. We recognize these types of considerations and consider "interests" to be subsumed under the term "values."

be a social problem in light of the value people place on their time. Communism is considered to be a social problem in light of the values people place on a capitalist economy and on certain types of personal freedom.

People are diverse and complex, however. Different people hold different values; and the same person may hold conflicting values. For these reasons, different people consider different things to be social problems. For example, while the environmentalist focuses on the problem of pollution, the auto manufacturer may be focusing on matters of profit and the economy. Thus, the auto manufacturer may see the government's requiring pollution control devices on cars as the real problem. Likewise, the driver who lives in a rural area where pollution is not apparent may value clean air, but he or she may also value good gas mileage. This driver, then, might agree with the auto manufacturer that the government's requiring pollution control devices, which cut gas mileage, is the problem.

Thus, what comes to be considered a social problem and the values that are involved are a complex matter. This is one of the most controversial aspects of the study of social problems, and it will be dealt with in more detail throughout this book.

A Significant Number of People. How many people are "a significant number"? This question has no clearcut answer. And, of course, some people are more "significant" than others. The President of the United States, for example, is more powerful than an ordinary citizen in determining whether or not a particular situation is defined as a social problem. Likewise, adults are more "significant" than children are in defining social problems, and middle-class people are more "significant" than are lower-class people.

Sociologists would agree that in general the more "significant" people for defining social problems are those who are more organized, are in positions of leadership, and/or are more powerful in economic, social, or political affairs. So it is not just a matter of numbers. The important point for the study of social problems, however, is this: when sociologists study social problems, they usually look at what other people in the society consider to be social problems. Thus, in studying social problems sociologists usually deal only with socially troublesome or deleterious situations that are recognized as problems by the public.[3]

3. It should be noted, however, that an increasing number of sociologists seem to object to the practice of studying only what the public recognizes as social problems. Such an approach, it has been argued, leads sociologists to neglect problems that are serious but unrecognized. Moreover, this approach is said to contain an implicit class bias in that troublesome conditions are more likely to be regarded as social problems when upper-class people label them as such. See, for example, Jerome G. Manis, "Assessing the Seriousness of Social Problems," *Social Problems* 22 (October 1974): 1–15; Alex Thio, "Class Bias in the Sociology of Deviance," *The American Sociologist* 8 (February 1973): 1–12; Alexander Liazos, "The Poverty of the Sociology of Deviance: Nuts, Sluts, and Preverts [sic]," *Social Problems* 20 (Summer

Action Is Needed.   Hand in hand with the definition of a situation as a social problem is the call for action to remedy the situation. People say among themselves that something must be done. They may write letters to the editor, circulate petitions, or hold rallies. Laws or ordinances may be passed and regulations enacted. And organizations may be formed to deal with the situation. Thus, sociologists generally regard social problems as situations that are not just troublesome but that, in addition, people want corrected and/or are trying to correct.

If there is no call for action, then, most sociologists would not conceptualize the situation as a social problem even though it may be troublesome to a large number of people. For example, the sociologist may see the doctor's waiting room as one of the more aggravating situations in our society. Patients often have to sit for hours in a small room with nothing to do. Many patients would rather be home in bed, and some dislike being exposed to the infections of other patients in the waiting room. Yet we hear no call for action. Complaints are numerous, but no demand is made that the situation be changed. Thus, the sociologist is not likely to consider the doctor's waiting room as one of our social problems.

THE DEVELOPMENT OF AMERICAN SOCIOLOGY

The study of social problems has been inextricably intertwined with the field of sociology as a whole. Changes in the study of social problems have been closely related to more general developments in the field of sociology, and the different perspectives on social problems reflect different perspectives on society in general. Before turning to these different perspectives, then, let us take a more general look at the field of sociology.

For centuries, people have thought about and studied their lives in society. But it remained for Auguste Comte in 1838 to give that activity a name. He coined the term "sociology," which means the scientific study of society.[4] Comte's interests, like those of Saint-Simon, Marx, Tocqueville, Spencer, and other early European sociologists, arose from the crises of industrialism. Accordingly, the big questions for these early European sociologists involved issues of social order and integration, on the one hand, and social development and change, on the other. The first of these questions asked, What holds a society together and makes it work? The second asked, Where is the society going, and how is it going there?

In the same way, the post-Civil War upheaval and the rise of industrialism in the United States spawned an interest in studying this society.

1972): 103–20; and Kenneth Westhues, "Social Problems as Systematic Costs," *Social Problems* 20 (Spring 1973): 419–31. An excerpt of Westhues' article is included in Chapter 4 of this book.

4. Auguste Comte, *Positive Philosophy,* trans. Harriet Martineau (London: George Bell & Sons, 1896).

In the two decades after the Civil War, books had begun to appear on the subject. By the middle of the 1890s, sociology courses were being taught in a number of American colleges. The first Ph.D. in sociology was granted in 1895, and the American Sociological Society was formed in 1905.

In the years that followed, American sociology continued to develop as an academic discipline, and it continued to deal with social problems. The ways in which sociologists dealt with such problems, however, changed from time to time. These changes reflect a succession of traditions in the development of sociology.

A "tradition" refers to beliefs, values, and customs. As new ideas are developed and as conditions change, these beliefs, values, and customs also change. In order to understand the study of social problems, and how it has changed over time, we must understand the changing traditions in the development of sociology.

The various traditions in the development of American sociology can be arbitrarily grouped into five stages: establishing a base (1905 to 1918); forming a scientific policy (1918 to 1935); integrating theory, research, and application (1935 to 1954); cultivating specialties (1954 to 1970); and the reemergence of macro theory (1970 on).[5] The changing perspectives on social problems outlined in this book reflect these basic changes in the development of sociology.

1. Establishing a Base (1905 to 1918).   During the years between 1905 and 1918, a hardy band of pioneers established the study of sociology in a number of American colleges. At that time, most of the leading American sociologists were ministers' sons who had moved from small towns to the rapidly growing cities and who had witnessed the changes resulting from America's recent conversion from a farm to a factory economy. Their primary emphasis was on the problems of society, and they saw urbanism as the main source of social problems.

These early American sociologists were guided in their thinking by the philosophy of moral progress—that is, the notion that in the long run, societies improve in quality. Thus, they were more or less convinced that progress and moral uplift would occur. At the same time, they wanted to take a hand in solving some of the problems they saw around them in their rapidly changing society. These early American sociologists tried very hard to eliminate these problems. Their conservative way of thinking, however, led them to advocate social reform rather than revolution.

5. This discussion uses all the dates for the first three stages, some but not all the arguments, and none of the titles that appear in Roscoe C. Hinkle and Gisela J. Hinkle, *The Development of Modern Sociology: Its Nature and Growth in the United States* (New York: Doubleday, 1954).

2. Forming a Scientific Policy (1918 to 1935). During this period, World War I dampened the optimism that had characterized the first period of American sociology. Increasingly, sociologists began to realize that if they were ever going to guide social action, they first had to develop a body of sociological knowledge. And the scientific method, rather than the values of small-town society, seemed more likely to produce such knowledge. Accordingly, during this period attention turned from solving the problems of society to developing sociology as a scientific discipline. The conviction grew among sociologists that science should be value-free, and working to solve social problems came to be regarded as somehow "unscientific."

3. Integrating Theory, Research, and Application (1935 to 1954). If the first period might be called an era of preaching, and the second period an era of retreat, then this period could be called an era of scientific contribution. During this period, sociologists became more professionalized, and they began to see theory, research, and applications as integrally related. As they did so, they began again to accept social reform as part of the sociological endeavor. Basic research and applied sociology came to be seen as two sides of the same coin, and the predominant attitude was that a scientific approach would both solve social problems and develop sociology as a science.

4. Cultivating Specialties (1954 to 1970). In the mid-1950s, sociology came of age. Both the number of sociologists and the number of sociology courses multiplied. For example, from 1926 to 1946, a total of 1,094 Ph.D.s in sociology were granted in the United States (an average of 55 per year); in the ten-year period from 1954 to 1964, 1,729 were granted (an average of 173 per year). At the same time, the sophistication of sociological work increased tremendously. Sociology became specialized, and within the various specialties sociologists began to develop bodies of theory and findings.

After 1954, however, rumblings began to be heard. Many sociologists began to feel that, in their race to answer basic theoretical questions, they had ignored the problems of society. These sociologists began to feel that sociology had neglected its social responsibility and become an instrument of the status quo. This attack was echoed by the next generation of college students. Thus, the recurrent tension between social problems and sociological problems became relevant to the students of sociology as well as to sociologists.

5. The Reemergence of Macro Theory (1970 on). The attack on sociology as a theoretical discipline, which reached its peak in the early 1970s, and Gouldner's *Coming Crisis of Western Sociology,* which was published in 1970, heralded the most recent stage in sociology's development. Gouldner argued that sociology had reached a dead end in its usefulness to a society increasingly in crisis. A critical point of view was seen to be necessary in order to grapple with the problems of both sociology and society. Gouldner himself, in a series of books, extended and deepened a critical Marxist approach. He also helped found the journal *Theory and Society,* which was to become the main scholarly voice of this view of society.

Such concerns as these were evident not only in the United States, but also in Europe, in particular in England and Germany. And, in some ways, this most recent synthesis of Marxist cultural and economic analyses has provided powerful resistance to the Americanization of sociology throughout the academic world and provided a strong push to return sociology to its European roots. In so doing, it has restored a macrosociological, rather than microsociological, view of social problems.

SOCIOLOGICAL PERSPECTIVES ON SOCIAL PROBLEMS

A perspective, generally speaking, is a way of looking at things. A sociological perspective includes a basic orienting idea from which one's conceptualization and analysis follow, and it reflects a particular set of ideas and assumptions regarding the nature of people and society. There are, of course, different ways of looking at social problems, and in sociology seven perspectives have been popular. In large part, these perspectives reflect the tension that has existed since sociology first developed—the tension between concentrating on the problems of society, on the one hand, and on the development of sociology as a scientific discipline, on the other. As sociologists emphasized first one and then another of these goals, they developed the perspectives dealt with in this book. These perspectives resolved for their proponents the questions of what should be studied, how it should be studied, and how the study would contribute to reforming society and to basic sociological knowledge.

The seven perspectives are Social Pathology, Social Disorganization, Value Conflict, Deviant Behavior, Labeling, the Critical Perspective, and the Social Constructionist Perspective. Each perspective contains its own notion of the definition, causes, conditions, consequences, and solutions of social problems. In order to better understand these alternative ways of looking at social problems, in the chapters that follow we will analyze each perspective in terms of these five elements. Before proceeding, we clarify what each element involves.

Definition. We have already presented one general definition of social problems (see page 4), and each of the seven perspectives does, implicitly, presuppose this definition. In addition, however, each perspective includes its own more specialized definition of social problems. These more specialized definitions vary in terms of which particular aspect of a socially troublesome phenomenon they focus on in defining that phenomenon as a social problem. For example, all social problems involve expectations, alleged violations of these expectations, and reactions to the violations. Nonetheless, the seven perspectives differ in terms of whether the definition of the social problem hinges on the expectations, the alleged violations, or the reactions.

Causes.   Each perspective includes its own causal imagery—that is, its own set of ideas about what types of factors produce social problems and how they do so.

Conditions.   Each perspective also has something to say, implicitly or explicitly, about the conditions under which social problems emerge and develop. These are not the immediate causes of social problems. Rather, they are the more general background features out of which the causes of social problems develop.

Consequences.   All seven perspectives view social problems as harmful. They differ, however, in terms of how the harmful effects of social problems are described.

Solutions.   Finally, each perspective includes its own implications about how we can solve social problems. The perspectives emerged at different points in the development of sociology. Thus, some are more explicitly concerned with social reform than are others. Nonetheless, all seven perspectives have some implications for the solution of social problems, and the characteristics of each perspective determine whether the solution focuses on expectations, violations, or reactions.[6]

PLAN OF THE BOOK

Each of the next seven chapters deals with one of the seven perspectives. Every chapter is organized along the following lines. First, there is a brief history of the perspective, including which sociologists contributed most to its development. Next, we give a summary of the perspective—its characteristics regarding the definition, causes, conditions, consequences, and solutions of social problems. Then we present readings that explicate and

6. The implications of each of the first five perspectives for the solution of social problems are more thoroughly examined, and illustrated by readings, in Martin S. Weinberg, Earl Rubington and Sue Kiefer Hammersmith, eds., *The Solution of Social Problems: Five Perspectives*, 2nd ed. (New York: Oxford University Press, 1981).

illustrate the perspective, followed by a selection that criticizes it. Questions for discussion and selected references complete the chapter.

As previously noted, these perspectives arose at different stages in the development of sociology. Thus, each has had periods of popularity and periods of relative neglect. Yet even today each is to some degree the basis for the thinking and writing of many sociologists. This, more than anything else, is the reason for this book.

SUMMARY AND CONCLUSION

Sociology began in the late 1800s with a dual mandate to study social relations, on the one hand, and social problems, on the other. Since then, there has been a recurrent tension in sociology over which of these should receive primary emphasis. In an effort to resolve this tension, sociologists have from time to time developed new perspectives for the study of social problems.

A perspective is basically a way of looking at things, and it clarifies for the sociologist the focus of his or her work. In the study of social problems, sociologists have fashioned seven popular perspectives: Social Pathology, Social Disorganization, Value Conflict, Deviant Behavior, Labeling, the Critical Perspective, and Social Constructionism. Each perspective has its own notion of the definition, causes, conditions, consequences, and solutions of social problems. Now, we look more closely at each of the perspectives.

Selected References

Bernard, Jessie. *Social Problems at Midcentury: Role, Status, and Stress in a Context of Abundance.* New York: Holt, Rinehart and Winston, 1957.

    A text that is extremely useful for its discussion of how middle-class reformers first formulated the concept of social problems.

Denzin, Norman K. "Who Leads: Sociology or Society?" *The American Sociologist* 5 (May 1970): 125–27.

    A concise argument that sociology should itself lead the society, rather than be led by it, in formulating problems for study.

Gusfield, Joseph R. "On the Side: Practical Action and Social Constructionism in Social Problems Theory." In *Studies in the Sociology of Social Problems,* ed. Joseph W. Schneider and John I. Kitsuse. Norwood, N.J.: Ablex, 1984, pp. 31–51.

    Recent discussions of social problems theory have argued that sociologists study social problems because they share the values of those offended by the existence of the problems and because they wish to solve these problems. Gusfield argues that the sociologist should only ascertain the conditions under which the situation came to be defined as a social problem. Such a position, he argues, ends up by clarifying values while remaining silent on the question of how to achieve them.

Hinkle, Roscoe C. *Founding Theory of American Sociology 1881–1915*. London: Routledge and Kegan Paul, 1980.

From its very inception as an academic discipline, sociologists were very concerned about solving the social problems that accompanied industrialization, immigration, and urbanization. But at the same time they were concerned about establishing sociology as a scientific discipline. Tension from this dual mandate continues to influence sociological work to this very day.

Hinkle, Roscoe, C. and Gisela J. Hinkle. *The Development of Modern Sociology: Its Nature and Growth in the United States*. New York: Doubleday, 1954.

One of the best discussions of the rise and development of American sociology. Admirable for the wealth of its scholarship and the brevity of its presentation.

Lazarsfeld, Paul F., William H. Sewell, and Harold L. Wilensky, eds. *The Uses of Sociology*. New York: Basic Books, 1967.

A collection of essays on the application of sociology for the solution of social problems.

Lynd, Robert S. *Knowledge for What? The Place of Social Science in American Culture*. Princeton, N.J.: Princeton University Press, 1939.

Perhaps the best argument to date for using scientific knowledge to help society.

Nisbet, Robert A. *The Social Bond*. New York: Knopf, 1970.

An introductory text that defines sociology as the study of social interaction and shows how sociological concepts are employed to analyze interaction. Contains a useful discussion of the distinction between sociological problems and social problems.

II / THE PERSPECTIVES

2/SOCIAL PATHOLOGY

The idea that there are social problems would appear to be as old as man. But actually, this is not the case at all. Though problems and suffering seem to be found in every society and every historical period, the notion that they are social problems about which something should be done is fairly recent.[1] Before examining the social pathology perspective, we consider briefly how the idea of social problems came into being.

THE CONCEPT OF SOCIAL PROBLEMS

Nineteenth-century America witnessed the ushering in of the urban-industrial order. People began to migrate from farms to cities, and emigration from Europe brought additional thousands to America's burgeoning cities. As the cities swelled, a number of troublesome conditions became more and more noticeable. Near the end of the Civil War, the notion arose that these conditions of suffering, pain, social disorder, institutional malfunctioning, and the like could be remedied. With this corrective attitude, the concept of social problems was born.

Primarily, it was middle-class reformers who perceived situations in the cities as social problems. Impressed with scientific ideology and imbued with the humanism of the Enlightenment, they felt that scientific study, which had solved the puzzles of the physical universe, could also solve the problems of society.

Around 1865, the American Social Science Association was formed. Social reform was the overall goal of the association, and the scientific study of social problems was its immediate objective.[2] In time, however, a

1. According to Arnold Green, a consciousness of social problems did not arise until the latter part of the eighteenth century. Four ideas—those of equality, humanitarianism, the goodness of human nature, and the modifiability of social conditions—made this consciousness possible. See Arnold Green, *Social Problems: Arena of Conflict (New York: McGraw-Hill, 1975)*.

2. For a more detailed discussion of the notion of social problems and the rise and fall of the American Social Science Association, see Jessie Bernard, *Social Problems at Mid-century: Role, Status, and Stress in a Context of Abundance* (New York: Holt, Rinehart, and Winston, 1957), pp. 90–102.

number of schisms took place within the association. First, several groups split off and formed more specialized associations in their respective academic disciplines—economics, political science, and so on. Second, within the association itself, distinctions arose between theory, on the one hand, and application, on the other. Eventually the association was disbanded. It left a legacy, however, of social problems courses, which were soon being given in American universities by a variety of disciplines. As sociology became better established, it took over more and more of these courses.

Very much a product of its times, early American sociology dove-tailed neatly with the objectives of the American Social Science Association, as well as with the attitudes of middle-class reformers. In particular, early American sociology was characterized by four popular beliefs of the late nineteenth century: natural law, progress, social reform, and individualism.[3] Thus, the founding fathers of American sociology believed that human behavior was governed by natural laws and that it was the task of sociology to discover these laws. Most early sociologists also believed in progress. In the course of social evolution, they thought, societies change from simple to complex, and people become freer, more rational, and happier. At the same time, however, these early sociologists saw industrialization and urbanization as the sources of some undesirable conditions, and they wanted to ameliorate those conditions. Thus, the early sociologists wanted to discover the natural laws of human behavior so that they could effect social reform. Finally, these early sociologists had an individualistic conception of social life. They assumed that, although a person belongs to groups, it is ultimately one's personal interests, motives, and characteristics that determine one's behavior.

ROOTS OF THE SOCIAL PATHOLOGY PERSPECTIVE

Essentially, the social pathology perspective is rooted in the organic analogy. Some early writers employed this analogy in a relatively primitive fashion; for example, some portrayed the government as the head of society, the postal service as the nervous system, the police as the "long arm of the law." Herbert Spencer, however, made a more sophisticated use of the organic analogy. In his view, society is like an organism in that it has mass, a complexity of structure that increases with its growth, interdependent parts, and a life that surpasses the life of any particular part.[4]

To the writers employing the organic analogy, persons or situations were considered to be social problems to the extent that they interfered with the "normal" workings of the social organism. In keeping with the

3. See Roscoe C. Hinkle, Jr., and Gisela J. Hinkle, *The Development of Modern Sociology: Its Nature and Growth in the United States* (New York: Doubleday, 1954), pp. 7–17.

4. Robert L. Cameiro, ed., *The Evolution of Society: Selections from Herbert Spencer's "Principles of Sociology"* (Chicago: University of Chicago Press, 1967).

organic analogy, such interference was viewed as a form of illness, or pathology.

The influence of the organic analogy on early American sociology can be seen in the following definition of social pathology, which appeared in an early and widely used sociology textbook.

> Since society is made up of individuals bound together in social re-lationships, social pathology refers to the maladjustments in social rela-tionships. The phrase is based on the analogy of bodily maladjustment of function in the organ. . . . If carefully guarded . . . the term "social pathol-ogy" may be used to denote the social conditions which result (1) from failure of individuals so to adjust themselves to social life that they function as independent self-supporting members of society, who contribute their fair share to its stability and progressive development; and (2) from the lack of adjustment of social structure, including ways of doing things and institutions, to the development of social personality.
>
> Pathological conditions in society may result from (1) natural lack of ability in individuals to keep pace with the changing ideals and institutions of society; or (2) from the failure of society to keep pace in its functional machinery with the changing conditions in the world in which it lives.[5]

The early social pathologists, then, saw both individual maladjustments (such as economic dependency) and institutional malfunctioning (such as economic depression) as obstacles in the forward march of social pro-gress. Thus, they thought that such maladjustments, whether individual or institutional, should be rooted out.

Two sociologists who helped to establish the basic outline of the social pathology perspective were Charles Henderson and Samuel Smith. Both wrote social pathology textbooks, and the line of reasoning set forth in these books dominated the field of sociology for at least a generation.[6] Central to the work of Henderson, Smith, and their many followers in the field of textbook writing was cultural borrowing. Since sociology was still a young and developing field, sociologists were inclined to borrow ideas and metaphors from disciplines that were already well established, such as medicine, philosophy, economics, and political science. The medical met-aphors of pathology and the organic analogy as developed in social phi-losophy helped to shape this perspective. In addition, most of these writers employed popular values in their sociological writings, saturating their text-books with the moral judgments of the day.

Most of the social pathology textbooks appeared during the first two stages of American sociology. These texts dominated the classroom for

5. John L. Gillin and Frank W. Blackmar, *Outlines of Sociology* (New York: Macmillan, 1930), p. 527.

6. Charles Henderson, *Introduction to the Study of Dependent, Defective, and Delinquent Classes, and of Their Social Treatment* (Boston: Heath, 1909); Samuel Smith, *Social Pathology* (New York: Macmillan, 1911).

years, with revisions appearing only every seven or eight years or more. This slow, settled pace of revision, coupled with the fact that only a few textbooks were available, perpetuated and strengthened the social pathology perspective. Today, in contrast, there are numerous textbooks representing different perspectives. Also, revisions appear every four years or so, allowing more opportunity to modify perspectives.

In addition, the slow and rather steady pace of social change during the early twentieth century probably made the original social pathology perspective seem more viable to early American sociologists than it may seem to us today. At that time, the status quo was more accepted as the normal, natural state of affairs. In such an atmosphere, it was easy for people to see anyone who deviated from the status quo as "sick."[7]

CHANGES IN THE SOCIAL PATHOLOGY PERSPECTIVE

In its early form, the social pathology perspective was based on the metaphor of society as an organism. The so-called normal functioning of society was assumed to be "healthy," and the social pathologists occupied themselves with classifying the "ills" of society.

This simplistic and conservative strand of social pathology had its heyday before World War I, especially between 1890 and 1910. After the war, it went into slow but steady decline. In the 1960s, however, there was a resurgence of the social pathology perspective, with some sociologists again writing about the "pathology" of our existence.[8] Also, many liberals and radicals were seeing the society as "sick." Ironically, the "counterculture" people (e.g., "hippies") who labeled society as sick were themselves the kinds of people whom the early social pathologists would have labeled "sick." Recently, however, there has been a blurring of these contrasting points of view in an attempt to make the pathology perspective more "objective" (e.g., see the selection by Kavolis in this chapter).

CHARACTERISTICS OF THE SOCIAL PATHOLOGY PERSPECTIVE

The more specific characteristics of this perspective are as follows:

7. From a contemporary point of view, "there is little disagreement about what constitutes a healthy state of the organism. But there is much less agreement when one uses the notion of pathology analogically, to describe kinds of behavior that are regarded as deviant. For people do not agree on what constitutes healthy behavior. It is difficult to find a definition that will satisfy even such a select and limited group as psychiatrists; it is impossible to find one that people generally accept as they accept criteria of health for the organism" (Howard S. Becker, *Outsiders: Studies in the Sociology of Deviance* [New York: Free Press, 1963], p. 5).

8. See, for example, Bernard Rosenberg, Israel Gerver, and F. William Howton, eds., *Mass Society in Crisis: Social Problems and Social Pathology* (New York: Macmillan, 1964).

Definition.   Desirable social conditions and arrangements are seen as healthy, while persons or situations that diverge from moral expectations are regarded as "sick," therefore bad. Thus, from the social pathology perspective, a social problem is a violation of *moral* expectations.

Causes.   The ultimate cause of social problems is a failure in socialization. Society, through its socializing agents, has the responsibility of transmitting moral norms to each generation. Sometimes, however, the socialization effort is ineffective. An early classification of deviants from the social pathology perspective portrayed them as defective, dependent, or delinquent.[9] Defectives cannot be taught; dependents are handicapped in receiving instruction; and delinquents reject the teachings. For later pathologists, social problems are the result of wrong values being learned. In this perspective's "tender" mood, the people who contribute to the social problem are viewed as "sick"; in its "tough" mood, they are viewed as "criminal." Behind both moods, however, is the notion that the person or situation is, at heart, "immoral."

Conditions.   The early social pathologists considered some people to be inherently defective. And, for the most part, the "defective, dependent, and delinquent" classes tended to perpetuate themselves through inbreeding.[10] Later, however, social pathologists began to see the social environment as the important condition contributing to social pathology. Indeed, Smith himself wrote, "social disease so prevalent as to create a social problem is rarely found without a bad environment of some sort or other, and so the social student is compelled to study the causes of social disease."[11] Whereas earlier pathologists tended to focus on the immoral properties of individuals, the recent pathologists have tended to focus on the immoral properties of societies and to see problems as developing from societal forces such as technology and population density.

Consequences.   In the early pathology view, social disturbances increase the cost of maintaining a legitimate social order. The early pathologists did believe, however, that ultimately the healthiest would survive. The more recent pathologists, in contrast, are morally indignant about the

---

9. Henderson, *Introduction to the Study.*

10. Lombroso claimed there was a definite "criminal type" and that these people were born criminal. The early social pathologists were much influenced by Lombroso's work, and they generalized his position to cover a host of "problem people." These dependent, defective, and delinquent people were viewed as the source of the great bulk of social problems. A summary of Lombroso's work may be found in Marvin E. Wolfgang, "Pioneers in Criminology: Cesare Lombroso (1835–1909)," *Journal of Criminal Law, Criminology, and Police Science* 52 (November–December 1961): 361–91.

11. Smith, *Social Pathology,* p. 8

defects of society and are less optimistic in their prognosis. The most indignant see societal pathology as total, spreading, and likely to dehuman-
ize the entire population.

Solutions.   Both the early and the recent versions of the social pathology
perspective suggest what form solutions to social problems might take.
The early sociologists who dwelt on the troubles caused by "genetically"
defective individuals, for example, turned to the eugenics movement as a
solution. Other sociologists thought the solution to social problems lay in
educating the troublemakers in middle-class morality. The recent variant,
which tends to regard the society rather than its nonconforming members
as "sick," has its roots in the Rousseauean view of human nature. Individuals are good; their institutions, on the other hand, are bad. Yet, even the
modern social pathologists see the remedy to "sick" institutions as a
change in people's values. Thus, according to this perspective, the only
real solution to social problems is moral education.[12]

SUMMARY AND CONCLUSION

The social pathology perspective organized the thinking of early American
sociologists with regard to social problems, and it has continued—in at
least some quarters—to be an influential point of view. It is rooted in the
organic analogy, and its primary concern is with the ills, or pathologies, of
society.

From this perspective, social problems are seen as violations of moral
expectations. Their cause is thought to be socialization failure, which was
attributed first to genetic inheritance and later to social environment. The
result of such failure is moral erosion; the solution, moral education.

Social pathologists can be grouped according to their period, orientation, and politics. Earlier pathologists tended to be conservative in their
orientation and politics. Later pathologists tended to be liberal or radical in
their orientation and politics. Most recently, a synthesis of these approaches has appeared, but it is difficult to say what direction this perspective will take or what its influence will be in the future.

12. For an early statement of this view, see Charles A. Ellwood, *The Social Problem: A Re-
constructive Analysis* (New York: Macmillan, 1919).

THE ORGANIC ANALOGY

Samuel Smith

This brief excerpt from Samuel Smith's Social Pathology *shows the considerable influence the organic analogy had on writers around the turn of the
century. Like medical doctors who study physical illness, social pathologists
undertook to study the "social diseases" of society. And Smith believed that
just as medical doctors study disease to learn how to treat it, so social
pathologists study social problems in order to learn how to "cure" them.*

Pathology in social science has a certain parallel to pathology in medical
science. As the study of physical disease is essential to the maintenance of
physical health, so social health can never be securely grounded without a
wider and more definite knowledge of social disease. General pathology in
medicine teaches that many diseases have much in common and there are
morbid processes which may be discussed, as well as particular diseases.

In social pathology the interrelation of the abnormal classes is one of
the most impressive facts. Paupers often beget criminals; the offspring of
criminals become insane; and to such an extent is the kinship of the defective, dependent, and delinquent classes exhibited, that some have gone
so far as to hold that under all the various forms of social pathology there
is a common ground in the morbid nervous condition of individuals.

Medical science classifies diseases and is not content with a study of
symptoms, but seeks to find out the causes of the maladies with which it
deals. Social students are coming to see with increasing clearness that the
study and treatment of mere symptoms in social disease have been among
the great defects of philanthropists and reformers who in times past, despite the generosity of their motives and the self-sacrifice of their labors,
have failed in their task because of a lack of accurate observation and definite knowledge, which are the only foundations of wise action. The social
doctrine is becoming clear and convincing to many minds that the individual can only be dealt with in his relationships. The weakness of the individual mind or will, the lack of development and the lack of self-control,
are all elements in the problem but social disease so prevalent as to create

From Samuel Smith, *Social Pathology*, pp. 8–9, 1911. The Macmillan Company.

a social problem is rarely found without a bad environment of some sort or other, and so the social student is compelled to study the causes of social disease.

Medical science teaches that the study of disease is only a step in the process leading to therapeutics, or the cure of disease, and instead of being the road to despair in the vast majority of physical ills, it is the only basis of hope. Nearly every disease can be cured if it is taken in time, but the crowning achievement of medical science is not in therapeutics, but in sanitation and in the prevention of disease.

Social pathology would be a gloomy study indeed if its accurate knowledge of facts and principles did not indicate pathways out of social difficulties leading to a discovery of the means by which the social causes of disease can be removed, the weak individual be socially reinforced so that finally, as an ideal at least, the social body shall exist in the minds of social workers, radiant with health, in which there is not a living being which does not share in the general glow of wholesomeness and power.

THE CRIMINAL AS A BORN CRIMINAL TYPE

Cesare Lombroso and William Ferrero

In this excerpt, Lombroso and Ferrero analyze the facial characteristics of twenty female criminals. In these twenty faces they note such irregularities as facial asymmetry, large jaws, overlapping teeth, canine incisors, cleft palate, and receding forehead. They present these observations in support of Lombroso's theory—formulated in the early part of his career—that there are "born criminals" who represent biologically primitive specimens of Homo sapiens. These "born criminals," Lombroso reasoned, resemble apes in their physical characteristics, and thus can be identified as "throwbacks"—reversions to an earlier evolutionary stage.

Among the most ridiculous of the prohibitions obtaining in Italy, or rather in the Italian bureaucracy, which is certainly not the first in Europe, is the absolute impossibility of measuring, studying, or photographing the worst criminals once they have been condemned.

From *The Female Offender* by Cesare Lombroso and William Ferrero. T. Fisher Unwin, London, 1895. Pp. 88–93.

So long as there is a presumption of innocence, so long as these persons are only suspected or accused, one can discredit them in every way, and hold them up to publicity by recording their answers to their judges.

But once it is admitted beyond question that they are reprobates, once the prison doors have closed for good upon them—oh, then they become sacred; and woe to him who touches, woe to him who studies them!

Consumptive patients, pregnant women, may be manipulated, even to their hurt, by thousands of students for the good of science; but criminals—Heaven forefend!

When one of the writers wished to publish photographs of male criminals in his "Uomo Delinquente," he was driven to the German prison "album"; and the difficulties thrown in his way by the Italian authorities were doubled in the case of female offenders and prostitutes, whose sense of shame it was considered necessary to respect in every way.

In Russian prisons Madame Tarnowsky was afforded every facility, and after making a complete study of the body and mind of the delinquents, she forwarded us their photographs.

FEMALE CRIMINALS

We will first take 5 homicides, of whom the two first have the true type of their class.

The first, aged 40, killed her husband with reiterated blows of a hatchet, while he was skimming the milk, then threw his body into a recess under the stairs, and during the night fled with the family money and her own trinkets. She was arrested a week later and confessed her crime. This woman was remarkable for the asymmetry of her face; her nose was hollowed out, her ears projecting, her brows more fully developed than is usual in a woman, her jaw enormous with a lemurian appendix.

No. 2, aged 60. Was constantly ill-treated by her husband, whom she finally joined with her son in strangling, hanging him afterwards so as to favour the idea of suicide.

Here again we have asymmetry of the face, breadth of jaw, enormous frontal sinuses, numerous wrinkles, a hollowed-out nose, a very thin upper lip, with deep-set eyes wide apart, and wild in expression.

No. 3, aged 21. Was married against her will, ill-treated by her husband, whom she killed, after a night altercation, with a hatchet while he slept.

In her we find only a demi-type. Her ears stand out, she has big jaws and cheek-bones, and very black hair, besides other anomalies which do not show in the photograph, such as gigantic canine teeth and dwarf incisors.

No. 4, aged 44. Strangled her husband by agreement with her lover, and threw him into a ditch. She denied her crime. Hollowed-out nose, black hair, deep-set eyes, big jaw. Demi-type.

No. 5, aged 50. A peasant. She killed her brother at supper, so as to inherit from him. She denied her guilt persistently. Was condemned, together with her hired accomplices, to twenty years' penal servitude. She had black hair, grey eyes, diasthema of the teeth, a cleft palate, precocious and profound wrinkles, thin lips, and a crooked face. Demi-type.

Passing now to poisoners, we find the following to be the most remarkable out of twenty-three:—

No. 6, aged 36. Of a rich family, with an epileptic mother, and a father addicted to alcohol. She poisoned her husband with arsenic after sixteen years of married life. Nose hollowed out and club-shaped, large jaws and ears, squint eyes, weak reflex action of left patella. She confessed nothing. Character resolute and devout. Type.

No. 7, aged 34. Also poisoned her husband with arsenic; also denied her guilt. An enormous under jaw. On close examination displayed gigantic incisors, and down so long as to resemble a beard. Demi-type.

No. 8, aged 64. Poisoned her son's wife and the mother of the same. Deep wrinkles, ears much higher than the level of the brows. A singularity is the size of the neck-muscles, exaggerated as in oxen. Thin lips, and a cleft palate. Demi-type.

No. 9, a peasant, aged 47. Poisoned her daughter-in-law because of inability to work. Fluent in speech, never confessed the crime. Asymmetrical face, oblique eyes (a feature, however, which might be ethnological), huge, unequal jaws, small ears, nose club-shaped and hollowed out. On a near view she displayed big canine teeth, and a great parieto-occipital depression. Her children like her grandfather were epileptic. Type.

No. 10, aged 20. Attempted to poison her husband, an old man, who treated her ill. Darwin's lobule was enormously developed in her ear, as may be seen even from the photograph. Hydrocephalic forehead, nose hollowed out and club-shaped, large, unequal jaws, eyes and hair black. Type.

No. 11, aged 35. Poisoned her daughter-in-law, for an unknown reason, with some medicine. Fair hair, asymmetrical face, overlapping teeth. Guilt confessed.

Now we come to the incendiaries, of whom there are 10, four of a striking type.

No. 12. Set fire to the village palisades to revenge herself on some malignant gossips. A large nose, thin lips, lowering expression, with incisors replaced by molars. Type.

No. 13, aged 63. Set fire to a neighbour's house because of a quarrel about money. Denied the offence. Defective teeth, big, feline eyes, very large ears, asymmetry of eyebrows. Demi-type.

No. 14, aged 25. Set fire, in concert with her husband, to a neighbour's house out of revenge. She accused her husband and denied her own complicity. Many wrinkles, projecting parietal bones, big ears and jaws, low forehead. Demi-type.

No. 15, aged 41. A peasant. Set fire to nine houses out of revenge; pretended to have done it while drunk. Very ferocious countenance, asymmetrical, with enormous ears and jaws. Sullen, very black eyes, fair hair, diasthema of the incisors, narrow arch of palate. Type.

No. 16, aged 45. Convicted more than once as a receiver, who had twice hidden convicts in her house. Crooked face and teeth, hollowed-out nose, large, prognathous face, enormous superciliary arches.

Out of 9 infanticides, 3 presented the salient type.

No. 17, aged 60. Killed a newborn babe to save her daughter's reputation. Cut the infant into pieces and hid it. Confessed nothing. A strong character. Many wrinkles, enormous cheek-bones, ears, and frontal sinuses. Right side of face higher than the left. Forehead receding as in savages. Canine teeth gigantic and badly placed. Sunken eyes, brownish-green in colour.

No. 18, aged 60. Assisted her daughter to drown the latter's newborn child; then afterwards accused the daughter, in consequence of a quarrel about a lover whom the two women shared.

Physiognomy relatively good, in spite of the subject's licentious tendencies which age could not eradicate. Nothing anomalous beyond the hollowed-out nose and very wrinkled skin. The face, however, though it does not appear so in the photograph, was really asymmetrical, and the woman had the cleft palate and fleshy lips which betray a luxurious disposition.

No. 19, aged 19, the domestic servant of a priest, had a child, of which the father was a stable-boy. Driven out of every house, she killed her child by beating it on the frozen ground. Crooked face, a hollowed-out nose, big ears and jaws, incisors overlapping.

Finally comes a female brigand—No. 20, aged 25. Was the companion in arms of a band of brigands, one of whom was her lover. A hollowed-out nose, large jaws and ears, a virile physiognomy; and in her also there is congenital division of the palate.

Many may find that after all these faces are not horrible, and I agree, so far, that they appear infinitely less repulsive when compared with corresponding classes among the men whose portraits were reproduced by us from the "Atlas de L'Homme Criminel." Among some of the females there is even a ray of beauty, as in Nos. 19 and 20; but when this beauty exists it is much more virile than feminine.

THE CHILD SAVERS

Anthony M. Platt

In this excerpt, Platt discusses the evolution of the social pathology per-spective. Among other things, he discusses the sources of its ideas and how these ideas changed with the development of the pathology perspective. One important source is the concept of the criminal as less than a complete human being (whether by nature or by nurture). Other features in the development of this perspective include the growth of professionalism in correctional work and the acceptance of a medical model and a "rehabili-tative ideal," particularly for the treatment of "delinquent" youth.

The . . . [social pathologists'] ideology was an amalgam of convictions and aspirations. From the medical profession, they borrowed the imagery of pathology, infection, immunization, and treatment; from the tenets of social Darwinism, they derived their pessimistic views about the intractability of human nature and the innate moral defects of the lower classes; finally, their ideas about the biological and environmental origins of crime can be attributed to the positivist tradition in European criminology and anti-urban sentiments associated with the Protestant, rural ethic.

American criminology in the last century was essentially a practical af-fair—a curious conglomeration of pseudo-scientific theory, Old World ideas, and religious humanitarianism. Theories of crime were imported from Europe and an indiscriminating eclecticism dominated the literature. Educated amateurs, physicians, clergymen, and scholar-technicians became the experts on crime. Before 1870, there were only a few American text-books on crime, and even the various penal and philanthropic organizations lacked specialized journals. Departments of law and sociology in the uni-versities were rarely concerned with more than the formal description and classification of crimes.[1]

American pioneers in criminology were either physicians, like Benjamin Rush or Isaac Ray, or at least guided by medical ideology. Their training

From Anthony M. Platt, *The Child Savers: The Invention of Delinquency*, pp. 18–21, 23–25, 29–31, 33–38, 40–41, 43–45. Copyright © 1969 by The University of Chicago Press. Reprinted by permission of the publisher and the author.

was often based on European methods and some, like Rush, actually attended European universities. With the notable exception of Ray's work, the authoritative literature on medical jurisprudence was of English origin.[2] The social sciences were similarly imported from Europe, and American criminologists fitted their data within the theoretical framework of criminal anthropology. Herbert Spencer's writings had an enormous impact on American intellectuals and made him even more popular in the United States than he was in his own country.[3] Cesare Lombroso, perhaps the most significant figure in nineteenth-century criminology, also sought recognition in the United States when he felt that his experiments had been neglected in Italy.[4]

Spencer and Lombroso, with their emphasis on Darwinist and biological images of human behavior, provided the ideological premise for crime workers and reformers. Anthropological explanations of crime complemented social Darwinism, which, in its most simple form, suggested that life is a competitive struggle for existence whereby the fittest survive and thus elevate the whole human race. The doctrine of "natural selection" also refuted revolutionary change and characterized human progress as a slow, natural, and inevitable process of evolution.[5] As Richard Hofstadter has observed, this view of social life was "seized upon as a welcome addition, perhaps the most powerful of all, to the store of ideas to which solid and conservative men appealed when they wished to reconcile their fellows to some of the hardships of life and to prevail upon them not to support hasty and ill-considered reforms."[6]

Spokesmen for conservative Darwinsim opposed welfare legislation and organized state care of the "dependent classes" on the grounds that all men, whatever their ability and resources, should engage in the competition for survival. The care and support of criminals, idiots, cripples, and the like, merely prolongs suffering, impedes human progress, and contradicts the laws of nature. The Darwinists, however, did not approve class warfare or the total elimination of the "unfit" through eugenic techniques. Hofstadter has pointed out that Spencer, accused of inhumanity in his application of biological principles to social life, "was compelled to insist over and over again that he was not opposed to voluntary private charity to the unfit, since it had an elevating effect on the character of the donors and hastened the development of altruism. . . ."[7]

Although Lombroso's theoretical and experimental studies were not translated into English until 1911, his findings were known by American academics in the early 1890s, and their popularity, as that of Spencer's, was based on the fact that they confirmed popular assumptions about the character and existence of a "criminal class." Lombroso's original theory suggested the existence of a criminal type distinguishable from noncriminals by observable physical anomalies of a degenerative or atavistic nature. He proposed that the criminal was a morally inferior human spe-

cies, one characterized by physical traits reminiscent of apes, lower pri-
mates, and savage tribes. The criminal was thought to be morally retarded
and, like a small child, instinctively aggressive and precocious unless re-
strained.[8] It is not difficult to see the connection between biological deter-
minism in criminological literature and the principles of "natural selection";
both of these theoretical positions, according to Leon Radzinowicz,
automatically justified the "eradication of elements that constituted a permanent and serious danger."[9]

Lombroso and his colleagues recognized other types of criminal behavior and even acknowledged the influence of social as well as biological
factors on criminals.[10] . . .

In England, the ideas and data of the so-called Italian school of criminology had already been summarized and publicized by Havelock Ellis.[11]
A similar, though much more superficial and less endurable, service was
provided by Robert Fletcher in an address before the Anthropological Society of Washington, D.C., in 1891. Fletcher told his audience that criminal
anthropology consisted of the study of individuals who are compelled to
commit crimes as a consequence of "physical conformation, hereditary
taint, or surroundings of vice, poverty, and ill example." The modern view
of the criminal depicts him as a "variety of human species who had degen-
erated physically and morally." . . .

American penologists supported this derogatory image of criminals and
enthusiastically welcomed pseudo-scientific proposals for their containment.[12] A typical medical view was expressed by Nathan Allen at the National Conference of Charities and Correction, where he observed that
criminals are usually incapable of overcoming their biological fate:

> All history proves that the criminal class as a body originates from a peculiar
> stratum or type in society—sometimes from the middle or common walks of
> life, but more generally from the lowest orders, especially from the ignorant,
> the shiftless, the indolent and dissipated. . . . If our object, then, is to prevent
> crime in a large scale, we must direct attention to its main sources—to the
> materials that make criminals; the springs must be dried up; the supplies
> must be cut off.

Allen further proposed that crime would be reduced if "certain classes of vicious persons could be hindered from propagation. What right have such individuals to bring upon the public so much misery, shame and cost?"[13] . . .

The organization of correctional workers—through their national representatives and their identification with the established professions, such
as law and medicine—operated to neutralize the pessimistic implications
of social Darwinism, because hereditary and fatalistic theories of crime
inevitably frustrated the professional aspirations of correctional functionaries. At the same time, even though the job of guard requires minimal
training, skill, or intelligence, crime workers did not wish to regard themselves as merely the custodians of a pariah class.[14]

The self-image of penal reformers as doctors rather than guards and the domination of criminological research in the United States by physicians, helped to encourage the acceptance of "therapeutic" strategies in prisons and reformatories. As Arthur Fink has observed, "the role of the physician in this ferment is unmistakable. Indeed, he was the dynamic agent. . . . Not only did he preserve and add to existing knowledge—for his field touched all borders of science—but he helped to maintain and extend the methodology of science."[15] Perhaps what is more significant is that physicians furnished the official rhetoric of penal reform. Admittedly, the criminal was "pathological" and "diseased," but medical science offered the possibility of miraculous cures. It was, therefore, the task of correctional agencies to make every individual self-supporting and independent by restraining "prodigality and extravagance of expenditure of human force and substance."[16] Although there was widespread belief in the existence of a "criminal class" separated from the rest of mankind by a "vague boundary line," there was no good reason why this class could not be identified, diagnosed, segregated, changed, and controlled. Crime, like disease, was revealed "in the face, the voice, the person and the carriage," so that a skillful and properly trained diagnostician could arrest criminal tendencies. . . .

Despite the wide acceptance of biological imagery, penal reformers stressed the possibility of redemption through religious and medical intervention. The desire to promote the "welfare of the community and future of the race," the stress on pseudo-scientific methods of eliminating criminality, and the ruthless, mechanistic classification of criminals had to be weighed against traditional Christian benevolence, the indulgence of the unfit, and the "optimism of Religion" (as compared with the "pessimism of Science").[17] Charles Henderson, professor of sociology at the University of Chicago and President of the National Conference of Charities and Correction for 1899, resolved this dilemma by observing that the laws of "natural selection" and the principles of educative reform were not antagonistic. To hurt the "defective classes," said Henderson, would be to hurt the social order itself; social progress must rest on the capacity of those persons who deal with this class to develop altruistic sentiments. . . .

Professional correctional workers and administrators gradually refuted monolithic explanations of crime based on biological imagery. . . . The superintendent of the Kentucky Industrial School of Reform, for example, was convinced by 1898 that hereditary theories of crime were over-fatalistic. "While I believe heredity, of both moral and physical traits, to be a fact," he told delegates to a national conference, "I think it is unjustifiably made a bugaboo to discourage efforts at rescue. We know that physical heredity tendencies can be neutralized and often nullified by proper counteracting precautions."[18] E.R.L. Gould, a sociologist at the University of Chicago, similarly objected to hereditary theories of crime, on the grounds that the empirical data was unconvincing. He criticized many so-called scientific studies for being unclear, morbid, and sentimental:

> There is great danger in emphasizing heredity, and by contrast minimizing the influence of environment and individual responsibility. Consequences doubly unfortunate must ensue. Individual stamina will be weakened, and society made to feel less keenly the duty of reforming environment. Is it not better to postulate freedom of choice than to preach the doctrine of the unfettered will, and so elevate criminality into a propitiary sacrifice?[19]

The problem confronting criminologists of "whether the man makes the circumstances or the circumstances make the man" was skillfully clarified by Charles Cooley in an address before the National Conference of Charities and Correction in 1896. He considered it unnecessary and pointless to create a dichotomy between "nature" and "nurture," inferring that there is a choice of alternatives.[20] "Like male and female, each is sterile without the other." Cooley took a dynamic and flexible position regarding the way in which social character is formed:

> The union of nature and nurture is not one of addition or mixture, but of growth, whereby the elements are altogether transformed into a new organic whole. One's nature acts selectively upon the environment, assimilating materials proper to itself; while at the same time the environment moulds the nature, and habits are formed which make the individual independent, in some degree, of changes in either. . . .

Cooley made the important observation that criminal behavior depended as much upon social experiences and economic circumstances as it did upon the inheritance of biological traits. The delinquent child is constrained by social rather than biological forces; in essence, however, he is normally constituted and the "criminal class is largely the result of society's bad workmanship upon fairly good material." Cooley criticized theories of crime based on physical peculiarities, noting that there was a "large and fairly trustworthy body of evidence" to support the fact that many so-called degenerates could be made "useful citizens by rational treatment."[21]

. . . [Thus], the concept of the natural criminal was modified with the rise of a professional class of correctional administrators and social servants who promoted a medical model of deviant behavior and suggested techniques of remedying "natural" imperfections. The pessimism of Darwinism was counterbalanced by the spirit of philanthropy, religious optimism, and a belief in the dignity of suffering. . . .

Another important influence on nineteenth-century images of crime was a disenchantment with urban life. The city was depicted as the main breeding ground of criminals: the impact of the physical horrors of urban ghettos on unskilled, poorly educated European immigrants "created" criminals. Immigrants were regarded as "unsocialized" and the city's impersonality compounded their isolation and degradation. "By some cruel alchemy," wrote Julia Lathrop, "we take the sturdiest of European peasantry and at once destroy in a large measure its power to rear to decent livelihood the first generation of offspring upon our soil."[22] . . .

Many penal and educational reformers considered that human nature operated in a radically different way in the city compared with the country. It was, therefore, the task of reformers to make city existence more like life on the farm, where social relationships were considered wholesome, honest, and free from depravity and corruption. Jenkin Lloyd Jones, in a speech before the Illinois Conference of Charities in 1898, expressed the hope that redistribution of the population would remedy some of the serious social problems associated with industrialism:

> The currents of industrial and commercial life have set in tremendously towards the city. Thither flows with awful precipitancy the best nerve, muscle and brain of the country, and the equilibrium will be permanently destroyed if there cannot be a counter current established, whereby the less competent, the unprotected, the helpless and the innocent can be passed back, to be restored and reinvigorated.[23] . . .

Children living in the city slums were described as "intellectual dwarfs" and "physical and moral wrecks" whose characters were predominantly shaped by their physical surroundings. Beverley Warner told the National Prison Association in 1898 that philanthropic organizations all over the country were

> making efforts to get the children out of the slums, even if only once a week, into the radiance of better lives. Seeing the beauties of a better existence, these children may be led to choose the good rather than the evil. Good has been done by taking these children into places where they see ladies well dressed, and with their hands and faces clean, and it is only by leading the child out of sin and debauchery, in which it has lived, into a circle of life that is a repudiation of things that it sees in its daily life, that it can be influenced.[24] . . .

SUMMARY

Important developments in the imagery of crime at the end of the last century were (1) the concept of the criminal as less than a complete human being, whether by nature or nurture, (2) the growth of professionalism in corrections work, and (3) the acceptance of the medical model and the "rehabilitative ideal," particularly with regard to the correction of "delinquent" children and adolescents.

1. Although there was a wide difference of opinion as to the precipitating causes of crime, it was generally agreed among experts that criminals

were *abnormally* conditioned by biological and environmental factors. Early theories stressed the permanent, irreversible, and inherited character of criminal behavior. To the image of natural depravity was added the image of urban corruption. Reformers emphasized the disorganized features of urban life and encouraged remedial programs which embodied rural and primary group concepts. Slum life was regarded as unregulated, vicious and lacking in social rules; its inhabitants were depicted as abnormal and maladjusted, living their lives in conflict and chaos.[25]

2. The element of fatalism in theories of crime was modified with the rise of a professional class of penal adminstrators and social servants who promoted a developmental view of human behavior. The pessimistic implications of Darwinist creeds were antagonistic not only to the Protestant ethic but also to crime workers who aspired to the professional status of doctors, lawyers, and other human service functionaries. It was fortunate, as John Higham has observed, that Darwinism was flexible enough to suit both philanthropic and misanthropic views of social life.[26]

3. There . . . [was] a shift . . . in official policies concerning crime. The warrant . . . shifted from one emphasizing the criminal nature of delinquency to the "new humanism," which speaks of disease, illness, contagion, and the like. The emergence of the medical warrant is of considerable significance, since it is a powerful rationale for organizing social action in the most diverse behavioral aspects of our society.

The "rehabilitative ideal"[27] presupposed that crime was a symptom of "pathology" and that criminals should be treated like irresponsible, sick patients. The older a criminal, the more chronic was his sickness; similarly, his chances of recovery were less than those of a young person. Adult criminals, particularly recidivists, were often characterized as nonhuman. Children, however, were less likely to be thought of as nonhuman since universalistic ethics, especially the ethic of Christianity, made it almost impossible to think of children as being entirely devoid of moral significance.

Social reformers emphasized the temporary and reversible nature of adolescent crime. As Charles Cooley observed, "when an individual actually enters upon a criminal career, let us try to catch him at a tender age, and subject him to rational social discipline, such as is already successful in enough cases to show that it might be greatly extended."[28] If, as the child savers believed, criminals are conditioned by biological heritage and brutish living conditions, then prophylactic measures must be taken early in life. Delinquent children—the criminals of the next generation—must be prevented from pursuing their criminal careers. "They are born to it," wrote the penologist Enoch Wines in 1880, "brought up for it. They must be saved."[29] Many new developments in penology took place at this time in the reformatory system where, it was hoped, delinquents would be saved and reconstituted.

Notes

1. Arthur E. Fink, *Causes of Crime: Biological Theories in the United States, 1800–1915* [(Philadelphia: University of Pennsylvania Press, 1938)]. Needless to say, histories of American criminological thought are hard to find. Fink's study makes a useful bibliographical contribution to the literature by assembling and condensing a vast amount of interesting primary sources. But he rarely attempts to interpret his data other than to make the occasional bow to the evolutionary perspective. There are of course numerous modern textbooks on the history of penology—such as H. E. Barnes and N. K. Teeters, *New Horizons in Criminology* ([New York: Prentice-Hall], 1943), Max Grünhut, *Penal Reform* ([Toronto: Oxford], 1948), and George B. Vold, *Theoretical Criminology* ([New York: Oxford], 1958)—but these are essentially compiled for undergraduate reading.

2. Isaac Ray, *A Treatise on the Medical Jurisprudence of Insanity* [(Cambridge: Belknap/Harvard University Press, 1962)]. The influence of English medical jurisprudence on American physicians is cursorily examined by Anthony M. Platt and Bernard L. Diamond, "The Origins of the 'Right and Wrong' Test of Criminal Responsibility and Its Subsequent Development in the United States," *California Law Review* 54 (1966): 1227–60. See also, Seymour Halleck, "American Psychiatry and the Criminal: A Historical Review," *American Journal of Psychiatry* 121, no. 9 (March, 1965): i–xxi.

3. Richard Hofstadter, *Social Darwinism in American Thought* (Boston: Beacon Press, 1960)], pp. 31–50.

4. See Lombroso's introduction to Arthur MacDonald, *Criminology* [(New York: Funk & Wagnalls, 1893)].

5. As Charles Cooley remarked, "most of the writers on eugenics have been biologists or physicians who have never acquired the point of view which sees in society a psychological organism with a life process of its own. They have thought of human heredity as a tendency to definite modes of conduct, and of environment as something that may aid or hinder, not remembering what they might have learned even from Darwin, that heredity takes on a distinctively human character only by renouncing, as it were, the function of predetermined adaptation and becoming plastic to the environment" (*Social Process* [(New York: Charles Scribner's Sons, 1918)], p. 206).

6. Hofstadter, *Social Darwinism*, p. 5.

7. *Ibid.*, p. 41.

8. An excellent critique of Lombroso's theories, findings and intellectual traditions is provided by Marvin E. Wolfgang, "Cesare Lombroso," in Hermann Mannheim, ed., *Pioneers in Criminology* [(Chicago: Quadrangle, 1960)], pp. 168–227.

9. *Ideology and Crime* ([New York: Columbia University Press, 1966]), p. 55.

10. This study is not the place to debate Lombroso's contributions to criminology or to measure his effect on European ideas; what I am concerned with here is how Lombroso was interpreted and simplified in the United States before 1900. It is well recognized that his later writings were more cautious and emphasized a multifactor approach.

11. Havelock Ellis, *The Criminal* [(London: Walter Scott, 1914)].

12. See, for example, Fink, *Causes of Crime,* pp. 188–210, on criminological attitudes toward sterilization.

13. Nathan Allen, "Prevention of Crime and Pauperism," *Proceedings of the Annual Conference of Charities* (PACC), 1878, pp. 111–24.

14. Analogous developments in the emergence of social work as a professional career are treated by [Roy] Lubove in *The Professional Altruist* [(Cambridge: Harvard University Press, 1965)].

15. Fink, *Causes of Crime,* p. 247.

16. *First Biennial Report of the Board of State Commissioners of Public Charities of the State of Illinois,* p. 18 (Springfield, Illinois: Illinois Journal Printing Office, 1871).

17. Charles Henderson, "Relation of Philanthropy to Social Order and Progress," [*Proceedings of the National Conference of Charities and Corrections (PNCCC)*], pp. 1–15. Cf. Charles E. Faulkner, "Twentieth Century Alignments for the Promotion of Social Order," with Frederick H. Wines, "The Healing Touch," *PNCCC, 1900,* pp. 1–9, 10–26.

18. Peter Caldwell, "The Duty of the State to Delinquent Children," *PNCCC, 1898,* pp. 404–10.

19. E.R.L. Gould, "The Statistical Study of Hereditary Criminality," *PNCCC, 1895,* pp. 134–43.

20. According to Hofstadter, "The new psychology . . . was a truly social psychology. . . . [I]nsistence upon the unreality of a personal psyche isolated from the social surroundings was a central tenet in the social theory of Charles H. Cooley. . . . The older psychology had been atomistic. . . . The new psychology, prepared to see the interdependence of the individual personality with the institutional structure of society, was destroying this one-way notion of social causation and criticizing its underlying individualism" (*Social Darwinism,* p. 150).

21. Charles H. Cooley, " 'Nature v. Nurture' in the Making of Social Careers," *PNCCC, 1896,* pp. 339–405.

22. Julia Lathrop, "The Development of the Probation System in a Large City," *Charities* 13 (January, 1905): 348.

23. "Who Are the Children of the State?" Illinois Conference of Charities (1898), *Fifteenth Biennial Report of the State Board of Commissioners of Public Charities of the State of Illinois,* pp. 286–87 (Springfield: Phillips Brothers, 1899).

24. Beverley Warner, "Child Saving," *Proceedings of the Annual Congress of the National Prison Association, Indianapolis, 1898,* pp. 377–78.

25. William Foote Whyte, "Social Disorganization in the Slums," *American Sociological Review* 8 (1943): 34–39.

26. ". . . the general climate of opinion in the early Darwinian era inhibited the pessimistic implications of the new naturalism. What stood out in the first instance, as the great social lesson of the theory of natural selection, was not the ravages of the struggle for survival but rather the idea of 'the survival of the fittest.' To a

generation of intellectuals steeped in confidence, the laws of evolution seemed to guarantee that the 'fittest' races would most certainly triumph over inferior competitors. . . . Darwinism, therefore, easily ministered to Anglo-Saxon pride, but in the age of confidence it could hardly arouse Anglo-Saxon anxiety.

"Secondly, Darwinism gave the race-thinkers little concrete help in an essential prerequisite of racism—belief in the preponderance of heredity over environment. Certainly the biological vogue of the late nineteenth century stimulated speculation along these lines, but the evolutionary theory by no means disqualified a fundamentally environmentalist outlook. Darwin's species struggled and evolved through adaptation to those settings" ([John] Higham, *Strangers in the Land,* pp. 135–36).

27. This term is used by Francis A. Allen, *The Borderland of Criminal Justice* [(Chicago: University of Chicago Press, 1964)].

28. Cooley, " 'Nature v. Nurture,' " p. 405.

29. Enoch C. Wines, *The State of Prisons and of Child-Saving Institutions in the Civilized World* [(Cambridge: University Press, 1880)], p. 132.

A UNIVERSAL CRITERION OF PATHOLOGY

Vytautas Kavolis

C. Wright Mills criticized the social pathology approach for cloaking the small-town values of conservative reformers in seemingly objective medical terms. In this excerpt, Kavolis argues that social pathology, carefully defined, can be a relatively objective and useful conception. Destructiveness to self or others, Kavolis holds, can be objectively identified, and such destructiveness is the core of social pathology. Thus, Kavolis believes, the study of social pathology should concern itself with people's destructive behavior and the conditions that give rise to such behavior.

The . . . [social pathology] conception of social problems . . . provides a universal criterion for evaluating social arrangements by their human costs. If it were possible to arrive at a cross-culturally valid definition of "destructive or self-destructive behavior," then conditions causally associated with such behavior could be identified as pathogenic (or having pathogenic aspects), regardless of whether they were institutionalized in a society and supported

From Vytautas Kavolis (ed.), *Comparative Perspectives on Social Problems,* pp. 2–6. Copyright © 1969 by Little, Brown and Company (Inc.). Reprinted by permission.

by its cultural traditions or not, and whether anyone in the society in which they occurred was aware of their pathogenic effects. With this perspective on social problems, no longer would the sociologist stand theoretically helpless—as the "deviationists" must—in relation to prejudice in South Africa, slavery in the pre-Civil War American South, Nazi concentration camps, genocide under Stalin, or the pathologies arising from conformity to "normal" middle-class values.[1]

I do not accept the view that to define pathology in terms of destructiveness is a culture-bound judgment. To regard *destruction of life, health, or sense of personal identity* (a definition with a hard core and stretchable boundaries) as the universal criterion of pathological behavior constitutes the most general extension of the implications of the major ethical systems of mankind. With respect to this criterion, exceptions have to be justified, not the criterion itself; but the criterion has been frequently held to apply only to members of one's own group. What we are doing is universalizing the criterion of pathology—applying it to all societies, including those that have not generalized their moral norms sufficiently to make them applicable to outsiders as much as to themselves.

Nor can it be legitimately assumed that the social-pathology approach necessarily incorporates a conservative bias in favor of preserving existing institutions.[2] What is pathological is not behavior which deviates from established custom or disrupts social stability but that which is destructive or self-destructive in its consequences. Whenever established institutions (or innovations) promote such behavior, they must be regarded as pathogenic. Conflict, in this theoretical perspective, is not in itself pathological (unless it generates violence). Lack of conflict may be pathogenic if it perpetuates a high incidence of self-destructive behavior.

The "field" of social pathology may be defined as the study of the destructive or self-destructive behavior of individuals (pathological behavior) and of the social and cultural conditions, or processes, which cause or contribute to such behavior (pathogenic conditions). If the goal is to understand how particular conditions have pathogenic effects on individuals, studying one type of pathological behavior in isolation from others is insufficient. It is only by investigating the overall effects of a social condition, on all types of pathological behavior, that the social pathologist can determine to what extent and in what manner the condition is pathogenic. A theoretical framework is needed within which any given social condition can be related to all types of pathological behaviors (if a relationship can be demonstrated to exist).

In organizing the data for such a framework, it is helpful to distinguish self-directed destructiveness from other-directed destructiveness, and spontaneous pathological behavior from organized pathologies. Self-destructiveness refers to all forms of behavior by which an individual destroys or damages his own life, health, or sense of personal identity. Such forms of behavior range from suicide at the highest level of intensity, through alcoholism and neurosis at intermediate levels, to various kinds of "inauthentic" actions, alien to the "true nature" of the personality, that the individual performs either because he is forced by external circumstances or because he does not "know" himself. Only the higher and intermediate levels of intensity will be considered systematically in this article, as little reliable cross-cultural research has been done on "inauthentic" behavior, except on alienation.

Other-directed destructiveness is another umbrella term referring to all activities by which an individual destroys or damages the life, health, or sense of personal identity of another person or persons. Such activities include, at one extreme, the various forms of murder (including socially sanctioned killing, as in warfare) and, at the other extreme, the withdrawal of social esteem from a specific person or group of persons. (This may be a rational action when it has been "earned" by the specific behavior of such a person or persons, but even then it is other-destructive.) I would classify racial discrimination and most forms of crime as other-directed destructive behavior of intermediate intensity. However, racial discrimination is easily intensified to the level of genocide; and the intensity of aggression inherent in crime varies from high to low. Some activities officially designated as crimes, such as school truancy, are purely self-destructive. Some crimes do not affect either the self or others destructively (e.g., the crime of offering a glass of wine to a seventeen-year-old in Pennsylvania). On the other hand, numerous other-destructive activities have historically not been regarded as crimes (war, economic exploitation of the easily victimized).

Spontaneous pathological behavior is exhibited when an individual "chooses," in part voluntarily, to engage in a destructive or self-destructive course of action, or when he unconsciously develops, without having the ability to choose, the symptoms of a self-destructive disease. Organized pathology exists when the individual is either "morally" obligated or "politically" coerced by the group or organization to whose authority or power he is subject to commit destructive or self-destructive acts (or to encourage others to commit such acts). The purest cases of organized pathology are found in concentration camps and the institution of slavery. While the victims of these institutions are coerced into self-destructive behavior, their masters, by accepting their position within these institutions, assume the obligation to engage in other-destructive behavior, essentially (though not wholly) regardless of their personal malevolence or lack thereof. Both the victims and the masters of pathological institutions are required, by the conditions of operation of such institutions, to engage in pathological behavior.

On a lower level of intensity, but with broadly comparable psychological effects, is the organized pathology of imperialism and colonialism, the most prominent representative of which, after the virtual demise of West European colonial empires, is the Soviet Union, with its at least fifteen nations held by force in the same relationship to the Great Russians as the natives of Mozambique are to the Portuguese—"crushed with their inessentiality."[3]

Organized pathology is not necessarily, at any given time, socially disreputable. Respected organizations may require their members to participate, or unintentionally promote, pathological behavior. The Catholic church does so when it requires its clerical members, against their growing opposition, to persuade its lay members not to use effective methods of fertility control. The rationale of this requirement is moral upgrading of the faithful. The socially relevant result is a sizable contribution to overpopulation, malnutrition of children, illegal abortions that damage the health or destroy the lives of pregnant women, and revolutionary political extremism, especially in Latin America. Some readers might find that the rats of Rajasthan constitute an emotionally more acceptable illustration of the point that is being made here.[4]

These examples suggest to what extent the deviance perspective may be irrelevant to understanding the causes of major social pathologies. Yet one of the measures of the rationality of a social order is the degree to which its definitions of socially unacceptable deviance correspond with what can be empirically shown to be pathological behavior. In a rational society, presumably, only the pathological would be regarded as seriously deviant, and the only socially consequential deviance would be that of demonstrably destructive or self-destructive behavior. However, since societies are not rationally organized, both the deviance and the pathology perspectives are necessary to understand their problems.

In studying social pathology, we aim at establishing the characteristics of social structure and process as well as those of cultural orientation which promote pathological behavior wherever they occur. To eliminate accidental patterns of findings that hold in a particular time and place but lack general validity, systematic cross-cultural study of the various forms of pathological behavior is necessary. Such studies should eventually lead to a theoretical integration of the knowledge of pathological behavior in preliterate, historical, and modern societies accumulated by half a dozen scholarly disciplines. It should be possible, on the basis of such a theoretical system, to predict how much of what types of pathology would be likely to occur if we constructed a society with certain specified characteristics.

Notes

1. Erich Fromm, *The Sane Society* (Greenwich, Conn.: Fawcett Publications, 1955).

2. An accusation that has been justly directed against an earlier generation of American social pathologists. C. Wright Mills, "The Professional Ideology of Social Path-

ologists," in his *Power, Politics and People,* ed. Irving Louis Horowitz (New York: Ballantine Books, 1963), pp. 525–552.

3. Frantz Fanon, *The Wretched of the Earth* (New York: Grove Press, 1966), p. 30.

4. "Food is scarce in this desert town, as it is in much of India. . . . But the rats in this desert state of Rajasthan face no food problem. They are considered to be holy creatures, and they are fed by faithful worshippers. The rodent population of Rajasthan is said to outnumber the human population: 25 million rats to 20.1 million people." *The New York Times,* August 21, 1968, p. 16.

THE PURSUIT OF LONELINESS

Philip Slater

American culture emphasizes individualism. According to Slater, this leads to competition, denial of interdependence with one's fellows, and a heightened need for privacy. Faced with these signs of social pathology, Americans respond with increased individualism, but this only makes them feel worse, because individualism cannot cure the pathologies it has itself produced.

We are so used to living in an individualistic society that we need to be reminded that collectivism has been the more usual lot of humans. Most people in most societies have lived and died in stable communities that took for granted the subordination of the individual to the welfare of the group. The aggrandizement of the individual at the expense of his neighbors was simply a crime.

This is not to say that competition is an American invention—all societies involve some mixture of cooperative and competitive institutions. But our society lies near the competitive extreme, and although it contains cooperative institutions, we suffer from their weakness and peripherality. Studies of business executives reveal a deep hunger for an atmosphere of trust and fraternity with their colleagues. The competitive life is a lonely one and its satisfactions short-lived, for each race leads only to a new one.

In the past our society had many oases in which one could take refuge from the frenzied invidiousness of our economic system—institutions such as the extended family and the stable local neighborhood in which people could take pleasure from something other than winning symbolic victories over their neighbors. But these have disappeared one by one, leaving us more and more in a situation in which we must try to satisfy our vanity and our needs for intimacy in the same place and at the same time. This has made the appeal of cooperative living more seductive, and the need to suppress our longing for it more acute.

The main vehicle for the expression of this longing has been the mass media. Popular songs and film comedies for fifty years have been engaged in a sentimental rejection of our dominant mores, maintaining that the best things in life are free, that love is more important than success, that keeping up with the Joneses is futile, that personal integrity should take precedence over winning, and so on. But these protestations must be understood for what they are: a safety valve. The same man who chuckles and sentimentalizes over a happy-go-lucky hero in a film would view his real-life counterpart as frivolous and irresponsible, and suburbanites who philosophized over the back fence with complete sincerity about their "dog-eat-dog-world," and "what-is-it-all-for," and "you-can't-take-it-with-you," and "success-doesn't-make-you-happy-it-just-gives-you-ulcers-and-a-heart-condition," were enraged in the sixties when their children began to pay serious attention to these ideas. To the young this seemed hypocritical, but if adults didn't feel these things they wouldn't have had to fight them so vigorously. The exaggerated hostility that young people aroused in the "flower child" era argues that the life they led was highly seductive to middle-aged Americans.

When a value is strongly held, as individualism is in America, the illnesses it produces tend to be treated in the same way an alcoholic treats a hangover or a drug addict his withdrawal symptoms. Technological change, mobility, and individualistic ways of thinking all rupture the bonds that tie a man to a family, a community, a kinship network, a geographical location—bonds that give him a comfortable sense of himself. As this sense of himself erodes, he seeks ways of affirming it. Yet his efforts accelerate the very erosion he seeks to halt.

This loss of a sense of oneself, a sense of one's place in the scheme of things, produces a jungle of competing egos, each trying to *create* a place. Huge corporations are fueled on this energy—the stockholders trying to buy place with wealth, executives trying to grasp it through power and prestige, public relations departments and advertisers trying to persuade people that the corporation can confer a sense of place to those who believe in it or buy its products.

Americans love bigness, mostly because they feel so small. They feel small because they're unconnected, without a place. They try to overcome that smallness by associating themselves with bigness—big projects, big organizations, big government, mass markets, mass media, "nationwide," "worldwide." But it's that very same bigness that rips away their sense of connectedness and place and makes them feel small. A vicious circle.

Notice the names of corporations: "Universal," "Continental," "International," "General," "National," "Trans-World"—the spirit of grandiosity and ego-inflation pervades our economic life. Corporations exist not to feed or supply the people, but to appease their own hungry egos. Advertising pays scant attention to price or quality and leans heavily on our needs for acceptance and respect. The economic structure of our society continually frustrates those needs, creating an artificial scarcity that in turn motivates the entire economy. This is why the quality of life in America is so unsatisfying. Since our economy is built on inflated vanity, rather than being grounded in the real material needs of the people, it must eventually collapse, when these illusions can no longer be maintained.

Much of the unpleasantness, abrasiveness, and costliness of American life comes from the fact that we're always dealing with strangers. This is what bureaucracy is: a mechanism for carrying on transactions between strangers. Who would need all those offices, all that paperwork, all those lawyers, contracts, rules and regulations, if all economic transactions took place between lifelong neighbors? A huge and tedious machinery has evolved to cope with the fact that we prefer to carry on our activities among strangers. The preference is justified, as are most of the sicknesses in American society, by the alleged economic benefits of bigness, but like many economic arguments, it's a con.

On the surface, it seems convincing. Any big company can undersell a little one. Corporations keep getting bigger and bigger and fewer and fewer. Doesn't that prove it? Survival of the fittest? Yet for some reason, what should be providing economic benefits to the consumer has in fact produced nothing but chronic inflation. If bigness lowers the cost of production, why does everything cost more and break sooner? Management, of course, blames it on labor, and each industry cites the rising prices of its own suppliers. Isn't it obvious that a few big nationwide companies can produce things cheaper than many local ones?

It all depends on what you leave out of your analysis (which is why a chimp pressing buttons randomly could predict as well as our economic forecasters). The fewer the companies, the less influence supply and demand have on prices. A heavy investment in advertising and public relations is necessary to keep a national reputation alive. And what about the transportation costs involved when all firms are national? Not to mention the air pollution costs, which are also passed on to the consumer. Chronic inflation suggests that someone is leaving something vital out of his analysis. How does one measure in dollars the cost of economic mistrust? It may be subtle, but it's clearly enormous.

THE GREAT ILLUSION

It's easy to produce examples of the many ways in which Americans try to minimize, circumvent, or deny the interdependence upon which all human societies are based. We seek a private house, a private means of transportation, a private garden, a private laundry, self-service stores, and do-it-yourself skills of every kind. An enormous technology seems to have set itself the task of making it unnecessary for one human being ever to ask anything of another in the course of going about his or her daily business. Even within the family Americans are unique in their feeling that each member should have a separate room, and even a separate telephone, television, and car, when economically possible. We seek more and more privacy, and feel more and more alienated and lonely when we get it. And what accidental contacts we do have seem more intrusive, not only because they're unsought, but because they're not connected with any familiar pattern of interdependence.

Most important, our encounters with others tend increasingly to be competitive as we search for more privacy. We less and less often meet our fellow humans to share and exchange, and more and more often encounter them as an impediment or a nuisance: making the highway crowded when we're rushing somewhere, cluttering and littering the beach or park or wood, pushing in front of us at the supermarket, taking the last parking place, polluting our air and water, building a highway through our house, blocking our view, and so on. Because we've cut off so much communication with each other we keep bumping into each other, so that a higher and higher percentage of our interpersonal contacts are abrasive.

We seem unable to foresee that the gratification of a wish might turn out to be a monkey's paw if the wish were shared by many others. We cheer the new road that shaves ten minutes off the drive to our country retreat but ultimately transforms it into a crowded resort and increases both the traffic and the time. We're continually surprised to find, when we want something, that thousands or millions of others want it, too—that other human beings get hot in summer and cold in winter. The worst traffic jams occur when a mass of vacationing tourists start home early to "beat the traffic." We're too enamored of the individualistic fantasy that everyone is, or should be, different—that a man could somehow build his entire life around some single eccentricity without boring himself and everyone else to death. We all have our quirks, which provide surface variety, but aside from this, human beings have little basis for their persistent claim that they are not all members of the same species.

THE FREEDOM FIX

Since our contacts with others are increasingly competitive, unanticipated, and abrasive, we seek still more apartness and thus accelerate the trend. The desire to be somehow special sparks an even more competitive quest for progressively more rare and expensive symbols—a quest that is ultimately futile since it is individualism itself that produces uniformity.

This is poorly understood by Americans, who tend to confuse uniformity with "conformity," in the sense of compliance with group demands. Many societies exert far more pressure on the individual to mold herself to play a sharply defined role in a total group pattern, but there is variation among these circumscribed roles. Our society gives more leeway to the individual to pursue her own ends, but since the culture defines what is worthy and desirable, everyone tends, independently but monotonously, to pursue the same things in the same way. Thus cooperation tends to produce variety, while competition generates uniformity.

The problem with individualism is not that it is immoral but that it is incorrect. The universe does not consist of a lot of unrelated particles but is an interconnected whole. Pretending that our fortunes are independent of each other may be perfectly ethical, but it's also perfectly stupid. Individualistic thinking is unflagging in the production of false dichotomies, such as "conformity *vs.* independence," "altruism *vs.* egoism," "inner-directed *vs.* other-directed," and so on, all of which are built upon the absurd assumption that the individual can be considered separately from the environment of which he or she is a part.

A favorite delusion of individualism—one that it attempts, through education and propaganda, to make real—is that only egoistic responses are spontaneous. But this is not so: collective responses—helping behavior, nurturance, supportiveness, the assumption of specialized roles in group tasks, rituals, or games—these are natural, not trained, even among animals. People are more *self-consciously* oriented toward others in competitive, individualistic societies—their behavior is calculated. They accommodate to others because they want to look good, impress people, protect themselves from shame and guilt, and avoid confronting people directly. In more organic and cooperative communities people respond spontaneously to impulses that are neither selfish nor unselfish, but more directly from the heart. Sometimes they look generous, sometimes grasping, but what's important is that the behavior is to others, not an effort to produce some sort of *effect* on others. Cooperative societies are unassuming—it's the competitive ones that are concerned with appearances.

Individualism in the United States is exemplified by the flight to the suburb and the do-it-yourself movement. Both attempt to deny human interdependence and pursue unrealistic fantasies of self-sufficiency. The first tries to overlook our dependence upon the city for the maintenance of the level of culture we demand. "Civilized" means, literally, "citified," and the state of the city is an accurate index of the condition of the culture as a whole. We behave toward our cities like an irascible farmer who never feeds his cow and then kicks her when she fails to give enough milk. But the flight to the suburb was in any case self-defeating, its goals subverted by the mass quality of the exodus. The suburban dweller sought peace, privacy, nature, community, good schools, and a healthy child-rearing environment. Instead, he found neither the beauty and serenity of the countryside, nor the stimulation of the city, nor the stability and sense of community of the small town. A small town, after all, is a microcosm, while the suburb is merely a layer, narrowly segregated by age and social class. A minor irony of the suburban dream is that, for many Americans, reaching the pinnacle of their social ambitions (owning a house in the suburbs) forces them to perform all kinds of menial tasks (carrying garbage cans, mowing lawns, shoveling snow, and so on) that were performed for them when they occupied a less exalted status.

Some of this manual labor, however, is voluntary—an attempt to deny the division of labor required in a complex society. Many Americans seem quite willing to pay the price rather than engage in encounters with workers. This do-it-yourself trend has accompanied increasing specialization in occupations. As one's job narrows, perhaps, he or she seeks the challenge of new skill-acquisition in the home. But specialization also means that one's encounters with artisans in the home proliferate and become more impersonal. It's no longer a matter of a few well-known people—smiths and grocers—who perform many functions, and with whom contact may be a source of satisfaction. One finds instead a multiplicity of narrow specialists, each perhaps a stranger—the same type of repair may even be performed by a different person each time. Every relationship, such as it is, must start from scratch, and it's small wonder the householder turns away from such an unrewarding prospect in apathy and despair.

Americans thus find themselves in a vicious circle in which their community relationships are increasingly competitive, trivial, and irksome, in part as a result of their efforts to avoid or minimize potentially irksome relationships. As the few vestiges of stable community life erode, the desire for a simple, cooperative lifestyle grows in intensity. The most seductive appeal of radical ideologies for Americans consists in the fact that all in one way or another attack the competitive foundations of our society.

Now it may be objected that American society is less competitive than it once was, and that the appeal of radical ideologies should hence be diminished. Social critics in the fifties argued that the entrepreneurial individualist of the past has been replaced by a bureaucratic Organization Man. Much of this historical drama was created by comparing yesterday's owner-president with today's assistant sales manager; certainly these nostalgia-merchants never visited a nineteenth-century company town. Another distortion is introduced by the fact that it was only the most ruthlessly competitive robber barons who survived to tell us how it was. Little is written about the neighborhood store that extended credit to the poor, or the small town industry that refused to lay off local workers in hard times. They all went under together. The meek may be blessed but they don't write memoirs.

Even if we grant that the business world was more competitive in the nineteenth century, the total environment was less so. The individual worked in a smaller firm with lower turnover in which his or her relationships were more enduring and more personal. The ideology of Adam Smith was tempered by the fact that the participants in economic struggles were neighbors and might have been childhood playmates. Even if the business world then was as "dog-eat-dog" as we imagine it, it occurred as a deviant episode in what was otherwise a more comfortable and familiar environment than the organization man can find today in or out of his office. The organization man is simply a carryover from the paternalistic environment of the family business and the company town; and the "other-directedness" of the suburban community just a desperate attempt to bring some old-fashioned small-town collectivism into the transient and impersonal lifestyle of the suburb. The social critics of the 1950s were so preoccupied with assailing these rather synthetic forms of human interdependence that they lost sight of the underlying sickness that produced them. Medical symptoms usually result from attempts made by the body to counteract disease, and attacking the symptoms often aggravates and prolongs the illness. This seems to be the case with the feeble and self-defeating efforts of twentieth-century Americans to create a viable social environment.

THE MORAL PREMISES
OF SOCIAL PATHOLOGY

Carl M. Rosenquist

Those who employ the social pathology perspective take an attitude toward social problems like that of the physician toward physical problems. They assume that society, like the individual, is an organism, and that there are normal and abnormal conditions for that organism.

Such an approach, Rosenquist argues, is untenable, for there is simply

From Carl M. Rosenquist, *Social Problems*, pp. 10–15, 20–22. Copyright © 1940 by Prentice-Hall, Inc. Englewood Cliffs, N.J. Reprinted by permission.

no way to define objectively states of social pathology. First of all, very often the "health" of one sector of society depends heavily on the "ill-health" of other sectors. In addition, since society is not an organism, there is no necessary set of relationships by which to define health (as there is, for example, between the nervous system and the digestive system). For these reasons, statements about what is "normal" or "healthy" for society reflect the ideals of the speaker, rather than any objective truth.

The most familiar explanation of social problems uses the analogy between the biological and social organisms. The study of pathology presupposes the existence of an organism in which the symptoms of disease may be observed. For the biologist the organism is a plant or an animal; for the social pathologist, a society.[1] The study of pathology further presupposes a condition of normality in the organism from which disease may be regarded as a deviation. As to the meaning of normality, it will suffice at this point to say that it ordinarily refers to the operation of the various organs in such a way as to secure or promote the welfare of the organism as a whole. Since the nature of the functions involved is dependent upon the structure of the organs, it follows that normality and, consequently, pathology, vary according to the kind of organism concerned. In the biological field, this means that each species of plant or animal has its own peculiar set of diseases; in sociology, it means that social ills differ from society to society and, since societies change, from time to time within the same society.

NORMAL SOCIETY

In the study of pathological manifestations, it is necessary first to know and recognize normality. . . . [It] may be assumed that society exists for its members and that they have certain ideas as to what society should provide. To the extent that these expectations are realized, society may be spoken of as normal or, for the purpose of the analogy, as healthy. This conception of normality does not necessarily find its expression in actual experience. Probably no society has ever provided complete satisfaction for all of its members. Yet the requirement remains as an ideal, from which we measure deviations, referred to as social ills.

When this concept of normality is compared with that of biology, a conspicuous difference is at once apparent. The animal organism is in health when as a whole it is functioning perfectly; the social organism is in health when all of its members are functioning perfectly. . . . It must be emphasized that the social organism exists for the benefit of the individuals who compose it, rather than for itself alone. Conceivably, a society might be healthy according to standards similar to those used in biology—this is, the group as a whole might be wealthy, successful in war, increasing in size, and long of life—but if the internal organization is based upon a system of exploitation in which some of the people make life miserable for the rest, the society is sick according to the usually accepted sociological viewpoint.

THE MEANING OF PATHOLOGY

. . . The discussion of pathology as ordinarily carried on makes it appear that disease is an enemy of the biological organism, existing outside the organism and always waiting for a favorable moment to launch an attack, just as a wolf prowls around a flock of sheep, waiting for the shepherd to relax his vigilance long enough to permit a raid on his charges. This notion has doubtless been strengthened by the discovery that micro-organisms are found in connection with many types of disease. To the human mind, with its strong predilection for personification, the minute organisms have appeared in the role of an attacking army bent on the destruction of its victims. Actually, the picture thus presented is far from the facts.

> Diseases are not entities: the classification of diseases is purely a matter of convenience: what are known as diseases are the results of what happens when the organism comes in contact with inimical agents.[2]

The word disease, then, does not properly refer to an attacking force, but to the response of the organism to certain conditions threatening its safety. The response consists of a series of physiological changes, described as the symptoms of the disease. They are but the indications that the organism has suffered from an injury or infection and is attempting to repair the damage. The symptoms are beneficent in character in the sense that they show active resistance on the part of the organism. To attempt to remove them may harm the organism instead of benefiting it. Disease may be tentatively defined therefore as a process of readjustment. . . .

THE CONCEPT OF NORMALITY

Since biologists invariably define disease in terms of deviation from a state of health, it becomes imperative to define health also. The definition of health as freedom from disease, is, of course, of no value. Substitution of the word "normality" does not remove the difficulty, for normality has no more specific meaning than health. It cannot mean the average condition of the organism, for perfect health is rarely if ever observed. Since normality does not exist as an actual condition, it must obviously refer to an imaginary condition, found only in the observer's mind. A brief inquiry shows this to be the case. Health or normality is an ideal state unattained and probably unattainable, but regarded as eminently desirable. It is taken for granted that good health and, consequently, a long life, are among the chief objectives of man, and that anything which militates against [their] attainment is pathological. This points plainly to the subjective and hedonistic elements in the definition of normality. From his own experience, the individual comes to certain conclusions regarding his own welfare. Sympathetically transferring his personal feelings to others, he produces a general notion of the kind of physical condition he considers ideal. To this he gives the name of normality. Not satisfied with this, he extends his anthropomorphism to all other forms of life, postulating norms for them as well as for himself. With these norms established for a given species, he can proceed at once to a study of its pathology. This is not to say that normality thus determined is without value. On the contrary, the results have amply justified working from postulates of this sort, as the triumphs of pathologists have shown many times; but it can hardly be maintained that the procedure is scientific, if by scientific we mean objective. . . .

This fairly well describes the status of the "pathology" which sociology has borrowed from biology. . . . As a basis for the study of social pathology, a "healthy" society is set up as a norm, from which deviations are observed. Unhappily for the comfort of sociologists, it appears to be much more difficult to arrive at an agreement as to the health of societies than as to the health of individuals. In this connection society is, of course, contemplated in its organic aspects, that is, it is considered as a whole composed of interrelated parts. Yet it is impossible to overlook the fact that there can be no social "health" apart from the health of individual members of society, and the further fact that the nature of the organization of society is determined by the members themselves. For example, it is possible to find described in history societies which have proved themselves very able in conflict with other societies and with nature, so that they have flourished and endured over long periods. From the viewpoint of society as an organism such a group might well be considered "healthy" or normal, whereas its internal organization might be of such a sort as to keep the vast majority of the members in a state of social degradation. On the other hand, it is possible to find societies which, because of looser controls, are less efficient and less secure, but in which the individual members find life highly agreeable. There can be hardly a doubt as to which society the ordinary individual would prefer to live in, and probably we cannot consider that society diseased which is, from the individual's point of view, the most desirable of all. . . .

What then is the most desirable society? What are we to take as the norms or ideals from which we may diagnose our social ills? The answers offered us in the numerous utopias in our literature are by no means unanimous. Some have war and others have peace; some are capitalistic and others are communistic; some are religious and others are unreligious. All have forms of family and community life. Each of them reflects its author's ideas as to what was wrong with the society he lived in. The variety presented makes instantly clear the fact that even in the planning of a new society, in which the authors are limited only by the powers of their own imagination, no agreement in form is possible. And if we were to question all the people in the world as to which of the several existing societies they would prefer, we should probably find no conclusive vote for any. . . .

CONCLUSION

In view of all these difficulties, it may well be wondered how social problems can be studied at all. Obviously we have no norm, real or imaginary, upon which we can agree. Nor is it likely, in view of the constantly changing character of society, that a norm can be established. How can we know what in society is really pathological? The only answer is: we do not and cannot know.

There is, however, a way in which social problems may be studied without answering these questions. They may be treated, not as the study of variations from a norm, but as manifestations of society itself. From this viewpoint popular recognition of any social condition or process as bad, followed by an attempt to eliminate or cure it, serves as the criterion for its inclusion in a study of social problems. The writer merely accepts the judgment of public opinion. . . . The question to be answered is not, then, whether poverty or any other condition is bad for society, and if so what is to be done about it, but what are the conditions of society which large numbers of people regard as harmful and remediable. Is poverty found among them? If so, what are its manifestations? How does it affect the individual? What is being done to remedy it? To these matters we address ourselves. Social problems are nothing more nor less than those conditions or aspects of society which considerable numbers of people are trying to change.[3]

Notes

1. That society is not an organism in the biological sense need not concern us here, but society must be seen as a mechanism of interacting parts if the concept of pathology is to be applied to a study of its ills.

2. William A. White, *The Meaning of Disease*, p. 171. Baltimore: The Williams and Wilkins Company, 1926.

3. "A social problem . . . is determined by group sanction, being the judgment of a group concerning the efficiency of a type of social organization in its structure or function. It is within the realm of folkways, mores, and opinions." George A. Lundberg, Read Bain, and Nels Anderson, Editors, *Trends in American Sociology;* Har-

old A. Phelps, "Sociology and Social Work," p. 332. New York: Harper and Brothers, 1929. Reprinted by permission of the publishers.

Questions for Discussion

1. Smith's statement appeared in 1911; Slater's, in 1970. What are the major differences between their statements?

2. What role did correctional workers play in the development of the social pathology perspective?

3. How did the "child savers" respond to Lombroso's work?

4. Does Rosenquist's critique apply to the contemporary social pathology approach exemplified by Slater and Kavolis? How about the approach described by Platt? How does it apply or not apply? In what ways do you agree or disagree with Rosenquist?

5. What are some of the implications of the social pathology perspective for sociology in general? What do you yourself think about the approach?

Selected References

Duster, Troy. *Backdoor to Eugenics.* New York: Routledge, 1990.

    Examines the resurgence of biological explanations for social problems and specifies the social conditions under which the social pathology perspective continues to flourish.

Fink, Arthur E. *Causes of Crime: Biological Theories in the United States, 1800–1915.* Philadelphia: University of Pennsylvania Press, 1938.

    A scholarly review of the work of thirty-five authors who attributed crime to various biological factors. This work demonstrates the influence of biocentric theorizing before World War I.

Gillin, John L. *Social Pathology.* 2nd ed. New York: Appleton-Century, 1939.

    Gillin's book represents the turning point in pathology texts. This was perhaps the first social pathology book to "attempt to treat social maladjustments in a framework of sociological theory." The middle-class bias is less pervasive in Gillin's book than in other texts, and the theory is more eclectic. (For an example of the prominence of the middle-class bias in some social pathology textbooks, see Stuart Alfred Queen and Jennette Rowe Gruener, *Social Pathology: Obstacles to Social Participation,* 2nd ed. New York: Crowell, 1940.)

Gove, Walter R. "The Effect of Age and Gender on Deviant Behavior: A Biopsychosocial Perspective." In *Gender and the Life Course,* ed. Alice Ross. New York: Aldine, 1985, pp. 115–44.

    Attributes the low rate of deviant behavior among females to their affiliative nature, their physique, and their lack of assertiveness, which also, according to him, have a biological base.

Henderson, Charles Richmond. *Introduction to the Study of the Dependent, Defective, and Delinquent Classes, and of Their Social Treatment.* Boston: Heath, 1909.

Henderson coined the expression "dependent, defective, and delinquent classes." The expression was quite popular in social pathology books for at least a generation. Henderson's book is typical of those that blame the characteristics of the individual for any violation of social rules.

Rafter, Nicole. *White Trash.* Boston: Northeastern University Press, 1988.

Rafter shows how early exponents of social pathology made the facts of defectiveness, dependency, and delinquency fit their beliefs about the causes of these problematic conditions.

Jeffery, C. Ray, ed. *Biology and Crime.* Beverly Hills, Calif.: Sage, 1979.

A collection of studies on the relationship between biology and crime. The editor, C. Ray Jeffery, himself a sociologist, says that sociologists have shied away from and denied the significance of biology as a cause or condition of crime. Reversing his earlier point of view, Jeffery now feels that while biology and society interact as causes of crime, biology is more often the cause while environment is one of its conditions.

Mednick, Sarnoff A., and Jan Volavka. "Biology and Crime." In *Crime and Justice: An Annual Review of Research,* ed. Norval Morris and Michael Tonry. Chicago: University of Chicago Press, 1980, pp. 85–158.

The authors review genetic, neurophysiological, biological, physiological, and biochemical studies. They conclude that biological and social factors combine to produce criminal behavior.

Mills, C. Wright. "The Professional Ideology of Social Pathologists." *American Journal of Sociology* 60 (September 1942): 165–80.

In this widely celebrated essay, Mills points out that most writers on social pathology came from small towns and were middle-class in their outlook, pragmatic in their approach, and conservative in their politics. He attacks their studies for being atheoretical and heavily biased.

Owen, D. R. "The 47-XYY Male: A Review." *Psychological Bulletin* 78 (September 1972): 209–33.

A review and assessment of the research that purports to show that males with an extra Y chromosome are more apt to commit crimes. The author's data suggest that despite the popularity of the XYY chromosome theory, the great majority of XYY males do not commit crimes and appear to lead normal lives.

Rosenberg, Bernard, Israel Gerver, and William Howton, eds. *Mass Society in Crisis: Social Problems and Social Pathology.* 2nd ed. New York: Macmillan, 1971.

A book of readings compiled in the framework of the more recent perspective on social pathology. Included is "A New Look at Mills' Critique," by Emil Bend and Martin Vogelfanger.

Wilson, James Q., and Richard J. Herrnstein. *Crime and Human Nature.* New York: Simon and Schuster, 1986.

An encyclopedic review of the sources of criminal behavior from the perspective of social pathology. The authors conclude that most criminals are mesomorphic, have low IQs, and poor impulse control. Criminality stems from defects in character, socialization, or both.

Zimbardo, Philip G. "The Pathology of Imprisonment." *Society* 9 (April 1972): 4–8.

A mock prison with college students as subjects was established to study the pathological effects of prison on both prisoners and guards. In less than a week, human values were suspended, and the most base pathological side of human nature surfaced. Written from the pathology perspective, the article provides an eloquent plea for prison reform.

3/SOCIAL DISORGANIZATION

The social disorganization perspective arose after World War I in response to a particular set of circumstances in both the larger society and the field of sociology. In this chapter, we look at the circumstances that gave rise to the social disorganization perspective, the sociologists who formulated it, and the basic features of the perspective.

PROBLEMS OF SOCIETY

Migration, urban living, and factory work are certainly nothing new. The ancestors of the American Indians, for example, migrated from Siberia across the Bering Strait and down into the Americas. The ancient Greeks and Egyptians lived in cities. And the ancient Romans are said to have established some of the earliest factories.

After World War I, however, these processes—migration, urbanization, and industrialization—began to occur in the United States at an unprecedented pace. And as they did so, many previously recognized social problems, such as poverty, delinquency and crime, mental illness, and alcoholism, seemed to become more and more prevalent.

Migration, for example, produced considerable culture conflict both for European immigrants and for native American migrants (e.g., people moving from the rural South to the northern cities). The European immigrants, for example, were likely to find considerable conflict between their native culture and the prevailing culture in their new home. Of course, many soon became "Americanized." Others, however, were less successful at the "Americanization process," and these people soon came to be seen as the source and substance of most American social problems. Urbanization also contributed to the sense of increasing social problems. The cities, for instance, included deviant subcultures that were not found in more rural areas—delinquent gangs, for example. Finally, industrialization brought with it many social problems. For example, working conditions were often poor, and technological advances put many people out of work.

Taken together, then, these three factors—migration, urbanization, and industrialization—established a broad social and cultural base for a host of undesirable conditions. Outgrowths of these conditions—such as crime, mental illness, alcoholism, drug addition, and juvenile delinquency—all came to be treated in the social problems textbooks of the day. When these problems had been smaller in scale, the social pathology perspective had seemed adequate. As they increased, however, the pathology perspective seemed less useful. Concomitantly, sociology was facing new problems as a discipline. In coping with these problems—both in society and in sociology—sociologists fashioned the social disorganization perspective.

PROBLEMS OF THE DISCIPLINE

Any fledgling discipline faces a number of difficulties. It has to state a rationale for its existence, it has to formulate what it will do that other disciplines do not do, and it has to make clear what its relationship to other disciplines will be. During its formative period (up to 1918), sociology had not yet resolved these issues.

When the Frenchman Auguste Comte coined the term "sociology," he envisioned it as the queen of the sciences, encompassing all the other scientific disciplines.[1] But Emile Durkheim, battling two generations later to establish sociology as a university discipline in France, took a quite different tack: he set out to make sociology a science with its own concepts and subject matter.[2]

Throughout its formative period, American sociology remained a hodgepodge of history, political science, economics, psychology, and social philosophy. It dealt with issues that overlapped these older disciplines or that they chose to ignore. Thus, some of the early critics called sociology a "science of leftovers." Throughout these years, sociology's concern with order, progress, and the philosophy of history ran strong.

As American sociology moved into its second period (1918 to 1935), it centered more and more on the formation of a scientific policy. Heavy emphasis was placed on the development of concepts and definitions, and much of this conceptual and definitional effort centered on showing how the subject matter of sociology differed from that of other disciplines.

The emergence of the social disorganization perspective during the 1920s reflects this effort to develop sociology as a scientific discipline. The very concept of social disorganization springs from a then-developing network of ideas centering on the concept of social organization. The notion of social organization implies, first of all, that there is a whole whose parts stand in some ordered relationship to one another. Second (and second-

1. Auguste Comte, *Positive Philosophy,* trans. Harriet Martineau (London: George Bell & Sons, 1896).
2. Emile Durkheim, *The Rules of Sociological Method,* trans. Sarah Solovay and John Mueller (Chicago: University of Chicago Press, 1938).

arily), it implies the concept of social disorganization—that is, that the various parts can get out of phase with one another.

Central to this entire conceptualization, implicitly or explicitly, is the notion of *rules*. Rules define not only the different parts of society, but also the way in which they interrelate. And by focusing on rules, sociologists succeeded in defining their subject matter as different from that of any other discipline.

The social disorganization perspective emerged from this developing sociological viewpoint, and in time it came to be the most popular way of studying social problems. To be more specific, sociologists began to see social problems as an index of social disorganization; as they developed a body of sociological concepts to deal with social organization, they also developed sister concepts to describe and explain social disorganization. In the end, sociology began to bloom as a discipline with its own subject matter, its own concepts, and its own way of describing reality.

DIFFERENCES BETWEEN THE PATHOLOGY AND THE DISORGANIZATION PERSPECTIVES

Compared with the earlier social pathology perspective, the social disorganization perspective is more complex, more intellectually distinct, and considerably more systematic—benefiting, of course, from the greater maturity of sociology as a discipline at the time it developed. It is instructive, at this point, to compare these two perspectives in terms of their subject matters, vocabularies, methods, and concerns with practical applications. The social pathologists, it will be recalled, studied social problems by looking at the failings of individuals and institutions. Their concepts and vocabularies, however, were borrowed from other disciplines, most notably medicine. Their methods were more philosophical than scientific. Finally, they wanted action; they wanted to apply their discoveries to the solution of social problems.

Writers using the social disorganization perspective, in contrast, studied social problems by examining social rules. They developed their own conceptualizations and vocabularies. They became more concerned with the development of theory and with precision in methodology. Finally, their emphasis on theory led them to be more concerned with acquiring knowledge than with finding practical solutions to social problems.

This comparison of the pathology and disorganization perspectives brings up the chronic division of opinion in sociology regarding whether sociologists should themselves make moral judgments or should merely study the moral judgments of others. Pathologists made moral judgments with regard to institutions and individuals alike. Disorganization writers, in contrast, chose to study moral judgments in a more detached, "objective" manner. (The social disorganization perspective, however, has since been criticized for not being objective. Critics have charged that nonconforming ways of life are often called disorganized when, in reality, they simply represent a different system of social organization. See, for example, the Clinard reading in this chapter.)

THE MAJOR SOCIAL DISORGANIZATION THEORISTS

The social disorganization perspective as we know it today stems largely from the writings of Charles H. Cooley, W. I. Thomas and Florian Znaniecki, and William F. Ogburn. To be sure, the idea of social disorganization has been considerably refined since these men first wrote about it. However, the major influences on current social disorganization writers can all be traced back to these four. All were primarily theorists, and all sought to explain why individuals sometimes fail to obey rules. And, as the following discussions show, they all pictured social problems as a function of social disorganization.

Cooley.   A very early but still influential writer, Cooley made some important conceptual contributions to the social disorganization perspective. First, he formulated the distinction between primary and secondary group relations. Primary relations refer to personal and enduring face-to-face relationships.[3] Secondary relationships, on the other hand, are less frequent, impersonal contacts. Given this distinction, sociologists quickly saw that the movement from rural to urban areas was accompanied by a breakdown in primary group controls. Second, Cooley conceptualized social disorganization as the disintegration of traditions. He argued that the worst aspect of social disorganization is that "the absence of social standards is likely to lower . . . [a person's] plane of achievement and throw him back upon sensibility and other primitive impulses."[4]

Thomas and Znaniecki.   In their major work on the Polish immigrant to America,[5] Thomas and Znaniecki defined social disorganization as the breakdown of the influence of rules on the individual. The bulk of their work consists of letters written by Polish immigrants to friends and relatives back home in Poland. The letters all give testimony to the conflict of cultures, ethnic as well as generational. According to Thomas and Znaniecki, the Polish immigrant faced either no rules or too many rules. In the case of a paucity of rules, the immigrant had no means of defining his or her situation. In the case of a plentitude of rules, the rules were either unclear or

3. Charles Horton Cooley, *Human Nature and the Social Order* (New York: Scribner's, 1902).

4. Charles Horton Cooley, *Social Organization: A Study of the Larger Mind* (New York: Scribner's, 1909), p. 348.

5. William I. Thomas and Florian Znaniecki, *The Polish Peasant in Europe and America,* 2 vols. (New York: Knopf, 1927).

in conflict with one another. Thus, the immigrant often did not know how to behave in America and lacked mutual understanding with native Americans. In their study of Polish immigrants, Thomas and Znaniecki conceptualized the experiences of millions who immigrated to the United States. They also indicated that a variety of social problems (e.g., delinquency, crime, mental illness, and alcoholism) could be attributed in large part to the failure of the immigrant family to control its members.

Ogburn. Ogburn's contribution lies primarily in his notion of cultural lag.[6] The different parts of a culture are interdependent, Ogburn said, and when different parts change at different rates, one part can get out of phase with another and produce disorder. Usually, Ogburn observed, people accept new tools more readily than new ideas; thus, material culture changes much more quickly than does nonmaterial culture. Stated another way, changes in customs and rules tend to lag behind those in technology, which is what Ogburn means by "cultural lag." The principal source of social disorganization, according to Ogburn, is this uneven rate of cultural change.

CHARACTERISTICS OF THE SOCIAL DISORGANIZATION PERSPECTIVE

People who work with this perspective view society as a social system— a complex, dynamic whole whose parts are coordinated. When events change one part of the system, there is a corresponding need for adjustment in other parts. "Social disorganization" refers to lack of adjustment, or poor adjustment, between the parts. The major elements of the social disorganization perspective are as follows:

Definition. Social disorganization is conceived of as a failure of rules. Three major types of disorganization are *normlessness, culture conflict,* and *breakdown.* With normlessness, no rules exist on how to act. With culture conflict, at least two opposing sets of rules exist on how to act. In such situations, persons who act in terms of one set of expectations may in so doing violate another set of expectations. Breakdown is a variation on this same theme. Here rules exist, but conformity to them either fails to produce the promised rewards or yields punishments instead.

Causes. The root cause of social disorganization is, broadly speaking, social change. As changes occur, the parts of the social system get out of tune with one another.

6. William F. Ogburn, *Social Change with Respect to Culture and Original Nature* (New York: Huebsch, 1922), pp. 199–280.

Conditions. The parts of a social system are never perfectly in tune. Nevertheless, there is usually a dynamic equilibrium. Any condition that upsets the equilibrium may precipitate social disorganization. Such conditions include technical, demographic, or cultural changes that generate social change (i.e., a change in social relationships).

Consequences. The social disorganization perspective predicts outcomes for the system and for persons in it. For persons, social disorganization produces stress, which in turn produces "personal disorganization"—for example, mental illness, alcoholism.[7] For the system, social disorganization may have three types of consequences. First, there can be change in the system (i.e., some response or adaptation may bring the various parts of the system back into equilibrium). Second, the system can continue to operate in a steady state (i.e., the disorganization may remain but the system continues to function anyway). Third, the system may break down (i.e., the disorganization may be so disruptive that it destroys the system).

Solutions. Attempts to reduce social disorganization can be put into effect once the proper diagnosis has been made. Thus, parts of the system that are out of phase can be brought back into equilibrium—for example, technical changes can be slowed down.

SUMMARY AND CONCLUSION

After World War I, American sociologists strove to establish sociology as an independent scientific discipline with its own concepts and subject matter. At the same time, migration, urban growth, and technological change seemed to be producing a number of social problems, and sociologists worked hard to devise a set of terms to describe and explain these problems.

Cooley taught a generation of sociologists to look for the signs of a breakdown of traditions, especially as reflected in the decreased hold of small, intimate groups on their members. Thomas and Znaniecki devised an important set of concepts and, in their study of Polish immigrants to America, showed how moving to a strange city in a foreign land disrupts families, sharpens generational conflict, and increases chances of criminality and mental illness. Ogburn examined the effects of technology on social organization, developed his influential theory of cultural lag, and fostered a whole school of technological determinists.

7. See, for example, Robert E. L. Faris and H. Warren Dunham, *Mental Disorders in Urban Areas: An Ecological Study of Schizophrenia and Other Psychoses* (Chicago: University of Chicago Press, 1939).

Briefly stated, social disorganization denotes a failure of rules. Social change is usually viewed as the cause, and technological, demographic, and cultural changes are viewed as the precipitating conditions. Personal disorganization and disequilibrium of the social system are seen as consequences of social disorganization, and the solution for disorganization is to bring the features of the social system back into equilibrium.

SOCIAL CHANGE AND SOCIAL DISORGANIZATION

Robert E. Park

The basis of social organization, Park says, is tradition and custom. And during periods of stability, the family, neighborhood, and community combine to exercise control over people. Urbanization, industrialization, and immigration disrupt these stabilizing influences, thereby undermining the authority of traditional social systems. The trends of modern society induce rapid changes that, in turn, produce social disorganization. Examples of social disorganization are found among migrants, delinquents, and derelicts, and in the rootlessness of life in areas where these people are found.

In the family and in the neighborhood such organization as exists is based upon custom and tradition, and is fixed in what Sumner calls the folkways and the mores. At this stage, society is a purely natural product; a product of the spontaneous and unreflective responses of individuals living together in intimate, personal, and face-to-face relations. Under such circumstances conscious efforts to discipline the individual and enforce the social code are directed merely by intuition and common sense.

In the larger social unit, the community, where social relations are more formal and less intimate, the situation is different. It is in the community, rather than in the family or the neighborhood, that formal organizations like the church, the school, and the courts come into existence and get their separate functions defined. With the advent of these institutions, and through their mediation, the community is able to supplement, and to some extent supplant, the family and the neighborhood as a means for the discipline and control of the individual. However, neither the orphan asylum nor any other agency has thus far succeeded in providing a wholly satisfactory substitute for the home. The evidence of this is that they have no alumni associations. They create no memories and traditions that those who graduate from them are disposed to cherish and keep alive.

It is in this community with its various organizations and its rational,

From Robert E. Park, Ernest W. Burgess, and Roderick D. McKenzie, *The City*, pp. 105–110. © 1967 by The University of Chicago Press. Reprinted by permission.

rather than traditional, schemes of control, and not elsewhere, that we have delinquency. Delinquency is, in fact, in some sense the measure of the failure of our community organizations to function.

Historically, the background of American life has been the village community. Until a few years ago the typical American was, and perhaps still is, an inhabitant of a middle western village; such a village, perhaps, as Sinclair Lewis describes in *Main Street*. And still, today, the most characteristic trait of Homo Americanus is an inveterate individualism which may, to be sure, have been temperamental, but in this case temperament has certainly been considerably reinforced by the conditions of life on the frontier.

But with the growth of great cities, with the vast division of labor which has come in with machine industry, and with movement and change that have come about with the multiplication of the means of transportation and communication, the old forms of social control represented by the family, the neighborhood, and the local community have been undermined and their influence greatly diminished.

This process by which the authority and influence of an earlier culture and system of social control is undermined and eventually destroyed is described by Thomas—looking at it from the side of the individual—as a process of "individualization." But looking at it from the point of view of society and the community it is social disorganization.

We are living in such a period of individualization and social disorganization. Everything is in a state of agitation—everything seems to be undergoing a change. Society is, apparently, not much more than a congeries and constellation of social atoms. Habits can be formed only in a relatively stable environment, even if that stability consists merely—as, in fact, it invariably does, since there is nothing in the universe that is absolutely static—in a relatively constant form of change. Any form of change that brings any measurable alteration in the routine of social life tends to break up habits; and in breaking up the habits upon which the existing social organization rests, destroys that organization itself. Every new device that affects social life and the social routine is to that extent a disorganizing influence. Every new discovery, every new invention, every new idea, is disturbing. Even news has become at times so dangerous that governments have felt it wise to suppress its publication.

It is probable that the most deadly and the most demoralizing single instrumentality of present-day civilization is the automobile. The automobile bandit, operating in our great cities, is much more successful and more dangerous than the romantic stage robber of fifty years ago. The connection of the automobile with vice is notorious. "The automobile is connected with more seductions than happen otherwise in cities altogether."[1]

The newspaper and the motion picture show, while not so deadly, are almost as demoralizing. If I were to attempt to enumerate all the social forces that have contributed to the disorganization of modern society I should probably be compelled to make a catalogue of everything that has introduced any new and striking change into the otherwise dull routine of our daily life. Apparently anything that makes life interesting is dangerous to the existing order.

The mere movement of the population from one part of the country to another—the present migration of the Negroes northward, for example—is a disturbing influence. Such a movement may assume, from the point of view of the migrants themselves, the character of an emancipation, opening to them new economic and cultural opportunities, but it is none the less disorganizing to the communities they have left behind and to the communities into which they are now moving. It is at the same time demoralizing to the migrating people themselves, and particularly, I might add, to the younger generation.

The enormous amount of delinquency, juvenile and adult, that exists today in the Negro communities in northern cities is due in part, though not entirely, to the fact that migrants are not able to accommodate themselves at once to a new and relatively strange environment. The same thing may be said of the immigrants from Europe, or of the younger generation of women who are just now entering in such large numbers into the newer occupations and the freer life which the great cities offer them.

"Progress," as I once heard William James remark, "is a terrible thing." It is a terrible thing in so far as it breaks up the routine upon which an existing social order rests, and thus destroys the cultural and the economic values, i.e., the habits of thrift, of skill, of industry, as well as the personal hopes, ambitions, and life-programs which are the content of that social order.

Our great cities, as those who have studied them have learned, are full of junk, much of it human, i.e., men and women who, for some reason or other, have fallen out of line in the march of industrial progress and have been scrapped by the industrial organization of which they were once a part.

A recent study by Nels Anderson of what he calls "Hobohemia," an area in Chicago just outside the "Loop," that is to say, the downtown business area, which is almost wholly inhabited by homeless men, is a study of such a human junk heap. In fact, the slum areas that invariably grow up just on the edge of the business areas of great cities, areas of deteriorated houses, of poverty, vice, and crime, are areas of social junk.

I might add, because of its immediate connection with the problems and interests of this association, that recent studies made in Chicago of boys' gangs seem to show that there are no playgrounds in the city in which a boy can find so much adventure, no place where he can find so much that may be called "real sport," as in these areas of general deterioration which we call the slums.

In order to meet and deal with the problems that have been created by the rapid changes of modern life, new organizations and agencies have sprung into existence. The older social agencies, the church, the school, and the courts, have not always been able to meet the problems which new conditions of life have created. The school, the church, and the courts have come down to us with their aims and methods defined under the influence of an older tradition. New agencies have been necessary to meet the new conditions. Among these new agencies are the juvenile courts, juvenile protective associations, parent-teachers' associations, Boy Scouts, Young Men's Christian Associations settlements, boys' clubs of various sorts, and I presume, playgrounds and playground associations. These agencies have taken over to some extent the work which neither the home, the neighborhood, nor the other older communal institutions were able to carry on adequately.

These new institutions, perhaps because they are not to the same extent hampered by our earlier traditions, are frankly experimental and are trying to work out a rational technique for dealing with social problems, based not on sentiment and tradition, but on science.

Largely on the basis of the experiments which these new agencies are making, a new social science is coming into existence. Under the impetus which the social agencies have given to social investigation and social research, sociology is ceasing to be a mere philosophy and is assuming more and more the character of an empirical, if not an exact, science.

As to the present condition of our science and of the devices that we have invented for controlling conduct and social life, I can only repeat what I said at the very outset of our paper: "The thing of which we still know least is the business of carrying on an associated existence."

Note

1. W. I. Thomas, *The Unadjusted Girl—with Cases and Standpoint for Behavior Analysis*, Criminal Science Monograph No. 4, Boston, 1923, p. 71.

THE ECOLOGY OF URBAN DISORGANIZATION

Robert E. L. Faris and H. Warren Dunham

Although urbanism and social disorganization tend to go together, the incidence of social problems varies within the ecological structure of the city. In looking at different areas of the city, Park, Burgess, and McKenzie found that rates of social disorganization and social problems were greatest in what they called the "zone in transition"—a zone characterized by boarding houses and tenements, transitory businesses, and dilapidated buildings. Social problems associated with these indices of disorganization included vice, poverty, crime, alcoholism, mental illness, and broken families. Faris and Dunham believe that social disorganization leads to social problems by breaking down primary group controls. Hence, rates of social problems are highest in the center of the city, where social disorganization is also highest; conversely, on the periphery the indices of social disorganization are at their lowest and so is the incidence of social problems.

A relationship between urbanism and social disorganization has long been recognized and demonstrated. Crude rural-urban comparisons of rates of dependency, crime, divorce and desertion, suicide, and vice have shown these problems to be more severe in the cities, especially the large rapidly expanding industrial cities. But as the study of urban sociology advanced, even more striking comparisons between the different sections of a city were discovered. Some parts were found to be as stable and peaceful as any well-organized rural neighborhood while other parts were found to be in the extreme stages of social disorganization. Extreme disorganization is confined to certain areas and is not characteristic of all sections of the city.

Out of the interaction of social and economic forces that cause city growth a pattern is formed in these large expanding American cities which is the same for all the cities, with local variations due to topographical and other differences. This pattern is not planned or intended, and to a certain

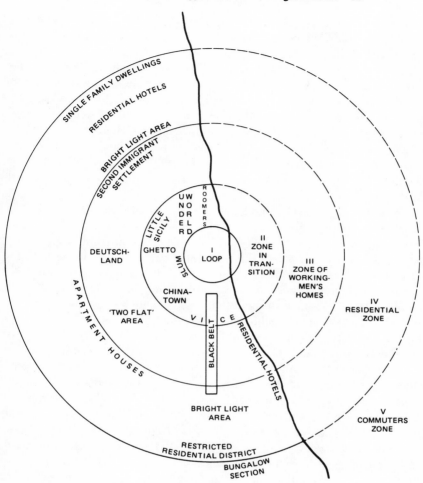

From Robert E. Park, Ernest W. Burgess and Roderick D. McKenzie, *The City*, Chart I, p. 42. Reprint 1966. Reprinted by permission of the University of Chicago Press.

extent resists control by planning. The understanding of this order is necessary to the understanding of the social disorganization that characterizes urban life.

THE NATURAL AREAS DEPICTED AS CIRCULAR ZONES

The most striking characteristics of this urban pattern, as described by Professor Burgess,[1] may be represented by a system of concentric zones, shown in Chart I. Zone I, at the center, is the central business district. The space is occupied by stores, business offices, places of amusement, light industry, and other business establishments. There are few residents in this area, except for transients inhabiting the large hotels, and the homeless men of the "hobohemia" section which is usually located on the fringe of the business district.

Zone II is called the zone in transition. This designation refers to the fact that the expanding industrial region encroaches on the inner edge. Land values are high because of the expectation of sale for industrial purposes, and since residential buildings are not expected to occupy the land permanently, they are not kept in an improved state. Therefore, residential buildings are in a deteriorated state and rents are low. These slums are inhabited largely by unskilled laborers and their families. All the settlements of foreign populations as well as the rooming-house areas are located in this zone.

Zone III, the zone of workingmen's homes, is inhabited by a somewhat more stable population with a higher percentage of skilled laborers and fewer foreign-born and unskilled. It is intermediate in many respects between the slum areas and the residential areas. In it is located the "Deutschlands," or second immigrant settlement colonies, representing the second generation of those families who have migrated from Zone II.

Zone IV and V, the apartment-house and commuters' zones, are inhabited principally by upper-middle-class families. A high percentage own their homes and reside for long periods at the same address. In these areas stability is the rule and social disorganization exceptional or absent.

The characteristics of the populations in these zones appear to be produced by the nature of the life within the zones rather than the reverse. This is shown by the striking fact that the zones retain all their characteristics as different populations flow through them. The large part of the population migration into the city consists of the influx of unskilled labor into the second zone, the zone in transition. These new arrivals displace the populations already there, forcing them to move farther out into the next zone. In general, the flow of population in the city is of this character, from the inner zones toward the outer ones. Each zone, however, retains its characteristics whether its inhabitants be native-born white, foreign-born, or Negro. Also each racial or national group changes its character as it moves from one zone to the next.

Within this system of zones, there is further sifting and sorting of economic and social institutions and of populations. In the competition for land values at the center of the city, each type of business finds the place in which it can survive. The finding of the place is not infrequently by trial and error, those locating in the wrong place failing. There emerge from this competition financial sections, retail department store sections, theater sections, sections for physicians' and dentists' offices, for specialized shops, for light industry, for warehouses, etc.

Similarly, there are specialized regions for homeless men, for rooming-houses, for apartment hotels, and for single homes. The location of each of these is determined ecologically and the characteristics also result from the interaction of unplanned forces. They maintain their characteristics in spite of the flow of various racial and national groups through them and invariably impress their effects on each of these groups. These have been called "natural areas" by Professor Park,[2] because they result from the interactions of natural forces and are not the result of human intentions.

Fortunately, the city of Chicago has been studied somewhat more intensively than most cities of its size. Certain of these areas are significant in relation to social disorganization. It is possible to define and describe these areas with certain kinds of objective data. The major divisions of the city can be seen in Map I. Extending outward from the central business district are the principal industrial and railroad properties. The rooming-house sections extend along three arms radiating from the center to the north, west, and south. The slum areas are roughly defined by the regions containing over 50 per cent foreign-born and native-born of foreign parentage and over 50 per cent Negro. Beyond these areas is the residential section. In the Lake Calumet section at the southeastern corner of the city is another industrial region inhabited by a foreign-born population.

Too small to be shown on this map are the areas of homeless men— the "hobohemia" areas.[3] These are located on three main radial streets and are just outside the central business district. Their inhabitants are the most unstable in the city. The mobility and anonymity of their existence produces a lack of sociability and in many cases deterioration of the personality. Although spending their time in the most crowded parts of the city, these homeless men are actually extremely isolated. For the most part they represent persons unable to obtain an economic foothold in society, and so they maintain themselves by occasional labor, by petty thievery, by begging, and by receiving charity. As they have no opportunity for normal married life, their sexual activities are limited to relations with the lowest type of prostitutes and to homosexuals. The rate of venereal infection is high among these men. Chronic alcoholism is also a common characteristic of the members of this group. Their lives are without goal or plan, and they drift aimlessly and alone, always farther from the conventional and normal ways of living.

Another area of importance is the rooming-house area. This is usually located along main arteries of transportation and a little farther from the center of the city. In Chicago there are several rooming-house sections, the three largest consisting of arms radiating to the north, west, and south, just beyond the hobohemia areas, each extending for something over two miles in length and from a half-mile to over a mile in width. The populations of these areas are principally young, unmarried white-collar workers, who are employed in the central business district during the day and live in low-priced rented rooms within walking distance or a short ride from their work.[4] Within the area the population is constantly shifting, turning

Types of Cultural and Economic Areas

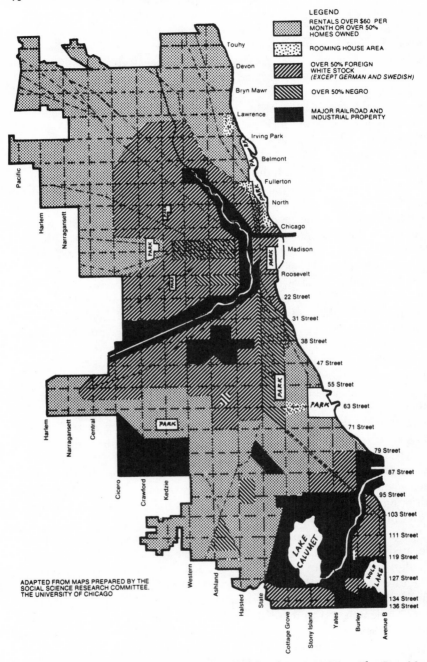

LEGEND

RENTALS OVER $60 PER MONTH OR OVER 50% HOMES OWNED

ROOMING HOUSE AREA

OVER 50% FOREIGN WHITE STOCK (EXCEPT GERMAN AND SWEDISH)

OVER 50% NEGRO

MAJOR RAILROAD AND INDUSTRIAL PROPERTY

ADAPTED FROM MAPS PREPARED BY THE SOCIAL SCIENCE RESEARCH COMMITTEE. THE UNIVERSITY OF CHICAGO

From Robert E. Park, Ernest W. Burgess and Roderick D. McKenzie, *The City*, Map I, p. 44. Reprint 1966. Reprinted by permission of the University of Chicago Press.

over entirely about once each four months. Anonymity and isolation also characterize the social relations in this area; no one knows his neighbors and no one cares what they might think or say. Consequently the social control of primary group relations is absent, and the result is a breakdown of standards of personal behavior and a drifting into unconventionality and into dissipations and excesses of various sorts. The rates of venereal diseases and of alcoholism are high in this area, and the suicide rate is higher than for any other area of the city.[5]

The foreign-born slum areas occupy a large zone surrounding the central business and industrial area. Within this zone there are a number of segregated ethnic communities, such as the Italian, Polish, Jewish, Russian, and Mexican districts. The newly arrived immigrants of any nationality settle in these communities with their fellow-countrymen. In these groups the language, customs, and many institutions of their former culture are at least partly preserved. In some of the most successfully isolated of these, such as the Russian-Jewish "ghetto," the Old-World cultures are preserved almost intact. Where this is the case, there may be a very successful social control and little social disorganization, especially in the first generation. But as soon as the isolation of these first-settlement communities begins to break down, the disorganization is severe. Extreme poverty is the rule; high rates of juvenile delinquency, family disorganization, and alcoholism reflect the various stresses in the lives of these populations.

Two distinct types of disorganizing factors can be seen in the foreign-born slum areas. The first is the isolation of the older generation, the foreign-born who speak English with difficulty or not all and who are never quite able to become assimilated to the point of establishing intimate friendships with anyone other than their native countrymen. Within the segregated ethnic communities these persons are well adapted to their surroundings, but as soon as they move away or are deserted by their neighbors, they suffer from social isolation.[6] The second type of disorganizing factor operates among the members of the second and third generations. The very high delinquency rate among the second-generation children has been shown by Shaw.[7] This disorganization can be shown to develop from the nature of the child's social situation. Also growing out of the peculiar social situation of the second generation is the mental conflict of the person who is in process of transition between two cultures—the culture of his ancestors and the culture of the new world in which he lives. As he attends American schools and plays with children of other than his own nationality, the child soon finds himself separated from the world of his parents. He loses respect for their customs and traditions and in many cases becomes ashamed of his own nationality, while at the same time he often fails to gain complete acceptance into the American group of his own generation. This is particularly true if he is distinguished by color or by features which betray his racial or national origin. This person is then a "man without a culture," for though he participates to some extent in two cultures, he rejects the one and is not entirely accepted by the other.[8]

The Negro areas are, in general, similar in character to the foreign-born slum areas. The principal Negro district in Chicago extends for several miles southward from the business district. Two smaller Negro districts are located on the Near West Side, as well as one on the Near North Side. In the larger area on the South Side, the social disorganization is extreme only at the part nearest the business district.[9] In the parts farther to the south live the Negroes who have resided longer in the city and who have become more successful economically. These communities have much the same character as the nearby apartment-house areas inhabited by native-born whites.

For some miles along the Lake Front in Chicago a long strip of apart-ment-hotel districts has grown up. These districts occupy a very pleasant and favorable location and attract residents who are able to pay high rentals. The rates of various indices of social disorganization are in general low in these sections.

The outlying residential districts of middle-class and upper-middle-class native-born white population live in apartments, two-flat homes, and single homes. In these districts, and especially the single home areas in which there is a large percentage of homes owned by the inhabitants, the popu-lation is stable and there is little or no social disorganization in comparison with those areas near the center of the city. . . .

Not only are such statistical facts as population composition, literacy, dependency rates, and disease rates known to vary greatly in the different sections of the city, but also mental life and behavior. In one of the most conclusive of these studies, the study of juvenile delinquency by Clifford R. Shaw and his associates,[10] sufficient control was obtained to establish with reasonable certainty that the high rates of delinquency were products not of the biological inferiority of the population stocks that inhabit the slum areas, nor of any racial or national peculiarity, but rather of the nature of the social life in the areas themselves. The delinquency rates remained constantly high in certain urban areas which were inhabited by as many as six different national groups in succession. Each nationality suffered from the same disorganization in these areas and each nationality alike improved after moving away from the deteriorated areas.

As has been shown, the natural areas which have been defined above can be identified by the use of certain mathematical indices for different types of social phenomena. Such indices as the percentage of foreign-born, the percentage of homes owned, the sex ratio, the median rentals paid, the density of population, the rate of mobility, the educational rate, the per-centage of rooming-houses and hotels, and the percentage of condemned buildings, roughly tend to identify these areas and to differentiate between them. These indices might be regarded as ones which measure the extent of social disorganization between the different communities and the natural areas of the city. Other types of objective data, representing such social problems as juvenile delinquency, illegitimacy, suicide, crime, and family disorganization, might be considered as indices representing effects or results of certain types of social processes. As in the research of Clifford Shaw which has been described above, the rates for these different social problems tend to fit rather closely into the ecological structure of the city as described by Park, Burgess, and others. In other words, in all of these social problems there is the concentration of high rates close to the center of the city, with the rates declining in magnitude as one travels in any direction toward the city's periphery. Shaw's study of juvenile delinquency gives one of the most complete pictures of this pattern. The other studies, in general, show the same pattern with certain variations which develop because of the location of certain ethnic groups in certain parts of the city.

The problem of mental disorder has been for the first time approached by the utilizing of this ecological technique. It is the attempt to examine the spatial character of the relations between persons who have different kinds of mental breakdowns. While this type of approach is used in this study, the authors wish to emphasize that they regard it as having definite limitations in understanding the entire problem of mental disorder. It can be looked upon as a purely cultural approach and as such does not tend to conflict with any understanding of this problem which may come from biological, physiological, or psychological approaches. However, in the light of these previous studies of social problems utilizing this method it does seem particularly desirable to study the distribution of the different types of mental disorders.

Notes

1. R. E. Park and E. W. Burgess, *The City* (Chicago: University of Chicago Press, 1925).

2. R. E. Park, "Sociology," in *Research in the Social Sciences*, ed. Wilson Gee (New York: Macmillan Co., 1929), pp. 28–29.

3. Nels Anderson, *The Hobo* (Chicago: University of Chicago Press, 1923).

4. H. W. Zorbaugh, *The Gold Coast and the Slum* (Chicago: University of Chicago Press, 1929).

5. R. S. Cavan, *Suicide* (Chicago: University of Chicago Press, 1928).

6. Louis Wirth, *The Ghetto* (Chicago: University of Chicago Press, 1928).

7. C. R. Shaw et al., *Delinquency Areas* (Chicago: University of Chicago Press, 1929).

8. Everett Stonequist, *The Marginal Man* (New York: Charles Scribner's Sons, 1937).

9. E. Franklin Frazier, *The Negro Family in Chicago* (Chicago: University of Chicago Press, 1932).

10. C. R. Shaw and H. D. McKay, *Report on the Causes of Crime,* National Commission on Law Observance and Enforcement (Washington, D.C.: U.S. Government Printing Office, 1931).

FAMILY DISORGANIZATION

W. I. Thomas and Florian Znaniecki

The rules for defining situations in traditional society require people to focus on what is best for the group, or the "we" attitude, as Thomas and Znaniecki call it. Immigration exposes people, especially children, to a new set of rules for defining situations in more modern society. Here, people are expected to focus more on what is best for them personally, or what Thomas and Znaniecki call the "I" attitude. The conflict of these two attitudes results in competing definitions and rules. And once groups are able to distinguish between the "I" and the "we" attitude, the ability of either set of rules to influence conduct is weakened immeasurably. This is the essence of family disorganization as Thomas and Znaniecki see it.

We can now draw certain general conclusions from our data which we shall hypothetically propose as sociological laws, to be verified by the observation of other societies.

1. The real cause of all phenomena of family disorganization is to be sought in the influence of certain new values—new for the subject—such as: new sources of hedonistic satisfaction, new vanity values, new (individualistic) types of economic organization, new forms of sexual appeal. This influence presupposes, of course, not only a contact between the individual and the outside world but also the existence in the individual's personality of certain attitudes which make him respond to these new values—hedonistic aspirations, desire for social recognition, desire for economic security and advance, sexual instinct. The specific phenomenon of family disorgan-

From W. I. Thomas and Florian Znaniecki, *The Polish Peasant in Europe and America* (2 vols.), New York Dover Publications, 1927, pp. 1167–1170.

ization consists in a definite modification of those preexisting attitudes under the influence of the new values, resulting in the appearance of new, more or less different attitudes. The nature of this modification can be generally characterized in such a way that, while the attitudes which existed under the family system were essentially "we"-attitudes (the individual did not dissociate his hedonistic tendencies, his desires for recognition or economic security, his sexual needs from the tendencies and aspirations of his family group), the new attitudes, produced by the new values acting upon those old attitudes, are essentially "I"-attitudes—the individual's wishes are separated in his consciousness from those of other members of his family. Such an evolution implies that the new values with which the individual gets in touch are individualistic in their meaning, appeal to the individual, not to the group as a whole; and this is precisely the character of most modern hedonistic, sexual, economic, vanity values. Disorganization of the family as primary group is thus an unavoidable consequence of modern civilization.

2. The appearance of the new individualistic attitudes may be counteracted, like every effect of a given cause, by the effects of other causes; the result is a combination of effects which takes the form of a suppression of the new attitude; the latter is not allowed to remain in full consciousness or to manifest itself in action, but is pushed back into the subconscious. Causes that counteract individualization within the family are chiefly influences of the primary community of which the family is a part. If social opinion favors family solidarity and reacts against any individualistic tendencies, and if the individual keeps in touch with the community, his desire for recognition compels him to accept the standards of the group and to look upon his individualistic tendencies as wrong. But if the community has lost its coherence, if the individual is isolated from it, or if his touch with the outside world makes him more or less independent of the opinion of his immediate milieu, there are no social checks important enough to counterbalance disorganization.

3. The *manifestations* of family disorganization in individual behavior are the effects of the subject's attitudes and of the social conditions; these social conditions must be taken, of course, with the meaning which they have for the acting individual himself, not for the outside observer. If the individual finds no obstacles in his family to his new individualistic tendencies, he will express the latter in a normal way; disorganization will consist merely in a loss of family interests, in a social, not anti-social action. If there are obstacles, but disorganization of the primary-group attitudes has gone far enough in the individual to make him feel independent of his family and community, the effect will probably be a break of relations through isolation or emigration. If, however, the individual meets strong opposition and is not sufficiently free from the traditional system to ignore it, hostility and anti-social behavior are bound to follow. In the measure

that the struggle progresses, the new attitude of revolt becomes a center around which the entire personality of the individual becomes reorganized, and this includes those of his traditional values which are not dropped, but reinterpreted to fit the new tendency and to give a certain measure of justification to his behavior. In the relatively rare cases where both the new attitude is very strong and the obstacles from the old system are powerfully resented and seem insuperable because the individual is still too much dependent on this system to find some new way out of the situation, the struggle leads to an internal conflict which may find its solution in an attempt to remove the persons by whom the old system is represented in this situation rather than in a complete rejection of the system itself.

4. It is evidently impossible to revive the original family psychology after it has been disintegrated, for the individual who has learned consciously to distinguish and to oppose to one another his own wishes and those of other members of his family group and to consider these wishes as merely personal cannot unlearn it and return to the primary "we"-attitudes. Reorganization of the family is then possible, but on an entirely new basis—that of a moral, reflective coordination and harmonization of individual attitudes for the pursuit of common purposes.

MORAL NORMS WITHOUT ENFORCEMENT

George C. Homans

In this study of a small town called "Hilltown," Homans demonstrates that moral norms, to be effective, must be backed by social control. Traditionally, frequent social contact among Hilltowners reinforced their moral norms, mainly through gossip. As changes in life style made contact less frequent, however, Hilltowners lost their sense of clearly agreed upon right and wrong. They became increasingly indifferent to their neighbors, and they lost interest in small-town gossip. Without reinforcement, the traditional norms lost their status in Hilltowners' eyes, and the eventual result was normlessness.

... We shall look first at changes in the environment in which Hilltown as a group has survived ... In the first place, the Hilltowners themselves

From George C. Homans, *The Human Group*, pp. 357–363, 365–368. Copyright © 1950 by Harcourt, Brace and Co. Reprinted by permission of the publisher.

brought about important changes in their physical environment. The land was cleared; the barns and houses built. The soil, once quite rich but always shallow, became depleted beyond the possibility of recovery by ordinary Yankee methods of farming. The forests were cut off, only timber for cordwood remaining.

Many other important changes, outside the control of Hilltowners, took place in the physical and technical environment. In particular, transportation was improved in scope, speed, and carrying capacity far beyond anything known at the beginning of the nineteenth century. Perhaps the most important event in the social history of Hilltown, and even in that of New England, was the opening of through railroads to the Great Lakes and the Ohio Valley. This meant that the products of Hilltown farms and shops had to compete in a national market with the products of richer areas. Later the appearance of the hard-surfaced road, the automobile, and the truck hastened the same process, but at the same time enabled Hilltowners to sell perishable produce, such as milk and chickens, more widely than they had before, and, with the rise of factory towns in the neighborhood, allowed them to sleep in town but work and play outside.

The physical and technical changes in the nation at large stimulated change in another field, the national standard of living. By a national standard of living we do not mean actual expenditures for different kinds of goods, but the scale of expenditure that many people feel to be appropriate: the standard of living is one of the norms of society. Suppose the people of one part of the country—Hollywood is a good example at the present day—are able to buy certain kinds of houses, clothes, gadgets, and entertainment that other people have not yet enjoyed. The knowledge of this fact is then, in one way and another, transmitted to, and acts as an influence on, the people of hundreds of other communities. They develop a new level of aspiration for the enjoyment of material goods. Certainly the rising standard of living of the nineteenth and twentieth centuries taught the Hilltowners to aspire to something better than subsistence farming. And national standards in such matters as road maintenance, poor relief, and children's schooling became so high that Hilltown could not meet those standards without help from outside. A concomitant of a rising standard of living is an increase in the scope and power of state and national government.

Finally, the Hilltowners were communicants in what the anthropologists would call New England culture. Its norms, far from checking the influence of rising living standards, encouraged Yankees to attain them. This effect of the cultural environment may be hard to describe but it cannot be ignored. We have said that the Yankees were, in effect, mere squatters on the land, content to till the soil only so long as no better opportunity presented itself. Unlike the French-Canadians, they were not indoctrinated in devotion to family, land, church, and tradition. Instead, their spiritual leaders, from John Wycliffe through Calvin to Emerson, had taught them for centuries the value of self-reliance and individual decision in the conduct of life. Translated from the spiritual plane to the half-conscious assumptions of everyday life, conveyed from parent to child, from teacher to pupil, from minister to churchgoer and even, for the Yankees were readers and their literature was flourishing, from writer to reader, this doctrine encouraged a conviction that every person should "make something of himself," "get ahead in the world," and submit to no group controls that might prevent his attaining these ends. At times Yankees seemed to believe, not that wealth came next to godliness, but that the two were identical. We are not arguing that even the kind of norms taught to French-Canadians will keep men subsistence farmers in the face of a rising standard of living. After all, a norm alone is not enough to preserve behavior unchanged; controls must back up the norm. We are arguing that the norms instilled in Yankees positively encouraged them to pursue the characteristic goals of American civilization in the nineteenth and twentieth centuries.

In short, the changes in the technical and physical environment made Hilltowners poorer, in comparison with other people, than they had once been, while the changes in the cultural environment made them anxious to get richer.

THE EXTERNAL SYSTEM

We turn now from the environment to the external system of social relationships in Hilltown, that is, the relationships determined by the survival of the group in its environment. We will remember that the sentiments entering the external system are those that men bring to a group rather than those that result from their membership in the group. These sentiments are often called individual self-interest. It is clear that in the course of Hilltown's history, *the number and strength of the sentiments that led members of the group to collaborate with other members had declined.* When the land had been cleared, and the barns and houses raised, the need for neighbors to work together became much less than it had been. As transportation improved, local industry declined, and mill towns grew up round about, the interests of Hilltowners led them to take part in organizations, such as markets and factories, outside the town rather than inside it.

At the same time, *the number of activities that members of the group carried on together decreased.* It is revealing just to count the number of activities in which Hilltowners collaborated with their fellow townsmen in the early part of the nineteenth century and then to count the ones that were still carried on in 1945. The farm bees had gone; farming itself was in decline; the local industries, first the small shops and then the factories, had been unable to survive; the general stores, once their customers began to trade in larger centers, lost money until finally only one of them was left. Though town government and town meeting remained, their activities were greatly curtailed. Militia training and the management of church affairs had vanished altogether; control of highways, schools, and relief was greatly reduced. Hilltown no longer sent its own representative to the state legislature—it was merely part of a larger electoral district. Finally, the church itself had been broken by schism.

This does not mean, of course, that individual Hilltowners had nothing to do. It does mean that they had much less to do with other Hilltowners. As the number of activities that members of the group carried on together declined, *so the frequency of interaction between members of the group decreased.* The sentiments, activities, and interactions of Hilltowners had become centrifugal rather than centripetal.

THE INTERNAL SYSTEM

The decline in the external system was accompanied by a decline in the internal. In studying the Bank Wiring Observation Room, we saw that when the wiremen were "thrown together" in the room, they soon developed "social" sentiments, activities, and interactions, over and above those necessary for the accomplishment of the wiring job itself. But if the process can run in one direction, it can also run in the other. *As the frequency of interaction between the members of a group decreases in the external system, so the frequency of interaction decreases in the internal system.* If we had known this rule and had been watching Hilltown at the turn of the century and afterwards, we should have been able to predict what happened. In a comparison of the Hilltown of 1850 or even 1900 with the Hilltown of 1945, even the crudest observations reveal an enormous impoverishment of social life. At the later date, there was much less informal visiting, and there were fewer parties. The decline was so great that some persons, particularly in the upper group, saw almost nobody outside of business. The fraternal orders disappeared, and the men stopped spending the time of day in the general store. The social occasions, such as church suppers, connected with the formal organs of Hilltown life, were much less frequent than they had once been. Even town meeting and church services were sparsely attended. Once again, it is important to state, in order to avoid misunderstanding, that this does not necessarily imply any lack of social life on the part of individual Hilltowners. It does imply that a citizen of the town today has fewer contacts with other Hilltowners than his ancestor had in the past. And it may imply something more, namely that, inside Hilltown or outside, the social life of an individual is made up of fewer occasions at every one of which substantially the same persons appear. There are fewer groups that come near being exclusive.

Just as an increase in the frequency of interaction between the members of a group will bring about an increase in the intensity of the sentiments they feel toward one another, *so a decrease in the frequency of interaction will bring about a decrease in the strength of interpersonal sentiments.* In Hilltown this rule seems to have held good for sentiments of antagonism as well as for sentiments of friendliness. Both retreated toward some neutral value. The words of informants suggest that, if there was less mutual good feeling in 1845 than in 1945, there was also, in certain fields, less mutual bad feeling. Certainly the attitudes of a townsman toward a member of a church different from his own were much more moderate. People were more nearly indifferent to one another. Again, this does not mean that people did not talk about one another. There is no evidence that gossip was in abeyance, but the gossip did not carry the same emotional tone.

This we should have been able to predict from what we know already. We have seen in the Bank Wiring group, and it is a commonplace of small-town life, that a sharp division into subgroups is quite compatible with a definite unity of the group as a whole. We should expect then that, if the unity of the group as a whole disintegrates, the division into subgroups disintegrates too. Something like this we find in Hilltown. If, in 1945, there was less positive antagonism dividing one subgroup from another than there had been in 1845, this did not bring positive good feeling within the group as a whole but rather emotional indifference, that is, the absence of social organization.

NORMS AND SOCIAL CLASS

The emotional indifference of persons toward one another may increase through two processes, one direct and the other indirect. Sheer decline in the frequency of interaction may be one: a man may have a hard time feeling strongly about someone he does not see. But the decline may also affect sentiments through the medium of norms. No more than other aspects of the social system do norms exist in a vacuum. Norms—notions of proper forms of behavior—are not left untouched by real behavior. The degree to which norms are held in common by the members of a group must bear a relation to the frequency of interaction of the members, and the definiteness of norms, to the frequency with which the activities, whose standard form they describe, are repeated. Thus in Hilltown, as elsewhere, *a decrease in the frequency of interaction between the members of a group and in the number of activities they participate in together entails a decline in the extent to which norms are common and clear.* In Hilltown this process is best illustrated in the decay of the Protestant churches, the guardians of the most important norms. The disintegration of the community led to a weakening of the norms and this in turn to a weakening of the churches.

But the circle is vicious, and the weakening of the churches led to a further weakening of the norms. Through ritual and preaching, churches drill people in norms, so that any decline in the churches contributes to social disintegration, since fewer people get the old thorough training in social standards. We can recognize this process at work in Hilltown, while still admitting that a general decline in the attitudes supporting the Protestant churches in America contributed to the decline in this single community. At least one point is clear: in the Hilltown of 1945 one important factor in the indifference of persons toward one another was their lack of an accepted standard for judging one another's behavior. A person is ready to look down on someone who has acted wrongly, but what if there is no definition of wrong? . . .

SOCIAL CONTROL

. . . Social control is not a separate department of group life; it is not a "function" that the group performs, or that someone performs for it. Instead, control, to a greater or lesser degree, is inherent in the everyday relationships between the members of the group. Now it is clear that social control was weaker in the Hilltown of 1945 than in the Hilltown of the nineteenth century. We do not have as much evidence as we should like, but we have enough. Reactions to the sexual irresponsibility of the young and to the misappropriation of town funds were very different in the two eras. When the tax collector, a few years ago, went off with town money, he was, to be sure, caught and put in jail, but so far as the town was concerned, nothing happened. The townspeople did nothing to catch him, and no one in town felt bound to make good the loss. When he got out of jail, he came back to town and was received as though everything was the same as before; no one was indignant and refused to associate with him; his social standing did not suffer. In short his action had none of the social consequences it would have had in an earlier generation. Yet it is a definition of stable equilibrium in a group that when a norm is violated something does happen. If a change takes place in a single element of behavior, there is a change in the other elements, and that of a certain kind: one tending to restore the previous state of the system. In the example we are using, the mere return of the funds would not have been enough to restore the previous state. If that had been enough, the equilibrium of Hilltown could have been preserved by a bonding company. Something more was needed: the supremacy of the violated norm should have been reestablished, and this certainly did not take place.

The reaction of the town to the pregnancy of young women before marriage was of much the same kind. But let us be perfectly clear. Although we use, for convenience, such words as "decline" and "disintegration," we are not taking a moral stand here. The point we are making is not that sexual continency in the young is, by absolute standards, a particularly valuable norm, but rather that it had once been a Hilltown norm and in 1945 was one no longer. There are plenty of societies in which the young people enjoy sexual freedom before marriage and in which, at the same time, social control is strong. The norms of these societies are not those of old-time New England, and yet a breach of the norms, such as they are, is at once met by a strong reaction. Hilltown, on the contrary, had been losing its old norms, and the controls associated with them, without acquiring others to take their place. No doubt we exaggerate, but this seems to have been the general direction of change.

We observe the fact that social control had weakened; *if, moreover, social control is implicit in the relationships of the social system, any change in the strength of control must be determined by changes in the relationships.* And this is just what we can begin to see in Hilltown. Control ultimately is a matter of the punishment or reward of individuals. If social interaction is rewarding to a man, then loss of social interaction will hurt him. But if loss of social interaction—that is, avoidance—does not follow a breach of a norm, where is the punishment, especially when, as in Hilltown, the frequency of interaction is low to start with? If the good opinion of his neighbors is a reward to a man, then a loss of their good opinion will hurt him, but if this loss does not follow a breach of a norm, where is the punishment? And how can it follow, when the norms themselves are not well defined? If social ranking in the community is not established, how can a man suffer loss of social rank? In short, the social system of Hilltown has become such as to bring very little automatic punishment upon a man if he departs from his existing degree of obedience to a norm.

Moreover, a decline in control to such an extent that a man who commits a serious offense is not driven out of town probably implies also that a good citizen is less apt to be kept in. If reward is the other side of punishment, a group that cannot induce the bad to leave cannot induce the good to stay. If a man enjoys working with others in a common enterprise, and cannot find one; if he wants to gain, by achievement, the good opinion of his neighbors, and there is no foundation, in a common body of norms, for that good opinion, then, in effect, his social system will not reward him sufficiently, and he will be apt to leave it. Emigration from Hilltown, which was partly determined by changes in environmental conditions, must also have been determined in part by changes in the social system. What we can see is that interaction, activity, sentiment, and norms in Hilltown, unlike some other groups we have studied, were not working together to maintain the *status quo* or to achieve further integration of the group. Instead the relationships between the elements of behavior were such as to lead, in time, toward the condition Durkheim called *anomie,* a lack of contact between the members of a group, and a loss of control by the group over individual behavior. Let us hasten to add, lest we be accused of a conservative bias, that changes in the *status quo* are not, in our view, always and necessarily in the direction of *anomie.*

Many people would see the problem of Hilltown as a moral one: a weakening of the moral fiber of its inhabitants or, in some way, an increasing flabbiness in the community considered as a person. But surely we have learned that conscience itself is, in part at least, a function of the social circumstances in which conscience develops, and that for conscience to decide on action in accord with community norms, the community must make conscience more, rather than less, easily able to choose right. Because Hilltown still has a name, geographical boundaries, and people who live within the boundaries, we assume that it is still a community and therefore judge that it is rotten. It would be wiser to see that it is no longer, except in the most trivial sense, a community at all.

The decline of a community means decreasing control by that community over individual behavior. Since the group can support the individual and help him to maintain his personal equilibrium under the ordinary shocks of life, this decline in control may mean damage to individual personalities, provided the individuals are members of no other community that will take up the slack. Extrapolating from Hilltown to modern America, or indeed to the modern world, we recognize that what we have been studying is very common. Civilization has fed on the rot of the village. This in itself is not the problem. It becomes a problem only when the organizations to which the former Hilltowners go, such as the big new industries, fail to develop some of the characteristics that Hilltown once had. If they do fail, then the disorders of personal behavior increase. To this question, the leaders of these organizations have, on the whole, failed to address themselves.

A DISORGANIZING CONCEPT

Marshall B. Clinard

Social disorganization started out as a sensitizing concept for sociologists, and those of the first generation who used the concept were able to understand a changing society better by means of the notion. The next generation of sociologists, however, often found the idea baseless and confusing. In this excerpt, Clinard summarizes the problems with the concept. Subjectively, writers tended to be unclear, whimsical, or biased when using the idea. Objectively, they tended to confuse change, deviant behavior, subcultures, and human variation with social disorganization.

. . . A state of disorganization is often thought of as one in which there is a "breakdown of social controls over the behavior of the individual" and a decline in the unity of the group because former patterns of behavior and social control no longer are effective.[1] There are a number of objections to this frame of reference. (1) Disorganization is too subjective and vague a concept for analyzing a general society. Effective use of the concept, however, may be made in the study of specific groups and institutions. (2) Social disorganization implies the disruption of a previously existing condition of organization, a situation which generally cannot be established. Social change is often confused with social disorganization without indicating why some social changes are disorganizing and others not. (3) Social disorganization is usually thought of as something "bad," and what is bad is often the value judgment of the observer and the members of his social class or other social groups. For example, the practice of gambling, the patronage of taverns, greater freedom in sex relations, and other behavior do not mean that these conditions are naturally "bad" or "disorganized." (4) The existence of forms of deviant behavior does not necessarily constitute a major threat to the central values of a society. The presence of suicide, crime, or alcoholism may not be serious if other values are being achieved. American society, for example, has a high degree of unity and integration despite high rates of deviant behavior if one considers such values as nationalism, a highly developed industrial production, and goals of material comfort. (5) What seems like disorganization actually may often be highly organized systems of competing norms. Many subcultures of deviant behavior, such as delinquent gangs, organized crime, homosexuality, prostitution, and white-collar crime, including political corruption, may be highly organized. The slum sex code may be as highly organized and normative regarding premarital relations in one direction as the middle-class sex code is in the other.[2] The norms and values of the slums are highly organized, as Whyte has shown in his *Street Corner Society*.[3] (6) Finally, as several sociologists have suggested, it is possible that a variety of subcultures may contribute, through their diversity, to the unity or integration of a society rather than weaken it by constituting a situation of social disorganization.[4]

Notes

1. Contemporary use of the concept "social disorganization" comes largely from W. I. Thomas and Florian Znaniecki, *The Polish Peasant in Europe and America* (New York: Alfred A. Knopf, Inc., 1927). For criticisms of this concept see John F. Cuber, Robert A. Harper, and William Kenkel, *Problems of American Society* (New York: Holt, Rinehart and Winston, Inc., 1956), Chap. 22; [Edwin M.] Lemert, *Social Pathology* (New York: McGraw-Hill, 1951), Chap. 1; and [Frank E.] Hartung, "Common and Discrete Values," *Journal of Social Psychology*, 38:3–22 (1953).

2. William F. Whyte, "A Slum Sex Code," *American Journal of Sociology*, 49:24–32 (1943).

3. William F. Whyte, *Street Corner Society* (Chicago: University of Chicago Press, 1943). Also see Marshall B. Clinard, *Slums and Community Development: Experiments in Self-Help* (New York: The Free Press, 1967).

4. See Robin Williams, Jr., "Unity and Diversity in Modern America," *Social Forces*, 36:1–8 (1957).

Questions for Discussion

1. What does Park see as the basic features of social disorganization?

2. Apply Park's conception of social disorganization (a) to Hilltown, (b) to the inner areas of cities, and (c) to Thomas and Znaniecki's description of family disorganization.

3. How does rapid social change precipitate social disorganization? Discuss the articles in this chapter in this light.

4. Do you agree with Clinard's critique of the social disorganization perspective? Is there any way a social disorganization analysis can avoid Clinard's criticisms? How so or why not?

Selected References

Bursik, Robert J., Jr. "Social Disorganization and Theories of Crime and Delinquency: Problems and Prospects." *Criminology* 26 (November 1988): 519–51.

In this study, Bursik shows how the Shaw-McKay perspective on social disorganization, as derived from Thomas and Znaniecki, can still help to account for reported variations in urban juvenile delinquency rates.

Carey, James T. *Sociology and Public Affairs: The Chicago School.* Beverly Hills, Calif.: Sage, 1975.

Chapter 4 ("The Social Disorganization Paradigm") tells how Thomas and Znaniecki first developed the social disorganization perspective, how students of theirs and their followers applied it to a variety of studies on social problems, and how the perspective came under critical attack in later years.

Cohen, Albert K. "The Study of Social Disorganization and Deviant Behavior." In *Sociology Today,* ed. Robert K. Merton, Leonard Broom, and Leonard S. Cottrell, Jr. New York: Basic Books, 1959, pp. 474–83.

According to Cohen, in order to understand social disorganization one must first examine the components of social organization. The basic conditions of social organization are the existence of rules to define events and the motivation of people to follow the rules. With regard to the first condition, social disorganization results from no rules, vague rules, or conflicting rules. With regard to the second condition, social disorganization may result from inadequate socialization or a failure in social control.

Coleman, James S. "Community Disorganization and Urban Problems." In *Contemporary Social Problems,* 4th ed., ed. Robert K. Merton and Robert Nisbet. New York: Harcourt Brace Jovanovich, 1976, pp. 557–601.

A description of the social processes leading to community organization or disorganization, as well as of the connection between social disorganization and urban problems.

Cooley, Charles Horton. *Social Organization: A Study of the Larger Mind.* New York: Scribner's, 1927, pp. 342ff.

Discusses the effects of disorganization—namely, chaos and lack of discipline in the lives of individuals.

Cottrell, W. F. "Death by Dieselization: A Case Study in the Reaction to Technological Change." *American Sociological Review* 16 (June 1951): 358–65.

A useful study of how changes in railroad technology disorganized a whole town centered around railroading.

Elliott, Mabel A., and Francis E. Merrill. *Social Disorganization.* 4th ed. New York: Harper, 1961.

An encyclopedic text on the interrelationship of personal and cultural problems in society. The authors make a vigorous effort to include all types of deviant behavior under the rubric of social disorganization.

Faris, Robert E. L., and H. Warren Dunham. *Mental Disorders in Urban Areas: An Ecological Study of Schizophrenia and Other Psychoses.* Chicago: University of Chicago Press, 1939.

An application of Burgess's concentric zone theory of the city. Near the heart of the city is the most socially disorganized area—the "zone of transition." Faris and Dunham show that, for certain mental illnesses, the rates are highest in this zone.

Linsky, Arnold S., and Murray A. Straus. *Social Stress in the United States: Links to Regional Patterns in Crime and Illness.* Dover, Mass.: Auburn House, 1986.

A study of crime, maladaptive behavior, and stress-related diseases as related to social conditions that reflect change, loss of stable relationships, and loss of secure normative guidelines. The authors discuss their findings in the framework of social disorganization theory.

Martindale, Don. "Social Disorganization: The Conflict of Normative and Empirical Approaches." In *Modern Sociological Theory,* ed. Howard Becker and Alvin Boskoff. New York: Holt, Rinehart and Winston, 1957, pp. 340–68.

In this chapter, Martindale gives perhaps the first detailed critical analysis of the concept of social disorganization as used by sociologists. He points out that the very notion of social disorganization is rooted in the society's values and has no real status as an objective scientific concept.

Obgurn, William F. *Social Change with Respect to Culture and Original Nature.* New York: Huebsch, 1922.

Ogburn presents his theory of cultural lag. Social disorganization arises out of a failure of groups to adapt to technological change.

Thomas, William I., and Florian Znaniecki. *The Polish Peasant in Europe and America.* 2 vols. New York: Knopf, 1927.

In the introduction to this famous book, Thomas and Znaniecki state that social disorganization consists of a breakdown in social rules. They then present letters written by recent immigrants from Poland to America, piling up abundant evidence of the anomalous situation they face in America.

Wirth, Louis. "Ideological Aspects of Social Disorganization." *American Sociological Review* 5 (August 1940): 472–82.

A distinguished American sociologist indicates that the term "social disorganization" frequently conceals a set of vested interests or special pleading.

4/VALUE CONFLICT

During the first two stages of American sociology's development (1905 to 1935), a number of theorists pointed to the prominence of conflict in society.[1] In addition, these early theorists were social critics. They found much that was wrong with American society, and they argued for basic changes in its structure.[2] Since American sociology was only in its infancy, however, all these writers addressed a reform-minded audience that was outside the academic setting.

During the 1930s and throughout the third period (1935 to 1954), American sociologists were to fashion a different role for themselves and were to begin addressing a different kind of audience. They became more concerned with developing sociology as a scientific discipline, and other academics became their audience. Instead of espousing social reform on behalf of an explicit set of values, they became more "objective" and detached in their analyses of social problems. And because the social disorganization perspective seemed the most congenial to the development of sociology as a scientific discipline, most sociologists subscribed to that perspective. Nonetheless, the conflict perspective was not forgotten, and during the third period in the development of American sociology the value conflict perspective was resurrected.

CONFLICT THEORISTS AND THE FORMULATION OF THE VALUE CONFLICT PERSPECTIVE

The value conflict perspective grew out of a synthesis of European and American theories of conflict. Among early European sociologists, conflict theorists abounded.[3] Karl Marx, for example, described history in terms of a struggle between the classes, and Georg Simmel analyzed conflict as a

1. Early American conflict theorists included Albion Small, Edward Ross, Lester Ward, Thorstein Veblen, and Robert Park.

2. Lewis A. Coser, *The Functions of Social Conflict* (New York: Free Press, 1956).

3. For example, Ludwig Gumplowicz, Karl Marx and Friedrich Engels, Gustav Ratzenhofer, and Georg Simmel.

form of social interaction.[4] Americans had studied European masters such as these and developed their own notions about social conflict,[5] but until the 1920s and 1930s, they did not apply the conflict perspective to the study of social problems. In 1925, Lawrence K. Frank advocated the value conflict approach to the study of social problems; applying this perspective to housing problems, Frank showed how a variety of social interests were entangled in housing questions and how changes introduced to solve the problems of the urban slum would involve a host of groups in endless conflicts of interests.[6]

The major formulation of the value conflict approach to social problems, however, was accomplished more than a decade later by Richard C. Fuller and Richard R. Myers. In two seminal papers published in 1941[7] (and reprinted in this chapter), Fuller and Myers held that conflicts of values usually figure in all phases of most social problems, regardless of the specific issues involved. They argued that all problems have a natural history with three stages—awareness, policy determination, and reform—and that at each of these stages, the values and interests of different groups clash.

The formulation of the value conflict perspective reflected the times. Fuller began to develop the approach during the Depression,[8] and his and Myers's papers were published during World War II.[9] The Depression and the war revived interest in conflict theory. In contrast to the disorganization perspective, conflict theory assumed that there is nothing wrong (or "disorganized") about people upholding their own interests and values against the competing interests and values of other groups.

In addition, when the nation went to war, sociologists found a patriotic

4. See, for example, Karl Marx and Friedrich Engels, *Selected Works,* 2 vols. (Moscow; Foreign Languages Publishing House, 1965), and Georg Simmel, "The Sociology of Conflict," trans. Albion Small, *American Journal of Sociology* 9 (1903–04): 490–525, 672–89, 798–811.

5. In America, the most important early conflict theorists were Albion Small and Robert Park. Small is largely responsible for introducing Simmel's writings to American sociologists. In addition, Small treated conflict as an important social process in his own writings. Park was also greatly influenced by Simmel. He treated conflict as one of the basic forms of interaction, and he used the notion of conflict at great length in his writings on community, city, and race relations. See Albion W. Small and George E. Vincent, *An Introduction to the Study of Society* (New York: American Book Company, 1894), and Robert E. Park and Ernest W. Burgess, *Introduction to the Science of Sociology* (Chicago: University of Chicago Press, 1921).

6. Lawrence K. Frank, "Social Problems," *American Journal of Sociology* 30 (January 1925): 463–75.

7. Richard C. Fuller and Richard R. Myers, "Some Aspects of a Theory of Social Problems," *American Sociological Review* 6 (February 1941): 24–32; Richard C. Fuller and Richard R. Myers, "The Natural History of a Social Problem," *American Sociological Review* 6 (June 1941): 320–28.

8. Richard C. Fuller, "Sociological Theory and Social Problems," *Social Forces* 15 (May 1937): 496–502; Richard C. Fuller, "The Problem of Teaching Social Problems," *American Journal of Sociology* 44 (November 1938): 415–28; Richard C. Fuller, "Social Problems," Part I, in *New Outline of the Principles of Sociology,* ed. R. E. Park (New York: Barnes & Noble, 1939), pp. 3–61.

9. Fuller and Myers, "Some Aspects of Theory," Fuller and Myers, "Natural History."

rationale for injecting social values into their sociology. In the early 1940s, two articles criticized the social disorganization perspective in a way that indirectly supported this school of thought. In these articles, the term "disorganization," like "pathology," was criticized for violating the norm of value neutrality.[10] More recently, as mentioned in the preceding chapter, what was labeled "disorganization" was said to reflect simply the sociologist's failure to recognize organization among people who did not have middle-class lifestyles.[11] Thus, it was suggested that sociologists using the disorganization approach were only deluding themselves when they claimed to deal with social problems in a value-free and "objective" manner. By pointing out that value judgments are implicit even when sociologists try to avoid them, these critiques gave solace to those sociologists who believed that they *should* inject their values into their sociology.

Consequently, the formulation of the value conflict perspective included the notion that sociologists' concern should be with service to society rather than scientific appearances. Fuller, for example, pointed out that the social problems course is a "service" course.[12] Most students who take it do not intend to go on to graduate work in sociology; thus what they need is a textbook and a point of view that will help them as citizens to understand, analyze, and take action regarding the social problems they are bound to face after graduation. (Fuller himself was planning a textbook along these lines when he died.) The notion of applied sociology was also echoed in another work of the period, a famous study of race relations that argued, among other things, that social scientists should labor explicitly in the service of their society.[13]

The first social problems textbook to be organized around the value conflict perspective appeared in 1948.[14] This book built on the papers by Fuller and Myers and by sociologists of the early 1940s. The authors differed from Fuller and Myers and others regarding the value conflict per-

---

10. Louis Wirth, "Ideological Aspects of Social Disorganization," *American Sociological Review* 5 (August 1940): 472–82; C. Wright Mills, "The Professional Ideology of Social Pathologists," *American Journal of Sociology* 49 (September 1942): 165–80.

11. See, for example, Marshall B. Clinard, *Sociology of Deviant Behavior,* 2nd ed. (New York: Holt, Rinehart and Winston, 1968), pp. 41–42, and Albert K. Cohen, "The Study of Social Disorganization and Deviant Behavior," in *Sociology Today: Problems and Prospects,* ed. Robert K. Merton, Leonard Broom, and Leonard S. Cottrell, Jr. (New York: Basic Books, 1959), p. 474. Two classic field studies refute the claim that slums are examples of social disorganization. See William Foote Whyte, *Street Corner Society: The Social Structure of an Italian Slum,* 2nd ed. (Chicago: University of Chicago Press, 1955), and Gerald D. Suttles, *The Social Order of the Slum: Ethnicity and Territory in the Inner City* (Chicago: University of Chicago Press, 1968).

12. Fuller, "Problem of Teaching."

13. Gunnar Myrdal, *An American Dilemma: The Negro Problem and Modern Democracy* (New York: Harper, 1944).

14. John F. Cuber and Robert A. Harper, *Problems of American Society: Values in Conflict* (New York: Henry Holt, 1948).

spective, however, by seeking to make the sociologist a detached analyst (and not, in addition, a therapist) of social problems. Thus, even within a perspective, there can be dissension regarding how sociology should fulfill its dual mandate.

CHARACTERISTICS OF THE VALUE CONFLICT PERSPECTIVE

Value conflict, as a perspective, is considerably sharper in focus than the social pathology perspective, yet less complex than the social disorganization perspective. Its essential characteristics are as follows:

Definition.   Social problems are social conditions that are incompatible with the values of some group whose members succeed in publicizing a call for action.

Causes.   The root causes of social problems are conflicts of values or interests. Various groups, because they have different interests, find themselves in opposition. Once opposition crystallizes into conflict, a social problem is born.

Conditions.   Background conditions affecting the appearance, frequency, duration, and outcome of social problems are competition and contact among groups. When two or more groups are in competition and in particular types of contact with one another, a conflict cannot be avoided. A number of kinds of social problems have arisen under these conditions. And once the problem has arisen, the competing groups can also be in conflict over how to resolve the problem.

Numerous writers have pointed out that social problems consist of an objective condition and a subjective definition. The objective condition is contact and competition; the subjective definition reflects different ways of defining and evaluating contact, competition, and the distribution of goods and rights. The social problem, then, emerges out of the volatile mixture of objective condition and subjective definition.

Consequences.   Conflicts can be abrasive and costly. Sometimes they result in the sacrifice of higher values on behalf of lesser-ranked values. More often, they result in abortive stalemates or in loss by the weaker party in the conflict. They also produce a tradition of "bad feeling" between the groups. In addition, however, as more liberal observers point out, conflicts can have the positive effect of helping groups clarify their values.

Solutions.   The value conflict perspective suggests three ways in which social problems arising out of clashing interests and values may be resolved: consensus, trading, and naked power. If the parties can resolve the conflict on behalf of a set of higher values shared by both parties, then consensus wins the day. If the parties can bargain, then a trade of values—all in the spirit of democratic process—can take place. If neither consensus nor trading works, then the group with the most power gains control.

SUMMARY AND CONCLUSION

Conflict has always figured in the thinking of important European and American sociologists. But as American sociologists sought to develop sociology as a science, they began to focus on social order and seemed to forget about conflict as a basic fact of social life and a major component of many social problems.[15] The Depression years, together with World War II, rekindled interest in conflict theory and in making sociology more "relevant" to society. Fuller and Myers produced the outstanding formulation of this view, which continues to be popular among sociologists.

From this perspective, social problems are seen as arising from conflicts of values. Competition and particular types of contact among groups are the conditions under which such conflicts develop. Value conflicts frequently lead to the polarization of groups and a clarification of their values. "Solutions" take the form of exerting power, bargaining, or reaching a consensus.

15. John Horton, "Order and Conflict Theories of Social Problems," *American Journal of Sociology* 71 (May 1966): 701–13.

THE CONFLICT OF VALUES

Richard C. Fuller and Richard R. Myers

Fuller and Myers, the two main theorists of the value conflict perspective, posit three kinds of social problems: the physical, the ameliorative, and the moral. The distinctions revolve around whether or not people agree on the undesirability of the condition and on what actions should be taken. With physical problems (such as tornadoes or hurricanes), people agree that the condition is undesirable and that nothing can be done about the physical cause of the problem. (They may disagree, however, about how to deal with the consequences of the event.) With ameliorative problems (such as crime or poverty), people agree that the condition is undesirable and that the condition can be corrected, but they disagree about what action should be taken. With moral problems (such as abortion or gambling), people do not agree about whether the condition is undesirable or about what action, if any, should be taken. As society changes, problems can shift from one category to another. Nonetheless, Fuller and Myers maintain, central to all social problems are "conflicts in the value scheme of the culture."

Social problems courses have too often fallen into disrepute because sociologists have had no clear understanding of the nature of the social phenomena out of which problems arise. Because of this lack of understanding, courses have been "informational" in character, the teaching lopsided and incomplete, and the textbooks primarily compendia of unrelated facts.

"Social Problems" has been a convenient heading under which a mass of data pertaining to crime, divorce, immigration, insanity, and the like, has been assembled and presented to the student in unsystematic and undigested form. In this lumping together, the contribution of the sociologist as such has been negligible. He has borrowed from the fields of history, economics, medicine, psychiatry, penology, and social work and has condensed findings from these various disciplines into a series of separate courses in miniature, but has added to the totality very little distinctly sociological analysis.

From Richard C. Fuller and Richard Myers, "Some Aspects of a Theory of Social Problems," *American Sociological Review*, 6, February 1941, quotes from pp. 24–25, 27–32. Copyright 1941 by the American Sociological Association. Reprinted by permission.

What justification is there for preserving in the sociology curriculum a course which surveys differentiated and discrete problems, catch-as-catch-can, without a unifying and systematic sociological interpretation? It may be that there is some place in the college curriculum for a survey course which considers a variety of social problems from a variety of viewpoints— biological, medical, economic, political—but a course of that type should be presented in collaboration by a number of different specialists. There is no reason why a sociologist should have any special competence to handle so many varied kinds of data with so many different scientific analyses.

Some may object that social problems do not have enough in common to be dealt with by one central thread of sociological theory. If such be the case, then each separate problem must be interpreted with a different set of sociological concepts and the only excuse for considering a number of problems together would be that of practical expediency—to satisfy students who desire a survey course because they have not the time or interest for more specialized study.

It seems worthwhile, therefore, to inquire whether sociology can work out a common orientation for the treatment of diverse social problems as "sociological phenomena," and whether this central thread of analysis can be maintained consistently throughout a course or textbook.

Attempts to achieve such common orientation have been made by certain textbook writers. The most popular climate of theory has been the application of cultural lag and social disorganization analyses to social problems.[1] We find this theory set up in skeleton form in first and last chapters of textbooks, but rarely, if ever, consistently applied throughout the book to all the problems with regard to which the author presents factual data. The result is that the theoretical discussion of the concept "social problem" is of little practical use to the student and is relegated to a minor role in the introduction or conclusion of the course.

The failure of sociologists to develop a workable sociological orientation stems from their inability to free themselves from the traditional concept "social problem" which is unrealistic because it is incomplete. Traditionally, sociologists have dealt with social problems as "givens," rather than as phenomena to be demonstrated. They have assumed certain conditions as inevitable social problems, either to suit their own scheme of values, or because such conditions have historically been discussed as problems in the textbooks.

A social problem is a condition which is an actual or imagined deviation from some social norm cherished by a considerable number of persons. But who is to say whether a condition is such deviation? The sociologist may say so, but that does not make the condition a social problem from the point of view of the layman. Sociologists, nonetheless, have been content to take deviations for granted, without bothering to consult the definitions of conditions which laymen make. . . .

A common sociological orientation for the analysis of all social problems may thus be found in the conflict of values which characterizes every social problem. These conflicts are mirrored in the failure of people to agree that a given condition is a social problem, or assuming such agreement, failure to reach an accord as to what should be done about it. It is exactly this disagreement in value-judgments that is the root cause of all social problems, both in the original definition of the condition as a problem and in subsequent efforts to solve it. May we suggest, tentatively, a threefold classification of social problems on the principle of different levels of relationship to the value-scheme?[2]

At the first level, we have what we may call the *physical* problem. The physical problem represents a condition which practically all people regard as a threat to their welfare, but value-judgments cannot be said to cause the condition itself. This is perhaps best demonstrated by such catastrophic problems as earthquakes, hurricanes, floods, droughts, locust plagues, and so forth. That these are "serious" problems from the standpoint of the people which they affect, we can have no doubt. However, we may raise the question whether or not they are "social" problems, since they do not usually occur because of conflicts in the value-scheme of the culture. We find no public forums debating the question of what to do about preventing earthquakes and hurricanes. There is no controversy over how to stop volcanic eruptions and cloudbursts. The causation is thought of as nonhuman, resting in natural forces outside the control of man. Perhaps we may call such causation noncultural or precultural.

Here, we must distinguish between the condition itself and the effects of the condition. While the earthquake itself may involve no value-judgments, its consequences inevitably will call for moral judgments and decisions of policy. People will not agree on how much should be spent in reconstruction, how it should be spent, or how the funds should be raised. There may be serious questions as to whether people in other unaffected areas of the same society should come to the aid of the stricken area. However, the earthquake itself is not a social problem in the same sense as illegitimacy and unemployment. The latter have cultural elements in their causation.

In the case of the physical problem, there is scientific ignorance of causation and control, and we cannot say that the value-judgments of the people are obstructing the solution of the problem. There is no social disorganization involved, no clash of social values, no lag between public opinion and scientific opinion. If scientific knowledge has ascertained the causes of the condition and for some reason the value-judgments of the people interfere with the acceptance and application of this knowledge, then we can say that value-judgments are a part of the causal pattern of the problem and that the problem is truly "social" and no longer belongs at our first level. Thus, if we may anticipate the time when scientists can tell us how to prevent earthquakes, control hurricanes, and make rain for drought-stricken areas, we may imagine some elements of the population who will oppose the application of scientific techniques on the ground that they are too costly and threaten budget-balancing, or that they interfere with nature and God's will, or for some other reason. At this point in the evolution of the culture, we do have a man-made problem, since the will of certain groups is a causal element in the occurrence of the condition itself.

Most diseases have at one time or another constituted physical or medical problems rather than social problems. Many years ago, the bubonic plague, small-pox, and syphilis were far beyond medical knowledge of prevention and control. Today, if the bubonic plague and small-pox should again sweep the world, they would not be essentially "medical" problems since medicine now knows how to deal with them. They would be "social problems" since their recurrence could be traced to the breakdown of our educational techniques, popular resistance against vaccination, confusion as to public policy in public health matters, or some other man-made situation. Likewise, the control of syphilis is now definitely a social problem. Medical knowledge of prevention and control is very nearly perfected, but the problem of changing social attitudes and removing social inertia is very much with us. . . .

As for locust plagues and floods, it is perhaps debatable whether or not they belong at this first level of the physical problem. To the degree that we know how to check boll weevil and grasshopper invasions and avoid floods, these things are social problems. To the degree that we lack such knowledge, they are merely technical, engineering, or physical problems.

At the second level, we have the *ameliorative* problem. Problems of this type represent conditions which people generally agree are undesirable in any instance, but they are unable to agree on programs for the amelioration of the condition. The essence of the ameliorative problem is one of solution and the administration of reform rather than original agreement that the condition constitutes a social problem which must be eradicated. Crime and delinquency fall in this category. Though there are individuals who offend the dominant community mores by robbing, murdering, raping, and petty thieving, there are no interest groups who openly in forum and legislature seek to perpetuate the interests which these individuals represent. All "right-thinking" people, regardless of race, nationality, religion, or economic status, look upon the ameliorative problem as intolerable. Among other problems which we may place in this class are most physical diseases, mental deficiency and insanity, and industrial and automobile accidents.

In contrast to the physical problem at the first level, the ameliorative problem is truly "social" in the sense that it is a man-made condition. By this we mean that value-judgments not only help to create the condition, but to prevent its solution. In the case of crime, certain moral judgments of our culture are to a large extent responsible for the criminal act in the first place. To the degree that our mores of conspicuous consumption enter into the motivation of crimes for pecuniary gain, there is a cultural responsibility for such criminal acts. Or again, traditional prison policies based on our belief in severity of punishment may become part of the causal pattern of further criminal behavior in the prisoner after his liberation. These same cherished notions of retribution in punishment of criminals operate to dissuade legislatures from adequately financing probation and parole systems, juvenile delinquency clinics, and the schools for problem children.

At this level, also, we have those physical and mental diseases where traditional beliefs obstruct the application of medical and psychiatric knowledge to the prevention and treatment of individual deficiencies. Certainly illness, disease, and industrial accidents among the low income groups reflect the failure of our culture both in preventing high incidences of risk to these people and in adequately insuring them against the costs of such risks. Specifically, the uneven distribution of wealth and income throughout our various social classes serves both to expose wage-earners and their families to malnutrition, disease, and accident, and to deprive them of the means to meet the economic costs of such disasters. . . .

It is true that all our ameliorative problems have their technical, medical, or engineering aspects similar to those involved in the physical problem. Venereal disease, tuberculosis, insanity, and automobile accidents all necessitate investigation by scientific specialists. The point is, of course, that in the case of such problems, even when the specialists have isolated the cause and are agreed upon programs of control, laymen still are hopelessly divided over questions of policy.

At the third level we have what we will call the *moral* problem. The moral problem represents a condition on which there is no unanimity of opinion throughout the society that the condition is undesirable in every instance. There is no general agreement that the condition is a problem and thus many people do not feel that anything should be done about it. With the moral problem, we have a basic and primary confusion in social values which goes much deeper than the questions of solution which trouble us in the ameliorative problem.[3] Of course, the ameliorative problem reflects confusion in the value-scheme and thus contains real elements of moral conflict, but such conflict centers more around techniques and means of reform than around fundamental agreement on objectives and ultimate values. Hence, though all "right-thinking" people regard such conditions as crime, insanity, and disease as bad, there are interest groups openly defending and perpetuating the conditions classified as moral problems. Witness the problems of child labor and low wage and hour standards. We have only to read the record of newspaper and Congressional debate on the recently enacted Fair Labor Standards Act to learn that many individuals and groups not only objected to the specific solution attempted in the legislation, but also refused to admit that the conditions themselves were problems over which we should be concerned. In one of the first cases heard under the child labor legislation, one Michigan judge defended the labor of a newsboy on the ground that when he was a boy such work was regarded as excellent character development and training in individual qualities of initiative and self-discipline. Certainly employers in the beet sugar fields of the middle-western states who rely heavily on the labor of children do not define the condition, insofar as it pertains to them, in terms of a social problem. In those families where the labor of children is considered necessary to the maintenance of the family budget, parents and children alike have a stake in the continuance of the condition so abhorred by others. Religious groups have even frowned on government control of child labor as an unjustifiable invasion of the home and a threat to the prerogatives of the church. As to long hours and low wages, the opposition of some dominant groups in the southern states to the enactment of the federal legislation indicated no "problem-conscious" attitude on their part. Classical economists and employers have been known to look upon unemployment and low wage and hours standards as the inevitable, if not the necessary, mechanics of competition in the labor market. . . .

The utility of this classification is in its relativity. The purpose is not to pigeonhole the different problems with finality at any one level, but rather to give us a working basis for observing the position of each problem relative to other problems, and to the value-scheme as a whole. Note that problems will move from one category to another with changes in the state of scientific knowledge and with shifts in the value-scheme. When the physical problems cease to be essentially problems of engineering and medical knowledge, and come to involve questions of social policy, they will move over into alignment with the ameliorative problems at the second level. As indicated, venereal disease has seemingly made this transition though infantile paralysis has not. When problems now classed as moral come to have wide disapproval throughout our culture as conditions which must in every instance be done away with, they will become essentially problems of solution rather than agreement on basic values and will be dealt with as ameliorative problems. Some day child labor may be looked upon as criminal in the same sense that robbery and murder are now regarded as criminal. Conceivably, war may sometime be defined as wrong as venereal disease.

Nor is there any finality about the problems tentatively classified as ameliorative. Many crimes, such as political corruption, gambling, liquor offenses, and traffic violations are condoned, tolerated, and even participated in by respected and otherwise responsible members of the community. White-collar crimes are conspicuous in this category. Crimes of this sort reflect the same fundamental confusion of values as the problems which we discussed as moral. Before such offenses can be said to be merely problems of police detection and judicial enforcement, the citizens of the community must get together and agree that something should be done.

It may well be that there are very few contemporary problems which can be said to be purely ameliorative in nature, since most of them reflect no underlying clarity of definition and moral evaluation. If such be the case, it is a revealing commentary on the absence of any firm tissue of cultural integration in the value-scheme. Cultural integration itself is a matter of degree. There is always more or less, but never complete integration. A complete homogeneity of social values would mean we would have no social problems at all unless we include only the purely physical problems discussed at the first level.

Notes

1. For a discussion of some of the limitations of the social disorganization theory in the analysis of social problems, see Richard C. Fuller, "The Problem of Teaching Social Problems," *Amer. J. Sociol.*, Nov. 1938, 415–25.

2. The elements of this classification were stated by Richard C. Fuller in the article, "The Problem of Teaching Social Problems," 419–20.

3. The term "moral problem" is used by Stuart A. Queen and Jennette R. Gruener in their *Social Pathology*, 38–42, New York, 1940. The moral problem, as they define it, pertains to questions of fundamental right and wrong.

THE STAGES OF A SOCIAL PROBLEM

Richard C. Fuller and Richard R. Myers

Social problems, according to Fuller and Myers, follow an orderly "career." The authors argue that all social problems go through the three stages of awareness, policy determination, and reform. In the first stage, groups begin to see a particular situation as a threat to important values. In the second stage, people choose sides, redefine values, and offer proposals for action. In the third stage, some group or groups succeed in rallying action

From Richard C. Fuller and Richard R. Myers, "The Natural History of a Social Problem," *American Sociological Review*, 6, June 1941, pp. 320–328. Copyright 1941 by the American Sociological Association. Reprinted by permission.

on behalf of their values. Thus, Fuller and Myers argue, values are clearly involved in all phases of the history of a social problem.

It is our thesis that every social problem has a natural history and that the natural history approach is a promising conceptual framework within which to study specific social problems.

Let us first clarify our usage of the terms "social problem" and "natural history." The concept "social problem" as used in this paper can be stated in a series of propositions.

1. A social problem is a condition which is defined by a considerable number of persons as a deviation from some social norm which they cherish. Every social problem thus consists of an objective condition and a subjective definition. The objective condition is a verifiable situation which can be checked as to existence and magnitude (proportions) by impartial and trained observers, e.g., the state of our national defense, trends in the birth rate, unemployment, etc. The subjective definition is the awareness of certain individuals that the condition is a threat to certain cherished values.

2. The objective condition is necessary but not in itself sufficient to constitute a social problem. Although the objective condition may be the same in two different localities, it may be a social problem in only one of these areas, e.g., discrimination against Negroes in the South as contrasted with discrimination in the North; divorce in Reno as contrasted with divorce in a Catholic community. *Social problems are what people think they are* and if conditions are not defined as social problems by the people involved in them, they are not problems to those people, although they may be problems to outsiders or to scientists, e.g., the condition of poor southern sharecroppers is a social problem to the braintrusters of the New Deal but not to many southern landowners.

3. Cultural values play an important causal role in the objective condition which is defined as a problem, e.g., the objective conditions of unemployment, race prejudice, illegitimacy, crime, divorce, and war come into being, in part at least, because people cherish certain beliefs and maintain certain social institutions which give rise to these conditions.

4. Cultural values obstruct solutions to conditions defined as social problems because people are unwilling to endorse programs of amelioration which prejudice or require abandonment of their cherished beliefs and institutions, e.g., one possible "solution" to illegitimacy would be social acceptance of contraception and abortion, practices which in themselves are now defined as violations of the mores.

5. Social problems thus involve a dual conflict of values: first, with regard to some conditions, people disagree as to whether the condition is a threat to fundamental values, e.g., race prejudice, divorce, child labor, war,

unorganized labor; second, with regard to other conditions, although there is a basic agreement that the condition is a threat to fundamental values, because of a disparity of other values relative to means or policy, people disagree over programs of reform, e.g., crime, mental and physical disease, motor car accidents.

6. In the last analysis, social problems arise and are sustained because people do not share the same common values and objectives.

7. Sociologists must, therefore, study not only the objective condition phase of a social problem but also the value-judgments of the people involved in it which cause them to define the same condition and means to its solution in different ways.[1]

The specific analytical frame which we have called the "natural history" is derived from the above conception of what constitutes a social problem. In our concept "social problem," we have attributed to all social problems certain common characteristics. These common characteristics imply a common order of development through which all social problems pass, consisting of certain temporal sequences in their emergence and maturation. The "natural history" as we use the term is therefore simply a conceptual tool for the examination of the data which constitute social problems.

Social problems do not arise full-blown, commanding community attention and evoking adequate policies and machinery for their solution. On the contrary, we believe that social problems exhibit a temporal course of development in which different phases or stages may be distinguished. Each stage anticipates its successor in time and each succeeding stage contains new elements which mark it off from its predecessor. A social problem thus conceived as always being in a dynamic state of "becoming" passes through the natural history stages of awareness, policy determination, and reform. As we proceed to discuss the qualitative differences between these stages, we will refer by way of illustration to data gathered by graduate students on the residence-trailer problem in Detroit.

AWARENESS

The genesis of every social problem lies in the awakening of people in a given locality to a realization that certain cherished values are threatened by conditions which have become acute. Definitions of alarm emerge only as these group values are thought to be involved. Without awareness or "problem consciousness" in certain groups of people, be they scientists, administrators, or likeminded neighbors, no identifiable problem can be said to exist. Before a social problem can be identified, there must be awareness on the part of people who express their concern in some communicable or observable form.[2] The outstanding characteristic of this initial phase of awareness inheres in the constantly recurrent statements of people involved in a challenging situation that "something ought to be done." As yet, these people have not crystallized their definition sufficiently to suggest or debate exact measures for amelioration or eradication of the undesirable condition. Instead, there is unsynchronized random behavior, with protest expressed in general terms.

The objective condition aspect of the residence-trailer problem is the residence-trailer camp or community. The earliest record of such a community in Detroit goes back to the spring of 1920. This was a small camp of eight or ten families located on the periphery of the city; the residents were industrial workers living in homemade trailers. At this time, no discernible residence-trailer problem existed in Detroit. The three Detroit newspapers contain no reference to the situation and the records of the police, health department, and social work agencies are equally silent. Although neighbors remember the camp, they insist it was "no trouble at all." However, the objective condition grew rapidly in proportions. By 1930, there were four well-established camps within the city limits and by 1935 the number had increased to nine. In five of these nine communities, the inhabitants made no pretense of temporary camping, but removed the wheels from their trailers, mounted them on saw horses and two-by-fours, and settled down to a semipermanent existence. As the visibility of trailers and trailerites increased, there came the dawn of a social problem awareness as measured by newspaper items, gossip of neighbors, formal complaints of neighbors to the press and to civic authorities, and the official utterances of these civic authorities.

A sampling of the three Detroit newspapers reveals no comment on the situation either in the form of news or editorials until January, 1925, when we have an item in one paper noting a "brawl" which occurred in one of the camps. During the next decade, 1925–35, there was a steadily increasing number of items and in the two-year period 1936–37, the items reached their greatest frequency. If a qualitative interpretation of these items is permissible, we can say that up to 1930 their tone was one of curiosity and amusement rather than alarm. Before 1930, the editorial columns and "letters to the editor" section gave very little attention to the situation. After 1930, the editorial departments of all three papers made frequent comment and "letters to the editor" became quite common. In both straight news reporting and in editorial page comment, the tone of the items rapidly took on a note of concern and alarm. In 1936–37, over one half of the items were editorials or letters to the editor; the remainder were news items concerned with crime, disease, fires, accidents, and humorous incidents in the camps. The letters to the editor were principally from people living in the neighborhoods close to the trailer communities, from school authorities, from real estate dealers, and from social workers.

Complaints of neighbors were articulated on the grounds of the unsightliness of the camps, noises, odors, immorality, crime, and property depreciation in the surrounding districts. The response of neighborhood groups to the condition was measured not only by formal complaints to police, health officials, and newspapers, but also by the participant observations of students living in local areas near trailer camps. One student reported:

> At first, none of us paid much attention when a number of families moved into the big open lot on the next corner below us. They were poor factory workers and the depression was pretty tough in 1932. They did not have to pay much rent. Most of us thought they would only stay a month or two and then be on their way. But after a year there were more trailers there than ever and neighbors began to say, "Well, it looks as if they were here to stay." But no one seemed to think that the camps were hurting any of us. Then we all began to miss certain small articles around the house. Newspapers, milk bottles, and tools began to disappear. We laid it to the trailer kids and blamed their parents for letting them run wild. Then someone said, "Why aren't these kids in school? That will keep them out of trouble." A neighbor wrote a letter to the truant officer about it but nothing came of it at first.
>
> [Another typical comment] Dad said Mother thought the trailer children were a bunch of sex perverted brats, but Dad said he did not worry half so much about that as how he would ever sell his house unless they got the campers out of the district. And Dad was always saying that he had nothing against the trailerites themselves. They could not help being poor, he said, but it was a "hell of a note why that should mean we all must be poor." [This statement referred to the situation in 1932.]

Awareness was registered in the official statements of organized civic authorities, such as health agencies, the police, and school functionaries, almost as soon as protests were being registered by local neighborhood groups. The health authorities were the first governmental unit to show concern in public statements and their information was given them first by social workers called into the camps to administer relief. The chief complaints of health inspectors to the Common Council were: families averaged two to each trailer and accommodations were scarcely large enough for one; several of the camps had no toilet accommodations and there was little or no privacy in such matters; water supply was low and residents were often dependent on sources outside the camp; in winter, the heating accommodations were deficient, small gas stoves serving most trailers and others had no heating whatsoever; garbage disposal was indiscriminate and dumping on nearby vacant lots was the usual expedient.

The police, as another organized official group, came to view trailer camps as potential danger spots, presenting a new challenge to the preservation of law and order. This awareness definition reflected in official police reports emerged as the police were increasingly called in to quell brawls, apprehend delinquents, and investigate reports of indignant neighbors.

School authorities became aware of the residence-trailer problem because the stability and routine of the school were affected. Some schools did not have the accommodations for the incoming trailer children, day to day attendance of the newcomers was extremely irregular, and, because of the impermanence of the trailer community, many children would depart before the school year was completed.

Thus, the stage of progressive awareness for Detroit's residence-trailer problem covered the approximate period of 1925–35, and is measurable by newspaper indexes as well as by the definitions of citizens and government officials who felt that group values of health, education, private property, and morals were threatened by the existence of the objective condition.

POLICY DETERMINATION

Very soon after the emergence of awareness comes debate over policies involved in alternative solutions. Ends and means are discussed and the conflict of social interests becomes intense. People who propose solutions soon find that these solutions are not acceptable to others. Even when they can get others to agree on solutions, they find agreement as to means a further difficulty. The stage of policy determination differs significantly from the stage of awareness in that interest groups are now concerned primarily with "what ought to be done" and people are proposing that "this and that should be done."[3] Specific programs occupy the focus of attention. The multi-sided protests have become organized and channelized.

Policy determination on the residence-trailer problem in Detroit indicated discussion on at least three interrelated levels: first, discussion by neighbors and other interested but unorganized groups; second, discussion by organized interest or pressure groups such as taxpayers, trailer manufacturers, real estate organizations, parent-teacher associations, women's clubs, and men's clubs; third, discussion among specialists and administrators in government or quasi governmental units—the police, health officials, Common Council, social workers, and school boards. The interinfluence and cross-fertilization of debate among and between these three levels of participating discussants represent the dynamics of policy determination.

Policy determination was preoccupied both with broad questions as to ends and with narrow, more specialized questions as to means. As to ends, should the trailer camps be prohibited entirely and expelled from the community, should they only be licensed, taxed, or otherwise restricted in growth, or should they be let alone in the hope that the situation would right itself? As to narrower questions of means, the more established, organized, and official the group, the more likely it was to agree on ends but to disagree on means. For instance, health officials debated periodic inspection, which would be costly but more efficient, as against sporadic inspection on complaints received, which would be less costly but involve more risk to the health of the community at large. Similarly, school officials debated the pros and cons of expansion, the pros and cons of vigorous truant officer activity, the pros and cons of a special class for trailer children. Police had to decide whether or not special details and augmented forces were necessary for trailer camp areas and whether a tough or lenient policy of arrest should be applied to trailer inhabitants.

Conflicts over policy determination can best be observed by charting the alignments of different interest groups who have various stakes in the solution of the difficulty. These groups represent certain institutional values, many of which appear incompatible with each other, all of which must be reconciled or compromised before the community can go ahead on a collective policy of reform. The official groups (police, health, school, social workers) can be said to be perpetuating basic organizational mores pertaining to the protection of private property, public health, education, and relief of the distressed. Then there are the special interest groups such as the real estate operators, hotel owners, and neighborhood taxpayers who want elimination or restriction of the homes on wheels because their pecuniary values of survival and status are threatened.

Lined up on the other side is the Coach Trailer Manufacturers' Association, a pressure group seeking the protection of the interests of trailerites, also motivated by self-interest and the profit mores. Then there are the interests of those who live in trailers. Though these trailer communities consist of low-income groups of migrant and transient workers, the casually employed, the chronic unemployable, factory wage earners, and the like, some of them are identified with an interest group of their own—The Mobile Home Owners' Association of America. This organization contends that trailer homes are the solution to the housing problems of the low-income family. With property and rental values held beyond their means, what is left for these people but the trailer house? There are citizens who are in sympathy with the position of trailer-residents, and although they favor some public control, they oppose abolition of these communities. Labor unions, civil rights groups, and other liberal organizations also are on record as championing the survival of trailer communities.

It seems, then, that the dynamics of policy determination on the residence-trailer problem, which became intensified during the approximate period of 1935–37, can be represented as an alignment of certain humanitarian interests with certain organizational interests to combat other humanitarian interests aligned with other organizational interests.

REFORM

The final stage in the natural history of a social problem is that of reform. Here we find administrative units engaged in putting formulated policy into action. General policies have been debated and defined by the general public, by special interest groups, and by experts. It is now the task of administrative experts specially trained in their jobs to administer reform. This is the stage of action, both public and private. The emphasis is no longer on the idea that "something ought to be done" or that "this or that should be done" but on the fact that "this and that are being done." Public action is represented in the machinery of government bodies, legislative, executive, and judicial; and in the delegated authority of administrative tribunals, special supervisory officers and boards. This is the institutionalized phase of the social problem in the sense that we have established policies carried out by publicly authorized policy-enforcing agencies. Reform may also be private in character, as witnessed by the activities of private clubs and organizations, private charities and other benevolent associations, and church groups.

Decisions of policy remain necessary at the reform stage, but such decisions usually involve quite technical matters pertaining to means and fall within the special bailiwick of the experts concerned with such questions. Of course, such policy questions may be taken out of the hands of the administrators whenever the general public exercises its powers of censorship, veto, or referendum. The already established public agencies may prove sufficient for the administration of reform in connection with a new community problem or it may be necessary to establish new agencies of administration.

The residence-trailer problem in Detroit is just beginning to enter the reform stage in its natural history. Although police and sanitation officials had sporadic contacts with the camps prior to 1937, their activities were not concerned with carrying out any special policies established for trailer communities. They were merely acting on community policies already established pertaining to crime and public health, wherever and whenever conditions called for bringing such old policies into action. Beginning about 1937, however, the Common Council enacted legislation which placed the trailer camps within the city under certain prohibitions and restrictions. These camps were absolutely prohibited from certain areas and allowed to survive only in specially designated areas. Also, special requirements as to licensing, inspection, and supervision of the camps were enforced on owners and/or leasees of the real estate where the camps were located. The health officials and sanitation inspectors were ordered to establish special rules of public health for the trailer communities. Reform has only begun, and many knotty legal problems remain to be ironed out before collective action can proceed further. There is no indication that the school authorities have taken any official action. The problem seems to be on the border of transition from policy determination to reform.

It should be fairly obvious from the statement of the residence-trailer problem that the stages in the natural history are not mutually exclusive and that they tend to overlap. For conceptual purposes, however, the three general phases may be set off from each other; in practical reality, the state of development of a problem at any one time usually contains elements of all three stages.

Is the natural history technique equally adaptable to all types of social problems? The residence-trailer problem is a situation which can be observed on a local and emergent basis in specific neighborhoods and communities. The factors of localism and emergence offer the investigator a delimited area and a timeliness of observation which permit a current, intimate focus on the items of awareness, policy determination, and reform. The data are fresh and immediate and the participant observer technique is available. Such problems are often transitory—that is, awareness, discussion, and conflict cease permanently with some arrangement for compromise or removal of the difficulty; or the abatement of conflict may be only momentary and the issue flares up again and again.

What of the traditional, older, more pervasive problems which have occupied the attention of teacher and student in social problems texts for the past fifty years or more? What of crime, poverty, insanity, war, family disorganization, prostitution, illegitimacy, and race prejudice? Obviously, we cannot go back into antiquity to record the first awareness of social groups defining such conditions as problems. We cannot trace the earliest conflicts over policy and the first attempts at solution. Anthropological, historical, and contemporary data may be used to demonstrate to the student the universal aspects of these problems in space and in time. Such materials, however, are inadequate in that they do not bring the student face to face with the dynamics of the problem. If the student is to understand why these old established problems persist and defy solution, he must examine the values of our social organization which bring the undesirable conditions into existence and which obstruct efforts to remove them. His laboratory for the study of these realities is the local community where the cross-sectional conflicts at the core of the problem can be observed most intimately.

The important fact which the textbooks overlook is that the old traditional problems are given relative emphases in the local community. At the awareness stage, a problem such as crime may be receiving very little attention in community A, whereas in the neighboring community B it is the all-absorbing focus of interest. Similarly, there may be no discussion of policies relative to race discrimination in B, whereas the people of A are intensely occupied with such discussion. The administration of relief for unemployment may be in an advanced stage in B, whereas little if anything is being done in A. Thus, even these problems which are persistently national in scope do not blanket the country with the same stage of development. Such conditions are only latent, dormant, or potential problems in the local area, and before they rise to local consciousness, debate, and control, a local issue is essential to set the natural history going. Although the conflicts of social values which make up the problem, once it has evolved, are much the same in all communities, the natural history technique provides a specific focus on these conflicts as they function in the concrete reality of a local situation.

CONCLUSION

We have presented the "natural history" interpretation of social problems as a broad conceptual frame for the examination of the dynamics of specific social problems. Obviously, before the natural history technique can be made a precise tool of research, the many implications of our statement must be refined and explored by further analysis.

Within our experience as teachers, the natural history approach has proved most valuable in bringing students to grips with the realities of social problems. These realities, as we see them, are the cross purposes at which people find themselves because they cherish incompatible and inconsistent objectives. The very norms of organization which give the community a working routine tend to produce conflicts of cultural values which create and sustain conditions defined as social problems.

In the search for temporal sequences in the "becoming" of a social problem, the student does not take problem conditions for granted, as objective "evils" caused by "evils." He seeks to explain social problems as emergents of the cultural organization of the community, as complements of the approved values of the society, not as pathological and abnormal departures from what is assumed to be proper and normal. As such, the natural history technique is a sociological orientation rather than a social welfare orientation. If social problems theory is to come of age, it must cease being a poor relation of sociological theory and become sociological theory in its own right.

Notes

1. The basic idea that the social problem is a conflict of values is not a new one. See Lawrence K. Frank, "Social Problems," *Amer. J. Sociol.*, 1925, 30:463–473, page 468 for Frank's definition; Harold A. Phelps, *Contemporary Social Problems*, rev. ed., 737, New York, 1938; Willard Waller, "Social Problems and the Mores," *Amer. Sociol. Rev.*, 1936, 1:922–933: Kingsley Davis, "The Sociology of Prostitution," *Amer. Socio. Rev.*, 1937, 2:749–755, and "Illegitimacy and the Social Structure," *Amer. J. Sociol.*, 1939, 45:215–233; Richard C. Fuller, "The Problem of Teaching Social Problems," *Amer. J. Sociol.*, 1938, 44:415–425, and [with Richard R. Myers], "Some Aspects of a Theory of Social Problems," *Amer. Sociol. Rev.*, 1941, 6:24–32; Stuart A. Queen and Jennette R. Gruener, *Social Pathology*, 38–42, New York,

1940; Louis Wirth, "Ideological Aspects of Social Disorganization," *Amer. Sociol. Rev.*, 1940, 5:472–482. Talcott Parsons, *The Structure of Social Action, passim*, New York, 1937, and "The Role of Ideas in Social Action," *Amer. Sociol. Rev.*, 1938, 3: 652–664, and Robert K. Merton, "Social Structure and Anomie," *Amer. Sociol. Rev.*, 1938, 3:672–682, have also analyzed the concepts of social problem and social disorganization from a general sociological point of view.

2. As yet, we have not perfected research techniques which can penetrate covert mental states very satisfactorily.

3. Newspaper comment on the residence-trailer problem subsequent to 1935 reveals this transition in emphasis from simple alarm to concrete proposals.

VALUES, POLITICS, AND SOCIAL PROBLEMS

Joseph A. Gusfield

The political process has a symbolic as well as an instrumental dimension. Gusfield shows that groups sometimes pass laws that reflect credit on their values while discrediting other groups with divergent values. Prohibition, for example, expressed rural, middle-class, Protestant values and fostered conflict with immigrant, urban, lower-class, Catholic values. Thus, laws that serve as social symbols foster value conflict and the emergence of a long-standing social struggle.

An action of a governmental agent takes on symbolic import as it affects the designation of public norms. A courtroom decision or a legislative act is a gesture which often glorifies the values of one group and demeans those of another. In their representational character, governmental actions can be seen as ceremonial and ritual performances, designating the content of public morality. They are the statement of what is acceptable in the public interest. Law can thus be seen as symbolizing the public affirmation of social ideals and norms as well as a means of direct social control. This symbolic dimension is given in the statement, promulgation, or announce-

From Joseph A. Gusfield, "Moral Passage," *Social Problems* 15:2 (Fall 1967), pp. 175–178. Reprinted by permission of The Society for the Study of Social Problems and the author.

ment of law unrelated to its function in influencing behavior through enforcement.

. . . The fact of affirmation through acts of law and government expresses the public worth of one set of norms of one sub-culture vis-à-vis those of others. It demonstrates which cultures have legitimacy and public domination, and which do not. Accordingly it enhances the social status of groups carrying the affirmed culture and degrades groups carrying that which is condemned as deviant. We have argued elsewhere that the significance of Prohibition in the United States lay less in its enforcement than in the fact that it occurred.[1] Analysis of the enforcement of Prohibition law indicates that it was often limited by the unwillingness of Dry forces to utilize all their political strength for fear of stirring intensive opposition. Great satisfaction was gained from the passage and maintenance of the legislation itself.[2]

Irrespective of . . . [enforcement,] public designation of morality is itself an issue generative of deep conflict. The designating gestures are dramatistic events, "since it invites one to consider the matter of motives in a perspective that, being developed in the analysis of drama, treats language and thought primarily as modes of action."[3] For this reason the designation of a way of behavior as violating public norms confers status and honor on those groups whose cultures are followed as the standard of conventionality, and derogates those whose cultures are considered deviant. My analysis of the American Temperance movement has shown how the issue of drinking and abstinence became a politically significant focus for the conflicts between Protestant and Catholic, rural and urban, native and immigrant, middle class and lower class in American society. The political conflict lay in the efforts of an abstinent Protestant middle class to control the public affirmation of morality in drinking. Victory or defeat were consequently symbolic of the status and power of the cultures opposing each other.[4] Legal affirmation or rejection is thus important in what it symbolizes as well or instead of what it controls. Even if the law was broken, it was clear whose law it was.

Notes

1. Joseph Gusfield, *Symbolic Crusade: Status Politics and the American Temperance Movement,* Urbana: University of Illinois Press, 1963, pp. 117–126.

2. Gusfield, "Prohibition: The Impact of Political Utopianism," in John Braeman, editor, *The 1920's Revisited,* Columbus: Ohio State University Press, forthcoming; Andrew Sinclair, *The Era of Excess,* New York: Harper Colophon Books, 1964, Chap. 10, pp. 13–14.

3. Kenneth Burke, *A Grammar of Motives,* New York: Prentice-Hall, 1945, p. 393. Burke's writings have been the strongest influence on the mode of analysis presented here. Two other writers, whose works have been influential, themselves influenced by Burke, are Erving Goffman and Hugh D. Duncan.

4. Gusfield, *Symbolic Crusade, op. cit.,* Chap. 5.

WORDS WITHOUT DEEDS

Willard Waller

In this classic statement on the role of values in social problems, Waller discusses the basic tension between humanitarian and organizational mores. People make value judgments on the basis of humanitarian mores. But, at the same time, they are often constrained in eliminating the problematic conditions because of the costs that would result vis-à-vis institutions that are important to them. Hence, many people can object to a situation without wanting to do what is necessary to change it. In terms of Fuller's and Myers's scheme, awareness and policy determination can exist without necessarily leading to reform. Thus, Waller claims, "social problems are not solved because people do not want to solve them."

If we are to treat social problems scientifically, we must try to understand why we consider them problems. We must subject to analysis our judgments of value as well as the social phenomena upon which these judgments are passed. We may do this by applying the concept of the mores to the problem of social problems as we have defined it. Social problems exist within a definite moral universe. Once we step out of our circle of accustomed moralities, social problems cease to exist for us. Likewise, if we consider the possibility of revolutionary change, social problems lose most of their complexity. A simple formulation of our standpoint, which we advance as roughly accurate for most social problems, rests upon the assumption of two conflicting sets of mores. Social problems result from the interaction of these two groups of mores, which we may call the *organizational* and the *humanitarian* mores.[1]

From Willard Waller, "Social Problems and the Mores," *American Sociological Review,* 1, December 1936, 924–33. Copyright 1936 by the American Sociological Association. Reprinted by permission.

The organizational, or basic, mores, are those upon which the social order is founded, the mores of private property and individualism, the mores of the monogamous family, Christianity, and nationalism. Conditions of human life which we regard as social problems emanate from the organizational mores as effective causes. Indeed, the fact that a certain condition is in some sense humanly caused is an unrecognized but essential criterion of the social problem. We are all, as Galsworthy remarked, under sentence of death, but death is not a social problem; death becomes a social problem only when men die, as we think, unnecessarily, as in war or by accident or preventable disease. Not all the miseries of mankind are social problems. Every condition which we regard as a social problem is in some sense a result of our institutions or we do not concern ourselves with it.

Alongside the organizational mores there exists a set of humanitarian mores; those who follow the humanitarian mores feel an urge to make the world better or to remedy the misfortunes of others.[2] Probably the humanitarian impulse has always existed, but it has apparently attained group-wide expression at a relatively late period in our history, following the breakdown of primary group society. Social problems in the modern sense did not exist when every primary group cared for its own helpless and unfortunate. Social problems as we know them are a phenomenon of secondary group society, in which the primary group is no longer willing and able to take care of its members. It was this breakdown which called group-wide humanitarianism into existence; it was this situation which brought it about that we were asked to feel sympathy for those whom we had never seen. Humanitarian mores are frequently expressed, for they are highly verbal, and they command the instant assent of almost any group.

The formula which crystallizes in our minds as we approach social problems from the angle of the mores is this: Social problems are social conditions of which some of the causes are felt to be human and moral. Value judgments define these conditions as social problems. Value judgments are the formal causes of social problems, just as the law is the formal cause of crime. Value judgments originate from the humanitarian mores, which are somewhat in conflict with the organizational mores. Social problems are moral problems; they are like the problems of a problem play. The existence of some sort of moral problem is the single thread that binds all social problems together. Any important social problem is marked by moral conflict in the individual and social conflict in the group. It is thus that the strain for consistency in the mores expresses itself.[3]

When someone has expressed a value judgment upon some condition of human life which originates from the organizational mores, and begins to reflect upon possible courses of action, he is at last in a position to understand the sense in which social problems are complex. For the same mores from which the deplored conditions originate continue to operate to limit any action which one takes in order to remedy them. Frank illustrates this limiting action of the organizational mores by showing how difficult it would be to explain our housing problem to a man from Mars.

> We should have to delegate an economist, a lawyer, a political scientist, a sociologist, and a historian to explain about the system of private property, the price system, popular government, congestion of population, transportation, and so on. And when they had severally and jointly expounded the complexities of the situation, pointing out that we cannot just build houses, but must rely upon individual initiative and private enterprise to enter the field of building construction, that we must use the "price system" to obtain the needed land which is someone's private property, to buy the necessary materials and to hire the skilled labor, that we must borrow capital on mortgages to finance these expenditures, paying a bonus to induce someone to lend that capital and also pay interest on the loan, together with amortization quotas and then we must contrive to rent these dwellings in accordance with a multiplicity of rules and regulations about leases and so on—after all these sundry explanations showing that to get houses built we must not infringe anyone's rights of private property or freedom to make a profit, and that what we want is to find a way of getting houses without interfering with anyone's customary activities, our visitor would suddenly exclaim, "Yes, I begin to see; have you any other such difficult problems, for this is exceedingly interesting?"[4]

In every social problem seek the moral problem; try to discover the complex processes of conflict, supplementation, and interference in our own moral imperatives. That is the principle which should guide the sociologist as he seeks to study social problems scientifically. Let us attempt to sketch the outlines of this conflict of mores with regard to a few typical social problems. Poverty is a social problem, when it exists in the midst of plenty, or in a world in which universal plenty is a technological possibility. The value judgment passed on poverty defines it as at least in part socially caused and as something which ought to be remedied. A simpleton would suggest that the remedy for poverty in the midst of plenty is to redistribute income. We reject this solution at once because it would interfere with the institution of private property, would destroy the incentive for thrift and hard work and disjoint the entire economic system. What is done to alleviate poverty must be done within the limits set by the organizational mores.

A slightly different type of conflict appears when a value judgment is passed, not upon the conditions of someone's life, but upon his behavior. An unmarried girl has a baby; her family and community take harsh and unreasoned action against her. The humanitarian comes in to save the pieces, but he cannot make things too easy for the girl or try to convince her family and community that she is not guilty of moral turpitude for fear of encouraging illegitimacy and injuring the morality upon which the monogamous family is founded. Likewise, venereal disease becomes a social problem in that it arises from our family institutions and also in that the medical means which could be used to prevent it, which would unquestionably be fairly effective, cannot be employed for fear of altering the mores of chastity. The situation is similar when it is a question of adjusting family relationships; Kingsley Davis has supplied a penetrating analysis of the "family clinic" as an agency operating within a circle of conflicting moral demands.[5]

Confusing conflicts of mores appear in those situations, frequent enough in unemployment relief, in which human misery and misbehavior are intermingled. When people suffer privation, the humanitarian mores dictate relief. If these people are willing to work, if the old live in strict monogamy and the young do not contract marriage until they are off the relief rolls, if they obey the law, if they do not conceal any assets, if they spend absolutely nothing for luxuries, if they are grateful and not demanding, if the level of relief does not approach the income of the employed, relatively few objections are raised to the giving of relief. But let any of the above violations of the organizational mores defining the situation of the recipient of charity arise, and the untrained investigator will quite possibly cut off relief in a storm of moral indignation. Herein he is in agreement with the moral sense of the greater part of the community. The trained social worker attempts at this point to bring the investigator over to a more broadly humanitarian point of view.[6]

It is necessary to remember that in all this the humanitarian is simply following his own mores, which he has received irrationally and which he obeys without reflection, being supported in this by the concurrence of his own group. When the social worker says, "One must not make moral judgments," she means that one must not make moral judgments of the conventional sort, but that it is perfectly all right to pass a moral judgment on the cruel judge or to hate the man who hates the Negro. Often the humanitarian has all the prejudices of his society upside down, and one who talks to him is reminded that there is still "a superstition in avoiding superstition, when men think to do best when they go furthest from the superstition formerly received." Among the sociologists, those who teach so-called "attitudes courses" are particularly likely to fall into this type of confusion.

A few further complications may be noted. The humanitarian often argues for his reforms on the basis of considerations which are consonant with the organizational mores but alien to the spirit of humanitarianism; he advocates a new system of poor relief, saying that it will be cheaper, while really he is hoping that it will prove more humane. As all of us must do sometimes, in order to communicate truth he has to lie a little. Great confusion is caused in the field of criminology by shuttling back and forth between practical and humanitarian universes of discourse. Orthodox economists have recognized the humanitarian impulse in an almost perverted manner; they owlishly assure us that prevalent economic practices are not what they seem to be, but are in the long run ultra-humanitarian.

Certain implications of this interpretation of social problems on the basis of conflict in the mores seem very clear. I should venture to suggest the following point:

The notion of conflict of mores enables us to understand why progress in dealing with social problems is so slow. Social problems are not solved because people do not want to solve them. From a thousand scattered sources the evidence converges upon this apparently unavoidable conclusion, from the history of reform movements, from the biographies and autobiographies of reformers, from politics, from the records of peace conferences, from the field of social work, from private discussions, and even from the debates of so-called radical groups. Even those who are most concerned about social problems are not quite at one with themselves in their desire to solve them. Solving social problems would necessitate a change in the organizational mores from which they arise. The humanitarian, for all his allegiance to the humanitarian mores, is yet a member of our society and as such is under the sway of its organizational mores. He wishes to improve the condition of the poor, but not to interfere with private property. Until the humanitarian is willing to give up his allegiance to the organizational mores, and in some cases to run squarely against them, he must continue to treat symptoms without removing their causes.[7]

Frequently the liberal humanitarian is brought squarely up against the fact that he does not really want what he says he wants. The difficulty which he faces is that the human misery which he deplores is a necessary part of a social order which seems to him good. A cruel person may amuse himself at the expense of humanitarians by suggesting simple and effective means to secure the ends which they believe they value above all others, or a cynical person may use this device to block reform. The means suggested, if adequate to the ends, are certain to involve deep changes in our society, and their cost terrifies the humanitarian so that he feels compelled to make excuses. The pacifist is sincerely concerned about war, and he will even assent to the general proposition that permanent peace requires, among other things, a redistribution of world population. But suggest that the United States should make a start by ceding the Philippines and Hawaii to Japan and opening its doors to Oriental immigration, and the pacifist usually loses heart! Indeed, one wonders whether there are many pacifists whose pacifism would not be shattered by a Japanese invasion of Mexico or Canada. The pacifist does not really want peace at its necessary price; he wants peace with the continuation of things in the present order which necessitate war. He wants a miracle. Lincoln Steffens tells how the shrewd but illiberal Clemenceau defeated Wilson by showing him the costs of peace; the incident is valuable, at any rate, as showing how the two men might have behaved.[8] Professing to be completely in sympathy with Wilson's ideals, Clemenceau stated that peace would involve giving up empire and the thought of empire; for England it would involve the loss of colonies; the French would have to come out of Morocco; the United States would have to surrender island possessions, give up spheres of influence, abrogate the Monroe doctrine, and so on. When Wilson replied that America was not ready to go quite so far, all at once, Clemenceau retorted that in that case the conference did not want peace, but war, and that the best time for France to make war was when she had one of her enemies down. One is reminded of Bacon's saying, "For it is the solecism of power to think to command the end, and yet not to endure the mean."

When one considers the conditions under which the humanitarian impulse comes to expression, he must realize that the urge to do something for others is not a very important determinant of change in our society, for any translation of humanitarianism into behavior is fenced in by restrictions which usually limit it to trivialities. The expression of humanitarian sentiments must remain almost wholly verbal, and because of this situation which is inherent in our acquisitive and possessive society: No one loses by giving verbal expression to humanitarianism or by the merely verbal expression of another, but many would lose by putting humanitarianism into practice, and someone would certainly lose by any conceivable reform. From the powerful someone who is certain to lose comes opposition to reform.

Notes

1. I have limited the present paper to discussion of the interaction of these mores at the present time. A lengthier treatment of the subject would have to pay considerable attention to the historical interrelations of these sets of mores.

2. While an explanation in terms of psychopathology would account for the fact that certain persons rather than certain others are the ones to pass value judgments, we must assume humanitarian mores in order to account for the fact that anyone passes them.

3. I should not like to be understood as making a claim for the originality of this conception of social problems. My interpretation is apparently not very far from Sumner's. L. K. Frank, in the paper quoted and in some other writings, appears to have anticipated my statement almost completely. Burgess makes use of a similar conception in one of his papers. (See E. W. Burgess, "Social Planning and the Mores," *Pub. Amer. Sociol. Soc.*, 29, No. 3, 1–18.) In numerous writings Woodard has attacked the same problem by means of a different type of analysis; I have in fact borrowed some terminology and certain interpretations from him. The Marxian conception of dialectic seems closely related to my interpretation; so, I am informed,

are certain passages of Bergson. It appears, then, that a great many thinkers have converged upon what is essentially the same interpretation, a fact which should serve, at any rate, to give the interpretation a certain added cogency.

4. L. K. Frank, "Social Problems," *Amer. J. Sociol.*, 30, Jan., 1925, 465–466.

5. Kingsley Davis, "The Application of Science to Personal Relations, A Critique of the Family Clinic Idea," *Amer. Sociol. Rev.*, 1, April, 1936, 236–247.

6. For a delightful discussion of a number of these situations, see the column, *Miss Bailey Says*, edited by Gertrude Springer, in *The Survey*.

7. Frank makes his intelligent Martian say: "If it is not indelicate of me to remark, every social problem you describe seems to have the same characteristics as every other social problem, namely, the crux of the problem is to find some way of avoiding the undesirable consequences of your established laws, institutions, and social practices, without changing those established laws, etc. In other words, you appear to be seeking a way to cultivate the flower without the fruit, which, in a world of cause and effect is somewhat difficult, to say the least." (*Op. cit.*, p. 467.)

8. Lincoln Steffens, *The Autobiography of Lincoln Steffens*, pp. 780–781.

A CRITIQUE OF THE VALUE CONFLICT PERSPECTIVE

Kenneth Westhues

Westhues makes three major criticisms of the value conflict perspective. First, it is class-biased, for it simply accepts the judgments of the more powerful social classes in defining what conditions are social problems. Second, the value conflict perspective does not contribute to a theoretical understanding of society; it tells us nothing about the structure of a society, how it works, and what it produces in the way of social problems. Third, Westhues claims that the perspective does not tell us how to resolve social problems. Westhues does suggest, however, that the sociologist can overcome these three shortcomings by studying cross-culturally the systemic costs of different forms of social organization.

PLEBISCITARY APPROACHES

Even when social pathology was still a respectable name for the social disorganization approach, various sociologists were discontented with it.

From Kenneth Westhues, "Social Problems as Systemic Costs," *Social Problems* 20:4 (Spring 1973), quotations from pp. 419, 422–426, 428–429. Reprinted by permission of The Society for the Study of Social Problems and the author.

The organic model of society on which it was based and its obvious bias toward the existing order led to a search for alternative approaches. Virtually all of those that have resulted choose "public opinion," "significant groups," or "a majority of people" as the actor with respect to whom the social problem is defined. The expert analysis of the sociologist is rejected as the criterion of what is or is not a social problem; instead the sociologist studies what others say are social problems. He then applies the tools of social science to the particular problems he is given; and the sociology of social problems proceeds in the same way as if its object were education, religion, the family, or any other facet of the given society.

Fuller, both alone (1937, 1938) and with Myers (1941a, 1941b), developed one early alternative to the social disorganization approach. In his "natural history" approach, the problem is defined by "a considerable number of persons." Then the job of the sociologist is to bring sociological theory to bear on the social problem and to study the stages through which the social problem passes, from initial formulation to eventual solution. Related to Fuller's approach is Blumer's (1970) portrayal of social problems as collective behavior; he argues (in contrast to the social disorganization proponents) that social problems are not objective phenomena but rather the result of subjective definition by some collectivity.

For Fuller and Blumer, the study of social problems becomes the study of *problematization*, the processes by which various publics define and solve problems; it is a field close to that of social movements. This orientation has the effect of insulating the sociologist from the kind of political implications with which the social disorganization approach is necessarily involved. It enhances the sociologist's claim that as sociologist he is free of evaluative biases and instead only an objective student of society. The study of social problems becomes another substantive course in the curriculum. . . .

Three problems of the plebiscitary approaches may be pointed out. First is that they are without a sophisticated theory of society or of history. This is not to say that a large number of logically-interrelated and empirically-supported hypotheses have not been accumulated. It is to say only that the theory has been mostly on the micro or social psychological level. There is no theoretically and empirically sound portrayal of what kind of society the United States (or any other society) is, as compared to alternatives. For this reason the plebiscitary approaches remain within the walls of the given society and do not result in policy-relevant theory.[1]

A second problem with plebiscitary approaches is that the definition of social problems is still largely dictated by the given society (this criticism has been developed at length by Liazos, 1972). If "significant groups" are relied upon to define what the social problems are, it is most likely that these are also the powerful groups who sit in central positions of the *status quo*. If—in order to become more democratic (see Finnigan, 1971)—representative samples of the population at large are asked to decide what the social problems are, the answers obtained are largely determined by the current whims of the mass media, which are in turn greatly influenced by the public opinion makers, namely those in power. In either case, as Liazos points out, the problems studied in the sociology of social problems are those given to the field by the existing order. As a result, plebiscitary approaches share at root the same biases as the social disorganization approach.

The third problem of approaches of this kind is that students are seldom satisfied to see the social problems course redefined as a substantive area, whether collective behavior or deviance. Students expect that the social problems course will be geared toward policy-relevant or applied sociology; they want to come out of the social problems course with knowledge they can use. . . .

SYSTEMIC COSTS

[An alternative] approach to the sociology of social problems can be termed the systemic costs approach, in which problems are defined as costs of the particular form of sociocultural organization a given society manifests. This approach, like the social disorganization approach, conceptualizes the given society as an ordered structure or system. Instead, however, of defining as problems those phenomena which do not fit into or satisfy the given order, problems are defined as those qualities or aspects of the given order that do not satisfy some outside criterion. Such a criterion is the actor with respect to which the problems are defined. The question raised in this approach is fundamentally, out of all possible gratifications, what does it cost members of a given society to be gratified according to the structure of their society. What this approach calls into question is not the behavior of deviants or dysfunctional sectors of the society; rather it calls into question the society itself, and asks what one has to forego in order to live in it, and why.

This approach is suggested to some extent in the social problems text of Bredemeier and Toby (1960:x), in which they "emphasize those aspects of American society which (we believe) produce problems, and necessarily, we ignore aspects of American society which (we believe) are achievements of the human spirit." The costs (their term) which they study are withdrawal from, submission to, relentless self-reliance upon, or rejection of what Bredemeier and Toby define as the four governing principles of American society. Congruity between these governing principles and people's behavior appears as the criterion or yardstick against which American society is evaluated. Thus, even while their approach is critical of the existing order, the perceptive student using the book cannot help but conclude that if only people were not frustrated there would be no problems. Even while they adopt a critical approach, Bredemeier and Toby's yardstick is not external to American society. Hence, their analysis of social problems remains trapped within the boundaries of American society.

Another example of a systemic costs approach is Mishan's (1967) *The Costs of Economic Growth*. He calls into question the compulsion for growth and the cult of efficiency which are integral to the workings of industrial societies and points out their undesirable effects. Although an economist, he does not limit himself to studying costs that can be quantified monetarily. The costs (or problems) he reviews are "the ways in which the organized pursuit and realization of technological progress themselves act to destroy the chief ingredients that contribute to man's well-being" (1969: 165). The yardstick by which Mishan evaluates industrial society is a humanistic model of man. Unfortunately, his book does not systematically describe what that model of man is.

In a similar vein is Lindenfeld's (1968:3) collection of readings, *Radical Perspectives on Social Problems*. This reader is grounded in the notion that "the sociologist's biases show through precisely in *what he takes for granted*." Lindenfeld is determined not to take the existing order for granted. The criterion by which the readings evaluate it varies from the Marxist model to other utopian ideals; in some articles the criterion appears simply as moral man, who is expected to be incensed at a portrayal of the United States as a garrison society or at the existence of an "Other America." While Lindenfeld's reader does take a critical approach, it risks being perceived as a collection of potshots at America, some of them hardly social scientific, that appeal to readers who already believe America is bad.

The most useful and policy relevant form of a systemic costs approach, it seems to me, is one in which the yardstick for assessing costs (and defining problems) is another existing society, or at least one that has existed at some point in time. Careful and systematic comparative analysis of alternative societies calls one's own society into question and at the same time prevents unrealistic utopian criticisms by forcing empirical thinking.

Comparative approaches to social problems are not unknown. Eisenstadt (1964:v) has produced a reader of this kind, prefaced with a statement of the utility of a comparative approach:

> Second, the organization that social problems are inherent in any social system, in any social organization, necessarily increases the importance of studying their manifestations and incidence in a variety of societies—be they primitive, historical, modernizing, or modern—and analyzing them in terms of these social structures.

Unfortunately, Eisenstadt limits his comparative approach largely to the conventional list of popularly regarded social problems: suicide, alcoholism, mental illness, family stability, etc. While a reader cannot be expected to offer a theoretically integrated framework, Eisenstadt's book does suggest the need for such frameworks for comparative analysis. The same can be said for Gerson's (1969) reader in social problems; while it takes a cross-cultural approach, its list of problems is quite conventional.

A good, albeit limited, example of a systemic costs approach is Faunce's (1968) *Problems of an Industrial Society*. The principal cost of industrial society on which Faunce concentrates is worker alienation. In the beginning of his book he analyzes the social structure of a Guatemalan peasant society, and later on he systematically compares craft production systems with mechanized and automated production systems. In this way he uses empirically observable alternative societies to evaluate the structure of work and production in modern industrial societies.

The matter of which problems should be chosen for study in a social problems class or for research priority outside the classroom is up to the sociologist himself in the systemic costs approach. Depending on which alternative society he might choose as the yardstick by which to measure costs, virtually any aspect of the given society can be regarded as a cost or problem. In choosing which costs or problems to examine, the sociologist may be aware of what the major problems are according to public opinion, but he may also decide upon problems not currently in the public vocabulary. He may, as it were, make students and readers aware of what they are missing and then explain with careful analytic techniques why they, in this particular society, are missing it.

The political implication of the systemic costs approach is social change. Through a theoretically integrated comparative analysis of his own and other societies, the students come to understand how variation in culture and social structure accounts for variation in the social problems experienced. Such a theory, provided it has an empirical basis, lends itself to effective social action in the manipulation of the cultural and structural variables which govern the particular area studied.[2] To the extent that students are given such a theory they are given power. Even if, by virtue of their social position, they lack the power to manipulate the variables that cause the particular social problem, at least they know that the problems are not inevitable or solvable only by the manipulation of personality variables. Such knowledge is itself a form of power, just as ignorance of social process is a form of powerlessness. . . .

CONCLUSION

A month or two before the beginning of each semester, literally thousands of sociologists have to choose what they will teach in their social problems classes. . . .

The choice is made to a great extent according to how one views the given society at present and the sociologist's role within it. If the given society is seen as good, and if the sociologist sees himself like Nisbet (1966:

16) as one "interested in making the protection of society his first responsibility," then the social disorganization approach (or one of its surrogates) will be chosen. If, whatever the evaluation of the given society, the role of sociologist is seen as one removed from the arena of public policy, then one of the plebiscitary approaches can be taken. If, finally, society is seen as in need of structural change, and the sociologist as one whose professional expertise can be used for that purpose, then the systemic costs approach is appropriate.

It is true that many critical sociologists, especially in the United States, have little interest in comparative research. Cannot their evaluation of given structures by the yardstick of utopian models or native deviant subcultures or the given society's stated ideology result in progressive and change-oriented thinking? The answer is certainly yes. The question, however, is whether this means is most effective. Utopian models risk on the one hand being too visionary to put into practice; on the other hand, utopian models which find their way into practice tend to be rather nasty and oppressive. With regard to the deviant subcultures, the problem is that they have been born out of reaction to the dominant order and are likely to be greatly conditioned by its way of doing things. To rely on deviant reactions for new ideas may result in ideas which appear much newer than they are. Evaluation of the given society by the yardstick of its own ideology may indeed disclose grievous problems, but why should the sociologist restrict his yardstick to a single society when he has a worldful to choose from? . . .

The reason why American sociologists in particular, and others in general, tend to limit themselves to their own society is that sociologists, like everybody else, internalize the values of their society and learn to take them for granted. The task of unlearning is not only the demand of personal growth but of good sociology and particularly of sociology that would lead to structural change. In the case of American sociologists, this is an even greater problem, since the careers of almost all American sociologists have been developed during the period of ascendancy of the United States in the international community. American culture, of which American sociologists are a part, has grown to take for granted the contention of *Fortune* magazine in 1940, "less by definition than by achievement, the United States is the greatest nation on earth." Given such a belief, American sociologists could scarcely need cross-cultural analyses of the kind that would call their own system into question: what could possibly be learned? Now that the knowledge has become more common, even within the United States, that this country is not in a class apart from all others, but rather lags behind on a range of indices, perhaps a comparative, systemic costs approach to the study of social problems will gain in popularity.[3] . . .

Notes

1. This criticism has been developed at length against Gouldner's moralism by Bredemeier (1971). The point is only that liberal values cannot substitute for careful
societal theory. Becker (1963), for example, attributes American anti-marijuana legislation largely to the "moral entrepreneurship" of Harry Anslinger, one-time head
of the Federal Narcotics Bureau. Becker's social-psychological explanation is happily
biased toward the pot-smoker, but the sympathetic reader is left with no policy
conclusion except to try to get rid of Harry Anslinger. Dickson (1968), on the other
hand, has offered an organizational analysis to explain the anti-marijuana legislation.
Not only is his analysis more convincing, it is grounded in macro-level theory. The
reader is left with some insight into how bureaucratic societies function; he learns
something about the *structure* of his society, not just about personalities within it.

2. This is not to say that the systemic costs approach limits its analysis to variables
that are manipulable—to applied sociology in the sense in which Gouldner (1957)
has used the term. A comprehensive theory includes variables of both kinds, theoretical or pure, manipulable or applied. The role of the social problems teacher,
as I see it, is to present comprehensive theory, realizing at the same time that not
all the variables in the theory will be relevant for political action.

3. It is interesting that two prominent "left-wing" sociologists, Howard Becker and
Irving L. Horowitz, in a 1972 article on the differences between radical political
positions and radical sociological research, still fail to suggest the need for comparative analysis of the United States with other sociocultural systems. Again and again
they write of "society" as if the United States were the only one or as if all societies
were alike. They propose, for example, studying communal living groups from a
sympathetic point of view, while they seem unaware that other societies have produced forms of family and kinship which the United States might possibly find
instructive, perhaps even more instructive than the deviant life-styles of its own sons
and daughters. The fact that Horowitz has himself done considerable research outside the United States, it may also be noted, illustrates the fact that cross-cultural
research does not necessarily lead to comparative frameworks that question the
structure of one's own society.

References

Becker, Howard. 1963. *Outsiders: Studies in the Sociology of Deviance.* Glencoe:
Free Press.

Blumer, Herbert. 1970. "Social problems as collective behavior." *Social Problems*
18 (Winter): 298–306.

Bredemeier, Harry C. 1971. "Banfield, Gouldner, and 'Social Problems'." *Social
Problems* 18 (Spring): 554–568.

———— and Jackson Toby. 1960. *Social Problems in America.* New York: John Wiley
and Sons.

Dickson, Donald. 1968. "Bureaucracy and morality: An organizational perspective on a moral crusade." *Social Problems* 16 (Fall): 143–156.

Eisenstadt, S. N. (ed.). 1964. *Comparative Social Problems.* New York: Free Press.

Faunce, William A. 1968. *Problems of an Industrial Society.* New York: McGraw-Hill.

Finnigan, B. W. 1971. "The relevance of sociological theory to Canadian social problems," paper presented at the Annual Meeting of the Western Association for Sociology and Anthropology, Calgary.

Fuller, Richard C. 1937. "Sociological theory and social problems." *Social Forces* 15 (May): 496–502.

———— 1938. "The problem of teaching social problems." *American Journal of Sociology* 44 (November): 415–435.

Fuller, Richard C. and Richard R. Myers. 1941a. "The natural history of a social problem." *American Sociological Review* 6 (June): 320–328.

———— 1941b. "Some aspects of a theory of social problems." *American Sociological Review* 6 (February): 24–32.

Gerson, Walter M. (ed.). 1969. *Social Problems in a Changing World.* New York: Thomas Y. Crowell.

Gouldner, Alvin W. 1957. "Theoretical requirements of the applied social sciences." *American Sociological Review* 22 (February): 92–102.

Liazos, Alexander. 1972. "The poverty of the sociology of deviance: Nuts, sluts and preverts." *Social Problems* 20 (Summer): 103–120.

Lindenfeld, Frank (ed.). 1968. *Radical Perspectives on Social Problems.* New York: Macmillan.

Mishan, E. J. 1967. *The Costs of Economic Growth.* Middlesex: Penguin.

Nisbet, Robert A. 1966. "The study of social problems," pp. 1–25 in R. K. Merton and R. A. Nisbet (eds.), *Contemporary Social Problems.* New York: Harcourt Brace and World.

Questions for Discussion

1. What type of social problem would Fuller and Myers consider the issue of equal rights for women to be? Why? Discuss the natural history of this problem.

2. What are the similarities between the natural history of the contemporary women's rights issue and the natural history of present-day racial problems? Discuss whether "symbolic struggles" play a role in these social problems?

3. What are the "organizational mores" involved in the problems of equal rights for women and for Afro-Americans? How do organizational mores

contribute to these problems? How do humanitarian mores "cause" these social problems?

4. Westhues presents three basic criticisms of the value conflict approach. Do you agree that these features are necessarily characteristic of the value conflict approach? Why or why not? Do you think these features are necessarily weaknesses? Why or why not? What perspective does Westhues employ?

Selected References

Becker, Howard S., ed. *Social Problems: A Modern Approach.* New York: Wiley, 1966, pp. 1–31.

A useful statement that succinctly presents the Fuller-Myers approach in terms of symbolic interaction. Most useful for people who subscribe to the value conflict approach.

Bernard, Thomas J. *The Cycle of Juvenile Justice.* New York: Oxford University Press, 1992.

Throughout U.S. history, according to Bernard, official responses to juvenile delinquency have cycled between harsh punishment and lenient treatment. The value conflict between justice and treatment personnel, Bernard says, accounts for the cycle.

Chambliss, William J., ed., *Problems of Industrial Society.* Reading, Mass.: Addison-Wesley, 1973.

A collection of social problems readings organized around the value conflict perspective.

Collins, Randall. *Conflict Sociology: Toward an Explanatory Science.* New York: Academic Press, 1974.

An important theoretical work that spells out the general conditions under which conflicts among groups with divergent interests and values produce social conditions that later give rise to serious social problems.

Cuber, John F., William F. Kenkel, and Robert A. Harper. *Problems of American Society: Values in Conflict.* 4th ed. New York: Holt, Rinehart and Winston, 1964.

This textbook first states the Fuller-Myers position, and then goes on to examine a series of social problems from this point of view.

Dahrendorf, Ralf. *Class and Class Conflict in Industrial Society.* Stanford, Calif.: Stanford University Press, 1959.

An important statement of conflict theory.

Green, Arnold W. *Social Problems: Arena of Conflict.* New York: McGraw-Hill, 1975.

A textbook that examines several different types of social problems from the value conflict perspective.

Lemert, Edwin M. "Is There a Natural History of Social Problems?" *American Sociological Review* 16 (April 1951): 217–23.

An empirical test of Fuller's and Myers's three stages in the natural history of social problems—awareness, policy formation, and reform. Based on case histories of California trailer camps, interviews with public officials, and newspaper items and Letters-to-the-Editor regarding trailer camps, Lemert concludes that the Fuller-Meyers formulation is not applicable to the trailer-camp situation in California cities.

Lemert, Edwin M. "Social Problems." In *International Encyclopedia of Social Sciences,* ed. David L. Sills. New York: Macmillan and The Free Press, 1968, vol. 14, pp. 452–59.

A scholarly review of the various strands of thought that have been interwoven in the sociological analysis of social problems. Lemert concludes that analysis of such problems can be objective only if the analysts are aware of their values and make them explicit. He also concludes that values are central to the development and resolution of problems.

McCaghy, Charles H. *Deviant Behavior: Crime, Conflict, and Interest Groups.* New York: Macmillan, 1982.

McCaghy analyzes various forms of deviance by means of the interest group conflict perspective; these include crimes against persons and property, assaults against children and spouses, deviance with regard to organizations, drug use, mental disorders, prostitution, and homosexuality.

Schur, Edwin M. "Recent Social Problems Texts: An Essay-Review." *Social Problems* 10 (Winter 1963): 287–93.

With Mills's criticisms in mind, Schur examines eleven recent textbooks. He shows that a distinctively sociological approach to social problems has emerged since the publication of Mills's article. More general sociological theory has been applied to analyzing social problems, and most social problems textbooks combine theory and data in a sophisticated manner. Schur argues, though, that sociologists should take a value position on social problems, drawing on their own discipline for factual support.

5/DEVIANT BEHAVIOR

From World War I until 1954, the social disorganization perspective dominated sociological thought regarding social problems. And during these years, sociology, like the larger society, underwent a number of changes, becoming increasingly complex. Departments of sociology expanded, concepts multiplied, theoretical systems matured, and research became a prime objective. Yet despite overall conceptual developments, social disorganization remained the dominant perspective for the study of social problems. Competitors emerged only to be defeated or incorporated into the framework of social disorganization, and the disorganization perspective continued to dominate the textbooks on social problems.[1]

Why did the social disorganization perspective enjoy such long-lived popularity? First, certain features of the perspective helped to sustain it. It was systematic; it represented the best attempt at that time to determine a special subject matter for sociology; and it appeared to be faithful to the developing norms of science. Another reason was textbook lag. The textbook is one vehicle for the transmission of a discipline's ideas and findings. Sifting through and organizing them into a comprehensible and useful book is a lengthy process, especially in the early stages of a discipline's development. Then, once in print, a textbook and a perspective can have a long life.

Eventually, however, other factors undermined the popularity of the social disorganization perspective. As sociology became a channel for so-

1. Fuller argued in 1937 that textbooks on social problems usually took one of two approaches—to be conceptual or to be community-oriented. Conceptual textbooks either used a battery of sociological concepts or tried to fit all problems under just one concept. Community-oriented textbooks showed how different kinds of problems affected the community. Conceptual textbooks labored more on behalf of sociology, while community-oriented textbooks sought to perform a service for society. Yet, in both approaches, the disorganization perspective remained dominant. Thus, conceptual textbooks—whether eclectic or monistic—made social disorganization the key concept, usually explicitly. Disorganization was also the key concept in community-oriented textbooks, though this was more often implicit than explicit.
Perhaps the most influential textbook during these years was Mabel Elliott and Francis Merrill, *Social Disorganization* (New York: Harper, 1931). This book began as a single-concept book, but later editions were revised to include a developing battery of sociological concepts.

cial mobility, the number of sociologists greatly increased.[2] And as the society became more affluent, it could afford more support for research. These factors were important in promoting an increase in social research that, in turn, was important in prompting a reformulation of the social disorganization perspective. This is discussed in more detail below.

THE REFOCUSING OF SOCIOLOGICAL THOUGHT

As more and more sociologists were trained, two schools of sociological thought developed. One school, centered at Harvard University, focused primarily on social structure. The other school, centered at the University of Chicago, emphasized social process. Both the Harvard and the Chicago sociologists recognized the importance of studying social problems in order to develop mature and systematic sociology theory. Controversy arose, however, over the correct approach to the study of social problems. The deviant behavior perspective has roots in both these sociological traditions. In order to understand how it developed, let us briefly review the character of sociology in each of these great universities.

Sociology at Harvard had a strongly theoretical bent. The work of classic European sociologists, such as Emile Durkheim, Max Weber, and Vilfredo Pareto, were studied. In addition, Talcott Parsons and some of his students developed a broad theoretical perspective that later came to be known as structural-functionalism, a theoretical orientation that, according to many, dominated the next three decades of American sociology.[3]

At Chicago, by contrast, more sociologists emphasized description than grand theory. Throughout the 1920s and early 1930s, Chicago faculty and students treated the city of Chicago as a natural laboratory for their studies.[4] Books on the hobo, the Gold Coast and the slum, the ghetto, the taxi dance hall, the hotel, mental disorders, and juvenile delinquency appeared in rapid succession.

Although the Chicago sociologists were more concerned with describing the facts than with developing broader theories, this department did develop the concentric zone theory of urban development, a theory that predicted different rates of social disorganization in different sectors of the

2. In 1935, for example, the American Sociological Association began with a membership of 1,169. By 1945, membership had grown only slightly to 1,309. In the next decade, however, membership increased by 240 percent—reaching 4,454 in 1955. (Since then, the association has continued to grow, with 8,892 members in 1965 and 12,300 members in 1988.)

3. For one important example, see Talcott Parsons, *The Social System* (Glencoe, Ill.: Free Press, 1951).

4. For an informal history of the Chicago department, see Robert E. L. Faris, *Chicago Sociology 1920–1932* (San Francisco: Chandler, 1967).

city.[5] Empirical studies found rates of juvenile delinquency and certain mental disorders to be consistent with this theory,[6] and numerous sociologists conducted other studies correlating various rates of deviance with census tracts or other ecological properties.

In 1950, however, a famous article pointed out that just because the rates of several characteristics are higher in some geographic areas than in others, one cannot conclude from this that the same people always manifest these various characteristics.[7] (For example, a census tract may have a large proportion of immigrants and a high rate of crime, but it does not necessarily follow that immigrants are more likely to be committing these crimes.) Recognition of the fact that individual correlations cannot be deduced from collective correlations helped to foster the deviant behavior perspective. Finding the conceptualizations of the disorganization perspective too broad for research on individuals, sociologists developed the deviant behavior perspective to discover why some people undertake a deviant line of conduct while others do not. As the deviant behavior perspective developed, the social disorganization approach became confined more to the discussion of social units than to the analysis of the behavior of individual persons.[8]

ROOTS IN CLASSICAL THEORY

Before examining the development of the deviant behavior perspective from these two traditions, a few words about its theoretical roots are in order. As numerous scholars in the history of science have pointed out, theory is often years ahead of its time. Theory must sometimes wait several decades before anyone develops the methodology and/or technology necessary to test its implications. Testing must sometimes await translation of the theory into another language, or the development of a scientific point of view with which later generations can grasp the essentials of the theory and formulate ways of testing, revising, extending, and generalizing it.

5. Robert E. Park, Ernest W. Burgess, and Roderick D. McKenzie, *The City* (Chicago: University of Chicago Press, 1925).

6. Clifford R. Shaw, with the collaboration of Harvey Zorbaugh, Henry D. McKay, and Leonard S. Cottrell, *Delinquency Areas: A Study of the Geographical Distribution of School Truants, Juvenile Delinquents, and Adult Offenders in Chicago* (Chicago: University of Chicago Press, 1929); Robert E. L. Faris and H. Warren Dunham, *Mental Disorders in Urban Areas: An Ecological Study of Schizophrenia and Other Psychoses* (Chicago: University of Chicago Press, 1939).

7. The article that first pointed out the "fallacy" of ecological correlations was W. S. Robinson, "Ecological Correlations and the Behavior of Individuals," *American Sociological Review* 15 (June 1950): 351–57.

8. See, for example, Robert K. Merton and Robert Nisbet, eds., *Contemporary Social Problems: An Introduction to the Sociology of Deviant Behavior and Social Disorganization,* 3rd ed. (New York: Harcourt Brace Jovanovich, 1971); Albert K. Cohen, "The Study of Social Disorganization and Deviant Behavior," in *Sociology Today,* ed. Robert K. Merton, Leonard Broom, and Leonard S. Coltrell, Jr. (New York: Basic Books, 1959).

All this is true for the concept of anomie, which first appeared in Emile Durkheim's study of suicide, published in France in 1897. This classic work was not translated into English until 1951.[9] Thus, more than fifty years passed before several variations on this theory began to produce an impressive and growing list of empirical studies testing it in a number of problem areas.

Durkheim formulated a typology of suicide that concentrated on the nature of the social bond. He called one type of suicide egoistic suicide. When people have weak social integration, there is little to deter them from taking their lives when stress arises. For example, responsibility to his family may deter a married man from committing suicide, while an unmarried man does not have this bond to restrain him. He called a second type of suicide altruistic suicide. When people have something positive to die for because of intense attachments to primary groups and strong social integration, they can be induced to sacrifice their lives—for example, the Kamikaze pilot. Egoistic and altruistic suicides reflect the two poles of extremely weak social integration and attachment, and extremely strong social integration and attachment, respectively. A third type of suicide—anomic suicide—reflects something else. This type of suicide occurs in response to sudden changes—for example, sudden wealth or sudden poverty. Others had noticed that suicide rates increase during times of economic hardship, but Durkheim found that suicide rates also increase during periods of increasing prosperity. Durkheim saw these suicides as a sign of anomie (that is, normlessness). During sudden prosperity, Durkheim reasoned, the traditional rules that ordinarily limit people break down, and people find it hard to put limits on themselves. They do not know what limits to accept; they want more and more and are never satisfied. The result is frustration that may lead to suicide. During sudden poverty, on the contrary, people can feel demoralized if they do not accept such changes as just, and this may also lead to suicide.

THE DEVELOPMENT OF ANOMIE THEORY

In 1938, Robert Merton (a Harvard student of Parsons) published an extremely important paper entitled "Social Structure and Anomie."[10] Developing one line of Durkheim's theory, Merton argued that anomie could be the normal state of affairs for persons in certain segments of society when cultural goals (for example, financial success) are overemphasized and legitimate opportunities to achieve those goals are blocked. Merton then

9. Emile Durkheim, *Le Suicide: Etude de Sociologie* (Paris: Felix Alcan, 1897). The American edition is Emile Durkheim, *Suicide: A Study in Sociology,* trans. John A. Spaulding and George Simpson (Glencoe, Ill.: Free Press, 1951).

10. Robert K. Merton, "Social Structure and Anomie," *American Sociological Review* 3 (October 1938): 672–82.

theorized that this disjunction between legitimate means and cultural goals produces four types of deviance: *innovation,* where new, usually illicit means are adopted to achieve the goals; *ritualism,* where people renounce the goals, only to overemphasize the means; *retreatism,* where they renounce both cultural goals and institutionalized norms; and *rebellion,* where they wish to replace the established system of goals and means with another system.

Several points are important here. First, this is a general theory applicable to many different social problems. For instance, white-collar crime, organized rackets, vice, cheating on exams, or doping horses or athletes can reflect innovation; psychosis, drug addiction, and Skid Row can reflect retreatism.

Second, given Americans' emphasis on the goal of success, anomie and some forms of deviant behavior may be construed as *normal* responses to abnormal situations (rather than as abnormal or "sick" responses). As such, no assumptions about biological or psychological abnormalities are required to explain the behavior.

Third, different segments of the population (America's lower classes, Merton suggested) have higher rates of deviance, presumably because the goals of success are held out for all to strive for, but the legitimate means of attaining them are not available to everyone. Thus, if people want things they cannot afford, they may steal.

Merton's anomie theory has become one of the two most powerful influences on the development of the deviant behavior perspective, and its influence grew as American sociologists began cultivating specialties. Merton's paper inspired ten pieces of empirical research between 1940 and 1944; and between 1955 and 1964, no fewer than sixty-four studies based on Merton's theory appeared in the sociological literature.[11]

THE DEVELOPMENT OF DIFFERENTIAL ASSOCIATION THEORY

The other profound influence on the development of the deviant behavior perspective was that of Edwin H. Sutherland, of the University of Chicago. Sutherland first published his deceptively simple theory of differential association in 1939.[12] Following Thomas and Znaniecki, he thought social disorganization played an important role in the production of deviance. In his work, however, Sutherland gave greater attention to the social process by which a person becomes deviant than to the social structural conditions that promote deviance. In his theory of differential association, Sutherland maintained that people learn deviant behavior(s) in primary groups. He

11. See Robert K. Merton, "Anomie, Anomia, and Social Interaction," in *Anomie and Deviant Behavior: A Discussion and Critique,* ed. Marshall B. Clinard (New York: Free Press, 1964), p. 216.

12. Edwin H. Sutherland, *Principles of Criminology* (Philadelphia: Lippincott, 1939), pp. 4–9.

identified four dimensions of contact with deviant and nondeviant patterns (frequency, duration, priority, and intensity), and he set forth seven propositions regarding such learning.

Later sociologists came to see that the differential association theory could be considered to be a complement to the anomie theory. Both theories extended Durkheim's axiom that deviant behavior is to be expected as a natural part of social life.[13] Merton's theory could explain why rates of deviant behavior are higher in some sectors of the society than in others; it could not, however, explain why some persons in these sectors engage in such acts, while others do not. Sutherland's theory, because it is essentially a theory based on social interaction, is silent on the question of rates but can explain why some people, but not others, commit deviant acts.

The first publication to synthesize anomie theory and differential association theory was by Albert Cohen in 1955.[14] In his theory of the development of the delinquent subculture, Cohen maintained that working-class boys faced a situation of anomie in middle-class school systems. As a result, they came together and devised a culture that was antithetical to middle-class values. Through the process of differential association, Cohen argued, they transmitted a set of norms that required the violation of legitimate codes, if only to achieve and maintain status in the gang.

In 1960, Richard Cloward and Lloyd Ohlin provided another synthesis of anomie theory and differential association theory.[15] They suggested that *illegitimate* opportunity structures must also be considered, and that different types of delinquent subcultures arise in response to the presence or absence of illegitimate as well as legitimate opportunities. This formulation is exceedingly important for devising solutions to social problems. Opportunity theory was the basis for the War on Poverty and most of the community action programs that appeared in the 1960s.

The first textbook written from the deviant behavior perspective appeared in 1957.[16] This book, *Sociology of Deviant Behavior* by Marshall Clinard, provided the first codification of the deviant behavior perspective. It called attention to the array of factors involved in the social production of deviant behavior, and while it drew heavily on Merton's and Sutherland's theories, other points of view were not neglected. Soon after this book appeared, social problems courses began to be redefined. Numerous

13. For the contributions of both structural-functional theory and the Chicago school to naturalism in American sociology, see David Matza, *Becoming Deviant* (Englewood Cliffs, N.J.: Prentice-Hall, 1969).

14. Albert K. Cohen, *Delinquent Boys: The Culture of the Gang* (Glencoe, Ill.: Free Press, 1955).

15. Richard A. Cloward and Lloyd E. Ohlin, *Delinquency and Opportunity: A Theory of Delinquent Gangs* (New York: Free Press, 1960).

16. Marshall B. Clinard, *Sociology of Deviant Behavior* (New York: Holt, Rinehart and Winston, 1957).

courses, once called either "Social Problems" or "Social Disorganization," were renamed "Sociology of Deviant Behavior." This renaming presented a new question—does the term "deviant behavior" denote all social problems or only some of them? For example, Clinard's book includes chapters on family maladjustment, old age, minority groups, and discrimination and prejudice. Not everyone would agree that these problems fall under the rubric "deviant behavior."

Another question that arose was this: If deviant behavior does not include all social problems, then what *is* its relationship to other types of problems—for example, problems of social disorganization? To Merton, Sutherland, and their followers, deviant behavior and social disorganization were separate and distinct; nonetheless, they tended to see each as causing the other.

Finally, since the deviant behavior perspective came into its own, sociologists have become aware of the difficulty of researching the causes of deviant behavior. As a result, this perspective has turned increasingly away from the study of etiology and toward the study of deviant behavior systems (which describe the characteristic social features of the particular deviant activity) and of social control (see the "Solutions" section below).

CHARACTERISTICS OF THE DEVIANT BEHAVIOR PERSPECTIVE

The key characteristics of the deviant behavior perspective are as follows:

Definition. Social problems reflect violations of normative expectations. Behavior or situations that depart from norms are deviant.

Causes. The cause of deviant behavior lies in inappropriate socialization—for example, when the learning of deviant ways is not outweighed by the learning of nondeviant ways. This socialization is viewed as taking place within the context of primary group relations.

Conditions. Restricted opportunities for learning so-called conventional ways, increased opportunities for learning deviant ways, restricted opportunities for achieving legitimate goals, a feeling of stress, and access to a deviant mode of relief are all important background conditions for the evolution of deviant patterns of behavior.

Consequences. The deviant behavior perspective postulates a variety of consequences. Many kinds of deviant behavior are costly to society. One outcome, for example, is the firm establishment of illegitimate social worlds. In addition, however, some observable deviant behavior is useful, if only because it establishes negative role models showing the kinds of behavior that will be punished.

Solutions. The principal solution for deviant behavior is resocialization, and the best way to resocialize is to increase meaningful primary group contact with legitimate patterns of behavior and reduce meaningful primary group contact with illegitimate patterns of behavior. At the same time, the opportunity structure must be opened in order to alleviate the strains that motivate people to behave in unacceptable ways. As legitimate opportunities increase, socially problematic behavior should decrease.

SUMMARY AND CONCLUSION

The social disorganization perspective dominated sociological thought on social problems during the second and third periods of American sociology—that is, from the end of World War I until the mid-1950s. During the third period, however, more and more sociologists were trained in scientific analysis, more and more research was conducted, and sociologists became increasingly concerned with integrating theory and research.

Some sociologists focused on social structure, while others concentrated on social process, and two traditions of sociological thought developed around this cleavage. The Harvard school centered on structure; the Chicago school, on process. From the former came Merton's anomie theory as a way of explaining rates of deviant behavior. From the latter came Sutherland's theory of differential association as a way of explaining how people learn deviant patterns. When these two conceptions were fused, the perspective of deviant behavior emerged.

The main postulate in this perspective is that the propensity for deviant behavior is socially learned within the context of the primary group. Its cause, broadly speaking, is inappropriate socialization. Its conditions are blocked opportunities, stress, access to a deviant mode of relief, and deviant role models. Its consequences are sometimes beneficial to society. And its solutions lie in redistributed access to opportunity, increased primary relations with legitimate role models, and reduction (if not complete elimination) of opportunities and contacts with deviant role models.

ROBERT MERTON: ANOMIE AND SOCIAL STRUCTURE

Marshall B. Clinard

In this excerpt, Clinard reviews Merton's anomie theory and discusses how it links deviant behavior to social structure. Material success is a highly valued goal in America, but the legitimate avenues for attaining this goal are unavailable to lower-class people. This discrepancy places lower-class people in a frustrating position that may lead psychologically normal people to engage in deviant behavior. Clinard reviews the several ways in which Merton says people may adapt to this disjunction between cultural goals and social structural opportunities. These adaptations are conformity, ritualism, rebellion, innovation, and retreatism.

. . . In the essay "Social Structure and Anomie," which first appeared in 1938, was revised in 1949, and was further extended eight years later, Robert Merton set forth his now well known social and cultural explanation of deviant behavior in terms of anomie.[1] The significance for sociology of this formulation has been great, one writer stating: "Without any doubt, this body of ideas, which has come to be known as 'anomic' theory, has been the most influential single formulation in the sociology of deviance in the last 25 years, and Merton's paper, in its original and revised versions, is possibly the most frequently quoted single paper in modern sociology."[2]

While derived from Durkheim's concept of anomie, Merton's formulation was at the same time both broader in orientation and more specific in application. Durkheim's view that a situation of normlessness may arise from a clash of aspirations and a breakdown of regulatory norms was reformulated into a general principle that "social structures exert a definite pressure upon certain persons in the society to engage in nonconforming rather than conforming conduct."[3] Merton emphasized normative structures and, like Durkheim, viewed behavior such as crime as a "normal" response to given social situations: pressures toward deviation in a society could be such that forms of deviant behavior were psychologically as normal as conformist behavior.

While Durkheim confined his application of anomie chiefly to suicide, Merton sought to explain not only suicide but crime, delinquency, mental disorder, alcoholism, drug addiction, and many other phenomena.[4]

Merton's definition of deviant behavior was never very clear in his two basic essays. In a later writing he said that it "refers to conduct that departs significantly from the norms set for people in their social statuses . . . [and] must be related to the norms that are socially defined as appropriate and morally binding for people occupying various statuses."[5]

Unlike Durkheim, Merton did not consider man's biological nature to be important in explaining deviation: what Durkheim considered the innate desires of man, such as ambition to achieve unattainable objectives, Merton felt were induced by the social structure. With an eye to the Freudians, he pointed out that man is not contending with society "in an unceasing war between biological impulse and social restraint. The image of man as an untamed bundle of impulses begins to look more like a caricature than a portrait."[6] Even if one were to grant some role to biological impulses, there still remained the question of "why it is that the frequency of deviant behavior varies within different social structures and how it happens that the deviations have different shapes and patterns in different social structures."[7]

In explaining anomie and deviant behavior, Merton therefore concentrated not on the individual but on the social order. He set what he admitted to be an arbitrary dichotomy between cultural goals and the institutional means to achieve these goals. For analytical purposes he first divided social reality into cultural structures, or culture, and social structure, or society. The cultural structure is "that organized set of normative values governing behavior which is common to members of a designated society or group."[8] The other element, the social structure, consists of institutional norms which define and regulate the acceptable mode of reaching these goals. This represents an "organized set of social relationships in which members of the society or social groups are variously implicated."[9]

Cultural goals and institutionalized norms do not bear a constant relation to one another, for "the cultural emphasis placed upon certain goals varies independently of the degree of emphasis upon institutionalized means."[10] There can be many dominant success goals—accumulation of wealth, scientific productivity, religious orthodoxy, and others—which may clash with the means open to those who are socially disadvantaged in the competitive race for achievement.[11] In fact, any cultural goal which is greatly emphasized in a society is likely to affect institutionalized means. Goals may take precedence at one time over the institutionally prescribed means to achieve them. On the other hand, one can have situations where sheer conformity becomes a central value; the original purpose of the cultural goals becomes forgotten and the institutional means become a ritual to be observed.[12] Actually, an effective equilibrium between these two phases of a society is usually maintained as long as individuals secure satisfactions from conforming to both cultural goals and institutional means.

The emphasis on a disequilibrium between cultural goals and institutional norms in a society is clear in Merton's definition. Anomie is "conceived as a breakdown in the cultural structure, occurring particularly when there is an acute disjunction between cultural norms and goals and the social structured capacities of members of the group to act in accord with them."[13] He goes on to add that "cultural values may help to produce behavior which is at odds with the mandates of the values themselves."[14] The malintegration of culture and social structure, one preventing what the other encourages, can lead to a breakdown of the norms and the development of a situation of normlessness.[15]

Merton assumes that rates of deviant behavior within a given society vary by social class, ethnic or racial status, and other characteristics. His explanation of deviant behavior hinges, then, on the validity of the proposition that the *strain toward anomie,* i.e., the inability to achieve the goals of society by available means, will be differentially distributed through a social system, and that different modes of deviant adaptation will be concentrated in varying social strata. The distribution of deviant behavior will depend on the accessibility of legitimate means to secure the goals and the degree of assimilation of goals and norms by the different social strata of society. Not all of those subject to pressures to achieve goals become deviant. "The theory only holds that those located in places in the social structure which are particularly exposed to such stresses are more likely than others to exhibit deviant behavior."[16] Those who conform despite stresses do so because alternative cultural goals are available to provide a basis for stabilizing the social and cultural systems. Schematically the relation of anomie to social structure can be summarized in this way:

1. *Exposure* to the cultural goal and norms regulating behavior oriented toward the goal.

2. *Acceptance* of the goal or norms as moral mandates and internalized values.

3. *Relative accessibility to the goal:* life chances in the opportunity structure.

4. *The degree of discrepancy* between the accepted goal and its accessibility.

5. *The degree of anomie.*

6. *The rates of deviant behavior* of the various types set out in the typology of modes of adaptation.[17]

In his writings, he confined his analysis of deviant behavior to those societies like the American, where certain goals tend to be stressed without a corresponding emphasis on institutional procedures to obtain them.

American culture is characterized by great emphasis on the accumulation of wealth as a success symbol without a corresponding emphasis on using legitimate means to march toward this goal.[18] "The culture may be such as to lead individuals to center their emotional convictions upon the complex of culturally acclaimed ends, with far less emotional support for prescribed methods of reaching out for these ends. . . . In this context, the sole significant question becomes 'Which of the available procedures is most efficient in netting the culturally approved value?' "[19]

At the other extreme from American society on the continuum are those societies where the emphasis is on goals which have been largely subordinated to institutional means and lack their original meaning, and where conformity has become an end in itself. Other, more integrated societies fall between these two types of "malintegrated cultures" where goals and means to achieve them are in some sort of rough balance.

It is important to recognize from Merton's analysis that the high frequency of deviant behavior among certain classes in American society cannot be explained by a lack of opportunity alone or by an exaggerated emphasis on a pecuniary value nexus. A more rigid class structure, such as a caste system, might restrict opportunities to achieve such goals even more, without resultant deviant behavior. It is the set of equalitarian beliefs in American society, stressing the opportunity for economic affluence and social ascent for all of its members, which makes for the difference.

As Merton points out, however, these are idealized goals: the same proportion of persons in all social classes does not internalize them. Since the number of persons in each of the social classes varies considerably, it is important to distinguish between absolute numbers and relative proportion. Only a substantial number or "a number sufficiently large to result in a more frequent *disjunction* between goals and opportunity among the lower-class strata than among the upper-class strata" need to be goal-oriented.[20] It is the restriction on the use of approved means for a considerable part of the population that is crucial to the discussion of adaptations which follows.

> It is only when a system of cultural values extols, virtually above all else, certain *common* success-goals *for the population at large* while the social structure rigorously restricts or completely closes access to approved modes of reaching these goals *for a considerable part of the same population,* that deviant behavior ensues on a large scale.[21]

The discussion so far has dealt, in general, with anomie: it has not explained the origin of particular forms of deviant behavior. This brings us to one of the perhaps most important and certainly most intriguing parts of Merton's theory, the ways in which a person can adapt to a situation where *legitimate* means to reach a goal are not available to him.

ADAPTATIONS

There are five types of individual adaptations to achieve culturally pre-scribed goals of success open to those who occupy different positions in the social structure. One is conformity; the other are the deviant adapta-tions of ritualism, rebellion, innovation, and retreatism. None of these ad-aptations, as Merton points out, is deliberately selected by the individual or is utilitarian, but rather, since all arise from strains in the social system, they can be assumed to have a degree of spontaneity behind them. The paradigm is the following.

A Typology of Modes of Individual Adaptation[22]

Modes of adaptation	Cultural goals	Institutionalized means
I Conformity	+	+
II Innovation	+	−
III Ritualism	−	+
IV Retreatism	−	−
V Rebellion	±	±

+ = acceptance; − = rejection; ± = rejection of prevailing values and substitution of new values.

Conformity.   Conformity to both cultural goals and institutional means is the most common adaptation, but can be passed in this discussion which deals with non-conformity, although Merton claims that all five forms of adaptation relate to deviant behavior. Conformity of commitment to goals and institutional norms on the part of a large proportion of people, how-ever, makes human society possible. It is not in focusing on conforming or normal behavior that it is possible to find out about the basic stresses of a society but rather by directing attention to deviant behavior.

Ritualism.   The abandoning or scaling down of the lofty goals of pecuniary success and rapid social mobility to the point where our aspirations can be satisfied is ritualism. "But though one rejects the cultural obligation to attempt 'to get ahead in the world,' though one draws in one's horizons, one continues to abide almost compulsively by institutional norms."[23] Ac-tually this adaptation seems also to have little direct relationship to devia-tion, except perhaps to some forms of compulsive neuroses, and Merton himself says that the behavior exhibited by the ritualist is not generally considered deviant. Still, he feels that those who "play it safe," who become "bureaucratic virtuosos," who avoid high ambitions and consequent frus-tration, clearly represent a departure from the cultural model in which men are obliged to strive actively, preferably through institutionalized proce-dures, to move onward and upward in the social hierarchy.

Rebellion.   In this form of adaptation persons turn away from the conventional social structure and seek to establish a new or greatly modified social structure. This form of adaptation arises when "the institutional system is regarded as a barrier to the satisfaction of legitimized goals. . . ."[24] If it goes on to organized political action, the allegiance of persons such as the radical or revolutionary must be withdrawn from the existing social structure and transferred to new groups with new ideologies. The adaptation through rebellion requires little further discussion; in fact, the radical seldom is treated in conventional texts on deviant behavior.[25] In a sense Merton recognizes this for he points out that rebellion is an adaptation which is on a clearly different plane from the others. "It represents a transitional response seeking to *institutionalize* new goals and new procedures to be shared by other members of the society. It thus refers to efforts to *change* the existing cultural and social structure rather than to accommodate efforts *within* this structure."[26]

Merton, in a later paper, modified his view that rebellion was deviation in the same sense as were the other adaptations. Using different terms, he distinguished between rebellion, on the one hand, and innovation, ritualism, and retreatism, on the other.[27] In this paper he divided deviant behavior into two types, non-conforming and aberrant behavior, on the basis of social structure and consequences for the social system. Nonconformity is quite different from aberrant behavior such as crime and delinquency. The non-conformist announces his dissent publicly; the aberrant hides behind his departure from norms. The non-conformist challenges the legitimacy of social norms he rejects; the aberrant acknowledges the legitimacy of the norms he violates. The non-conformist tries to change the norms and may appeal to a higher morality; the aberrant merely wishes to escape the sanctioning force of present society. The non-conformist is often acknowledged by conventional society as departing from norms for disinterested purposes; the aberrant deviates to serve his own interests. Finally, the non-conformist draws upon the ultimate basic values of society for his goals, as distinguished from the aberrant whose interests are private, self-centered, and definitely antisocial.

Innovation.   Societies where the culture emphasizes pecuniary success and the social structure places undue limitations on approved means provide numerous situations for the development of socially disapproved departures from institutional norms, in the form of innovative practices. The use of such illegitimate means as crime to achieve culturally prescribed goals of success, power, and wealth, therefore, has become common in our society. Such a form of adaptation presupposes that individuals have been inadequately socialized with respect to cultural goals emphasizing success-aspirations. As evidence Merton maintains that unlawful behavior such as delinquency and crime appears to be most common in the lower strata of our society and this is "a 'normal' response to a situation where the cultural emphasis upon pecuniary success has been absorbed, but where there is little access to conventional and legitimate means for becoming success-ful."[28] These pressures tend to result in the gradual reduction in efforts to use legitimate means and an increase in the use of more or less expedient illegitimate means. The opportunities of the lower class are largely re-stricted to manual labor, and this is often stigmatized. Consequently, "the status of unskilled labor and the consequent low income cannot readily compete *in terms of established standards of worth* with the promise of power and high income from organized vice, rackets and crime."[29]

Illegitimate innovations are not restricted to crime among the lower socioeconomic classes. Similar pressures for ever greater monetary status symbols are exerted on the upper socioeconomic groups and give rise to unethical business practices and what has been termed white collar crime. "On the top economic levels, the pressure toward innovation not infre-quently erases the distinction between business-like striving this side of the mores and sharp practices beyond the mores."[30] He points out, however, that "whatever the differential rates of deviant behavior in several social strata . . . the greatest pressures toward deviation are exerted on the lower social strata."[31]

In his second basic essay on anomie, Merton attempted to qualify his earlier all-embracing explanation of delinquency and crime as a form of anomie. He recognized that various types of behavior are included in the legal rubrics of delinquency and crime, and therefore that "the foregoing theory of anomie is designed to account for some, not all, forms of deviant behavior customarily described as criminal or delinquent."[32] Except, how-ever, for specifically indicating that a theory of anomie does not account for much of the nonutilitarian character of behavior occurring in delinquent groups, he is vague as to which behavior is covered by his explanation and which is not.

The effect of innovative adaptation such as delinquency can be dynamic. Some individuals, because of their disadvantaged positions or personality patterns, are subjected more than others to the strains of the discrepancy between cultural goals and institutional means. They are, consequently, more vulnerable to deviant behavior. This "successful" adjustment tends to affect others and to lessen the legitimacy of the institutional norms for others. Others who did not respond to the original, rather slight anomie now do so. "This, in turn, creates a more acutely anomic situation for still other and initially less vulnerable individuals in the social system. In this way anomie and mounting rates of deviant behavior can be conceived as interacting in a process of social and cultural dynamics, with cumulatively disruptive consequences for the normative structure, unless counteracting mechanisms of control are called into play."[33]

Not all deviations in the form of innovation are dysfunctional for society.[34] Some may form the basis for new institutions better equipped to function than older ones. In any event, innovation, even of a deviant nature, is likely to be dynamic. "Social dysfunction is not a latter-day terminological substitute for 'immorality' or 'unethical practice.' "[35] In some cases it may even be "the norms of the group which are at fault, and not the innovator who rejects them." Although the extent is unknown, some deviation from current norms is probably functional for the basic goals of a group.[36] As Merton has written later:

> In the history of every society, one supposes, some of its culture heroes eventually come to be regarded as heroic in part because they are held to have had the courage and the vision to challenge the beliefs and routines of their society. The rebel, revolutionary, non-conformist, heretic or renegade of an earlier day is often the culture hero of today. Moreover, the accumulation of dysfunctions in a social system is often the prelude to concerted social change that may bring the system closer to the values that enjoy the respect of members of the society.[37]

Retreatism.   The adaptation to disjunctive means and goals through retreatism is significant in understanding certain specific forms of deviant behavior. In a sense one might say this is not so much an adaptation but a rejection of both cultural goals and institutional means. "The retreatist pattern consists of substantial abandoning both of the once-esteemed cultural goals and of institutionalized practices directed toward those goals."[38] The individual has internalized fully the cultural goals of success but finds inaccessible the institutionalized means to obtain them. Under internalized pressure not to obtain the goal by illegitimate means such as innovation provides, the individual finds himself frustrated and handicapped. He [thus] ... adopts escape mechanisms such as "defeatism, quietism and retreatism."

Retreatism constitutes some of the adaptive activities of "psychotics, autists, pariahs, outcasts, vagrants, tramps, chronic drunkards and drug addicts."[39] Their mode of adaptation in many cases is derived from the social structure which, in a sense, they have sought to repudiate. The retreatist form of adaptation is particularly condemned by conventional society because it is nonproductive, nonstriving, attaches no value to the success-goal of a society and does not use institutional means. The conformist keeps the wheels of society running; the innovator is at least "smart" and actively striving; the retreatist at least conforms to the mores.[40]

Retreatism is a private rather than a collectivized form of adaptation. "Although people exhibiting this deviant behavior may gravitate toward centers where they come into contact with other deviants and although they may come to share in the sub-culture of these deviant groups, their adaptations are largely private and isolated rather than unified under the aegis of a new cultural code."[41]

Notes

1. See Robert K. Merton, "Social Structure and Anomie: Revisions and Extensions," in Ruth Nanda Anshen, *The Family: Its Function and Destiny* (New York: Harper & Row, 1949), 275–312; "Social Structure and Anomie," 131–60, and "Continuities in the Theory of Social Structure and Anomie," 161–94, in Robert K. Merton, *Social Theory and Social Structure* [(Glencoe: The Free Press, 1957)]. The original essay was reprinted in the first edition (1949, rev. 1957) as "Social Structure and Anomie."

2. Albert K. Cohen, "Towards a Theory of Deviant Behavior: Continuities Continued," paper presented to session on deviant behavior, American Sociological Association meeting, August 28, 1963.

3. Merton, *Social Theory and Social Structure, op. cit.*, 132.

4. In this volume we are concentrating arbitrarily on behavior accompanied by a strong, negative societal reaction. Such deviant behavior includes delinquency and crime, mental disorder, alcoholism, and drug addiction. While Merton explained all as anomic adaptations, it should be emphasized that his analysis includes other behavior. It is, as he says, a theory "that distinguishes forms of deviant behavior which may be far removed from those which represent violations of law." To him deviant behavior includes, for example, the over-conformist with norms, the radical and the revolutionary, the "bureaucratic virtuosos," the person caught in the net of conformity, widows and aged persons who retreat into the past, and workers who develop passivity in response to anomic situations.

5. Robert K. Merton, "Social Problems and Sociological Theory," in Robert K. Merton and Robert A. Nisbet, *Contemporary Social Problems* [(New York: Harcourt, Brace & World, 1961)], 723–24.

6. Merton, *Social Theory and Social Structure, op. cit.*, 131.

7. *Ibid.*

8. *Ibid.*, 162.

9. *Ibid.*

10. *Ibid.*, 133.

11. *Ibid.*, 181.

12. *Ibid.*, 134.

13. *Ibid.*, 162. Robert Bierstedt, in his review of the original 1949 edition of *Social Theory and Social Structure*, questioned the applicability of the word "anomie" in Merton's sense to situations which exhibit opposing norms rather than no norms. *Amer. Sociological Rev.*, 15 (February, 1950), 140–41. In another connection Merton has suggested three other potential sources of anomie but they have never been incorporated into his basic theoretical position. Anomie may arise (1) in a situation where there is a system of contradictory norms, (2) where there are many values but individuals are not afforded any way of determining which is appropriate, (3) where norms are insufficiently defined in relation to others so that this ambiguity may result in difficulties in predicting environmental responses. "The Social-Cultural Environment and Anomie," in Helen L. Witmer and Ruth Kotinsky, Eds.,

New Perspectives for Research in Juvenile Delinquency (Washington, D.C.: U.S. Government Printing Office, 1956), 63–67.

14. Merton, *Social Theory and Social Structure, op. cit.,* 162.

15. The existence of a situation of anomie resulting from a conflict between important cultural values and sanctioned institutional means is not the same, however, as "value conflict." The conflict between goals and institutional means is the source of anomie. In fact, conflicts between members of various subgroups, rather than resulting in anomie, may cause the members of each group to comply more fully with their own norms.

16. Merton, *Social Theory and Social Structure, op. cit.,* 183.

17. *Ibid.,* adapted from 175.

18. *Ibid.,* 135. This emphasis on wealth is not peculiar to an economic system. As Max Weber has pointed out, the impulse to gain money has nothing to do with capitalism. "This impulse exists and has existed among waiters, physicians, coachmen, artists, prostitutes, dishonest officials, soldiers, nobles, crusaders, gamblers, and beggars. One may say that it has been common to all sorts and conditions of men at all times and in all countries of the earth, wherever the objective possibility of it is or has been given." Max Weber, *The Protestant Ethic and the Spirit of Capitalism,* tr. Talcott Parsons (New York: Charles Scribner's Sons, 1930), 17.

19. As a simple illustration of an anomic situation, Merton cites instances where winning the game may become the paramount goal. Rather than follow the rules of the game, universities may resort to illegitimate means, such as "surreptitiously slugging the star of the opposing team." The university alumni may "covertly subsidize 'students' whose talents are confined to the athletic field." Merton, *Social Theory and Social Structure, op. cit.,* 134–35.

20. *Ibid.,* 174.

21. *Ibid.,* 146.

22. *Ibid.,* 140.

23. *Ibid.,* 150.

24. *Ibid.,* 156.

25. An exception is Edwin M. Lemert's *Social Pathology* (New York: McGraw-Hill Book Co., 1951), which contains the chapter "Radicalism and Radicals."

26. Merton, *Social Theory and Social Structure, op. cit.,* 140.

27. "The foregoing account of non-conforming behavior develops somewhat the pattern of behavior identified as 'rebellion' in the typology set forth in 'Social Structure and Anomie.' In that same typology, innovation, ritualism, and retreatism would comprise forms of aberrant behavior." Robert K. Merton, "Social Problems and Sociological Theory," *op. cit.,* 727.

28. Merton, *Social Theory and Social Structure, op. cit.,* 145.

29. *Ibid.*

30. *Ibid.,* 144.

31. *Ibid.,* 141.

32. *Ibid.*, 178.

33. *Ibid.*, 180.

34. There are a number of theoretical problems inherent in the terms "functional" and "dysfunctional," but since the terms are used by Merton and currently used extensively in sociological literature, we have employed them in this paper. See, for example, "Functionalism in Social Science," in Ernest Nagel, *The Structure of Science: Problems in the Logic of Scientific Explanation* (New York: Harcourt, Brace & World, 1961), 530–35, and Llewellyn Gross, Ed., *Symposium on Sociological Theory* (New York: Harper & Row, 1959).

35. *Ibid.*, 182.

36. The latent positive functions of deviance, such as innovation, have been developed by Lewis Coser, who has pointed out that the deviant helps to arouse the community to the consequences of the breach of norms, and that deviance from this point of view may have the aspects of "normalcy." Lewis A. Coser, "Some Functions of Deviant Behavior and Normative Flexibility," *Amer. J. Sociology*, 68 (September, 1962), 172–81.

37. Merton, "Social Problems and Sociological Theory," *op. cit.*, 736.

38. Merton, *Social Theory and Social Structure, op. cit.*, 187.

39. *Ibid.*, 153.

40. *Ibid.*, 154. Merton later included in this adaptive response those whose social relations and norms had become seriously disturbed. Examples of this include widows and persons forced into retirement, and those experiencing the anomie of prosperity and depression, where disruptions in status may occur with great rapidity.

41. *Ibid.*, 155.

LEARNING TO BE DEVIANT

Edwin H. Sutherland and Donald R. Cressey

Although Durkheim had maintained that crime is normal in any society, many sociologists continued to regard deviant behavior as the result of individual pathology. Merton and Sutherland, however, helped to revive the Durkheimian notion of deviant behavior as a normal occurrence. On the level of social structure, Merton showed that deviant behavior can be seen as a normal response to an abnormal social situation. On the level of

From Edwin H. Sutherland and Donald R. Cressey, *Principles of Criminology*, seventh edition, pp. 77–83. Copyright © 1966 by the J. B. Lippincott Company. Reprinted by permission of the publisher.

social interaction, Sutherland argued that people learn to be criminal in the same way that they learn to be law-abiding. Thus, Sutherland concluded, deviant behavior is best explained by the principles of social learning rather than the principles of abnormal psychology.

If criminology is to be scientific, the heterogeneous collection of "multiple factors" known to be associated with crime and criminality should be organized and integrated by means of an explanatory theory which has the same characteristics as the scientific explanations in other fields of study. That is, the conditions which are said to cause crime should always be present when crime is present, and they should always be absent when crime is absent. Such a theory would stimulate, simplify, and give direction to criminological research, and it would provide a framework for understanding the significance of much of the knowledge acquired about crime and criminality in the past. Furthermore, it would be useful in control of crime, providing it could be "applied" in much the same way that the engineer "applies" the scientific theories of the physicist.

There are two complementary procedures which may be used to put order into criminological knowledge, to develop a causal theory of criminal behavior. The first is logical abstraction. Negroes, urban-dwellers, and young adults all have comparatively high crime rates. What do they have in common that results in these high crime rates? Research studies have shown that criminal behavior is associated in greater or less degree with the social and personal pathologies, such as poverty, bad housing, slum-residence, lack of recreational facilities, inadequate and demoralized families, feeble-mindedness, emotional instability, and other traits and conditions. What do these conditions have in common which apparently produces excessive criminality? Research studies have also demonstrated that many persons with those pathological traits and conditions do not commit crimes and that persons in the upper socio-economic class frequently violate the law, although they are not in poverty, do not lack recreational facilities, and are not feeble-minded or emotionally unstable. Obviously, it is not the conditions or traits themselves which cause crime, for the conditions are sometimes present when criminality does not occur, and they also are sometimes absent when criminality does occur. A causal explanation of criminal behavior can be reached by abstracting, logically, the mechanisms and processes which are common to the rich and the poor, Negroes and whites, urban and rural dwellers, young adults and old adults, and the emotionally stable and the emotionally unstable who commit crimes.

In arriving at these abstract mechanisms and processes, criminal behavior must be precisely defined and carefully distinguished from non-criminal behavior. The problem in criminology is to explain the criminality of behavior, not behavior as such. The abstract mechanisms and processes common to the classes of criminals indicated above should not also be common to non-criminals. Criminal behavior is human behavior, has much in common with non-criminal behavior, and must be explained within the same general framework used to explain other human behavior. However, an explanation of criminal behavior should be a specific part of a general theory of behavior. Its specific task should be to differentiate criminal from non-criminal behavior. Many things which are necessary for behavior are not for that reason important to the criminality of behavior. Respiration, for instance, is necessary for any behavior, but the respiratory process cannot be used in an explanation of criminal behavior, for it does not differentiate criminal behavior from non-criminal behavior.

The second procedure for putting order into criminological knowledge is differentiation of levels of analysis. This means that the problem is limited to a particular part of the whole situation, largely in terms of chronology. The causal analysis must be held at a particular level. For example, when physicists stated the law of falling bodies they were not concerned with the reasons why a body began to fall except as this might affect the initial momentum. It made no difference to the physicist whether a body began to fall because it was dropped from the hand of an experimental physicist or rolled off the edge of a bridge because of vibration caused by a passing vehicle. Also, a round object would have rolled off the bridge more readily than a square object, but this fact was not significant for the law of falling bodies. Such facts were considered as existing on a different level of explanation and were irrelevant to the problem with which the physicists were concerned. Much of the confusion regarding criminal behavior is due to a failure to define and hold constant the level of explanation. By analogy, many criminologists would attribute some degree of causal power to the "roundness" of the object in the illustration above. However, consideration of time sequences among the factors associated with crime and criminality may lead to simplicity of statement. In the heterogeneous collection of factors associated with criminal behavior, one factor often occurs prior to another factor (in much the way that "roundness" occurs prior to "vibration," and "vibration" occurs prior to "rolling off a bridge"), but a theoretical statement about criminal behavior can be made without referring to those early factors. By holding the analysis at one level, the early factors are combined with or differentiated from later factors or conditions, thus reducing the number of variables which must be considered in a theory.

A motion picture several years ago showed two boys engaged in a minor theft; they ran when they were discovered; one boy had longer legs, escaped, and became a priest; the other had shorter legs, was caught, committed to a reformatory, and became a gangster. In this comparison, the boy who became a criminal was differentiated from the one who did not become a criminal by the length of his legs. But "length of legs" need not be considered in a criminological theory for, in general, no significant relationship has been found between criminality and length of legs and certainly many persons with short legs are law-abiding and many persons with long legs are criminals. The length of the legs does not determine criminality and has no necessary relation to criminality. In the illustration, the differential in the length of the boys' legs may be observed to be significant to subsequent criminality or non-criminality only to the degree that it determined the subsequent experiences and associations of the two boys. It is in these experiences and associations, then, that the mechanisms and processes which are important to criminality or non-criminality are to be found. A "one-level" theoretical explanation of crime would be concerned solely with these mechanisms and processes, not with the earlier factor "length of legs."

TWO TYPES OF EXPLANATIONS OF CRIMINAL BEHAVIOR

Scientific explanations of criminal behavior may be stated either in terms of the process which are operating at the moment of the occurrence of crime or in terms of the processes operating in the earlier history of the criminal. In the first case, the explanation may be called "mechanistic," "situational," or "dynamic"; in the second, "historical" or "genetic." Both types of explanation are desirable. The mechanistic type of explanation has been favored by physical and biological scientists, and it probably could be the more efficient type of explanation of criminal behavior. However, criminological explanations of the mechanistic type have thus far been notably unsuccessful, perhaps largely because they have been formulated in connection with the attempt to isolate personal and social pathologies among criminals. Work from this point of view has, at least, resulted in the conclusion that the immediate determinants of criminal behavior lie in the person-situation complex.

The objective situation is important to criminality largely to the extent that it provides an opportunity for a criminal act. A thief may steal from a fruit stand when the owner is not in sight but refrain when the owner is in sight; a bank burglar may attack a bank which is poorly protected but refrain from attacking a bank protected by watchmen and burglar alarms. A corporation which manufactures automobiles seldom or never violates the Pure Food and Drug Law, but a meat-packing corporation might violate this law with great frequency. But in another sense, a psychological or sociological sense, the situation is not exclusive of the person, for the situation which is important is the situation as defined by the person who is involved. That is, some persons define a situation in which a fruit-stand owner is out of sight as a "crime-committing" situation, while others do not so define it. Furthermore, the events in the person-situation complex at the time a crime occurs cannot be separated from the prior life experiences of the criminal. This means that the situation is defined by the person in terms of the inclinations and abilities which the person has acquired up to date. For example, while a person could define a situation in such a manner that criminal behavior would be the inevitable result, his past experiences would for the most part determine the way in which he defined the situation. An explanation of criminal behavior made in terms of these past experiences is an historical or genetic explanation.

The following paragraphs state such a genetic theory of criminal behavior on the assumption that a criminal act occurs when a situation appropriate for it, as defined by the person, is present. The theory should be regarded as tentative. . . .

GENETIC EXPLANATION OF CRIMINAL BEHAVIOR

The following statement refers to the process by which a particular person comes to engage in criminal behavior.

1. *Criminal behavior is learned.* Negatively, this means that criminal behavior is not inherited, as such; also, the person who is not already trained in crime does not invent criminal behavior, just as a person does not make mechanical inventions unless he has had training in mechanics.

2. *Criminal behavior is learned in interaction with other persons in a process of communication.* This communication is verbal in many respects but includes also "the communication of gestures."

3. *The principal part of the learning of criminal behavior occurs within intimate personal groups.* Negatively, this means that the impersonal agencies of communication, such as movies and newspapers, play a relatively unimportant part in the genesis of criminal behavior.

4. *When criminal behavior is learned, the learning includes (a) techniques of committing the crime, which are sometimes very complicated, sometimes very simple; (b) the specific direction of motives, drives, rationalizations, and attitudes.*

5. *The specific direction of motives and drives is learned from definitions of the legal codes as favorable or unfavorable.* In some societies an individual is surrounded by persons who invariably define the legal codes as rules to be observed, while in others he is surrounded by persons whose definitions are favorable to the violation of the legal codes. In our American society these definitions are almost always mixed, with the consequence that we have culture conflict in relation to the legal codes.

6. *A person becomes delinquent because of an excess of definitions favorable to violation of law over definitions unfavorable to violation of law.* This is the principle of differential association. It refers to both criminal and anti-criminal associations and has to do with counteracting forces. When persons become criminal, they do so because of contacts with criminal patterns and also because of isolation from anti-criminal patterns. Any person inevitably assimilates the surrounding culture unless other patterns

are in conflict; a Southerner does not pronounce "r" because other Southerners do not pronounce "r." Negatively, this proposition of differential association means that associations which are neutral so far as crime is concerned have little or no effect on the genesis of criminal behavior. Much of the experience of a person is neutral in this sense, e.g., learning to brush one's teeth. This behavior has no negative or positive effect on criminal behavior except as it may be related to associations which are concerned with the legal codes. This neutral behavior is important especially as an occupier of the time of a child so that he is not in contact with criminal behavior during the time he is so engaged in the neutral behavior.

7. *Differential associations may vary in frequency, duration, priority, and intensity.* This means that associations with criminal behavior and also associations with anti-criminal behavior vary in those respects. "Frequency" and "duration" as modalities of associations are obvious and need no explanation. "Priority" is assumed to be important in the sense that lawful behavior developed in early childhood may persist throughout life, and also that delinquent behavior developed in early childhood may persist throughout life. This tendency, however, has not been adequately demonstrated, and priority seems to be important principally through its selective influence. "Intensity" is not precisely defined but it has to do with such things as the prestige of the source of a criminal or anti-criminal pattern and with emotional reactions related to the associations. In a precise description of the criminal behavior of a person these modalities would be stated in quantitative form and a mathematical ratio be reached. A formula in this sense has not been developed, and the development of such a formula would be extremely difficult.

8. *The process of learning criminal behavior by association with criminal and anti-criminal patterns involves all of the mechanisms that are involved in any other learning.* Negatively, this means that the learning of criminal behavior is not restricted to the process of imitation. A person who is seduced, for instance, learns criminal behavior by association, but this process would not ordinarily be described as imitation.

9. *While criminal behavior is an expression of general needs and values, it is not explained by those general needs and values since noncriminal behavior is an expression of the same needs and values.* Thieves generally steal in order to secure money, but likewise honest laborers work in order to secure money. The attempts by many scholars to explain criminal behavior by general drives and values, such as the happiness principle, striving for social status, the money motive, or frustration, have been and must continue to be futile since they explain lawful behavior as completely as they explain criminal behavior. They are similar to respiration, which is necessary for any behavior but which does not differentiate criminal from noncriminal behavior.

It is not necessary, at this level of explanation, to explain why a person has the associations which he has; this certainly involves a complex of many things. In an area where the delinquency rate is high, a boy who is sociable, gregarious, active, and athletic is very likely to come in contact with the other boys in the neighborhood, learn delinquent behavior from them, and become a gangster; in the same neighborhood the psychopathic boy who is isolated, introverted, and inert may remain at home, not become acquainted with the other boys in the neighborhood, and not become delinquent. In another situation, the sociable, athletic, aggressive boy may become a member of a scout troop and not become involved in delinquent behavior. The person's associations are determined in a general context of social organization. A child is ordinarily reared in a family; the place of residence of the family is determined largely by family income; and the delinquency rate is in many respects related to the rental value of the houses. Many other aspects of social organization affect the kinds of associations a person has.

The preceding explanation of criminal behavior purports to explain the criminal and noncriminal behavior of individual persons. As indicated earlier, it is possible to state sociological theories of criminal behavior which explain the criminality of a community, nation, or other group. The problem, when thus stated, is to account for variations in crime rates and involves a comparison of the crime rates of various groups or the crime rates of a particular group at different times. The explanation of a crime rate must be consistent with the explanation of the criminal behavior of the person, since the crime rate is a summary statement of the number of persons in the group who commit crimes and the frequency with which they commit crimes. One of the best explanations of crime rates from this point of view is that a high crime rate is due to social disorganization. The term "social disorganization" is not entirely satisfactory and it seems preferable to substitute for it the term "differential social organization." The postulate on which this theory is based, regardless of the name, is that crime is rooted in the social organization and is an expression of that social organization. A group may be organized for criminal behavior or organized against criminal behavior. Most communities are organized both for criminal and anti-criminal behavior and in that sense the crime rate is an expression of the differential group organization. Differential group organization as an explanation of variations in crime rates is consistent with the differential association theory of the processes by which persons become criminals.

ILLEGITIMATE OPPORTUNITIES
AND DEVIANT BEHAVIOR

Richard A. Cloward and Lloyd E. Ohlin

Cloward and Ohlin claim that the emergence of delinquent subcultures and the forms they take depend on illegitimate as well as legitimate opportunities. When adolescents are denied legitimate opportunities for success, for example, their response to this status frustration depends on the opportunity structures open to them. If criminal opportunities are readily available, they may form or participate in a criminal subculture to solve their status problem. If criminal opportunities are not readily available, the youths may turn to violence or fighting. And if drugs and the knowledge of how to use them are available, then a drug culture may very likely emerge.

THE AVAILABILITY OF ILLEGITIMATE MEANS

Social norms are two-sided. A prescription implies the existence of a prohibition, and *vice versa*. To advocate honesty is to demarcate and condemn a set of actions which are dishonest. In other words, norms that define legitimate practices also implicitly define illegitimate practices. One purpose of norms, in fact, is to delineate the boundary between legitimate and illegitimate practices. In setting this boundary, in segregating and classifying various types of behavior, they make us aware not only of behavior that is regarded as right and proper but also of behavior that is said to be wrong and improper. Thus the criminal who engages in theft or fraud does not invent a new way of life; the possibility of employing alternative means is acknowledged, tacitly at least, by the norms of the culture.

This tendency for proscribed alternatives to be implicit in every prescription, and *vice versa*, although widely recognized, is nevertheless a reef upon which many a theory of delinquency has foundered. Much of the criminological literature assumes, for example, that one may explain a criminal act simply by accounting for the individual's readiness to employ illegal alternatives of which his culture, through its norms, has already made him generally aware. Such explanations are quite unsatisfactory, however, for they ignore a host of questions regarding the *relative availability* of illegal alternatives to various potential criminals. The aspiration to be a physician is hardly enough to explain the fact of becoming a physician; there is much that transpires between the aspiration and the achievement. This is no less true of the person who wants to be a successful criminal. Having decided that he "can't make it legitimately," he cannot simply choose among an array of illegitimate means, all equally available to him. . . . It is assumed in the theory of anomie that access to conventional means is differentially distributed, that some individuals, because of their social class, enjoy certain advantages that are denied to those elsewhere in the class structure. For example, there are variations in the degree to which members of various classes are fully exposed to and thus acquire the values, knowledge, and skills that facilitate upward mobility. It should not be startling, therefore, to suggest that there are socially structured variations in the availability of illegitimate means as well. In connection with delinquent subcultures, we shall be concerned principally with differentials in access to illegitimate means within the lower class.

Many sociologists have alluded to differentials in access to illegitimate means without explicitly incorporating this variable into a theory of deviant behavior. This is particularly true of scholars in the "Chicago tradition" of criminology. Two closely related theoretical perspectives emerged from this school. The theory of "cultural transmission," advanced by Clifford R. Shaw and Henry D. McKay, focuses on the development in some urban neighborhoods of a criminal tradition that persists from one generation to another despite constant changes in population.[1] In the theory of "differential association," Edwin H. Sutherland described the processes by which criminal values are taken over by the individual.[2] He asserted that criminal behavior is learned, and that it is learned in interaction with others who have already incorporated criminal values. Thus the first theory stresses the value systems of different areas; the second, the systems of social relationships that facilitate or impede the acquisition of these values.

Scholars in the Chicago tradition, who emphasized the processes involved in learning to be criminal, were actually pointing to differentials in the availability of illegal means—although they did not explicitly recognize this variable in their analysis. This can perhaps best be seen by examining Sutherland's classic work, *The Professional Thief*. "An inclination to steal," according to Sutherland, "is not a sufficient explanation of the genesis of the professional thief."[3] The "self-made" thief, lacking knowledge of the ways of securing immunity from prosecution and similar techniques of defense, "would quickly land in prison; . . . a person can be a professional thief only if he is recognized and received as such by other professional thieves." But recognition is not freely accorded: "Selection and tutelage are the two necessary elements in the process of acquiring recognition as a professional thief. . . . A person cannot acquire recognition as a professional thief until he has had tutelage in professional theft, *and tutelage is given only to a few persons selected from the total population.*" For one thing, "the person must be appreciated by the professional thieves. He must be appraised as having an adequate equipment of wits, front, talking-ability, honesty, reliability, nerve and determination." Furthermore, the aspirant is judged by high standards of performance, for only "a very small percentage of those who start on this process ever reach the stage of professional thief. . . ." Thus motivation and pressures toward deviance do not fully account for deviant behavior any more than motivation and pressures toward conformity account for conforming behavior. The individual must have access to a learning environment and, once having been trained, must be allowed to perform his role. Roles, whether conforming or deviant in content, are not necessarily freely available; access to them depends upon a variety of factors, such as one's socioeconomic position, age, sex, ethnic affiliation, personality characteristics, and the like. The potential thief, like the potential physician, finds that access to his goal is governed by many criteria other than merit and motivation.

What we are asserting is that access to illegitimate roles is not freely available to all, as is commonly assumed. Only those neighborhoods in which crime flourishes as a stable, indigenous institution are fertile criminal learning environments for the young. Because these environments afford integration of different age-levels of offender, selected young people are exposed to "differential association" through which tutelage is provided and criminal values and skills are acquired. To be prepared for the role may not, however, ensure that the individual will ever discharge it. One important limitation is that more youngsters are recruited into these patterns of differential associations than the adult criminal structure can possibly absorb. Since there is a surplus of contenders for these elite positions, criteria and mechanisms of selection must be evolved. Hence a certain proportion of those who aspire may not be permitted to engage in the behavior for which they have prepared themselves.

Thus we conclude that access to illegitimate roles, no less than access to legitimate roles, is limited by both social and psychological factors. We shall here be concerned primarily with socially structured differentials in illegitimate opportunities. Such differentials, we contend, have much to do with the type of delinquent subculture that develops.

LEARNING AND PERFORMANCE STRUCTURES

Our use of the term "opportunities," legitimate or illegitimate, implies access to both learning and performance structures. That is, the individual must have access to appropriate environments for the acquisition of the values and skills associated with the performance of a particular role, and he must be supported in the performance of the role once he has learned it.

Tannenbaum, several decades ago, vividly expressed the point that criminal role performance, no less than conventional role performance, presupposes a patterned set of relationships through which the requisite values and skills are transmitted by established practitioners to aspiring youth:

> It takes a long time to make a good criminal, many years of specialized training and much preparation. But training is something that is given to people. People learn in a community where the materials and the knowledge are to be had. A craft needs an atmosphere saturated with purpose and promise. The community provides the attitudes, the point of view, the philosophy of life, the example, the motive, the contacts, the friendships, the incentives. No child brings those into the world. He finds them here and available for use and elaboration. The community gives the criminal his materials and habits, just as it gives the doctor, the lawyer, the teacher, and the candlestick-maker theirs.[4]

Sutherland systematized this general point of view, asserting that opportunity consists, at least in part, of learning structures. Thus "criminal behavior is learned" and, furthermore, it is learned "in interaction with other persons in a process of communication." However, he conceded that the differential-association theory does not constitute a full explanation of criminal behavior. In a paper circulated in 1944, he noted that "criminal behavior is partially a function of opportunities to commit [*i.e.*, to perform] specific classes of crime, such as embezzlement, bank burglary, or illicit heterosexual intercourse." Therefore, "while opportunity may be partially a function of association with criminal patterns and of the specialized techniques thus acquired, it is not determined entirely in that manner, and consequently differential association is not the sufficient cause of criminal behavior."[5]

To Sutherland, then, illegitimate opportunity included conditions favorable to the performance of a criminal role as well as conditions favorable to the learning of such a role (differential associations). These conditions, we suggest, depend upon certain features of the social structure of the community in which delinquency arises.

DIFFERENTIAL OPPORTUNITY: A HYPOTHESIS

We believe that each individual occupies a position in both legitimate and illegitimate opportunity structures. This is a new way of defining the situation. The theory of anomie views the individual primarily in terms of the legitimate opportunity structure. It poses questions regarding differentials in access to legitimate routes to success-goals; at the same time it assumes either that illegitimate avenues to success-goals are freely available or that differentials in their availability are of little significance. This tendency may be seen in the following statement by Merton:

> Several researches have shown that specialized areas of vice and crime constitute a "normal" response to a situation where the cultural emphasis upon pecuniary success has been absorbed, but where there is little access to conventional and legitimate means for becoming successful. The occupational opportunities of people in these areas are largely confined to manual labor and the lesser white-collar jobs. Given the American stigmatization of manual labor *which has been found to hold rather uniformly for all social classes*, and the absence of realistic opportunities for advancement beyond this level, the result is a marked tendency toward deviant behavior. The status of unskilled labor and the consequent low income cannot readily compete *in terms of established standards of worth* with the promises of power and high income from organized vice, rackets and crime. . . . [Such a situation] leads toward the gradual attenuation of legitimate, but by and large ineffectual, strivings and the increasing use of illegitimate, but more or less effective, expedients.[6]

The cultural-transmission and differential-association tradition, on the other hand, assumes that access to illegitimate means is variable, but it does not recognize the significance of comparable differentials in access to legitimate means. Sutherland's "ninth proposition" in the theory of differential association states:

> *Though criminal behavior is an expression of general needs and values, it is not explained by those general needs and values since non-criminal behavior is an expression of the same needs and values.* Thieves generally steal in order to secure money, but likewise honest laborers work in order to secure money. The attempts by many scholars to explain criminal behavior by general drives and values, such as the happiness principle, striving for social status, the money motive, or frustration, have been and must continue to be futile since they explain lawful behavior as completely as they explain criminal behavior.[7]

In this statement, Sutherland appears to assume that people have equal and free access to legitimate means regardless of their social position. At the very least, he does not treat access to legitimate means as variable. It is, of course, perfectly true that "striving for social status," "the money motive," and other socially approved drives do not fully account for either deviant or conforming behavior. But if goal-oriented behavior occurs under conditions in which there are socially structured obstacles to the satisfaction of these drives by legitimate means, the resulting pressures, we contend, might lead to deviance.

The concept of differential opportunity structures permits us to unite the theory of anomie, which recognizes the concept of differentials in access to legitimate means, and the "Chicago tradition," in which the concept of differentials in access to illegitimate means is implicit. We can now look at the individual, not simply in relation to one or the other system of means, but in relation to both legitimate and illegitimate systems. This approach permits us to ask, for example, how the relative availability of illegitimate opportunities affects the resolution of adjustment problems leading to deviant behavior. We believe that the way in which these problems are resolved may depend upon the kind of support for one or another type of illegitimate activity that is given at different points in the social structure. If, in a given social location, illegal or criminal means are not readily available, then we should not expect a criminal subculture to develop among adolescents. By the same logic, we should expect the manipulation of violence to become a primary avenue to higher status only in areas where the means of violence are not denied to the young. To give a third example, drug addiction and participation in subcultures organized around the consumption of drugs presuppose that persons can secure access to drugs and knowledge about how to use them. In some parts of the social structure, this would be very difficult; in others, very easy. In short, there are marked differences from one part of the social structure to another in the types of illegitimate adaptation that are available to persons in search of solutions to problems of adjustment arising from the restricted availability of legitimate means.[8] In this sense, then, we can think of individuals as being located in two opportunity structures—one legitimate, the other illegitimate. Given limited access to success-goals by legitimate means, the nature of the delinquent response that may result will vary according to the availability of various illegitimate means.[9]

Notes

1. See esp. C. R. Shaw, *The Jack-Roller* (Chicago: University of Chicago Press, 1930); Shaw, *The Natural History of a Delinquent Career* (Chicago: University of Chicago Press, 1931); Shaw *et al.*, *Delinquency Areas* (Chicago: University of Chicago Press, 1940); and Shaw and H. D. McKay, *Juvenile Delinquency and Urban Areas* (Chicago: University of Chicago Press, 1942).

2. E. H. Sutherland, ed., *The Professional Thief* (Chicago: University of Chicago Press, 1937); and Sutherland, *Principles of Criminology*, 4th Ed. (Philadelphia: Lippincott, 1947).

3. All quotations on this page are from *The Professional Thief*, pp. 211–13. Emphasis added.

4. Frank Tannenbaum, "The Professional Criminal," *The Century*, Vol. 110 (May–Oct. 1925); p. 577.

5. See A. K. Cohen, Alfred Lindesmith, and Karl Schuessler, eds., *The Sutherland Papers* (Bloomington, Ind.: Indiana University Press, 1956), pp. 31–35.

6. R. K. Merton, *Social Theory and Social Structure*, Rev. and Enl. Ed. (Glencoe, Ill.: Free Press, 1957), pp. 145–46.

7. *Principles of Criminology, op. cit.*, pp. 7–8.

8. For an example of restrictions on access to illegitimate roles, note the impact of racial definitions in the following case: "I was greeted by two prisoners who were to be my cell buddies. Ernest was a first offender, charged with being a 'hold-up' man. Bill, the other buddy, was an old offender, going through the machinery of becoming a habitual criminal, in and out of jail. . . . The first thing they asked me was, 'What are you in for?' I said, 'Jack-rolling.' The hardened one (Bill) looked at me with a superior air and said, 'A hoodlum, eh? An ordinary sneak thief. Not willing to leave jack-rolling to the niggers, eh? That's all they're good for. Kid, jack-rolling's not a white man's job.' I could see that he was disgusted with me, and I was too scared to say anything" (Shaw, *The Jack-Roller, op. cit.,* p. 101).

9. For a discussion of the way in which the availability of illegitimate means influences the adaptations of inmates to prison life, see R. A. Cloward, "Social Control in the Prison," *Theoretical Studies of the Social Organization of the Prison,* Bulletin No. 15 (New York: Social Science Research Council, March 1960), pp. 20–48.

ANOMIE: THEORY AND FACT

Marshall B. Clinard

Most influential theories generate a good deal of criticism. Criticism usually focuses on the clarity and consistency of the concepts and on how well the theory fits the facts. In this excerpt, Clinard summarizes the criticisms of anomie theory that six sociologists made during a special symposium on the subject. The major criticisms are as follows: uniform values seem most unlikely in a complex society; there is no evidence of higher rates of deviant behavior among the lower classes; status discontent does not uniformly lead to deviant behavior; the so-called deviant's role in selecting a deviant style is much more complex than the theory allows for; and social control, as either cause or deterrent of deviant behavior, is completely overlooked by the theory.

THE UNIFORMITY OF CULTURAL VALUES

Merton's theory of anomie tends to consider the social structure as consisting of more uniform values than an empirical examination of the diverse nature of most societies shows, according to Lemert. His main criticism of anomie is directed at the difficulty of identifying a set of values that could

From Marshall B. Clinard, *Anomie and Deviant Behavior,* pp. 40–47, 49–52. Copyright © 1964 by The Free Press of Glencoe, a division of The Macmillan Company. Reprinted by permission.

be considered universal in most societies today. There are not many societies, even pre-literate ones, in which "values learned in childhood, taught as a pattern, and reinforced by structured controls, serve to predict the bulk of the everyday behavior of members and to account for prevailing conformity to norms."[1] He adds also that to maintain that contemporary, urban, secular, and technologically based societies, such as the United States, "have a common value hierarchy, either culturally transmitted or structurally induced, strains credulity."[2] In societies where there is ethnic pluralism or newly migrant groups, or where a set of foreign values has been imposed, as on a colonial population, criminal behavior, for example, can be explained in the same way as conformity among members of the dominant group, i.e., by reference to traditionally patterned values and norms where there is *no* structural restriction of means.[3]

Rather than assuming "goals" to exist in American culture, as Merton does, Lemert believes that the "ends sought" grow out of the nature of associations in modern complex societies, the multi-value claims made on individuals, and the influence of modern technology. In this way it is possible to explain conformity as well as deviations without assuming "inherent" qualities or goals which apply to all members of a modern society. Individual members of a modern complex society may, as a result of interaction with diverse groups, modify their cultural values or change the order of their satisfaction. Consequently, it is doubtful whether study of the "ideal pattern" or those values and norms presumably indoctrinated into individuals, will generally predict conformity in modern society.

EVIDENCE OF CLASS VARIATIONS IN THE DISTRIBUTION OF DEVIANT BEHAVIOR

In his discussion, Lemert claims that Merton over-emphasizes one aspect of social structure, class-limited access to means, in explaining deviant behavior. He questions whether we even have sufficient empiric evidence to support the contention that deviant behavior is disproportionately more common at lower class levels of society. A more discriminating concept or concepts than social class should, therefore, be utilized in explaining how social structure influences deviation. Moreover, there is insufficient evidence to support the view that deviation is the result of individual adaptations. . . .

PRESSURES TOWARD DEVIATION DEPENDENT ON POSITION IN THE SOCIAL STRUCTURE

Several authors are critical of Merton's position that limited access to the goals of society through legitimate means by the lower socioeconomic groups is a principal source of deviance. For example, while recognizing that social position may play an important role in determining what means become available to reach certain ends, Lemert feels that other factors are equally important, namely, group or collective adaptations, technology, psychic processes, and socio-biological handicaps. All of these factors Merton largely neglects in his emphasis on social class.

Lemert, moreover, maintains that "the discrete individual remains for Merton the unit of analysis; the group as an arena of interaction, influencing conformity and deviation, nowhere comes to the fore in his treatment."[4] Many forms of deviant behavior such as professional crime, prostitution, and opiate addiction, are collective acts in which group-maintained values, as well as private values, are involved. Much of white collar crime is of this order, as several studies have demonstrated. Likewise, much of what is termed conformity is a collective rather than an individual phenomenon or form of adaptation.

In their implementation of Merton's theory, Cohen, Cloward, and Ohlin made much of gang delinquency as a reflection of position or status discontent. In a test of this hypothesis, Short found this to be a chief component of those pressures toward deviant behavior, as measured by the magnitude of the mean discrepancy between the boys' occupational aspirations and occupational expectations; position discontent orders the boys in approximately the same manner as does their delinquency involvement, as measured by police records.[5] When position discontent was measured by a comparison of the occupational aspirations and expectations of the boys with the occupational achievements of their fathers, the Negro boys as a group had aspirations and expectations much higher than that of the white boys. On the other hand, there was an even higher degree of such position discontent among non-gang lower class boys, who had a lower rate of delinquency. A similar overall picture was presented for perceiving educational opportunities as closed, but again, there were internal contradictions.

These contradictory findings suggest to Short the difficulty of conducting research on anomie theory. "High educational and occupational aspirations . . . seem clearly not to pressure the boys toward deviance, despite limitations, perceived and objective, in opportunities for achievement of these aspirations."[6] He offers a possible hypothesis that "high aspirations are indicative of identification with conventional values and institutions. The stake in conformity . . . serves to protect the boys from delinquency involvement."[7]

Again, contrary to Cohen and Cloward and Ohlin, Short found that gang boys recognized the moral validity and legitimacy of middle class values. As opposed to Cohen, no rebellion against the social system nor evidence of reaction against middle class values was found. Short then advanced a significant point when he maintained that the conception of "social" which is basic to the anomie paradigm of opportunity structures and status dep-

rivation must be "broadened to include situations which are more immediate to the boys, such as local community norms and opportunities, and
normative and status considerations *within* the group."[8]

Short goes on to argue that while status considerations are important
in explaining a gang boy's behavior, they do not have to be sought in middle
class institutions and criteria of success. Status deprivation can also be important in a more immediate context, such as the boy's status as a male or
as a member of a particular gang. As a tentative conclusion therefore, let
us take the position that the "behavior of gang boys may be understood as
an attempt by these boys to seek and create alternative status systems in
the form of the gang, and that delinquency arises sometimes as a by-
product and sometimes as a direct product of this attempt."[9] He enlarges
the thesis that while gang boys encounter status deprivation within "respectable society," the status situations which are of immediate concern
are those which relate to ongoing processes which involve their daily lives.
Each boy then must adjust to a variety of statuses, a process which Short
terms "status management."

This view is far removed from one which seeks to explain delinquency
by the economic, educational, and other deprivations of the larger social
structure, although Short says one may consider his explanation as an extension of the larger theory. He believes that the social structure operates
to determine or to influence strongly economic and educational goals, aspirations, and opportunities. The theory of anomie, however, fails to take
into account the ongoing group processes of interaction, from which delinquent behavior may develop. . . .

THE ROLE OF THE ACTOR

Lemert has a major objection to Merton's view of choice and action by
individuals in our type of society. He feels that Merton simplifies something
that is actually quite complex. The individual is not a free agent in his
choice of values, but rather is restricted by the claims of various groups to
which he belongs. The "pressures" on individuals come from these conflicting claims rather than from cultural emphasis on goals. Special interest
groups in our society attempt to advance or protect their own sets of values.
. . . As Lemert says, . . . the "emphasis placed on normative means is determined by their cost, that is, by the *particular* values that must be sac-
rificed in order to adopt means."[10] . . .

In his paper on delinquency, Short states that anomie is too mechanical
a theory and that it disregards the actor. "What is lacking in most models
of gang behavior is precisely this type of Meadian act, in which behavior
is seen as a process of *continuous adjustment* of actors to one another,
rather than as a sort of mechanical reaction to some one factor or combination of factors in the situation, whether they be characteristics of actors,

or subcultures, or other features. It is this conception, too, which is lacking in anomie theory."[11] What the theory of anomie refers to as "pressures toward deviance" needs both theoretical and empirical specification. . . .

RETREATISM AS AN ADAPTATION OF MEANS AND GOALS

Three characteristic types of retreatism are generally considered by anomie theory to be drug addiction, alcoholism, and mental disorder. Lindesmith and Gagnon maintain that drug addicts are not retreatists but rather claim that difficulties in securing the drug make the addict of necessity an "active" rather than retreatist person. Snyder, while recognizing the research difficulties in studying the phenomenon of alcoholism, which has a prolonged history and by definition is "retreatist," feels that there is evidence to support the contention that the alcoholic was anomic even before his addiction began. . . .

Lindesmith and Gagnon point out that while some of the characteristics ascribed to retreatism apply to some drug addicts, none is accurate as a general description. Addicts are not persons who have abandoned both goals and means and who are characterized, in Merton's terms, by "defeatism, quietism, and resignation." In actuality, there are substantial numbers of addicts to whom such a description does not apply; there are addicts who are "responsible and productive members of society, who share the common frame of values, who have not abandoned the quest for success and are not immune to the frustrations involved in seeking it."[12] They go on to point out that Merton's description of the retreatist, while it does not adequately describe the actual addict, "does provide a reasonably accurate portrait of the current popular stereotype of the addict."

The "double failure" hypothesis of drug addiction advanced by Cloward and Ohlin, and in part implicit by Merton, namely, that the addict cannot achieve success goals by either legitimate or illegitimate means, comes in for pointed criticism by Lindesmith and Gagnon. They state: (1) It is not clear whether there is an actual objective performance failure or whether the individual tends to feel simply frustrated by a perceived block to success. (2) The hypothesis is not applicable to the doctor addict, among others. (3) The addicted person is not necessarily a failure in crime. (4) One cannot judge early adolescents, among whom such phenomena might occur, as double failures because of the age factor. . . . (5) While it may be conceded that there are many addicts who are failures in both the criminal and noncriminal world, it may be argued that addiction is probably more potent as a cause of failure than failure is a cause of addiction.[13]

For the addict in American society, the pursuit of drugs becomes a stimulus to action, not an escape from the requirements of society. One might describe the successful drug user as a "double success" rather than a double failure, the conventional rewards of accomplishment being an assured and adequate supply of drugs. In fact, one of the defects in the theory of anomie is the contention that the inner strain of anomie supposedly is reduced by the use of drugs, when actually, addiction ordinarily widens the "gap between aspirations and the means of achievement and to intensify, rather than resolve, inner anomie-generated conflict."[14]

The use of opiates by real addicts does not have the euphoric effect often described by those who assume that drugs are used for escape. As Lindesmith and Gagnon maintain, "The paradox anomie theory faces is that while opiates can be used for retreatist motives, they are used in this way primarily by those who are not addicted to them."[15] Addiction to opiates is not retreatism; rather, many persons are able to overcome retreatism through the use of drugs and to carry on their daily activities.

In an analytical paradigm they show that there is no invariant relationship between anomie, deviance, retreatism, and drug addiction. Not all drug addiction arises from anomie or is retreatist or deviant, and drug addiction may produce anomia. Addiction may, therefore, occur in any combination with the other three and also when all are absent. Likewise, anomie, deviance, and retreatism might also occur singly or in combination in the absence of addiction. Anomie as a theory does not, therefore, "specify the conditions under which the phenomenon being explained will occur and in the absence of which will not occur."[16]

Lindesmith and Gagnon disagree with the assumption that the use of drugs necessarily constitutes deviation, whether retreatist or otherwise, for like other forms of deviant behavior, the definition may shift according to time, place, the definer, and other considerations. They cite evidence that a substantial part of marijuana and opiate use today cannot be viewed as deviant behavior. Similarly, the nondeviant use of opiates can be illustrated by their wide use in Western society, in the past and today, either in therapy or to relieve pain. This may lead to addiction without the patient having voluntarily administered the drug. Their conclusion is: "Since the theory of anomie is proposed as a theory of deviance, and since some drug use is not deviant, the theory can hardly be relevant to the non-deviant portion. If the theory is applied to the non-deviant drug use, or if it is restricted to 'deviant drug use,' it meets substantial difficulties."[17]

Notes

1. Marshall B. Clinard, *Anomie and Deviant Behavior: A Discussion and Critique,* New York: The Free Press, 1964, p. 64.

2. *Ibid.,* 66.

3. *Ibid.,* 65.

4. *Ibid.*, 76.

5. *Ibid.*, 111–113.

6. *Ibid.*, 115.

7. *Ibid.*, 116.

8. *Ibid.*, 115.

9. *Ibid.*, 117.

10. *Ibid.*, 70.

11. *Ibid.*, 124.

12. *Ibid.*, 178.

13. *Ibid.*, 177.

14. *Ibid.*, 180.

15. *Ibid.*, 183.

16. *Ibid.*, 188.

17. *Ibid.*, 163.

AN EVALUATION OF THE THEORY OF DIFFERENTIAL ASSOCIATION

Donald R. Cressey

Sutherland's differential association theory is fifty years old. It is very influential and has inspired a good deal of research. Yet it is also misunderstood and widely criticized. In this excerpt, Cressey answers some critics and evaluates its current status as a theory of crime. He points out that Sutherland derived the theory of differential association from the principle of normative conflict and showed how it made sense of the data on crime rates. As a statement of how people become criminal, however, it is neither complete nor precise, and the lack of precision makes it difficult to test. At the same time, since accurate predictors of criminal behavior can be deduced from the theory of differential association, Cressey concludes, it goes further than any other current theory in explaining how people become criminals.

From pp. 87–97 in *Criminology*, Tenth Edition, by Edwin H. Sutherland and Donald R. Cressey. Copyright © 1978 by J. B. Lippincott Company. Reprinted by permission of Harper & Row, Publishers, Inc.

One popular form of criticism of differential association is not, strictly speaking, criticism at all. A number of scholars have speculated that some kinds of criminal behavior are exceptions to the theory. Thus, it has been said that the theory does not apply to rural offenders, to landlords who violate rent control regulations, to criminal violators of financial trust, "naïve check forgers," to white-collar criminals, to certain delinquents,[1] to perpetrators of "individual" and "personal" crimes, to irrational and impulsive criminals, to "adventitious" and/or "accidental" criminals, to "occasional," "incidental," and "situational" offenders, to murderers, nonprofessional shoplifters and noncareer types of criminals, to persons who commit crimes of passion and to persons whose crimes were perpetrated under emotional stress.[2] It is important to note that only the first six comments—those referring to rural offenders, landlords, trust violators, check forgers, some white-collar criminals, and some delinquents—are based on research. . . .

The fact that most of the comments are not based on research means that the criticisms are actually proposals for research. Should a person conduct research on a particular type of offender and find that the theory does not hold, then a revision of the theory is called for, provided the research actually tested the theory, or part of it. As indicated, this procedure has been used in six instances, and these instances need to be given careful attention. Hirschi, for example, has concluded on the basis of empirical research that *absence* of control, not the presence of behavior patterns favorable to delinquency, is what increases the likelihood that delinquent acts will be committed.[3] But in most cases, there is no evidence that the kind of behavior said to be exceptional is exceptional. For example, we do not know that "accidental" or "incidental" or "occasional" criminals have not gone through the process specified in the theory. Perhaps it is sometimes assumed that some types of criminal behavior are "obviously exceptional." However, one theoretical analysis indicated that a type of behavior that appears to be obviously exceptional—"compulsive criminality"—is not necessarily exceptional at all.[4]

A second principal kind of criticism attacks the theory because it does not adequately take into account the "personality traits," "personality factors," or "psychological variables" in criminal behavior. This is real criticism, for it suggests that the statement neglects an important determinant of criminality. Occasionally, the criticism is linked with the apparent assumption that some kinds of criminality are "obviously" exceptional. However, at least a dozen authors have proposed that the statement is defective because it omits or overlooks the general role of personality traits in determining criminality.

In an early period Sutherland stated that his theory probably would have to be revised to take account of personality traits.[5] Later he pointed out what he believed to be the fundamental weakness in his critics' argument: *Personality traits* and *personality* are words that merely specify a condition, like mental retardation, without showing the relationship between that condition and criminality. He posed three questions for advocates of personality traits as supplements to differential association: (1) What are the personality traits that should be regarded as significant? (2) Are there personal traits to be used as supplements to differential association, which are not already included in the concept of differential association? (3) Can differential association, which is essentially a *process* of learning, be combined with personal traits, which are essentially the *product* of learning?[6]

Sutherland did not attempt to answer these questions, but the context of his discussion indicates his belief that differential association does explain why some persons with a trait like "aggressiveness" commit crimes, while other persons possessing the same trait do not. It also reveals his conviction that terms like *personality traits, personality,* and *psychogenic trait components* are, when used with no further elaboration to explain why a person becomes a criminal, synonyms for *unknown conditions.*[7]

Closely allied with the "personality trait" criticism is the assertion that the theory does not adequately take into account the "response" patterns, "acceptance" patterns, and "receptivity" patterns of various individuals. The essential notion here is that differential association emphasizes the social process of transmission but minimizes the individual process of reception. Stated in another way, the idea is that the theory deals only with external variables and does not take into account the meaning to the recipient of the various patterns of behavior presented in situations which are objectively quite similar but nevertheless variable, according to the recipient's perception of them. One variety of this type of criticism takes the form of asserting that criminals and noncriminals are sometimes reared in the "same environment"—criminal behavior patterns are presented to two persons, but only one of them becomes a criminal.

Sutherland was acutely aware of the social psychological problem posed by such concepts as "differential response patterns." Significantly, his proposed solution to the problem was his statement of the theory of differential association.[8] One of the principal objectives of the theory is to account for differences in individual responses to opportunities for crime and in individual responses to criminal behavior patterns presented. To illustrate, one person who walks by an unguarded and open cash register, or who is informed of the presence of such a condition in a nearby store, may perceive the situation as a "crime-committing" one, while another person in the identical circumstances may perceive the situation as one in which the owner should be warned against carelessness. The difference in these two perceptions, the theory holds, is due to differences in the prior associations with the two types of definition of situation, so that the alternatives in behavior are accounted for in terms of differential association. The differential in "response pattern," or the difference in "receptivity" to the criminal behavior pattern presented, then, is accounted for by differential association itself.[9] Cressey has argued that one of the greatest defects in the theory is its implication that receptivity to any behavior pattern presented is determined by the patterns presented earlier, that receptivity to those early presentations was determined by even earlier presentations, and so on back to birth.[10] But this is an assertion that the theory is difficult to test, not an assertion that it does not take into account the differential response patterns of individuals.

If receptivity is viewed in a different way, however, the critics appear to be on firm ground.[11] The theory does not identify what constitutes a definition favorable to or unfavorable to the violation of law. The same objective definition might be favorable or unfavorable, depending on the relationship between the donor and the recipient. Consequently, the theory indicates that differential associations may vary in "intensity," which is not precisely defined but "has to do with such things as the prestige of the source of a criminal or anticriminal pattern and with emotional reactions related to the associations." This statement tells us that some associations are to be given added *weight*, but it does not tell us how, or whether, early associations affect the *meaning* of later associations. If earlier associations determine whether a person will later identify specific behavior patterns as favorable or unfavorable to law violation, then these earlier associations determine the very meaning of the later ones, and do not merely give added weight to them. In other words, whether a person is prestigeful or not prestigeful to another may be determined by experiences that have nothing to do with criminality and anticriminality. Nevertheless, these experiences affect the meaning (whether favorable or unfavorable) of patterns later presented to the person and, thus, they affect receptivity to the behavior patterns.[12] For example, in one experiment a rich-looking person and a poor-looking person were employed as models. The models crossed a street against a traffic light, and the experimenters noted how many pedestrians followed them in their lawbreaking. More people imitated the rich-looking model, possibly because to many persons, observing another person crossing the street against the light is not objectively favorable or unfavorable. If a poor person does it, it might be a behavior pattern unfavorable to law violation, but if a rich person does it, the pattern might have a quite different meaning.[13]

A fourth kind of criticism is more damaging than the first three, for it insists that the ratio of learned behavior patterns used to explain criminality cannot be determined with accuracy in specific cases. Short, for example, has pointed out the extreme difficulty of operationalizing terms such as "favorable to" and "unfavorable to"; nevertheless, he has devised various measures of differential association and has used the term in a series of significant studies.[14] Glaser has noted that the "phrase 'excess of definitions' itself lacks clear denotation in human experience." Glueck has asked, "Has anybody actually counted the number of definitions favorable to violation of law and definitions unfavorable to violation of law, and demonstrated that in the predelinquency experience of the vast majority of delinquents and criminals, the former exceeds the latter?" And Hirschi has concluded both that the theory is "virtually nonfalsifiable" and that predictions from it "tend to be trivial."[15] In a study of trust violators, Cressey found that embezzlers could not identify specific persons or agencies from whom they learned their behavior patterns favorable to trust violation. The general conclusion was, "It is doubtful that it can be shown empirically that the differential association theory applies or does not apply to crimes of financial trust violation or even to other kinds of criminal behavior."[16] Similarly, Stanfield has noted the extreme difficulty of measuring the variation and content of "frequency, duration, priority, and intensity."[17]

It should be noted that these damaging criticisms of the theory of differential association as a precise statement of the mechanism by which persons become criminals do not affect the value of the theory as a general principle which organizes and makes good sense of the data on crime rates. As we shall see below, a theory accounting for the distribution of crime, delinquency, or any other phenomenon can be valid even if a presumably coordinate theory specifying the process by which deviancy occurs in individual cases is *incorrect*, let alone untestable.

The fifth kind of criticism states in more general terms than the first four that the theory of differential association oversimplifies the process by which criminal behavior is learned. At the extreme are assertions that the theory is inadequate because it does not allow for a process in which criminality is said to be "chosen" by the individual actor. Some such assertions maintain that a social psychology and sociology of criminals and crime is impossible, and their authors ask for a return to something like the "free will" tenets of the classical school of criminology. Interestingly enough, such assertions have in recent years been announced by social psychologists and sociologists.[18] More realistic criticism ranges from simple assertions that the learning process is more complex than the theory states or implies, to the idea that the theory does not adequately take into account some specific type of learning process, such as differential identification or operant conditioning.

But it is one thing to criticize the theory for failure to specify the learning process accurately and another to specify which aspects of the learning process should be included and in what way.[19] Clinard, Glaser, and Matthews, among others, have introduced the process of identification.[20] Weinberg, Sykes and Matza, Cressey and Frazier, among others, have stressed other aspects of more general social psychological theory.[21] Adams has, on the basis of a laboratory experiment, noted the importance of such "non-

social" variables as money, drugs, and sex in the reinforcement and maintenance of delinquent behavior.[22] Jensen consistently found that boys who
associate with delinquents are more likely to be delinquent than boys who
do not, but this occurs independently of the effect of these associations on
their attitudes and beliefs.[23] Even these attempts are, like the differential
association statement itself, more in the nature of general indications of
the kind of framework or orientation one should use in formulating a theory
of criminality than they are statements of theory. Burgess and Akers have
given a most promising lead in this area by specifying that the conditions
and mechanisms through which delinquent and criminal behavior are
learned are those indicated in the theory of human learning variously referred to as reinforcement theory, operant behavior theory, and operant
conditioning theory.[24]

The theory of differential association does not concentrate exclusively
on individual criminality. It is also concerned with making sense of the
gross facts about delinquency and crime.[25] Examination of Sutherland's
writings clearly indicates that when he formulated the theory he was
greatly, if not primarily, concerned with organizing and integrating the factual information about crime rates. In his account of how the theory of
differential association developed, he made the following three relevant
points:

> More significant for the development of the theory were certain questions
> which I raised in class discussions. One of these questions was, Negroes,
> young-adult males, and city dwellers all have relatively high crime rates: What
> do these three groups have in common that places them in this position?
> Another question was, even if feeble-minded persons have a high crime rate,
> why do they commit crimes? It is not feeble-mindedness as such, for some
> feeble-minded persons do not commit crimes. Later I raised another question
> which became even more important in my search for generalizations. Crime
> rates have a high correlation with poverty if considered by areas of a city but
> a low correlation if considered chronologically in relation to the business
> cycle; this obviously means that poverty as such is not an important cause of
> crime. How are the varying associations between crime and poverty ex-
> plained?[26]
>
> It was my conception that a general theory should take account of all the
> factual information regarding crime causation. It does this either by organ-
> izing the multiple factors in relation to each other or by abstracting them
> from certain common elements. It does not, or should not, neglect or elim-
> inate any factors that are included in the multiple-factor theory.[27]
>
> The hypothesis of differential association seemed to me to be consistent
> with the principal gross findings in criminology. It explained why the Mol-
> laccan children became progressively delinquent with length of residence in
> the deteriorated area of Los Angeles, why the city crime rate is higher than
> the rural crime rate, why males are more delinquent than females, why the
> crime rate remains consistently higher in deteriorated areas of cities, why the
> juvenile delinquency rate in a foreign nativity group is high while the group
> lives in a deteriorated area and drops when the group moves out of the area,

why second-generation Italians do not have the high murder rate their fathers had, why Japanese children in a deteriorated area of Seattle had a low delinquency rate even though in poverty, why crimes do not increase greatly in a period of depression. All of the general statistical facts seem to fit this hypothesis.[28]

The formal statement of the theory indicates, for example, that a high crime rate in urban areas can be considered the end product of criminalistic traditions in those areas. Similarly, the fact that the rate for all crimes is not higher in some urban areas than it is in some rural areas can be attributed to differences in conditions which affect the probabilities of exposure to criminal behavior patterns.[29] The important general point is that in a multigroup type of social organization, alternative and inconsistent standards of conduct are possessed by various groups, so that an individual who is a member of one group has a high probability of learning to use legal means for achieving success, or learning to deny the importance of success, while an individual in another group learns to accept the importance of success and to achieve it by illegal means. Stated in another way, there are alternative educational processes in operation, varying with groups, so that a person may be educated in either conventional or criminal means of achieving success. As indicated above, this situation may be called "differential social organization" or "differential group organization." "Differential group organization" should explain the crime rate while differential association should explain the criminal behavior of a person. The two explanations must be consistent with each other.

It should be noted that, in the three quotations above, Sutherland referred to the differential association statement as both a "theory" and a "hypothesis," and did not indicate any special concern for distinguishing between differential association as it applies to the epidemiology of crime and differential association as it applies to individual conduct. In order to avoid controversy about the essential characteristics of theories and hypotheses, it seems preferable to call differential association, as it is used in reference to crime rates, a principle. Many "theories" in sociology are in fact principles that order facts about rates—now called epidemiology—in some way. Durkheim, for example, invented what may be termed a "principle of group integration" to account for, organize logically, and integrate systematically the data on variations in suicide rates. He did not invent a theory of suicide, derive hypotheses from it, and then collect data to determine whether the hypotheses were correct or incorrect. He tried to make sense of known facts about rates, and the principle he suggested remains the most valuable idea available to understand the differences in the rates of suicide between Protestants and Jews, urban-dwellers and rural-dwellers, and so on.

The differential association statement, similarly, is a "principle of normative conflict" which proposes that high crime rates occur in societies and groups characterized by conditions that lead to the development of extensive criminalistic subcultures. The principle makes sense of variations in crime rates by observing that modern societies are organized for crime as well as against it, and then observing further that crime rates are unequally distributed because of differences in the degree to which various categories of persons participate in this normative conflict.[30] Sutherland invented the principle of normative conflict to account for the distribution of high and low crime rates; he then tried to specify the mechanism by which this principle works to produce individual cases of criminality. The mechanism proposed is differential association:

> The second concept, differential association, is a statement of [normative] conflict from the point of view of the person who commits the crime. The two kinds of culture impinge on him or he has association with the two kinds of cultures and this is differential association.[31]

THE VALUE OF DIFFERENTIAL ASSOCIATION

As an organizing principle, normative conflict makes understandable most of the variations in crime rates discovered by various researchers and observers, and it also focuses attention on crucial research areas.[32] The principle of normative conflict does not make good sense out of all the statistical variations, but it seems to make better sense out of more of them than do any of the alternative theories.

On the other hand, it also seems safe to conclude that differential association is not a precise statement of the process by which one becomes a criminal. The idea that criminality is a consequence of an excess of intimate associations with criminal behavior patterns is valuable because, for example, it negates assertions that deviation from norms is simply a product of being emotionally insecure or living in a broken home, and then indicates in a general way why only some emotionally insecure persons and only some persons from broken homes commit crimes. Also, it directs attention to the idea that an efficient explanation of individual conduct is consistent with explanations of epidemiology. Yet the statement of the differential association process is not precise enough to stimulate rigorous empirical test, and it therefore has not been proved or disproved. This defect is shared with broader social psychological theory. Although critics agree, as we have indicated, that the differential association statement oversimplifies the process by which normative conflict "gets into" persons and produces criminality, an acceptable substitute that is consistent with the principle of normative conflict has not appeared.

It is important to observe, however, that the "individual conduct" part of the theoretical statement does order data on individual criminality in a general way and, consequently, might be considered a principle itself. Thus, "differential association" may be viewed as a restatement of the principle of normative conflict, so that this one principle is used to account for the distribution of criminal and noncriminal behavior in both the life of the individual *and* in the statistics on collectivities. In this case, both individual behavior data and epidemiological rate data may be employed as indices of the variables in the principle, thus providing two types of hypotheses for testing it.[33] Glaser has shown that differential association makes sense of both the predictive efficiency of some parole prediction items and the lack of predictive efficiency of other items.[34] In effect, he tested the principle by determining whether parole prediction procedures which could have proven it false actually failed to prove it false. First, he shows that a majority of the most accurate predictors in criminology prediction research are deducible from differential association theory, while the least accurate predictors are not deducible at all. Second, he shows that this degree of accuracy does not characterize alternative theories. Finally, he notes that two successful predictors of parole violation—type of offense and noncriminal employment opportunities—are not necessarily deducible from the theory, and he suggests a modification that would take this fact into account.

Notes

1. Marshall B. Clinard, "The Process of Urbanization and Criminal Behavior," *American Journal of Sociology,* 48: 202–13, 1942; idem, "Rural Criminal Offenders," *American Journal of Sociology,* 50: 38–45, 1944; idem, "Criminological Theories of Violations of Wartime Regulations," *American Sociological Review,* 11: 258–70, 1946; Donald R. Cressey, "Application and Verification of the Differential Association Theory," *Journal of Criminal Law, Criminology, and Police Science,* 43: 43–52, 1952; Edwin M. Lemert, "Isolation and Closure Theory of Naïve Check Forgery," *Journal of Criminal Law, Criminology, and Police Science,* 44: 293–307, 1953; Daniel Glaser, "Criminality Theories and Behavioral Images," *American Journal of Sociology,* 61: 441, 1956; and Travis Hirschi, *Causes of Delinquency* (Berkeley: University of California Press, 1969), pp. 14–15, 229–30.

2. See [Gwynn] Nettler, *Explaining Crime* [New York: McGraw-Hill, 1974], p. 197; and Steven Giannell, "Criminosynthesis," *International Journal of Social Psychiatry,* 16: 83–95, 1970.

3. Hirschi, *Causes of Delinquency,* p. 229. See also Gary F. Jensen, "Parents, Peers, and Delinquent Action: A Test of the Differential Association Perspective," *American Journal of Sociology,* 78: 562–75, 1972; John R. Hepburn, "Testing Alternative Models of Delinquency Causation," *Journal of Criminal Law and Criminology,* 67: 450–60, 1977; and Joseph H. Rankin, "Investigating the Interrelations Among Social Control Variables and Conformity," *Journal of Criminal Law and Criminology,* 67: 470–80, 1977.

4. Donald R. Cressey, "The Differential Association Theory and Compulsive

Crimes," *Journal of Criminal Law, Criminology, and Police Science,* 45: 49–64, 1954.

5. Sutherland, "Development of the Theory," pp. 25–27.

6. Edwin H. Sutherland, *White Collar Crime* (New York: Dryden Press, 1949), p. 272. See also Harwin L. Voss, "Differential Association and Containment Theory— a Theoretical Convergence," *Social Forces,* 47: 381–91, 1969.

7. See the discussion in Chapter 7 [of *Criminology,* the source of this excerpt].

8. See Edwin H. Sutherland, "Susceptibility and Differential Association," in *Edwin H. Sutherland on Analyzing Crime,* ed. Schuessler, pp. 42–43. See also Solomon Kobrin, "The Conflict of Values in Delinquency Areas," *American Sociological Review,* 16: 653–61, 1951.

9. Cf. Elihu Katz, Martin L. Levin, and Herbert Hamilton, "Traditions of Research on the Diffusion of Innovation," *American Sociological Review,* 28: 237–52, 1963.

10. Cressey, "Application and Verification of the Differential Association Theory."

11. I am indebted to Albert K. Cohen for assistance with this paragraph and with other points.

12. See also Don C. Gibbons, *Society, Crime and Criminal Careers: An Introduction to Criminology* (Englewood Cliffs, N.J.: Prentice-Hall, 1968), pp. 204–6.

13. M. M. Lefkowitz et al., "Status Factors in Pedestrian Violation of Traffic Signals," *Journal of Abnormal and Social Psychology,* 51: 704–6, 1955.

14. James F. Short, Jr., "Differential Association and Delinquency," *Social Problems,* 4: 233–39, 1957; and James F. Short, Jr. and Fred L. Strodtbeck, *Group Process and Gang Delinquency* (Chicago: University of Chicago Press, 1965).

15. Glaser, "Criminality Theories and Behavioral Images"; Glueck, "Theory and Fact in Criminology," p. 96; and Hirschi, *Causes of Delinquency,* pp. 14–15.

16. Cressey, "Application and Verification of the Differential Association Theory," p. 52.

17. Robert E. Stanfield, "The Interaction of Family Variables and Gang Variables in the Aetiology of Delinquency," *Social Problems,* 13: 411–17, 1966.

18. David Matza, *Becoming Deviant* (Englewood Cliffs, N.J.: Prentice-Hall, 1969), p. 107; Steven Box, *Deviance, Reality, and Society* (London: Holt, Rinehart and Winston, 1971), p. 21; Ian Taylor, Paul Walton, and Jock Young, *The New Criminology: For a Social Theory of Deviance* (London: Routledge and Kegan Paul, 1973), p. 128.

19. Despite the fact that Sutherland described a learning process, it should be noted that he also said, "The process of learning criminal and anticriminal behavior patterns involves all the mechanisms that are involved in any other learning."

20. Clinard, "The Process of Urbanization and Criminal Behavior"; idem, "Rural Criminal Offenders"; idem, "Criminological Theories of Violations of Wartime Regulations"; Glaser, "Criminality Theories and Behavioral Images"; idem, "Differential Association and Criminological Prediction," *Social Problems,* 8:6–14, 1960; idem, "The Differential Association Theory of Crime," in *Human Behavior and Social Process,* ed. Arnold Rose (Boston: Houghton Mifflin, 1962), pp. 425–43; Victor

Matthews, "Differential Identification: An Empirical Note," *Social Problems*, 15: 376–83, 1968.

21. S. Kirson Weinberg, "Theories of Criminality and Problems of Prediction," *Journal of Criminal Law, Criminology, and Police Science*, 45: 412–29, 1954; idem, "Personality and Method in the Differential Association Theory," *Journal of Research in Crime and Delinquency*, 3: 165–72, 1966; Gresham Sykes and David Matza, "Techniques of Neutralization: A Theory of Delinquency," *American Sociological Review*, 22: 664–70, 1957; Cressey, "Application and Verification of the Differential Association Theory"; idem, "The Differential Association Theory and Compulsive Crimes"; idem, "Social Psychological Foundations for Using Criminals in the Rehabilitation of Criminals," *Journal of Research in Crime and Delinquency*, 2: 49–59, 1965; idem, "The Language of Set Theory and Differential Association," *Journal of Research in Crime and Delinquency*, 3: 22–26, 1966; Charles E. Frazier, *Theoretical Approaches to Deviance* (Columbus, Ohio: Bobbs-Merrill, 1976), pp. 113–114.

22. Reed Adams, "The Adequacy of Differential Association Theory," *Journal of Research in Crime and Delinquency*, 11: 1–8, 1974. See also Clarence Ray Jeffery, "Criminal Behavior and Learning Theory," *Journal of Criminal Law, Criminology, and Police Science*, 56: 294–300, 1965.

23. Jensen, "Parents, Peers and Delinquent Action."

24. Robert L. Burgess and Ronald L. Akers, "A Differential Association—Reinforcement Theory of Criminal Behavior," *Social Problems*, 14: 128–47, 1968. See also Ronald L. Akers, Robert L. Burgess, and Weldon T. Johnson, "Opiate Use, Addiction, and Relapse," *Social Problems*, 15: 459–69, 1968.

25. One of the Sutherland's own students, colleagues, and editors has said, "Much that travels under the name of sociology of deviant behavior or of social disorganization is psychology—some of it very good psychology, but psychology. For example, Sutherland's theory of differential associations, which is widely regarded as preeminently sociological, is not the less psychological because it makes much of the cultural milieu. It is psychological because it addresses itself to the question: How do people become the kind of individuals who commit criminal acts? A sociological question would be: What is it about the structure of social systems that determines the kinds of criminal acts that occur in these systems and the way in which such acts are distributed within these systems?" (Albert K. Cohen, "The Study of Social Disorganization and Deviant Behavior," chap. 21 in *Sociology Today*, ed. Robert K. Merton, Leonard Broom, and Leonard S. Cottrell, Jr. [New York: Basic Books, 1959], p. 462).

26. Sutherland, "Development of the Theory," p. 15.

27. Ibid., p. 18.

28. Ibid., pp. 19–20.

29. Cf. Henry D. McKay, "Differential Association and Crime Prevention: Problems of Utilization," *Social Problems*, 8: 25–37, 1960.

30. See Raymond D. Gastil, "Homicide and a Regional Culture of Violence," *American Sociological Review*, 36: 412–27, 1971.

31. Sutherland, "Development of the Theory," pp. 20–21.

32. Cf. Llewellyn Gross, "Theory Construction in Sociology: A Methodological Inquiry," chap. 17 in *Symposium on Sociological Theory*, ed. Llewellyn Gross (Evanston, Ill.: Row, Peterson, 1959), pp. 548–55. See also Donald R. Cressey, "The State of Criminal Statistics," *National Probation and Parole Association Journal*, 3: 230–41, 1957; and DeFleur and Quinney, "Reformulation of Sutherland's Differential Association Theory."

33. I am indebted to Daniel Glaser for calling this point to my attention.

34. Glaser, "Differential Association and Criminological Prediction." See also idem, "A Reconsideration of Some Parole Prediction Factors," *American Sociological Review*, 19: 335–41, 1954; and idem, "The Efficiency of Alternative Approaches to Parole Prediction," *American Sociological Review*, 20: 283–87, June, 1955; and Daniel Glaser and Richard R. Hangren, "Predicting the Adjustment of Federal Probationers," *National Probation and Parole Association Journal*, 4: 258–67, 1958; and David M. Downes, *The Delinquent Solution: A Study in Subcultural Theory* (London: Routledge and Kegan Paul, 1966), pp. 97–98.

Questions for Discussion

1. Sutherland and Cressey discuss different levels of causal analysis. How do Merton's anomie and Sutherland's differential association theories differ in their levels?

2. How does Sutherland's theory integrate the multiple factors that may help to explain criminal behavior?

3. How does Cloward and Ohlin's theory of delinquent subcultures synthesize Merton's and Sutherland's theories?

4. Consider Clinard's critique of Merton's anomie theory. Do you see it as a plea for integration with differential association theory? How so, or why not? Do you agree with any of the criticisms of Sutherland's theory? If yes, which one(s) and why?

Selected References

Agnew, Robert. "A Longitudinal Test of Social Control Theory and Delinquency." *Journal of Research in Crime and Delinquency* 28 (May 1991): 126–56.

    A study which shows, among the variables researched, the best predictions of delinquency to be prior delinquent involvement and deviant peer associations, results which support social learning theory.

Agnew, Robert. "Foundation for a General Strain Theory of Crime and Delinquency." *Criminology* 30 (February 1992): 47–87.

    Robert Agnew has revitalized and extended Merton's theory. He amplifies the strain concept so that it might explain all forms of delinquent behavior.

Akers, Ronald L. *Deviant Behavior. A Social Learning Approach.* 3rd ed. Belmont, Calif.: Wadsworth, 1985.

A text that analyzes alcohol and drug use, mental illness, suicide, sexual deviance, and several varieties of criminal behavior by means of an extension or reformulation of Sutherland's differential association theory.

Blake, Judith, and Kingsley Davis. "Norms, Values, and Sanctions." In *Handbook of Modern Sociology,* ed. Robert E. L. Faris. Chicago: Rand McNally, 1964, pp. 456–84.

Focuses on the sources of unintentional deviance, the sources of deviant motivation, and the factors preventing deviant motives from erupting into deviant behavior. The answers are provided from existing sociological literature.

Clinard, Marshall B., ed. *Anomie and Deviant Behavior: A Discussion and Critique.* New York: Free Press, 1964.

A useful dialogue regarding anomie theory. Clinard restates Merton's anomie theory and its implications. Six sociologists then give criticisms of the application of anomie theory to particular types of deviant acts. Finally, Merton responds to these critics. A useful appendix inventories eighty-eight empirical and theoretical studies of anomie—a testimony to the tremendous influence of this theory.

Clinard, Marshall B., and Robert F. Meier. *Sociology of Deviant Behavior.* 6th ed. New York: Holt, Rinehart and Winston, 1985.

Clinard and Meier point out that Sutherland's differential association theory can be applied not only to crime, but also to both the causes and the distribution of many different varieties of deviance among various groups in the population. Broadening his conception to a more general socialization theory, they apply it to numerous forms of deviant behavior, including physical disabilities.

Cohen, Albert K. *Delinquent Boys: The Culture of the Gang.* Glencoe, Ill.: Free Press, 1955.

A creative synthesis of the theories of anomie and differential association in which Cohen develops an influential theory of delinquent subcultures. A landmark in the tradition of deviant behavior analysis.

Cohen, Albert K. "Deviant Behavior." In *International Encyclopedia of Social Sciences,* ed. David L. Sills. New York: Macmillan and The Free Press, 1968, vol. 4, pp. 148–55

A scholarly essay on the rise and development of the deviant behavior perspective.

Cohen, Albert K., Alfred Lindesmith, and Karl Schuessler, eds. *The Sutherland Papers.* Bloomington: Indiana University Press, 1956.

Unsolicited self-criticism is rare. In this book, Sutherland examines his own theory of differential association, and his criticisms are almost as trenchant as the theory itself.

Durkheim, Emile. *Suicide: A Study in Sociology.* Trans. John A. Spaulding and George Simpson. Glencoe, Ill.: Free Press, 1951.

The classic statement regarding anomie. Durkheim shows that rates of suicide are higher under certain types of social conditions. One such condition is anomie, or normlessness.

Hirschi, Travis. *The Causes of Delinquency.* Berkeley: University of California Press, 1968.

Hirschi devises a systematic deviant behavior perspective on why teenagers become delinquent and then proceeds to test his hypothesis on some 4,000 California high-school students. His results offer ample support for his contention that the weakening of social bonds is the major cause of juvenile delinquency.

Kornhauser, Ruth Rosner. *Social Sources of Delinquency: An Appraisal of Analytic Models.* Chicago: University of Chicago Press, 1978.

After a systematic review of numerous studies of juvenile delinquency, Kornhauser finds that control theories (such as Hirschi's and others) explain delinquency much better than disorganization, anomie, or differential association.

Leonard, Eileen B. *Women, Crime and Society: A Critique of Criminology Theory.* New York: Longman, 1982.

According to Leonard, as more women aim to achieve financial success, thus challenging traditional restrictions and expectations, this can lead to anomie and, hence, to an increase in female crime.

Simon, William, and John H. Gagnon. "The Anomie of Affluence: Post-Mertonian Conception." *American Journal of Sociology* 82 (September 1976): 356–78.

The authors maintain that Merton's famous anomie theory presupposes an economy of scarcity. Since 1938, when Merton first presented his typology of responses to strains between culture and social structure, most of the societies in the Western world have become affluent. The situation of affluence produces different kinds of strains between means and goals, and the authors posit nine types of responses to the strains experienced in the affluent society, a number of which contribute to social problems.

Warr, Mark, and Mark Stafford. "The Influence of Delinquent Peers: What They Think or What They Do?" *Criminology* 29 (November 1991): 851–66.

In studying marijuana use, the authors find that in addition to attitude transmission (Sutherland's version of social learning) such mechanisms as "imitation" can be involved in the effect peers have on one's behavior.

6/LABELING

Perspectives differ in the questions they ask and the answers they yield. The sociology of deviant behavior, for example, initially asks *why people commit* crimes or other deviant acts. Sociologists in this tradition attempt to determine the necessary and sufficient conditions that produce deviant acts. The labeling perspective,[1] on the contrary, examines the social definition of deviance. Sociologists in this tradition want to know *how people define* situations, persons, processes, or events as problematic.

Inspired by Fuller, most sociologists agree that a social problem consists of a subjective definition and an objective condition. But, with few exceptions, sociologists have paid more attention to the objective condition than to the subjective definition. Students of labeling, however, have in recent years reversed the emphasis by taking a closer look at the process of subjective definition, and this has led to an entirely different line of sociological questioning.

This chapter discusses the people who developed the labeling perspective, the questions they raised, and the events in sociology that contributed to the development of this perspective.

FOCUS AND CONCERNS OF THE LABELING PERSPECTIVE

Included in the labeling perspective is a set of assumptions about how people define situations. Perhaps the principal assumption is that people define all the recurrent situations in which they find themselves by means of interests and values. If so, then of course all definitions are related to people's positions in a given situation, the values they hold, and the interests they wish to further.

One line of attack of the labeling approach has been to look at the

1. A growing number of sociologists now prefer to call this approach the "interactionist perspective" rather than "labeling theory." The newer name was first used by Earl Rubington and Martin S. Weinberg, eds., *Deviance: The Interactionist Perspective* (New York: Macmillan, 1968) to connote that the "labeling" perspective fits into the broader tradition of "symbolic interactionism." Becker now also prefers the term "interactionist."

world from the vantage point of persons who have been socially defined by others as deviant, as well as from the vantage point of those who do the defining. Another has been to study the making of social rules (laws, organizational definitions, and so on) and the practices by which they are enforced. Both lines of attack have led to some very important research findings. They have also, however, led some sociologists to accuse the labeling approach of having a vested interest in the underdog, almost to the point of accepting a "distorted" view of social reality.[2] We turn now to some of the conditions that gave rise to the labeling perspective.

THE DISCIPLINE AND ITS PROBLEMS

The labeling perspective arose relatively late in American sociology's fourth period (cultivating specialties: 1954–1970). During this period, the study of crime, deviance, and social control became specialties. Thus, sociologists working from both the deviant behavior and the labeling perspectives generally restricted themselves to the study of these social problems.

What transpired during this period to foster the labeling perspective? Three factors contributed: extension of concepts, conflict between schools, and interest in questions left unanswered by the deviant behavior perspective.

Extension of Concepts.   The drive to refine and extend concepts characterizes the history of most sciences because of the efforts of scientists to explain a greater number of phenomena by means of a smaller number of concepts. During sociology's fourth period, theorists worked on refining concepts while researchers extended these concepts to new areas. This combination of labors contributed to the growing body of sociological knowledge. As a tradition called symbolic interactionism developed, researchers began to extend its concepts to the study of social problems, and the labeling perspective evolved out of this extension. (The role of the interactionist tradition in the development of the labeling perspective is dealt with more fully in the section on philosophical sources.)

Conflict Between Schools.   Competition between Chicago sociology and Harvard sociology, noted in the preceding chapter, grew out of different conceptions of the sociological enterprise. Harvard emphasized structure, and many of its students developed, refined, and extended the concepts of structural-functionalism. Chicago, on the contrary, emphasized

2. See, for example, David Bordua, "Deviant Behavior and Social Control," *The Annals* 369 (January 1967): 149–63, and Alvin W. Gouldner, "The Sociologist as Partisan," *The American Sociologist* 3 (May 1968): 103–16.

social process and developed, refined and extended the concepts of symbolic interactionism. Of course, notions of the differences between these schools of thought were exaggerated and frequently bordered on caricature. Nonetheless, opposition between the two schools almost required that one segment of sociologists study the processes involved in social problems, while the others look for their sources in social structure. Thus, the politics of sociology, as it were, led sociologists congenial to the Chicago school to join the labeling camp and followers of the Harvard school to oppose it.

Unanswered Questions. There are limitations in the deviant behavior perspective related to the specialized and complex nature of the society. In a multigroup society, conforming to the rules of one's own group sometimes requires violating another group's rules, whether legal, moral, or social. Similarly, not all violators are caught or punished, even though their offenses may be widely known. Finally, of those who are officially caught, not everyone is classified and treated in the same way.

These aspects of social problems seemed inexplicable from the deviant behavior perspective, leading some sociologists to begin to ask different sorts of questions: When are violations sanctioned, by whom, regarding whom, and with what social consequences? With these questions, the labeling perspective was born.

For those in the deviant behavior tradition, the labeling perspective stereotypes and oversimplifies the phenomenon of deviance. For those in the labeling tradition, it signifies a legitimate extension of interactionist concepts. Some differences between the interests of the two perspectives are summarized below.

Etiology. Whereas the underlying causes of deviant behavior (for example, broken homes, social class, anomie, psychiatric disorder) are of great interest from the deviant behavior perspective, they are of little interest from the labeling perspective.

Initiating Factor. The initiating factor, or the last act in the etiological chain, is of considerable interest to those who use the deviant behavior perspective, but of less interest to students of labeling.

Social Reactions. Social reactions to alleged deviance are the central concern of labeling theory but not of the deviant behavior perspective.

The Official Record. The deviant behavior perspective takes official records for granted, using them as indicators of deviant behavior. Labeling finds official records interesting in and of themselves.[3] The acts that are recorded, how they are categorized, as well as where, when, and with what consequences, constitute a major focus of attention. The labeling perspective assumes that official records reflect primarily the processes of the organization compiling them. Thus, they are not assumed to present literal descriptions of the behaviors that they supposedly document.

In summary, the labeling perspective focuses on process rather than structure, on subjectivity rather than objectivity, and on reactions to deviance rather than the initiation of deviance.

PHILOSOPHICAL SOURCES OF THE LABELING PERSPECTIVE

The labeling approach is an outgrowth of the social philosophies of George Herbert Mead[4] and Alfred Schutz.[5] Although both men were philosophers, each exerted tremendous influence on sociologists. Mead's influence has been felt for a longer period of time by a wider circle of sociologists, while Schutz's influence has been more recent and limited. Together, Mead and Schutz constitute the major background sources of the labeling perspective.

Mead.   Mead taught philosophy at the University of Chicago. In his lectures, Mead presented a model of people and of social reality that, as adopted and developed by members of the Chicago department of sociology, came to be known as symbolic interactionism.

Mead held that the sense of self arises in the course of social interaction. People learn to take the "attitude of the other" toward themselves. In so doing, they come to see themselves as social objects, and they subsequently behave according to that self-conception.

Mead also conceived of social interaction as emergent and dynamic rather than static in character. By reading gestures and symbols, he stressed, people continually adjust their behavior to what others seem about to do. The labeling perspective highlights the relevance of this concept for the study of deviance.

Schutz.   Schutz sought to explain social order by showing that people produce a set of typifications about the world.[6] These typifications include

3. A good example is John I. Kitsuse and Aaron V. Cicourel, "A Note on the Uses of Official Statistics," *Social Problems* 11 (Fall 1963): 131–39.

4. George Herbert Mead, *Mind, Self, and Society from the Standpoint of a Social Behaviorist* (Chicago: University of Chicago Press, 1934).

5. Alfred Schutz, *Collected Papers I: The Problem of Social Reality,* ed. Maurice Natanson (The Hague: Martinus Nijhoff, 1962).

6. In his work, Schutz provides an important synthesis of the thought of Edmund Husserl, George Herbert Mead, and Max Weber.

persons, places, things, and events; and insofar as people assume that other people are defining situations in much the same way, social order is produced. Schutz concerned himself with three important questions: What is the essence of any particular phenomenon in question? How do people make typifications? By what processes do typifications come to be considered as shared? The labeling perspective picks up on these interests and asks related questions: What is the essence of deviance as a *sociological* phenomenon? What are the processes by which people typify others as deviant? How do people come to share these typifications?

FOUNDERS OF THE LABELING PERSPECTIVE

The "grandfather" of labeling theory is Edwin Lemert. In 1951, Lemert published a book titled (or mistitled) *Social Pathology.*[7] In this book he set forth a systematic theory of deviant behavior based on the notion that deviance is defined by social reactions and that the frequency and character of deviation, together with the role of the deviant, are in large part shaped by the social reaction.

The labeling perspective was christened, however, in a book by Howard S. Becker, *Outsiders,* which appeared in 1963. The statement that helped to name the approach was:

> Social groups create deviance by making the rules whose infraction constitutes deviance, and by applying those rules to particular people and labeling them as outsiders. From this point of view, deviance is not a quality of the act the person commits, but rather a consequence of the application by others of rules and sanctions to an "offender." The deviant is one to whom that label has successfully been applied; deviant behavior is behavior that people so label.[8]

Though a change in thought on social problems was already under way, Becker's *Outsiders* crystallized it. Becker showed that becoming sociologically deviant is a dynamic interactive process, drawn out over time in sequences orderly enough to be called a career. He also observed that not everyone who breaks the rules gets labeled deviant, that ultimately the definition and the enforcement of moral rules are political acts, and that the meaning of a deviant act can change over time for the people involved.

In the years since Becker's book appeared in 1963, a number of other sociologists have contributed to the labeling perspective. These sociologists have dealt primarily with the applications of rules to people who have apparently breached them, the conditions under which rules or labels are

7. Edwin M. Lemert, *Social Pathology: A Systematic Approach to the Theory of Sociopathic Behavior* (New York: McGraw-Hill, 1951).

8. Howard S. Becker, *Outsiders: Studies in the Sociology of Deviance* (New York: Free Press, 1963), p. 9.

applied, and the consequences for the labeled person's self-image and future.[9]

CHARACTERISTICS OF THE LABELING PERSPECTIVE

Central to the labeling perspective is the notion that social problems and deviance exist in the eye of the beholder. The perspective seeks to study the process of and responses to social differentiation. The principal elements in the labeling perspective are as follows:

Definition. A social problem or social deviant is defined by social reactions to an alleged violation of rules or expectations. This perspective focuses on the conditions under which behaviors or situations come to be defined as problematic or deviant.

Causes. The cause of a social problem is ultimately *the attention it receives* from the public or from social control agents, for social reactions cannot occur until the alleged behavior or situation is recognized.

Conditions. When a person or situation is labeled problematic or deviant, the labeler is usually in a position to gain by affixing such a label. The labeler must have a negative label to apply and the power to make it stick. Very often, the labeling is done by someone whose job it is to apply labels (for example, social control agents, journalists), and assigning labels is often a mark of success in such jobs.[10] Occasionally, people may label themselves, and in doing so they may gain some advantages (for example, people have reported that they are homosexual in order to be discharged from the military).[11]

Consequences. The definition of a person or situation as socially problematic or deviant may lead to a reordering of human relations in a way that promotes further "deviance." For example, after a person has been labeled "deviant," most people expect him or her to continue violating norms of conventional behavior. This may limit the labeled person's life chances and lead him or her to elaborate the deviant role; for example, an ex-convict may be unable to obtain employment in a conventional job and may thus return to crime in order to make a living. This elaboration of

9. Despite their contributions, several of these writers disavow that they are proponents of labeling theory. For a useful discussion, see Erich Goode, "On Behalf of Labeling Theory," *Social Problems* 22 (June 1975): 570–83.

10. Examples are provided in Rubington and Weinberg, *Deviance.*

11. For example, see Colin J. Williams and Martin S. Weinberg, *Homosexuals and the Military: A Study of Less than Honorable Discharge* (New York: Harper & Row, 1971).

deviant roles because of other people's reactions is called "secondary deviance."[12]

Solutions. The labeling perspective suggests two solutions: definitions can be changed, and the profit can be taken out of labeling. Changing definitions would mean becoming more tolerant, so that people stop labeling certain people and situations as problematic. Taking the profit out of labeling would presumably mean a consequent decrease both in people's labeling of themselves and others as deviant, and in the problems that result from such labeling.

SUMMARY AND CONCLUSION

In the period after 1954, sociology was characterized as *the cultivation of specialties*. Early in this period, the deviant behavior perspective became prominent. Nonetheless certain problems remained unexplained by that perspective, and these unexplained problems generated the labeling perspective. The labeling point of view was rooted in symbolic interactionism, formulated by Mead and later elaborated by Schutz. As symbolic interactionism was extended to the study of the social processes surrounding deviance, the gap between structure and process views in sociology widened.

The labeling perspective examines certain taken-for-granted aspects of social problems. Sociologists working within this perspective focus on the people who define problems, the conditions under which a person or situation is labeled problematic, and the consequences of this labeling. Thus, social problems and deviance are defined by social reactions to a presumed violation of rules or expectations. The cause is presumed knowledge of the violation, and the conditions affecting the labeling process are power relations and the gains to be made by labeling. The major consequences of successful labeling are an elaboration of deviance (secondary deviance) and expectations of continued violations. Solutions suggested by the labeling perspective are to change definitions and to eliminate labeling profits.

12. For an extended discussion of secondary deviance, see Edwin M. Lemert, *Human Deviance, Social Problems, and Social Control,* 2nd ed. (Englewood Cliffs, N.J.: Prentice-Hall, 1972), pp. 62–92.

OUTSIDERS

Howard S. Becker

Traditionally, sociologists studied deviance by examining the attributes of persons who violated rules, why they did so, what distinguished violators from nonviolators, and what could be done about it in a practical sense. Becker's excerpt exemplifies a more recent trend, in which deviance is studied in terms of the successful application of labels. With this reconceptualization, many sociologists have turned their attention from studying deviant behaviors to studying the social definition of deviance and the consequence of such definitions.

DEVIANCE AND THE RESPONSES OF OTHERS

[One sociological view] . . . defines deviance as the infraction of some agreed-upon rule. It then goes on to ask who breaks rules, and to search for the factors in their personalities and life situations that might account for the infractions. This assumes that those who have broken a rule constitute a homogeneous category, because they have committed the same deviant act.

Such an assumption seems to me to ignore the central fact about deviance: it is created by society. I do not mean this in the way it is ordinarily understood, in which the causes of deviance are located in the social situation of the deviant or in "social factors" which prompt his action. I mean, rather, the *social groups create deviance by making the rules whose infraction constitutes deviance*, and by applying those rules to particular people and labeling them as outsiders. From this point of view, deviance is *not* a quality of the act the person commits, but rather a consequence of the application by others of rules and sanctions to an "offender." The deviant is one to whom that label has successfully been applied; deviant behavior is behavior that people so label.[1]

Since deviance is, among other things, a consequence of the responses of others to a person's act, students of deviance cannot assume that they are dealing with a homogeneous category when they study people who have been labeled deviant. That is, they cannot assume that these people have actually committed a deviant act or broken some rule, because the process of labeling may not be infallible; some people may be labeled deviant who in fact have not broken a rule. Furthermore, they cannot assume that the category of those labeled deviant will contain all those who actually have broken a rule, for many offenders may escape apprehension and thus fail to be included in the population of "deviants" they study. Insofar as the category lacks homogeneity and fails to include all the cases that belong in it, one cannot reasonably expect to find common factors of personality or life situation that will account for the supposed deviance.

What, then, do people who have been labeled deviant have in common? At the least, they share the label and the experience of being labeled as outsiders. I will begin my analysis with this basic similarity and view deviance as the product of a transaction that takes place between some social group and one who is viewed by that group as a rule-breaker. I will be less concerned with the personal and social characteristics of deviants than with the process by which they come to be thought of as outsiders and their reactions to that judgment.

Malinowski discovered the usefulness of this view for understanding the nature of deviance many years ago, in his study of the Trobriand Islands:

> One day an outbreak of wailing and a great commotion told me that a death had occurred somewhere in the neighborhood. I was informed that Kima'i, a young lad of my acquaintance, of sixteen or so, had fallen from a coconut palm and killed himself. . . . I found that another youth had been severely wounded by some mysterious coincidence. And at the funeral there was obviously a general feeling of hostility between the village where the boy died and that into which his body was carried for burial.
>
> Only much later was I able to discover the real meaning of these events. The boy had committed suicide. The truth was that he had broken the rules of exogamy, the partner in his crime being his maternal cousin, the daughter of his mother's sister. This had been known and generally disapproved of but nothing was done until the girl's discarded lover, who had wanted to marry her and who felt personally injured, took the initiative. This rival threatened first to use black magic against the guilty youth, but this had not much effect. Then one evening he insulted the culprit in public—accusing him in the hearing of the whole community of incest and hurling at him certain expressions intolerable to a native.
>
> For this there was only one remedy; only one means of escape remained to the unfortunate youth. Next morning he put on festive attire and ornamentation, climbed a coconut palm and addressed the community, speaking from among the palm leaves and bidding them farewell. He explained the reasons for his desperate deed and also launched forth a veiled accusation against the man who had driven him to his death, upon which it became the duty of his clansmen to avenge him. Then he wailed aloud, as is the custom, jumped from a palm some sixty feet high and was killed on the spot. There followed a fight within the village in which the rival was wounded; and the quarrel was repeated during the funeral. . . .

If you were to inquire into the matter among the Trobrianders, you would find . . . that the natives show horror at the idea of violating the rules of exogamy and that they believe that sores, disease and even death might follow clan incest. This is the ideal of native law, and in moral matters it is easy and pleasant strictly to adhere to the ideal—when judging the conduct of others or expressing an opinion about conduct in general.

When it comes to the application of morality and ideals to real life, however, things take on a different complexion. In the case described it was obvious that the facts would not tally with the ideal of conduct. Public opinion was neither outraged by the knowledge of the crime to any extent, nor did it react directly—it had to be mobilized by a public statement of the crime and by insults being hurled at the culprit by an interested party. Even then he had to carry out the punishment himself. . . . Probing further into the matter and collecting concrete information, I found that the breach of exogamy—as regards intercourse and not marriage—is by no means a rare occurrence, and public opinion is lenient, though decidedly hypocritical. If the affair is carried on *sub rosa* with a certain amount of decorum, and if no one in particular stirs up trouble—"public opinion" will gossip, but not demand any harsh punishment. If, on the contrary, scandal breaks out—everyone turns against the guilty pair and by ostracism and insults one or the other may be driven to suicide.[2]

Whether an act is deviant . . . depends on how other people react to it. You can commit clan incest and suffer from no more than gossip as long as no one makes a public accusation; but you will be driven to your death if the accusation is made. The point is that the response of other people has to be regarded as problematic. Just because one has committed an infraction of a rule does not mean that others will respond as though this had happened. (Conversely, just because one has not violated a rule does not mean that he may not be treated, in some circumstances, as though he had.)

The degree to which other people will respond to a given act as deviant varies greatly. Several kinds of variation seem worth noting. First of all, there is variation over time. A person believed to have committed a given "deviant" act may at one time be responded to much more leniently than he would be at some other time. The occurrence of "drives" against various kinds of deviance illustrates this clearly. At various times, enforcement officials may decide to make an all-out attack on some particular kind of deviance, such as gambling, drug addiction, or homosexuality. It is obviously much more dangerous to engage in one of these activities when a drive is on than at any other time. (In a very interesting study of crime news in Colorado newspapers, Davis found that the amount of crime reported in Colorado newspapers showed very little association with actual changes in the amount of crime taking place in Colorado. And, further, the people's estimate of how much increase there had been in crime in Colorado was associated with the increase in the amount of crime news but not with any increase in the amount of crime.)[3]

The degree to which an act will be treated as deviant depends also on who commits the act and who feels he has been harmed by it. Rules tend to be applied more to some persons than others. Studies of juvenile delinquency make the point clearly. Boys from middle-class areas do not get as far in the legal process when they are apprehended as do boys from slum areas. The middle-class boy is less likely, when picked up by the police, to be taken to the station; less likely when taken to the station to be booked; and it is extremely unlikely that he will be convicted and sentenced.[4] This variation occurs even though the original infraction of the rule is the same in the two cases. Similarly, the law is differentially applied to Negroes and whites. It is well known that a Negro believed to have attacked a white woman is much more likely to be punished than a white man who commits the same offense; it is only slightly less well known that a Negro who murders another Negro is much less likely to be punished than a white man who commits murder.[5] This, of course, is one of the main points of Sutherland's analysis of white-collar crime: crimes committed by corporations are almost always prosecuted as civil cases, but the same crime committed by an individual is ordinarily treated as a criminal offense.[6]

Some rules are enforced only when they result in certain consequences. The unmarried mother furnishes a clear example. Vincent[7] points out that illicit sexual relations seldom result in severe punishment or social censure for the offenders. If, however, a girl becomes pregnant as a result of such activities, the reaction of others is likely to be severe. (The illicit pregnancy is also an interesting example of the differential enforcement of rules on different categories of people. Vincent notes that unmarried fathers escape the severe censure visited on the mother.)

Why repeat these commonplace observations? Because, taken together, they support the proposition that deviance is not a simple quality, present in some kinds of behavior and absent in others. Rather, it is the product of a process which involves responses of other people to the behavior. The same behavior may be an infraction of the rules at one time and not at another; may be an infraction when committed by one person, but not when committed by another; some rules are broken with impunity, others are not. In short, whether a given act is deviant or not depends in part on the nature of the act (that is, whether or not it violates some rule) and in part on what other people do about it.

Some people may object that this is merely a terminological quibble, that one can, after all, define terms any way he wants to and that if some people want to speak of rule-breaking behavior as deviant without reference to the reactions of others they are free to do so. This, of course, is true. Yet it might be worthwhile to refer to such behavior as *rule-breaking behavior* and reserve the term *deviant* for those labeled as deviant by some segment of society. I do not insist that this usage be followed. But it should be clear that insofar as a scientist uses "deviant" to refer to any rule-breaking behavior and takes as his subject of study only those who have been *labeled* deviant, he will be hampered by the disparities between the two categories.

If we take as the object of our attention behavior which comes to be labeled as deviant, we must recognize that we cannot know whether a given act will be categorized as deviant until the response of others has occurred. Deviance is not a quality that lies in behavior itself, but in the interaction between the person who commits an act and those who respond to it. . . .

In any case, being . . . branded as deviant has important consequences for one's further social participation and self-image. The most important consequence is a drastic change in the individual's public identity. Committing the improper act and being publicly caught at it place him in a new status. He has been revealed as a different kind of person from the kind he was supposed to be. He is labeled a "fairy," "dope fiend," "nut" or "lunatic," and treated accordingly.

In analyzing the consequences of assuming a deviant identity let us make use of Hughes' distinction between master and auxiliary status traits.[8] Hughes notes that most statuses have one key trait which serves to distinguish those who belong from those who do not. Thus the doctor, whatever else he may be, is a person who has a certificate stating that he has fulfilled certain requirements and is licensed to practice medicine; this is the master trait. As Hughes points out, in our society a doctor is also informally expected to have a number of auxiliary traits: most people expect him to be upper middle class, white, male, and Protestant. When he is not there is a sense that he has in some way failed to fill the bill. Similarly, though skin color is the master status trait determining who is Negro and who is white, Negroes are informally expected to have certain status traits and not to have others; people are surprised and find it anomalous if a Negro turns out to be a doctor or a college professor. People often have the master status trait but lack some of the auxiliary, informally expected characteristics; for example, one may be a doctor but be female or Negro.

Hughes deals with this phenomenon in regard to statuses that are well thought of, desired and desirable (noting that one may have the formal qualifications for entry into a status but be denied full entry because of lack of the proper auxiliary traits), but the same process occurs in the case of deviant statuses. Possession of one deviant trait may have a generalized symbolic value, so that people automatically assume that its bearer possesses other undesirable traits allegedly associated with it.

To be labeled a criminal one need only commit a single criminal offense, and this is all the term formally refers to. Yet the word carries a number of connotations specifying auxiliary traits characteristic of anyone bearing the label. A man who has been convicted of house-breaking and thereby labeled criminal is presumed to be a person likely to break into other houses; the police, in rounding up known offenders for investigation after a crime has been committed, operate on this premise. Further, he is considered likely to commit other kinds of crimes as well, because he has shown himself to be a person without "respect for the law." Thus, apprehension for one deviant act exposes a person to the likelihood that he will be regarded as deviant or undesirable in other respects.

There is one other element in Hughes's analysis we can borrow with profit: the distinction between master and subordinate statuses.[9] Some statuses, in our society as in others, override all other statuses and have a certain priority. Race is one of these. Membership in the Negro race, as socially defined, will override most other status considerations in most other situations; the fact that one is a physician or middle-class or female will not protect one from being treated as a Negro first and any of these other things second. The status of deviant (depending on the kind of deviance) is this kind of master status. One receives the status as a result of breaking a rule, and the identification proves to be more important than most others. One will be identified as a deviant first, before other identifications are made. . . .

Notes

1. The most important earlier statements of this view can be found in Frank Tannenbaum, *Crime and the Community* (New York: McGraw-Hill Book Co., Inc., 1951), and E. M. Lemert, *Social Pathology* (New York: McGraw-Hill Book Co., Inc., 1951). A recent article stating a position very similar to mine is John Kitsuse, "Societal Reaction to Deviance: Problems of Theory and Method," *Social Problems,* 9 (Winter 1962), 247–256.

2. Bronislaw Malinowski, *Crime and Custom in Savage Society* (New York: Humanities Press, 1926), pp. 77–80. Reprinted by permission of Humanities Press and Routledge & Kegan Paul, Ltd.

3. F. James Davis, "Crime News in Colorado Newspapers," *American Journal of Sociology,* LVII (January 1952), 325–330.

4. See Albert K. Cohen and James F. Short, Jr., "Juvenile Delinquency," in Robert K. Merton and Robert A. Nisbet, editors, *Contemporary Social Problems* (New York: Harcourt, Brace and World, Inc., 1961), p. 87.

5. See Harold Garfinkel, "Research Notes on Inter- and Intra-Racial Homicides," *Social Forces,* 27 (May 1949), 360–381.

6. Edwin H. Sutherland, "White Collar Criminality," *American Sociological Review,* V (February 1940), 1–12.

7. Clark Vincent, *Unmarried Mothers* (New York: The Free Press of Glencoe, 1961), pp. 3–5.

8. Everett C. Hughes, "Dilemmas and Contradictions of Status," *American Journal of Sociology,* L (March 1945), 353–359.

9. *Ibid.*

PRIMARY AND SECONDARY DEVIATION

Edwin M. Lemert

The causes of deviant acts, Lemert claims, must be distinguished from the causes of deviant roles. The latter phenomenon, which he calls "secondary deviation," arises out of social interaction between the deviant and his community. If the deviant behavior continues long enough and the community responds with escalating social penalties, then the sequence culminates in "a stigmatizing of the deviant . . . in the form of name calling, labeling, or stereotyping" and a resulting "deviant role." In the absence of severe social reaction, however, a deviant role is less likely since the person is not assigned a disvalued role which would require him to defend himself against real or imagined social punishment.

There has been an embarrassingly large number of theories, often without any relationship to a general theory, advanced to account for various specific [deviations] in human behavior. For certain types of [deviance], such as alcoholism, crime, or stuttering, there are almost as many theories as there are writers on these subjects. This has been occasioned in no small way by the preoccupation with the origins of [deviant] behavior and by the fallacy of confusing *original* causes with *effective* causes. All such theories have elements of truth, and the divergent viewpoints they contain can be reconciled with the general theory here if it is granted that original causes or antecedents of deviant behaviors are many and diversified. This holds especially for the psychological processes leading to similar [deviance], but it also holds for the situational concomitants of the initial aberrant conduct. A person may come to use excessive alcohol not only for a wide variety of subjective reasons but also because of diversified situational influences, such as the death of a loved one, business failure, or participating in some sort of organized group activity calling for heavy drinking of liquor. Whatever the original reasons for violating the norms of the community, they are important only for certain research purposes, such as assessing the extent of the "social problem" at a given time or determining the requirements for a rational program of social control. From a narrower *sociological viewpoint* [Italics added] . . . deviations are not significant until they are organized subjectively and transformed into active roles and become the social criteria for assigning status. The deviant individuals must react symbolically to their own behavior aberrations and fix them in their sociopsychological patterns. The deviations remain primary deviations or symptomatic and situational as long as they are rationalized or otherwise dealt with as functions of a socially acceptable role. Under such conditions normal and pathological behaviors remain strange and somewhat tensional bedfellows in the same person. Undeniably a vast amount of such segmental and partially integrated [deviant] behavior exists in our society and has impressed many writers in the field of [deviance].

Just how far and for how long a person may go in dissociating his [deviant] tendencies so that they are merely troublesome adjuncts of normally conceived roles is not known. Perhaps it depends upon the number of alternative definitions of the same overt behavior that he can develop. . . . However, if the deviant acts are repetitive and have a high visibility, and if there is a severe societal reaction, which, through a process of identification is incorporated as part of the "me" of the individual, the probability is greatly increased that the integration of existing roles will be disrupted and that reorganization based upon a new role or roles will occur. (The "me" in this context is simply the subjective aspect of the societal reaction.) Reorganization may be the adoption of another normal role in which the tendencies previously defined as ["deviant"] are given a more acceptable social expression. The other general possibility is the assumption of a deviant role, if such exists; or, more rarely, the person may organize an aberrant sect or group in which he creates a special role of his own. *When a person begins to employ his deviant behavior or a role based upon it as a means of defense, attack, or adjustment to the overt and covert problems created by the consequent societal reaction to him, his deviation is secondary.* Objective evidences of this change will be found in the symbolic appurtenances of the new role, in clothes, speech, posture, and mannerisms, which in some cases heighten social visibility, and which in some cases serve as symbolic cues to professionalization.

ROLE CONCEPTIONS OF THE INDIVIDUAL MUST BE REINFORCED BY REACTIONS OF OTHERS

It is seldom that one deviant act will provoke a sufficiently strong societal reaction to bring about secondary deviation, unless in the process of introjection the individual imputes or projects meanings into the social situation which are not present. In this case anticipatory fears are involved. For example, in a culture where a child is taught sharp distinctions between "good" women and "bad" women, a single act of questionable morality might conceivably have a profound meaning for the girl so indulging. However, in the absence of reactions by the person's family, neighbors, or the larger community, reinforcing the tentative "bad-girl" self-definition, it is questionable whether a transition to secondary deviation would take place. It is also doubtful whether a temporary exposure to a severe punitive reaction by the community will lead a person to identify himself with a [deviant] role, unless, as we have said, the experience is highly traumatic. Most frequently there is a progressive reciprocal relationship between the deviation of the individual and the societal reaction, with a compounding of the societal reaction out of the minute accretions in the deviant behavior, until a point is reached where ingrouping and outgrouping between society and the deviant is manifest.[1] At this point a stigmatizing of the deviant occurs in the form of name calling, labeling, or stereotyping.

The sequence of interaction leading to secondary deviation is roughly as follows: (1) primary deviation; (2) social penalties; (3) further primary deviation; (4) stronger penalties and rejections; (5) further deviation, perhaps with hostilities and resentment beginning to focus upon those doing the penalizing; (6) crisis reached in the tolerance quotient, expressed in formal action by the community stigmatizing of the deviant; (7) strengthening of the deviant conduct as a reaction to the stigmatizing and penalties; (8) ultimate acceptance of deviant social status and efforts at adjustment on the basis of the associated role.

As an illustration of this sequence the behavior of an errant schoolboy can be cited. For one reason or another, let us say excessive energy, the schoolboy engages in a classroom prank. He is penalized for it by the teacher. Later, due to clumsiness, he creates another disturbance and again he is reprimanded. Then, as sometimes happens, the boy is blamed for something he did not do. When the teacher uses the tag "bad boy" or "mischief maker" or other invidious terms, hostility and resentment are excited in the boy and he may feel that he is blocked in playing the role expected of him. Thereafter, there may be a strong temptation to assume his role in the class as defined by the teacher, particularly when he discovers that there are rewards as well as penalties deriving from such a role. There is, of course, no implication here that such boys go on to become delinquents or criminals, for the mischief-maker role may later become integrated with or retrospectively rationalized as part of a role more acceptable to school authorities.[2] If such a boy continues this unacceptable role and becomes delinquent, the process must be accounted for in the light of the general theory of this volume. There must be a spreading corroboration of a [deviant] self-conception and societal reinforcement at each step in the process.

The most significant personality changes are manifest when societal definitions and their subjective counterpart become generalized. When this happens, the range of major role choices becomes narrowed to one general class.[3] This was very obvious in the case of a young girl who was the daughter of a paroled convict and who was attending a small Middle Western college. She continually argued with herself and with the author, in whom she had confided, that in reality she belonged on the "other side of the railroad tracks" and that her life could be enormously simplified by acquiescing in this verdict and living accordingly. While in her case there was a tendency to dramatize her conflicts, nevertheless there was enough societal reinforcement of her self-conception by the treatment she received in her relationship with her father and on dates with college boys to lend it a painful reality. Once these boys took her home to the shoddy dwelling in a slum area where she lived with her father, who was often in a drunken condition, they abruptly stopped seeing her again or else became sexually presumptive. . . .

Notes

1. Mead, G., "The Psychology of Punitive Justice," *American Journal of Sociology,* 23, March, 1918, pp. 577–602.

2. Evidence for fixed or inevitable sequences from predelinquency to crime is absent. Sutherland, E. H., *Principles of Criminology,* 1939, 4th ed., p. 202.

3. Sutherland seems to say something of this sort in connection with the development of criminal behavior. *Ibid.,* p. 86.

LABELING THE MENTALLY RETARDED

Jane R. Mercer

A central tenet of the labeling perspective is that deviance is behavior that some person or persons have labeled deviant. Mercer examines this proposition by comparing and contrasting how retardates from two different social classes came to be defined as retarded. She finds that parental definitions of retardation, age at which children are officially defined as retarded, institutionalization, prognosis, and willingness to accept retardates back in the family all vary with the family's social class. Higher-class par-

Reprinted from "Social System Perspective and Clinical Perspective: Frames of Reference for Understanding Career Patterns of People Labelled as Mentally Retarded," *So-*

ents are more apt to know the label, to define their children as retarded, to do so at an early age, to institutionalize them, to be pessimistic about their future life chances and less willing to accept them back in the family fold. Lower-class parents, by contrast, are less apt to have a concept of mental retardation, their children are more apt to be defined as retarded later in life by police or welfare agencies, are more apt to be institutionalized later in life, and are more likely to be reaccepted by their families who remain optimistic about their future life chances. Her study supports the general labeling proposition that though peoples' behaviors may be similar, the response to those behaviors may vary with the definition significant others and officials place upon them.

The clinical perspective is the frame of reference most commonly adopted in studies of mental deficiency, mental illness, drug addiction, and other areas which the students of deviance choose to investigate.[1,2] This viewpoint is readily identified by several distinguishing characteristics.

First, the investigator accepts as the focus for study those individuals who have been labeled deviant. In so doing, he adopts the values of whatever social system has defined the person as deviant and assumes that its judgments are the valid measure of deviance. . . . Groups in the social structure sharing the values of the core culture tend to accept the labels attached as a consequence of the application of these values without serious questioning. . . .

A second distinguishing characteristic of the clinical perspective is the tendency to perceive deviance as an attribute of the person, as a meaning inherent in his behavior, appearance, or performance. Mental retardation, for example, is viewed as a characteristic of the person, a lack to be explained. This viewpoint results in a quest for etiology. Thus, the clinical perspective is essentially a medical frame of reference, for it sees deviance as individual pathology requiring diagnostic classification and etiological analysis for the purpose of determining proper treatment procedures and probable prognosis.

Three additional characteristics of the clinical perspective are the de-

cial Problems, 13:1 (Summer 1965), pp. 21–30, 33–34, by permission of the Society for the Study of Social Problems and the author.

Supported in part by the National Institute of Mental Health, Grant No. 3M-9130: Population Movement of Mental Defectives and Related Physical, Behavioral, Social, and Cultural Factors; and Grant No. MH-5687: Mental Retardation in a Community, Pacific State Hospital, Pomona, California. Appreciation for assistance is expressed to the Western Data Processing Center, Division of the Graduate School of Business Administration, University of California, Los Angeles.

velopment of a diagnostic nomenclature, the creation of diagnostic instruments, and the professionalization of the diagnostic function.

When the investigator begins his research with the diagnostic designations assigned by official defining agents, he tends to assume that all individuals placed in a given category are essentially equivalent in respect to their deviance. . . . Individuals assigned to different categories of deviance are compared with each other or with a "normal" population consisting of persons who, for whatever reason, have escaped being labeled. The focus is on the individual.

Another characteristic of the clinical perspective is its assumption that the official definition is somehow the "right" definition. . . .

Finally, when deviance is perceived as individual pathology, social action tends to center upon changing the individual or, that failing, removing him from participation in society. Prevention and cure become the primary social goals. . . .

The social system [labeling] perspective, on the other hand, attempts to see the definition of an individual's behavior as a function of the values of the social system within which he is being evaluated. The professional definers are studied as one of the most important of the evaluating social systems but within the context of other social systems which may or may not concur with official definitions.

Defining an individual as mentally ill, delinquent, or mentally retarded is viewed as an interpersonal process in which the definer makes a value judgment about the behavior of the persons being defined. . . . Deviation is not seen as a characteristic of the individual or as a meaning inherent in his behavior, but as a socially derived label which may be attached to his behavior by some social systems and not by others.[3]

. . . Thus, it follows that a person may be mentally retarded in one system and not mentally retarded in another. He may change his label by changing his social group. This viewpoint frees us from the necessity of seeing the person as permanently stigmatized by a deviant label and makes it possible to understand otherwise obscure patterns in the life careers of individuals. . . . The research reported in this paper attempts to answer these questions about a group of persons who shared the common experience of having been labeled retarded by official defining agencies and placed in a public institution for the retarded. . . .

The specific question which this study seeks to investigate within the above framework is: "Why do the families of some individuals take them back home after a period of institutionalization in a hospital for the retarded while other families do not, when, according to official evaluations, these individuals show similar degrees of deviance, that is, have comparable intelligence test scores, and are of equivalent age, sex, ethnic status, and length of hospitalization?" . . .

METHOD

Two groups of labeled retardates were studied. One group consisted of patients who had been released to their families from a state hospital for the retarded and the other group consisted of a matched group of patients still resident in the hospital at the time of the study.[4]

Specifically, the released group was made up of all patients released to their families during a three year period (1957–59), who had not been readmitted to another institution for the retarded at the time of the study, and who were reported to be living within a one hundred mile radius of the hospital. Only those cases in which the family had assumed responsibility for the patient were included. Of the 76 patients who met these qualifications, it was possible to complete interviews with 63 of the families. Six families refused to be interviewed and seven could not be located.

The resident group was selected to match the released group in intelligence quotient, age, sex, ethnic status, and year of admission, other studies having demonstrated that these factors are related to the probability of release.[5]

The matched group of resident patients was selected in the following manner: all patients on the hospital rolls were sorted into two groups by sex, two groups by age, three groups by ethnic status, three groups by intelligence quotient, and two groups by year of admission. All released patients were likewise assigned to the proper category. Resident patients were then chosen at random from within each cell in sufficient numbers to correspond to the number of discharged patients also falling in that cell. Each resident case was required to have a family living within a one hundred mile radius of the hospital. If a case did not meet this requirement, another case was drawn randomly from the appropriate cell until there was an equal number of discharged and resident cases in each cell. Sex distribution in each group was 53 males and 23 females; ethnic distribution, 47 Caucasians, 20 Mexicans, and 9 Negroes.

. . . Of the 76 resident cases selected to match the released cases, interviews were completed with 70 families. Two refused to be interviewed and four families could not be located. Using a Kolmogorov-Smirnov Test of two independent samples, we found that all differences between the interviewed groups could be accounted for by chance.

When the 19 non-interviewed cases were compared with the 133 interviewed cases, no significant differences were found in the sex, age, I.Q., or ethnic status of the patients, or the socioeconomic level of the families. . . .

The hospital file for each patient selected for study was searched for relevant data and an interview was held with a family member. In 75% of the cases the mother was interviewed; in 8% the father was interviewed; and in the remaining cases some other relative served as informant. . . .

To clarify the circumstances under which members of the released group returned to their families, the respondent was asked two questions: "Who was the most important person in getting you to take————out of the hospital?" and "What were the main reasons you decided to have ————discharged from the hospital?"

In 12 cases the parents reported that someone in the hospital, i.e., a social worker, family care mother, or a ward technician, had first suggested that the patient could be released to the family. In the 51 remaining cases the families were the active agents in release. . . .

It is clear . . . that most of the patients who returned to their families returned because the family made an effort to secure their release. . . .

FINDINGS

Social Status of Released Patients.   Several indices were used to measure the socioeconomic level of the family of each retardate. A socioeconomic index score based on the occupation and education of the head of the household, weighted according to Hollings-head's system, was used as the basic measure. In addition, the interviewer rated the economic status of the street on which the patient's home was located, rated the physical condition of the housing unit, and completed a checklist of equipment present in the household. . . . [T]he families of the released patients rated significantly lower than the families of the resident patients on every measure. The heads of the households in the families of released patients had less education and lower level jobs, the family residence was located among less affluent dwellings, the housing unit was in a poorer state of repair, and the dwelling was less elaborately furnished and equipped. Contrary to the pattern found in studies of those placed as mentally ill,[6] it is the "retardate" from lower socioeconomic background who is most likely to be released to his family while higher status "retardates" are more likely to remain in the hospital.

From the clinical perspective, several explanations may be proposed for these differences. It has been found in hospital populations that patients with an I.Q. below 50 are more likely to come from families which represent a cross-section of social levels, while those with an I.Q. between 50 and 70 are more likely to come from low status families.[7] Since persons with higher I.Q.'s have a higher probability of release, this could account for higher rates of release for low status persons. However, in the present study, the tested level of intelligence was equal for both groups, and this hypothesis cannot be used as an explanation.

A second possible explanation from a clinical perspective might be based on the fact that persons who have more physical handicaps tend to be institutionalized for longer periods of time than persons with few handicaps.[8] Should it be found that high status patients have more physical handicaps than low status patients, then this could account for the latter's shorter hospitalization. Data from the present sample were analyzed to determine whether there was a significant relationship between physical handicap and social status. Although released patients tended to have fewer physical handicaps than resident patients, this was irrespective of social status. When high status patients were compared with low status patients, 50% of the high status and 56% of the low status patients had no physical handicaps . . .

A third explanation from the clinical perspective may hinge on differences in the diagnostic categories to which retardates of different social status were assigned. . . . A diagnostic label of "familial" or "undifferentiated" ordinarily indicates that the individual has few or no physical stigmata and is essentially normal in body structure. All other categories ordinarily indicate that he has some type of physical symptomatology. Although released patients were more likely to be diagnosed as familial or undifferentiated than resident patients . . . this, like physical handicap, was irrespective of social status. Fifty-seven per cent of the high status retardates, and 69% of the low status retardates were classified as either undifferentiated or familial, a difference which could be accounted for by chance. . . .

Divergent Definitions. In analyzing social status, four types of situations were identified. The modal category for resident patients was high social status with a smaller number of resident patients coming from low status families. The modal category for released patients was low status with a smaller number of released patients coming from higher status families. If we are correct in our hypothesis (that higher release rates for low status patients are related to the fact that the family social system [labeling] is structurally more distant from the core culture and that its style of life, values, and definitions of the patient are more divergent from official definitions than that of high status families), we would expect the largest differences to occur when high status resident families are compared to low status released families.

. . . [T]hree questions [were] asked to determine the extent to which family members concurred in the official label of "retardation," the extent to which they believed the patient's condition amenable to change, and the extent to which they anticipated that the individual could live outside the hospital and, perhaps, fill adult roles. The patterns of the divergent definitions of the situation which emerged for each group are illuminating.

When asked whether *he* believed the patient to be retarded, the high status parent more frequently concurred with the definitions of the official defining agencies while the low status parent was more prone to disagree outright or to be uncertain. This tendency is especially marked when the two modal categories are compared. While 33.3% of the parents of the low

status released patients stated that they did not think the patient was retarded and 25.6% were uncertain whether he was retarded, only 4.6% of
the parents of high status resident patients felt he was not retarded and
20.9% were uncertain.

When parents were asked whether they believed anything could change
the patient's condition, the differences between all groups were significant
at the .02 level or beyond. The high status parent was most likely to believe
that nothing could change his child's condition, and this was significantly
more characteristic of parents whose children were still in the hospital than
those who had taken their child from the hospital on both status levels.

When asked what they saw in the future for their child, all groups again
differed significantly in the expected direction. The modal, high status
group was least optimistic and the modal, low status group, most optimistic
about the future. Fully 46% of the parents of the latter group expressed
the expectation that their child would get a job, marry, and fulfill the usual
adult roles while only 6.9% of the modal, high status group responded in
this fashion. High status parents, as a group, more frequently see their
child playing dependent roles. It is interesting to note that, although a large
percentage of parents of released patients believe the patient will be dependent, they demonstrate their willingness to accept responsibility for the
retarded child themselves by their responding that they foresee him having
a future in which he is dependent at home. Only 9.3% of the high status
and 22.2% of the low status parents of the resident patients see this as a
future prospect. Release to the family clearly appears to be contingent upon
the willingness of the family to accept the patient's dependency, if they do
not foresee him assuming independent adult roles.

Factors in the Labeling Process.   From the social system [labeling] perspective, retardation is viewed as a label placed upon an individual after
someone has evaluated his behavior within a specific set of norms. Retardation is not a meaning necessarily inherent in the behavior of the individual. We have seen that the parents of low status, released patients tend to
reject the label of retardation and to be optimistic about the future. We
surmised that this divergent definition could well be related to factors in
the process by which the child was first categorized as subnormal, such as
his age at the time, the type of behavior which was used as a basis for
making the evaluation, and the persons doing the labeling. Consequently,
parents were asked specifically about these factors. . . .

Children from lower status families were labeled as mentally subnormal
at a significantly later age than children from high status families. Seventy-
nine per cent of the patients in the high status, modal group were classified
as retarded by the age of six while only 36.1% of those in the low status,
modal group were identified at such an early age. The largest percentage
of low status retardates were first classified after they reached public school

age. This indicates that relatives and friends, who are the individuals most likely to observe and evaluate the behavior of young children, seldom saw anything deviant in the early development of lower status children later labeled retarded, but that the primary groups of higher status children did perceive early deviation.

This is related to the responses made when parents were asked what first prompted someone to believe the patient retarded. The modal, high status group reported slow development in 48.8% of the cases and various types of physical symptoms in an additional 20.9%, while only 14.7% and 11.8% of the modal, low status parents gave these responses. On the other hand, 55.9% of the modal, low status group were first labeled because they had problems learning in school, while this was true of only 9.3% of the modal high status group.

When parents were asked who was the most important person influencing them in placing the child in the hospital, a parallel pattern emerged. Medical persons are the most important single group for the modal, high status persons while the police and welfare agencies loom very significant in 64.1% of the cases in the modal, low status group. These findings are similar to those of Hollingshead and Redlich in their study of paths of the hospital for the mentally ill.[9] Of additional interest is the fact that the person important in placement differentiates the low status released from the low status resident patient at the .01 level. The resident low status patient's path to the hospital is similar to that of the high status patient and markedly different from released low status persons. When authoritative figures such as police and welfare are primary forces in placement, the patient is more likely to return home.

We interpret these findings to mean that when the family—or persons whose advice is solicited by the family, i.e., medical persons—is "most important" in placing a person in a hospital for the retarded, the primary groups have themselves first defined the individual as a deviant and sought professional counsel. When their own suspicions are supported by official definitions, they are more likely to leave the patient in an institution.

Conversely, when a person is labeled retarded by an authoritative, governmental agency whose advice is not solicited and who, in the case of the police, may be perceived as a punishing agent, the family frequently rejects the official definition of the child as retarded and withdraws him from the institution at the first opportunity. This attitude was clearly exemplified by one mother who, when asked why the family had taken the child from the hospital, replied, "Why not? He had served his time."

The police [are more of] a factor in labeling the low status person as retarded. . . . Fifty per cent of the low status retardates had some type of police record while only 23% of the high status subnormals were known to the police. . . .

DISCUSSION AND CONCLUSIONS

The life space of the individual may be viewed as a vast network of inter-locking social systems [labeling] through which the person moves during the course of his lifetime. Those systems which exist close to one another in the social structure tend, because of overlapping memberships and frequent communication, to evolve similar patterns of norms. Most individuals are born and live out their lives in a relatively limited segment of this social network and tend to contact mainly social systems which share common norms. When an individual's contacts are restricted to a circumscribed segment of the structure, this gives some stability to the evaluations which are made of his behavior and to the labels which are attached to him.

However, when the person's life career takes him into segments of the social network which are located at a distance from his point of origin, as when a Mexican-American child enters the public school or a Negro child gets picked up by the police, he is then judged by a new and different set of norms. Behavior which was perfectly acceptable in his primary social systems [labeling] may now be judged as evidence of "mental retardation." At this point, he is caught up in the web of official definitions. However, because he has primary social systems [labeling] which may not agree with these official labels, he may be able to return to that segment of the social structure which does not label him as deviant after he has fulfilled the minimal requirements of the official system. That is, he can drop out of school or he can "serve his time" in the state hospital and then go home. By changing his location in social space, he can change his label from "retarded" to "not much different from the rest of us." For example, the mother of a Mexican-American, male, adult patient who had been released from the hospital after being committed following an incident in which he allegedly made sexual advances to a young girl, told the author, "There is nothing wrong with Benny. He just can't read or write." Since the mother spoke only broken English, had no formal schooling, and could not read or write, Benny did not appear deviant to her. From her perspective, he didn't have anything wrong with him.

The child from a high status family has no such recourse. His primary social systems [labeling] lie structurally close to the official social systems and tend to concur on what is acceptable. Definitions of his subnormality appear early in his life and are more universal in all his social groups. He cannot escape the retarded label because all his associates agree that he is a deviant.[10]

In conclusion, tentative answers may be given to the three questions raised earlier in this discussion. "Who sees whom as retarded?" Within the social system perspective, it becomes clear that persons who are clinically similar may be defined quite differently by their primary social systems.

The person from lower status social systems is less likely to be perceived as mentally subnormal.

"What impact does this differential definition have on the life career of the person?" Apparently, these differential definitions do make a difference because the group which diverges most widely from official definitions is the group in which the most individuals are released from the institution to their families.

Finally, "What are the characteristics of the social systems [labeling] which diverge most widely from official definitions?" These social systems [labeling] seem to be characterized by low educational achievement, high levels of dependency, and high concentrations of ethnic minorities.

A social system [labeling] perspective adds a useful dimension to the label "mental retardation" by its focus on the varied definitions which may be applied to behavior by different groups in society. For those interested in the care and treatment of persons officially labeled as mentally subnormal, it may be beneficial in some cases to seek systematically to relocate such individuals in the social structure in groups which will not define them as deviant. Rather than insisting that family members adopt official definitions of abnormality, we may frequently find it advisable to permit them to continue to view the patient within their own frame of reference and thus make it easier for them to accept him.

Notes

1. August B. Hollingshead and Frederick C. Redlich, *Social Class and Mental Illness*, New York: John Wiley and Sons, 1958, Chapter 11.

2. H. E. Freeman and O. G. Simmons, "Social Class and Posthospital Performance Levels," *American Sociological Review*, 2 (June 1959), p. 348.

3. Howard S. Becker, editor, *The Other Side: Perspectives on Deviance*, New York: The Free Press, 1964.

4. Pacific State Hospital, Pomona, California, is a state supported hospital for the mentally retarded with a population of approximately 3,000 patients.

5. G. Tarjan, S. W. Wright, M. Kramer, P. H. Person, Jr., and R. Morgan, "The Natural History of Mental Deficiency in a State Hospital. I: Probabilities of Release and Death by Age, Intelligence Quotients, and Diagnosis," *AMA J. Dis. Childr.*, 96 (1958), pp. 64–70.

6. August B. Hollingshead and Frederick C. Redlich, 1958, *op. cit.*, Chapter 11.

7. Georges Sabagh, Harvey F. Dingman, George Tarjan, and Stanley W. Wright, "Social Class and Ethnic Status of Patients Admitted to a State Hospital for the Retarded," *Pacific Sociological Review*, 2 (Fall 1959), pp. 76–80.

8. G. Tarjan, S. W. Wright, M. Kramer, R. H. Person, Jr., and R. Morgan, 96, 1958, *op. cit.*, pp. 64–70.

9. August B. Hollingshead and Frederick C. Redlich, 1958, *op. cit.*, Chapter 11.

10. Lewis Anthony Dexter, "On the Politics and Sociology of Stupidity in Our Society" in *The Other Side: Perspectives on Deviance*, edited by Howard S. Becker, New York: The Free Press, 1964, pp. 37–49.

THE SAINTS AND THE ROUGHNECKS

William J. Chambliss

Becker had argued in Outsiders *that one contingency of labeling was social class. This, he said, was particularly true in the case of juvenile delinquency, control agents showing more tolerance for middle-class delinquents, much less for working-class delinquents. Chambliss, in this oft-reprinted field study, documents how class background can make a big difference when it comes to being labeled a juvenile delinquent. The Saints and the Roughnecks engaged in roughly the same amount of deviant behavior. But because of class bias, visibility of delinquent acts, and behavior when in the presence of control agents, the Roughnecks were tagged as troublemakers, young men whose future lay in only more deviant behavior. By contrast, the community expected the Saints to be successes after high school. Where six of the eight Saints went on to higher degrees, five of the seven Roughnecks lived up to the community's expectation that none of them would come to a good end. As Chambliss notes: "The community responded to the Roughnecks as boys in trouble, and the boys agreed with that perception."*

Eight promising young men—children of good, stable, white upper-middle-class families, active in school affairs, good pre-college students—were some of the most delinquent boys at Hanibal High School. While community residents and parents knew that these boys occasionally sowed a few wild oats, they were totally unaware that sowing wild oats completely occupied the daily routine of these young men. The Saints were constantly occupied with truancy, drinking, wild driving, petty theft and vandalism.

Reprinted by permission of Transaction, Inc., from *Society*, 11:1 (November/December 1973), pp. 24–31. Copyright © 1973 by Transaction, Inc.

Yet not one was officially arrested for any misdeed during the two years I observed them.

This record was particularly surprising in light of my observations during the same two years of another gang of Hanibal High School students, six lower-class white boys known as the Roughnecks. The Roughnecks were constantly in trouble with police and community even though their rate of delinquency was about equal with that of the Saints. What was the cause of this disparity? The result? The following consideration of the activities, social class and community perceptions of both gangs may provide some answers.

THE SAINTS FROM MONDAY TO FRIDAY

The Saints' principal daily concern was with getting out of school as early as possible. The boys managed to get out of school with minimum danger that they would be accused of playing hookey through an elaborate procedure for obtaining "legitimate" release from class. The most common procedure was for one boy to obtain the release of another by fabricating a meeting of some committee, program or recognized club. Charles might raise his hand in his 9:00 chemistry class and ask to be excused—a euphemism for going to the bathroom. Charles would go to Ed's math class and inform the teacher that Ed was needed for a 9:30 rehearsal of the drama club play. The math teacher would recognize Ed and Charles as "good students" involved in numerous school activities and would permit Ed to leave at 9:30. Charles would return to his class, and Ed would go to Tom's English class to obtain his release. Tom would engineer Charles' escape. The strategy would continue until as many of the Saints as possible were freed. After a stealthy trip to the car (which had been parked in a strategic spot), the boys were off for a day of fun.

Over the two years I observed the Saints, this pattern was repeated nearly every day. There were variations on the theme, but in one form or another, the boys used this procedure for getting out of class and then off the school grounds. Rarely did all eight of the Saints manage to leave school at the same time. The average number avoiding school on the days I observed them was five.

Having escaped from the concrete corridors the boys usually went either to a pool hall on the other (lower-class) side of town or to a cafe in the suburbs. Both places were out of the way of people the boys were likely to know (family or school officials), and both provided a source of entertainment. The pool hall entertainment was the generally rough atmosphere, the occasional hustler, the sometimes drunk proprietor and, of course, the game of pool. The cafe's entertainment was provided by the owner. The boys would "accidentally" knock a glass on the floor or spill cola on the counter—not all the time, but enough to be sporting. They would also bend spoons, put salt in sugar bowls and generally tease whoever was working in the cafe. The owner had opened the cafe recently and was dependent on the boys' business which was, in fact, substantial since between the horsing around and the teasing they bought food and drinks.

THE SAINTS ON WEEKENDS

On weekends, the automobile was even more critical than during the week, for on weekends the Saints went to Big Town—a large city with a population of over a million, 25 miles from Hanibal. Every Friday and Saturday night most of the Saints would meet between 8:00 and 8:30 and would go into Big Town. Big Town activities included drinking heavily in taverns or nightclubs, driving drunkenly through the streets, and committing acts of vandalism and playing pranks.

By midnight on Fridays and Saturdays the Saints were usually thoroughly high, and one or two of them were often so drunk they had to be carried to the cars. Then the boys drove around town, calling obscenities to women and girls; occasionally trying (unsuccessfully so far as I could tell) to pick girls up; and driving recklessly through red lights and at high speeds with their lights out. Occasionally they played "chicken." One boy would climb out the back window of the car and across the roof to the driver's side of the car while the car was moving at high speed (between 40 and 50 miles an hour); then the driver would move over and the boy who had just crawled across the car roof would take the driver's seat.

Searching for "fair game" for a prank was the boys' principal activity after they left the tavern. The boys would drive alongside a foot patrolman and ask directions to some street. If the policeman leaned on the car in the course of answering the question, the driver would speed away, causing him to lose his balance. The Saints were careful to play this prank only in an area where they were not going to spend much time and where they could quickly disappear around a corner to avoid having their license plate number taken.

Construction sites and road repair areas were the special province of the Saints' mischief. A soon-to-be-repaired hole in the road inevitably invited the Saints to remove lanterns and wooden barricades and put them in the car, leaving the hole unprotected. The boys would find a safe vantage point and wait for an unsuspecting motorist to drive into the hole. Often, though not always, the boys would go up to the motorist and commiserate with him about the dreadful way the city protected its citizenry.

Leaving the scene of the open hole and the motorist, the boys would then go searching for an appropriate place to erect the stolen barricade. An "appropriate place" was often a spot on a highway near a curve in the road where the barricade would not be seen by an oncoming motorist. The boys would wait to watch an unsuspecting motorist attempt to stop and (usually) crash into the wooden barricade. With saintly bearing the boys might offer help and understanding.

A stolen lantern might well find its way onto the back of a police car or hang from a street lamp. Once a lantern served as a prop for a reenactment of the "midnight ride of Paul Revere" until the "play," which was taking place at 2:00 A.M. in the center of a main street of Big Town, was interrupted by a police car several blocks away. The boys ran, leaving the lanterns on the street, and managed to avoid being apprehended.

Abandoned houses, especially if they were located in out-of-the-way places, were fair game for destruction and spontaneous vandalism. The boys would break windows, remove furniture to the yard and tear it apart, urinate on the walls and scrawl obscenities inside.

Through all the pranks, drinking and reckless driving the boys managed miraculously to avoid being stopped by police. Only twice in two years was I aware that they had been stopped by a Big City policeman. Once was for speeding (which they did every time they drove whether they were drunk or sober), and the driver managed to convince the policeman that it was simply an error. The second time they were stopped they had just left a nightclub and were walking through an alley. Aaron stopped to urinate and the boys began making obscene remarks. A foot patrolman came into the alley, lectured the boys and sent them home. Before the boys got to the car one began talking in a loud voice again. The policeman, who had followed them down the alley, arrested this boy for disturbing the peace and took him to the police station where the other Saints gathered. After paying a $5.00 fine, and with the assurance that there would be no permanent record of the arrest, the boy was released.

The boys had a spirit of frivolity and fun about their escapades. They did not view what they were engaged in as "delinquency," though it surely was by any reasonable definition of that word. They simply viewed themselves as having a little fun and who, they would ask, was really hurt by it? The answer had to be no one, although this fact remains one of the most difficult things to explain about the gang's behavior. Unlikely though it seems, in two years of drinking, driving, carousing and vandalism no one was seriously injured as a result of the Saints' activities.

THE SAINTS IN SCHOOL

The Saints were highly successful in school. The average grade for the group was "B," with two of the boys having close to a straight "A" average. Almost all of the boys were popular and many of them held offices in the school. One of the boys was vice-president of the student body one year. Six of the boys played on athletic teams.

At the end of their senior year, the student body selected ten seniors for special recognition as the "school wheels"; four of the ten were Saints.

Teachers and school officials saw no problem with any of these boys and anticipated that they would all "make something of themselves."

How the boys managed to maintain this impression is surprising in view of their actual behavior while in school. Their technique for covering truancy was so successful that teachers did not even realize that the boys were absent from school much of the time. Occasionally, of course, the system would backfire and then the boy was on his own. A boy who was caught would be most contrite, would plead guilty and ask for mercy. He inevitably got the mercy he sought.

Cheating on examinations was rampant, even to the point of orally communicating answers to exams as well as looking at one another's papers. Since none of the group studied, and since they were primarily dependent on one another for help, it is surprising that grades were so high. Teachers contributed to the deception in their admitted inclination to give these boys (and presumably others like them) the benefit of the doubt. When asked how the boys did in school, and when pressed on specific examinations, teachers might admit that they were disappointed in John's performance, but would quickly add that they "knew he was capable of doing better," so John was given a higher grade than he had actually earned. How often this happened is impossible to know. During the time that I observed the group, I never saw any of the boys take homework home. Teachers may have been "understanding" very regularly.

One exception to the gang's generally good performance was Jerry, who had a "C" average in his junior year, experienced disaster the next year and failed to graduate. Jerry had always been a little more nonchalant than the others about the liberties he took in school. Rather than wait for someone to come get him from class, he would offer his own excuse and leave. Although he probably did not miss any more classes than most of the others in the group, he did not take the requisite pains to cover his absences. Jerry was the only Saint whom I ever heard talk back to a teacher. Although teachers often called him a "cut up" or a "smart kid," they never referred to him as a troublemaker or as a kid headed for trouble. It seems likely, then, that Jerry's failure his senior year and his mediocre performance his junior year were consequences of his not playing the game the proper way (possibly because he was disturbed by his parents' divorce). His teachers regarded him as "immature" and not quite ready to get out of high school.

THE POLICE AND THE SAINTS

The local police saw the Saints as good boys who were among the leaders of the youth in the community. Rarely, the boys might be stopped in town for speeding or for running a stop sign. When this happened the boys were always polite, contrite and pled for mercy. As in school, they received the mercy they asked for. None ever received a ticket or was taken into the precinct by the local police.

The situation in Big City, where the boys engaged in most of their delinquency, was only slightly different. The police there did not know the boys at all, although occasionally the boys were stopped by a patrolman. Once they were caught taking a lantern from a construction site. Another time they were stopped for running a stop sign, and on several occasions they were stopped for speeding. Their behavior was as before: contrite, polite and penitent. The urban police, like the local police, accepted their demeanor as sincere. More important, the urban police were convinced that these were good boys just out for a lark.

THE ROUGHNECKS

Hanibal townspeople never perceived the Saints' high level of delinquency. The Saints were good boys who just went in for an occasional prank. After all, they were well dressed, well mannered and had nice cars. The Roughnecks were a different story. Although the two gangs of boys were the same age, and both groups engaged in an equal amount of wild-oat sowing, everyone agreed that the not-so-well-dressed, not-so-well-mannered, not-so-rich boys were heading for trouble. Townspeople would say, "You can see the gang members at the drugstore night after night, leaning against the storefront (sometimes drunk) or slouching around inside buying cokes, reading magazines, and probably stealing old Mr. Wall blind. When they are outside and girls walk by, even respectable girls, these boys make suggestive remarks. Sometimes their remarks are downright lewd."

From the community's viewpoint, the real indication that these kids were in for trouble was that they were constantly involved with the police. Some of them had been picked up for stealing, mostly small stuff, of course, "but still it's stealing small stuff that leads to big time crimes." "Too bad," people said. "Too bad that these boys couldn't behave like the other kids in town; stay out of trouble, be polite to adults, and look to their future."

The community's impression of the degree to which this group of six boys (ranging in age from 16 to 19) engaged in delinquency was somewhat distorted. In some ways the gang was more delinquent than the community thought; in other ways it was less.

The fighting activities of the group were fairly readily and accurately perceived by almost everyone. At least once a month, the boys would get into some sort of fight, although most fights were scraps between members of the group or involved only one member of the group and some peripheral hanger-on. Only three times in the period of observation did the group fight together: once against a gang from across town, once against two blacks and once against a group of boys from another school. For the first two fights the group went out "looking for trouble"—and they found it both times. The third fight followed a football game and began spontaneously with an argument on the football field between one of the Roughnecks and a member of the opposition's football team.

Jack had a particular propensity for fighting and was involved in most of the brawls. He was a prime mover of the escalation of arguments into fights.

More serious than fighting, had the community been aware of it, was theft. Although almost everyone was aware that the boys occasionally stole things, they did not realize the extent of the activity. Petty stealing was a frequent event for the Roughnecks. Sometimes they stole as a group and coordinated their efforts; other times they stole in pairs. Rarely did they steal alone.

The thefts ranged from very small things like paperback books, comics and ballpoint pens to expensive items like watches. The nature of the thefts varied from time to time. The gang would go through a period of systematically lifting items from automobiles or school lockers. Types of thievery varied with the whim of the gang. Some forms of thievery were more profitable than others, but all thefts were for profit, not just thrills.

Roughnecks siphoned gasoline from cars as often as they had access to an automobile, which was not very often. Unlike the Saints, who owned their own cars, the Roughnecks would have to borrow their parents' cars, an event which occurred only eight or nine times a year. The boys claimed to have stolen cars for joy rides from time to time.

Ron committed the most serious of the group's offenses. With an unidentified associate the boy attempted to burglarize a gasoline station. Although this station had been robbed twice previously in the same month, Ron denied any involvement in either of the other thefts. When Ron and his accomplice approached the station, the owner was hiding in the bushes beside the station. He fired both barrels of a double-barreled shotgun at the boys. Ron was severely injured; the other boy ran away and was never caught. Though he remained in critical condition for several months, Ron finally recovered and served six months of the following year in reform school. Upon release from reform school, Ron was put back a grade in school, and began running around with a different gang of boys. The Roughnecks considered the new gang less delinquent than themselves, and during the following year Ron had no more trouble with the police.

The Roughnecks, then, engaged mainly in three types of delinquency: theft, drinking and fighting. Although community members perceived that this gang of kids was delinquent, they mistakenly believed that their illegal activities were primarily drinking, fighting and being a nuisance to passersby. Drinking was limited among the gang members, although it did occur, and theft was much more prevalent than anyone realized.

Drinking would doubtless have been more prevalent had the boys had ready access to liquor. Since they rarely had automobiles at their disposal, they could not travel very far, and the bars in town would not serve them. Most of the boys had little money, and this, too, inhibited their purchase of alcohol. Their major source of liquor was a local drunk who would buy them a fifth if they would give him enough extra to buy himself a pint of whiskey or a bottle of wine.

The community's perception of drinking as prevalent stemmed from the fact that it was the most obvious delinquency the boys engaged in. When one of the boys had been drinking, even a casual observer seeing him on the corner would suspect that he was high.

There was a high level of mutual distrust and dislike between the Roughnecks and the police. The boys felt very strongly that the police were unfair and corrupt. Some evidence existed that the boys were correct in their perception.

The main source of the boys' dislike for the police undoubtedly stemmed from the fact that the police would sporadically harass the group. From the standpoint of the boys, these acts of occasional enforcement of the law were whimsical and uncalled for. It made no sense to them, for example, that the police would come to the corner occasionally and threaten them with arrest for loitering when the night before the boys had been out siphoning gasoline from cars and the police had been nowhere in sight. To the boys, the police were stupid on the one hand, for not being where they should have been and catching the boys in a serious offense, and unfair on the other hand, for trumping up "loitering" charges against them.

From the viewpoint of the police, the situation was quite different. They knew, with all the confidence necessary to be a policeman, that these boys were engaged in criminal activities. They knew this partly from occasionally catching them, mostly from circumstantial evidence ("the boys were around when those tires were slashed"), and partly because the police shared the view of the community in general that this was a bad bunch of boys. The best the police could hope to do was to be sensitive to the fact that these boys were engaged in illegal acts and arrest them whenever there was some evidence that they had been involved. Whether or not the boys had in fact committed a particular act in a particular way was not especially important. The police had a broader view: their job was to stamp out these kids' crimes; the tactics were not as important as the end result.

Over the period that the group was under observation, each member was arrested at least once. Several of the boys were arrested a number of times and spent at least one night in jail. While most were never taken to court, two of the boys were sentenced to six months' incarceration in boys' schools.

THE ROUGHNECKS IN SCHOOL

The Roughnecks' behavior in school was not particularly disruptive. During school hours they did not all hang around together, but tended instead to spend most of their time with one or two other members of the gang who were their special buddies. Although every member of the gang attempted to avoid school as much as possible, they were not particularly successful and most of them attended school with surprising regularity. They considered school a burden—something to be gotten through with a minimum of conflict. If they were "bugged" by a particular teacher, it could lead to trouble. One of the boys, Al, once threatened to beat up a teacher and, according to the other boys, the teacher hid under a desk to escape him.

Teachers saw the boys the way the general community did, as heading for trouble, as being uninterested in making something of themselves. Some were also seen as being incapable of meeting the academic standards of the school. Most of the teachers expressed concern for this group of boys and were willing to pass them despite poor performance, in the belief that failing them would only aggravate the problem.

The group of boys had a grade point average just slightly above "C." No one in the group failed either grade, and no one had better than a "C" average. They were very consistent in their achievement or, at least, the teachers were consistent in their perception of the boys' achievement.

Two of the boys were good football players. Herb was acknowledged to be the best player in the school and Jack was almost as good. Both boys were criticized for their failure to abide by training rules, for refusing to come to practice as often as they should, and for not playing their best during practice. What they lacked in sportsmanship they made up for in skill, apparently, and played every game no matter how poorly they had performed in practice or how many practice sessions they had missed.

TWO QUESTIONS

Why did the community, the school and the police react to the Saints as though they were good, upstanding, nondelinquent youths with bright futures but to the Roughnecks as though they were tough, young criminals who were headed for trouble? Why did the Roughnecks and the Saints in fact have quite different careers after high school—careers which, by and large, lived up to the expectations of the community?

The most obvious explanation for the differences in the community's and law enforcement agencies' reactions to the two gangs is that one group of boys was "more delinquent" than the other. Which group *was* more delinquent? The answer to this question will determine in part how we explain the differential responses to these groups by the members of the community and, particularly, by law enforcement and school officials.

In sheer number of illegal acts, the Saints were the more delinquent. They were truant from school for at least part of the day almost every day of the week. In addition, their drinking and vandalism occurred with surprising regularity. The Roughnecks, in contrast, engaged sporadically in delinquent episodes. While these episodes were frequent, they certainly did not occur on a daily or even a weekly basis.

The difference in frequency of offenses was probably caused by the Roughnecks' inability to obtain liquor and to manipulate legitimate excuses from school. Since the Roughnecks had less money than the Saints, and teachers carefully supervised their school activities, the Roughnecks' hearts may have been as black as the Saints', but their misdeeds were not nearly as frequent.

There are really no clear-cut criteria by which to measure qualitative differences in antisocial behavior. The most important dimension of the difference is generally referred to as the "seriousness" of the offenses.

If seriousness encompasses the relative economic costs of delinquent acts, then some assessment can be made. The Roughnecks probably stole an average of about $5.00 worth of goods a week. Some weeks the figure was considerably higher, but these times must be balanced against long periods when almost nothing was stolen.

The Saints were more continuously engaged in delinquency but their acts were not for the most part costly to property. Only their vandalism and occasional theft of gasoline would so qualify. Perhaps once or twice a month they would siphon a tankful of gas. The other costly items were street signs, construction lanterns and the like. All of these acts combined probably did not quite average $5.00 a week, partly because much of the stolen equipment was abandoned and presumably could be recovered. The difference in cost of stolen property between the two groups was trivial, but the Roughnecks probably had a slightly more expensive set of activities than did the Saints.

Another meaning of seriousness is the potential threat of physical harm to members of the community and to the boys themselves. The Roughnecks were more prone to physical violence; they not only welcomed an opportunity to fight; they went seeking it. In addition, they fought among themselves frequently. Although the fighting never included deadly weapons, it was still a menace, however minor, to the physical safety of those involved.

The Saints never fought. They avoided physical conflict both inside and outside the group. At the same time, though, the Saints frequently endangered their own and other people's lives. They did so almost every time they drove a car, especially if they had been drinking. Sober, their driving was risky; under the influence of alcohol it was horrendous. In addition, the Saints endangered the lives of others with their pranks. Street excavations left unmarked were a very serious hazard.

Evaluating the relative seriousness of the two gangs' activities is difficult. The community reacted as though the behavior of the Roughnecks was a problem, and they reacted as though the behavior of the Saints was not. But the members of the community were ignorant of the array of delinquent acts that characterized the Saints' behavior. Although concerned citizens were unaware of much of the Roughnecks' behavior as well, they were much better informed about the Roughnecks' involvement in delinquency than they were about the Saints'.

VISIBILITY

Differential treatment of the two gangs resulted in part because one gang was infinitely more visible than the other. This differential visibility was a direct function of the economic standing of the families. The Saints had access to automobiles and were able to remove themselves from the sight of the community. In as routine a decision as to where to go to have a milkshake after school, the Saints stayed away from the mainstream of community life. Lacking transportation, the Roughnecks could not make it to the edge of town. The center of town was the only practical place for them to meet since their homes were scattered throughout the town and any noncentral meeting place put an undue hardship on some members. Through necessity the Roughnecks congregated in a crowded area where everyone in the community passed frequently, including teachers and law enforcement officers. They could easily see the Roughnecks hanging around the drugstore.

The Roughnecks, of course, made themselves even more visible by making remarks to passersby and by occasionally getting into fights on the corner. Meanwhile, just as regularly, the Saints were either at the cafe on one edge of town or in the pool hall at the other edge of town. Without any particular realization that they were making themselves inconspicuous, the Saints were able to hide their time-wasting. Not only were they removed from the mainstream of traffic, but they were almost always inside a building.

On their escapades the Saints were also relatively invisible, since they left Hanibal and travelled to Big City. Here, too, they were mobile, roaming the city, rarely going to the same area twice.

DEMEANOR

To the notion of visibility must be added the difference in the responses of group members to outside intervention with their activities. If one of the Saints was confronted with an accusing policeman, even if he felt he was truly innocent of a wrongdoing, his demeanor was apologetic and penitent. A Roughneck's attitude was almost the polar opposite. When confronted with a threatening adult authority, even one who tried to be pleasant, the Roughneck's hostility and disdain were clearly observable. Sometimes he might attempt to put up a veneer of respect, but it was thin and was not accepted as sincere by the authority.

School was no different from the community at large. The Saints could manipulate the system by feigning compliance with the school norms. The availability of cars at school meant that once free from the immediate sight of the teacher, the boys could disappear rapidly. And this escape was well enough planned that no administrator or teacher was nearby when the boys left. A Roughneck who wished to escape for a few hours was in a bind. If it were possible to get free from class, downtown was still a mile away, and even if he arrived there, he was still very visible. Truancy for the Roughnecks meant almost certain detection, while the Saints enjoyed almost complete immunity from sanctions.

BIAS

Community members were not aware of the transgressions of the Saints. Even if the Saints had been less discreet, their favorite delinquencies would have been perceived as less serious than those of the Roughnecks.

In the eyes of the police and school officials, a boy who drinks in an alley and stands intoxicated on the street corner is committing a more serious offense than is a boy who drinks to inebriation in a nightclub or a tavern and drives around afterwards in a car. Similarly, a boy who steals a wallet from a store will be viewed as having committed a more serious offense than a boy who steals a lantern from a construction site.

Perceptual bias also operates with respect to the demeanor of the boys in the two groups when they are confronted by adults. It is not simply that adults dislike the posture affected by boys of the Roughneck ilk; more important is the conviction that the posture adopted by the Roughnecks is an indication of their devotion and commitment to deviance as a way of life. The posture becomes a cue, just as the type of the offense is a cue, to the degree to which the known transgressions are indicators of the youths' potential for other problems.

Visibility, demeanor and bias are surface variables which explain the day-to-day operations of the police. Why do these surface variables operate as they do? Why did the police choose to disregard the Saints' delinquencies while breathing down the backs of the Roughnecks?

The answer lies in the class structure of American society and the control of legal institutions by those at the top of the class structure. Obviously, no representative of the upper class drew up the operational chart for the police which led them to look in the ghettoes and on street corners—which led them to see the demeanor of lower-class youth as troublesome and that of upper-middle-class youth as tolerable. Rather, the procedures simply developed from experience—experience with irate and influential upper-middle-class parents insisting that their son's vandalism was simply a prank and his drunkenness only a momentary "sowing of wild oats"—experience with cooperative or indifferent, powerless, lower-class parents who acquiesced to the laws' definition of their son's behavior.

ADULT CAREERS OF THE SAINTS AND THE ROUGHNECKS

The community's confidence in the potential of the Saints and the Roughnecks apparently was justified. If anything, the community members underestimated the degree to which these youngsters would turn out "good" or "bad."

Seven of the eight members of the Saints went on to college immediately after high school. Five of the boys graduated from college in four years. The sixth one finished college after two years in the army, and the seventh spent four years in the air force before returning to college and receiving a B.A. degree. Of these seven college graduates, three went on for advanced degrees. One finished law school and is now active in state politics, one finished medical school and is practicing near Hanibal, and one boy is now working for a Ph.D. The other four college graduates entered submanagerial, managerial or executive training positions with larger firms.

The only Saint who did not complete college was Jerry. Jerry had failed to graduate from high school with the other Saints. During his second senior year, after the other Saints had gone on to college, Jerry began to hang around with what several teachers described as a "rough crowd"—the gang that was heir apparent to the Roughnecks. At the end of his second senior year, when he did graduate from high school, Jerry took a job as a used-car salesman, got married and quickly had a child. Although he made several abortive attempts to go to college by attending night school, when I last saw him (ten years after high school) Jerry was unemployed and had been living on unemployment for almost a year. His wife worked as a waitress.

Some of the Roughnecks have lived up to community expectations. A number of them were headed for trouble. A few were not.

Jack and Herb were the athletes among the Roughnecks and their athletic prowess paid off handsomely. Both boys received unsolicited athletic scholarships to college. After Herb received his scholarship (near the end of his senior year), he apparently did an about-face. His demeanor became very similar to that of the Saints. Although he remained a member in good standing of the Roughnecks, he stopped participating in most activities and did not hang out on the corner as often.

Jack did not change. If anything, he became more prone to fighting. He even made excuses for accepting the scholarship. He told the other gang members that the school had guaranteed him a "C" average if he would come to play football—an idea that seems far-fetched, even in this day of highly competitive recruiting.

During the summer after graduation from high school, Jack attempted suicide by jumping from a tall building. The jump would certainly have killed most people trying it, but Jack survived. He entered college in the fall and played four years of football. He and Herb graduated in four years, and both are teaching and coaching in high schools. They are married and have stable families. If anything, Jack appears to have a more prestigious position in the community than does Herb, though both are well respected and secure in their positions.

Two of the boys never finished high school. Tommy left at the end of his junior year and went to another state. That summer he was arrested and placed on probation on a manslaughter charge. Three years later he was arrested for murder; he pleaded guilty to second degree murder and is serving a 30-year sentence in the state penitentiary.

Al, the other boy who did not finish high school, also left the state in his senior year. He is serving a life sentence in a state penitentiary for first degree murder.

Wes is a small-time gambler. He finished high school and "bummed around." After several years he made contact with a bookmaker who employed him as a runner. Later he acquired his own area and has been working it ever since. His position among the bookmakers is almost identical to the position he had in the gang; he is always around but no one is really aware of him. He makes no trouble and he does not get into any. Steady, reliable, capable of keeping his mouth closed, he plays the game by the rules, even though the game is an illegal one.

That leaves only Ron. Some of his former friends reported that they had heard he was "driving a truck up north," but no one could provide any concrete information.

REINFORCEMENT

The community responded to the Roughnecks as boys in trouble, and the boys agreed with that perception. Their pattern of deviancy was reinforced, and breaking away from it became increasingly unlikely. Once the boys acquired an image of themselves as deviants, they selected new friends who affirmed that self-image. As that self-conception became more firmly entrenched, they also became willing to try new and more extreme deviances. With their growing alienation came freer expression of disrespect and hostility for representatives of the legitimate society. This disrespect increased the community's negativism, perpetuating the entire process of commitment to deviance. Lack of a commitment to deviance works the same way. In either case, the process will perpetuate itself unless some event (like a scholarship to college or a sudden failure) external to the established relationship intervenes. For two of the Roughnecks (Herb and Jack), receiving college athletic scholarships created new relations and culminated in a break with the established pattern of deviance. In the case of one of the Saints (Jerry), his parents' divorce and his failing to graduate from high school changed some of his other relations. Being held back in school for a year and losing his place among the Saints had sufficient impact on Jerry to alter his self-image and virtually to assure that he would not go on to college as his peers did. Although the experiments of life can rarely be reversed, it seems likely in view of the behavior of the other boys who did not enjoy this special treatment by the school that Jerry, too, would have "become something" had he graduated as anticipated. For Herb and Jack outside intervention worked to their advantage; for Jerry it was his undoing.

Selective perception and labelling—finding, processing and punishing some kinds of criminality and not others—means that visible, poor, non-mobile, outspoken, undiplomatic "tough" kids will be noticed, whether their actions are seriously delinquent or not. Other kids, who have established a reputation for being bright (even though underachieving), disciplined and involved in respectable activities, who are mobile and monied, will be invisible when they deviate from sanctioned activities. They'll sow their wild oats—perhaps even wider and thicker than their lower-class cohorts—but they won't be noticed. When it's time to leave adolescence most will follow the expected path, settling into the ways of the middle class, remembering fondly the delinquent but unnoticed fling of their youth. The Roughnecks and others like them may turn around, too. It is more likely that their noticeable deviance will have been so reinforced by police and community that their lives will be effectively channelled into careers consistent with their adolescent background.

A CRITIQUE OF LABELING

Gwynn Nettler

The labeling perspective is more interested in definitions of deviance than in deviant behaviors per se. Thus, it is less concerned with what so-called deviants actually do than with how others react. The advantage of the labeling perspective, Nettler says, is that it helps us see that in some cases people respond more to labels than to actual behaviors, and that by doing so they sometimes produce the very behaviors they condemn. In terms of explaining crime, however, Nettler does not think the labeling perspective is very useful. Specifically, it fails to predict or explain criminal behavior, it uses circular reasoning in treating the response to crime as the cause of crime, and it cannot tell us how to reduce criminal behavior.

The most popular new set of ideas employed by sociologists to explain crime is a bundle of assumptions known as the "labeling" hypothesis. This hypothesis depends heavily upon the belief that social relations are "constructed," that reality is defined and interpreted before it becomes meaningful. This is a way of saying that we act in terms of the *meanings* attributed to events rather than to objective events. Conditions, it is said, are *defined* before they are reacted to. How we respond to each other is a function of the way we have categorized each other and of the significance we have assigned to our interactions.

From this point of view, "crime" is a word, not an act. Crime is socially defined and criminals are socially "produced" in a process which allows majorities to apply labels to minorities and which, in many cases, permits majorities to enforce the consequences of this labeling. As a result, the "labeled" person—the stigmatized person—may be unable to act in any way different from the role ascribed to him.

THE TRANSCENDENCE OF ROLES OVER BEHAVIORS

Labeling theory emphasizes the processes of human interaction that result in the attribution and acceptance of *roles*. The emphasis upon role con-

From Gwynn Nettler, *Explaining Crime*, pp. 202–12. Copyright © 1974 by McGraw-Hill, Inc. Reprinted by permission of the McGraw-Hill Book Company.

struction calls attention to the way behavior may be shaped by the expectations of those with whom one is interacting and to the way our perceptions of each other are reinforced by the early assignment of labels to samples of our acts. Once roles are defined, clusters of attributes are inferred. Such inference stimulates a selective perception that permits a linking together of diverse acts under some meaningful label (Turner, 1972, p. 310).

The emphasis upon role formation means that less attention is paid to how people behave than to how they categorize each other on the basis of small segments of behavior. The tendency of the labeling theorist, then, is to deny or ignore differences in the ways in which people act and to stress the utility and the consequences of having the power to categorize. Throughout the literature, the prevailing sentiment is to deny differences and to cast doubt upon the validity and the justice of popular images of minorities.

TRANSLATING "CRIMINALITY" INTO "DEVIANCE"

Given this attitude toward difference, the labeling theorists find it more convenient to talk about "deviance" than about "criminality." This translation directs attention to the fact that majorities are reacting to minorities and that it is being different in the sense of being powerless because of small numbers that permits arrest, censure, and punishment to be attached to a difference.

Such a viewpoint is, obviously, sympathetic to minorities. The labeling school has, consequently, been termed an "underdog philosophy." Its spokesmen ask, "Whose side are we on?" (Becker, 1967).

The philosophy of the underdog turns the tables on conventional thought. Instead of assuming that it is the deviant's difference which needs explanation, it asks why the majority responds to *this* difference as it does. This shift of the question reverses the normal conception of causation; the labeling school suggests that the other person's peculiarity has not caused us to regard him as different so much as our labeling has caused his peculiarity. This reversal, among other characteristics of the labeling hypothesis, has made the theory interesting and has contributed to its popularity (Davis, 1971).

Proponents of the labeling hypothesis distinguish between "primary deviance," that is, some offensive act, and "secondary deviance" (Lemert, 1951), that is, the process by which the reaction of society to an initial difference may confirm the deviant in the stigmatized behavior. Being cast out means being an outcast and makes it comfortable for stigmatized persons to band together in defense of their egos and in justification of their "peculiar" interests.

The labeling theorist deemphasizes the difference in the deviant. He holds that "initially" everyone deviates somewhat from some standards some of the time. What confirms the difference is some official attachment of a label to the apprehended deviant. The labeling theorist is concerned, then, to study how much deviance is produced by the very correctional agencies that are supposed to reduce difference. How much delinquency do reform schools manufacture? How much crime do prisons create? How much psychosis is perpetuated by mental hospitals?

What is to be explained is not so much the deviant as the people who have the power to attach the scarlet letter and thus to confirm the deviation. The labeling theorist sees the judicial response to crime as "the dramatization of evil" (Tannenbaum, 1938).

IMPLICATIONS FOR METHODOLOGY

The research method advocated by the labeling theorist is intensive observation of labelers and their victims. Field work is preferred to the collection of statistics. The result of such study is a description of how the labeler comes to recognize and define the deviant and of how the deviant reacts to and interprets his own world. The test of the adequacy of such a description is understanding and insight rather than prediction and control.

As compared with statistical and experimental studies, the reportorial field work recommended by the labeling theorist is more fun for students. It is good sport to engage in "participant observation," particularly among people who are "different." To this element of pleasure, labeling theory has added the advocacy of the "rights" of minorities. Its appreciative methodology and its political stance have combined to make it a fashionable way of thinking about undesirable behaviors and "social problems." The fashion has spread from its application to crime and has been extended, with variations, to attempts to understand blindness (Scott, 1969), stuttering (Lemert, 1967), illness (Lorber, 1967), civil disturbances (Turner, 1969), "welfarism" (Beck, 1967), paranoia (Lemert, 1962), death and dying (Sudnow, 1966), mental retardation (Mercer, 1965), and neurosis and psychosis (Braginsky et al., 1969; Plog and Edgerton, 1969; Scheff, 1966). An evaluation of this popular mode of explanation must recognize both its advantages and its liabilities.

THE ADVANTAGES OF THE LABELING HYPOTHESIS

The value of the labeling hypothesis lies in its attention to the possibilities that (1) people may respond more to their definitions of others than to the behaviors of others and (2) stigmatizing definitions may produce the bad behaviors they condemn.

1. *The labeling hypothesis asks "society" whether it is reacting to the deviant's behavior or to its own definition of the deviance.* The idea that deviance is produced in some process of interaction that results in our pinning tags on each other calls attention to the possible inaccuracy of the names we apply. To say that "deviance" is created by labeling is to suggest that the labels may be inappropriate, and to raise the question whether we are responding more to what the other person did or more to the image of the other person that is called up by the name we have given him.

This is a valuable question, and it deserves a scientific answer. Thus far, the answer has been assumed by the labeling theorists rather than tested. This assumption partakes of a tradition in social psychology that has itself applied a label to the common-sense categories which most of us use to order our social worlds. The label applied by social psychologists to such popular concepts is "stereotype." Calling a popular image a "stereotype" assumes, without adequate evidence, that the ordinary citizen's notions about the "different" kinds of people around him are mostly wrong. However, the sociopsychological assumption itself seems more false than true. The few studies that have attempted to test the accuracy of popular images have shown that "stereotypes" are more accurate than inaccurate. This has been found true of popular perceptions of occupations (Rice, 1928) and of ethnic groups (Mackie, 1971, 1973). No adequate research has yet been completed on the validity of popular images of various kinds of criminals, although one such study is under way (Solhaug, 1972). Until some research on this matter has been completed, we can appreciate the point made by the labeling theorists without subscribing to it.

2. *The labeling hypothesis alerts us to the possibility that official reactions to some disapproved behaviors may do more harm than good.* The chief value of the labeling hypothesis has been to call attention to the possibility that official reactions to some kinds of disapproved behaviors may confirm the actors in their deviant ways. It is suggested, for example, that some "sick behaviors" improve more rapidly when they are untreated and that some cures are worse than the diseases they treat.

The labeling theorist emphasizes how minor events in the stream of life may become major events through official reaction. The careers of some different kinds of people are made even more different by the fact that some portion of their lives must be spent in dodging the consequences of the official response to their deviance. The model here is that of the marijuana user,[1] whose life may be changed by the criminalization of his preference.

Labeling theory gains credence as it develops biographies showing that being "officially handled" increases the chances of future official attention. There is evidence that some part of this risk is incurred by the discrimination associated with a criminal label. *There is no way of knowing, however, how much of repeated offense is so caused.*

The labeling hypothesis could prove more useful if its ideas were associated with a taxonomy of offenders in such a way that we might know who could be best "saved" from future criminality by ignoring his present offense. This is not an easy question.[2] It is, however, part of what probation is about.

The labeling hypothesis is politically important because it challenges the *status quo*. This is congenial to revolutionaries, of course, whose ideology translates the label "convict" as "political prisoner." Less radically, the labeling hypothesis stimulates thinking about the costs of applying the criminal law to certain categories of disapproved behaviors. It suggests that there may be limits to the efficacy of the legal sanction (Packer, 1968) and urges assessment of the relative costs and benefits of the criminalization or decriminalization of immoral, peculiar, or unhealthful conduct.

THE LIABILITIES OF THE LABELING PERSPECTIVE

(1) Labeling theory has been criticized for ignoring the differences in behavior described by labels. The labeling schema draws attention from deeds to the public definitions of those deeds. Such diversion means that (2) labeling theory does not increase, and may well decrease, our ability to predict individual behavior. Its low predictive power is a result not only of its neglect of individual differences but also of the fact that (3) it contains a defective model of causation. This in turn means that (4) its relevance to social policy is lessened. Each of these points will be amplified.

1. *Labeling theory does not explain the behaviors that lead to the application of labels.* The labeling theorists argue as if popular and legal categories were devoid of content, as if they were never "well earned." The labeling explanation pays little or no attention to the fact that people do *not* behave similarly. It slights the possibility that a label may *correctly* identify consistent differences in conduct, and it pays little attention to the reasons why "society" continues to apply a label once it has been used.

Labeling theory denies, therefore, the causal importance and explanatory value of personality variables. In fact, labeling theorists regard as futile the search for personality differences that might distinguish categories of more or less criminal persons. The labeling hypothesis prefers a political interpretation to such a psychological one. It prefers to believe that deviants are minorities lacking power to challenge the rules by which a majority has labeled them. The theory denies, then, that a label may be properly applied to describe personality differences which may underlie real behavioral differences. This denial has unfortunate consequences for the prediction of individual behavior.

It has unfortunate consequences, too, for the development of public policy. The prescription that follows from the labeling hypothesis is to change the attitudes of majorities toward misbehaving minorities. In reply, majorities tell us that they are not yet convinced that a more compassionate attitude toward the robber or the burglar will change the offender's behavior and reduce the pain he gives.

2. *When applied to the understanding of individual behavior, the labeling hypothesis has low predictive power.* The low predictive power of labeling theory results from its denial of personality differences. The interactional bias of the labeling theorist encourages such optimistic but risky beliefs as these:

> He will be honest if I trust him.
> She will be reasonable if you are.
> He will be pacific if we are.
> Her psychosis is not "in her," but "in her situation." When the mirrors in which she sees herself are changed, she will change.

On the contrary, there *are* personality differences that are reliably associated with behavioral differences and that are remarkably persistent. These persistent ways of feeling and acting are not readily changeable with changes in the labels attached to them. Regardless of what we have been called, *most of us continue to be what we have been a long time becoming.*

The research literature on this subject is vast. It may be sampled in the works of Honzik (1966), Kelly (1963), Mischel (1969), Robins and O'Neal (1958), Roff (1961), Schaefer and Bayley (1960), Thomas et al. (1970), Witkin (1965), and Zax et al. (1968). The point is made in the autobiography of the playwright S. N. Behrman (1972) who, after years of failure and impoverished struggle, wrote a play that was a hit. Behrman comments, "With the production of a successful play, . . . you acquire overnight a new identity—a public label. But this label is pasted on you. It doesn't obliterate what you are and have always been—doesn't erase the stigmata of temperament" (p. 37).

The statement that there are persistent temperamental and cognitive differences underlying our behaviors can be qualified by adding that such personality variables have more of an impact upon behavior as circumstances are equalized. Nevertheless, most of us can tell the difference between behavior—our own and others'—that is only situationally reactive and behavior that is characteristic. All of us operate, implicitly or explicitly, with the idea of *character*—the idea that there *are* enduring personal predispositions relevant to moral behavior. This means that, unless there are tremendous changes in environments, people are likely to continue to behave as they have behaved. Against the optimistic recommendations of the interactionist, it seems more sensible to believe that:

> The embezzler may need to be arrested, and stigmatized, before he "turns honest."
> Being reasonable with a fanatic is futile.

A soft answer turns away the wrath of some men, but not of others, and there is no point in pleading for your life with a Charles Manson.

The cures of psychoses are exceptional. Most people who are "peculiar" are not disordered in all ways, all the time. Misbehavior may be episodic; but ordinarily, safety lies in the assumption of behavioral continuity.

3. *The model of causation implicit in the labeling hypothesis is questionable.* Every explanation of human behavior makes assumptions about its causes. The labeling theory locates the causes of adult behavior in an unusual place—in the people who respond to it. It shifts the "responsibility" for my action from me to you. It stresses how much of what I do is a result of what you have done to me, and for me. My "self," it is said, is reflected to me by the social mirrors available to me. My "self" is the presumed agent of my actions, but my "self" is itself largely constructed by the responses of "significant others" to my initial efforts.

This is a shorthand statement of the hypothesis of "socialization." In its general formulation, there is no quarrel with such a hypothesis. All theories that would explain human behavior, including popular theories, assume that our behavior has been shaped by the actions of others. The sociopsychological hypotheses of the "control" variety pay particular attention to the "how" of this socialization process.

It is not denied, then, that how people respond to us when we misbehave may affect our subsequent conduct. The lively questions are, however, at what periods of our development, and to what degree, others mould us. What is at issue is *how much* of the adult behavior to be explained varies with the response of others to it.

It is our ignorance that permits the continuing quarrel, for no one knows which kinds of behaviors, in which kinds of personalities, at which "stage" of life, are affected how much, by which kinds of response, from which others, in which situations. Some generalization about this is part of our popular wisdom, but much of that is truistic. We expect more than truisms from criminological theories.

The valuable contributions of the labeling hypothesis have tended to obscure its deficiencies. It is one thing to study the way in which a defining process affects our response to the behavior of others. It is another matter to study the causes of the events we are defining. Studying how we respond to deviant others may suggest to us a more economical (more rational) mode of reacting. This suggestion should not be confused, however, with information about the causes of the crimes that concern us.

Such confusion is created when spokesmen of the labeling theory tell us, for example, that *"social groups create deviance by making the rules whose infraction constitutes deviance,* and by applying those rules to particular people and labeling them as outsiders" (Becker, 1963, p. 9). Some readers will translate statements like this as saying that "social groups create crime by making the laws whose infraction constitutes crime." This translation is slippery: it slides between the truth that social groups create the *definition* of "crime" and the falsehood that the *injuries* condemned by these definitions would disappear (or would not have been "created") if the definition had not been formulated. To the layman, it sounds as though the labeling theorist believed that people would not wish to defend themselves against burglary or murder if they had not learned a rule defining these acts as crimes. It sounds, also, as though the labeling theorist believed that there would be less "burglary" if we did not use that term. The non-professional consumer of criminological explanations recognizes this for the semantic trick that it is—the trick of saying, "If a crime is a breach of a rule, you won't have the crime if you don't have the rule." The ordinary reaction to this sematic sleight of hand is to say, "A mugging by any other name hurts just as much."

Applied to "real life" the labeling hypothesis functions as another of the "power of positive thinking" philosophies: "If disease is an error of thought, positive thinking will cure it." "If crime resides in our definitions of deviance, redefining it will change it."

Our question has to do with the location of causation. When the causation implied by the labeling hypothesis is tested, it fails. The causes specified by this schema do not account for the production of the behaviors that disturb us. "Mental hospitals" do not cause "mental illness" (Gove, 1970), nor do the agencies of social control, or the labels they apply, account for crime (Ward, 1971).

The assumption of labeling theory is that those who become "criminal" are mostly those who, while behaving much like everyone else, just happened to get tagged, or that those labeled "criminals" were more liable to the tagging because they fit some public's prejudiced stereotype of the criminal. Contrary to these assumptions, however, studies of the operation of the system of justice show that it works like a sieve: as we have seen, the people who end up caught in the sieve tend to be the more serious and persistent lawbreakers (Black and Reiss, 1970; Bordua, 1967; Terry, 1967).

In summary, the labeling theorist does not think about causes and effects, about antecedents and consequents; he prefers to think about interactions. This preference does not eliminate the idea of causation; it only obscures it by shifting the locus of causes from actors to their judges. This shift has some moral and political value in the fight between outsiders and insiders. It justifies a challenge of the police and the courts, or any other mechanism of social control, that would condemn the conduct of minorities. When the labeling hypothesis is applied to the explanation of the serious crimes, however, its model of causation reduces its value for public policy.

4. *On the level of social concerns, the labeling hypothesis does not an-*

swer the perennial questions about crime. We are reminded that explanatory theories are only as good as the questions they answer. The answers provided by the labeling theorists are not addressed to the questions about crime that are asked by most people. These questions are, again, "What causes crime?" "What accounts for increases or decreases in crime rates?" "How can crime be reduced?"

To these questions, the labeling theorists give no good reply. The policy recommendation of the labeling hypothesis comes down to "Avoid unnecessary labeling" (Schur, 1971, p. 171). This may be helpful in decriminalizing some activities. It is a recommendation that is already being followed in some areas, as in the euphemistic use of language that substitutes kind words for harsh ones—"sanitary engineer" for "garbage collector" and "special child" for "imbecile." Such transitions bespeak a change in attitude, yet the categories persist. Categorizing is an inevitable part of our response to the world. We should wish our categories to be clean, accurate, and useful, as social psychologists have urged. It is doubtful, however, whether attention to our vocabularies will tell citizens and public officials how better to reduce robbery and rape.

Notes

1. The labeling theorist's point can be made by substituting for marijuana the criminalization of any other chemical, like tobacco or alcohol, that many people habitually use.

2. The answer to this question is made difficult by the possible antagonism among the various goals of justice. The antagonism is the desire to rehabilitate some apprehended offenders, the need to deter others, and the need to express, through the symbolism of punishment, society's rejection of criminal conduct.

References

Beck, B. 1967. "Welfare as a moral category." *Social Problems* 14 (Winter): 258–277.

Becker, H.S. 1963. *Outsiders: Studies in the Sociology of Deviance.* Glencoe, Ill.: The Free Press.

———. 1967. "Whose side are we on?" *Social Problems* 14 (Winter): 239–247.

Behrman, S. N. 1972. "People in a diary, I." *The New Yorker* 48 (13 May): 36–94.

Black, D. J., and A. J. Reiss, Jr. 1970. "Police control of juveniles." *American Sociological Review* 35 (February): 63–77.

Bordua, D. J. 1967. "Recent trends: Deviant behavior and social control." *The An-*

nals of the American Academy of Political and Social Science 369 (January): 149–163.

Braginsky, B. M., et al. 1969. *Methods of Madness: The Mental Hospital as a Last Resort.* New York: Holt, Rinehart, and Winston, Inc.

Davis, M. S. 1971. "That's interesting!" *Philosophy of the Social Sciences* 1 (December): 309–344.

Gove, W. R. 1970. "Societal reaction as an explanation of mental illness: An evaluation." *American Sociological Review* 35 (October): 873–884.

Honzik, M. P. 1966. "Prediction of behavior from birth to maturity." In J. Rosenblith and W. Allinsmith (Eds.), *The Causes of Behavior.* Second Edition. Boston: Allyn and Bacon.

Kelly, E. L. 1963. "Consistency of the adult personality." *American Psychologist* 10 (November): 659–681.

Lemert, E. M. 1951. *Social Pathology.* New York: McGraw-Hill Book Company.

————. 1962. "Paranoia and the dynamics of exclusion." *Sociometry* 25 (March): 2–20.

————. 1967. *Human Deviance, Social Problems and Social Control.* Englewood Cliffs, N. J.: Prentice-Hall.

Lorber, J. 1967. "Deviance as performance: The case of illness." *Social Problems* 14 (Winter): 302–310.

Mackie, M. M. 1971. *The Accuracy of Folk Knowledge Concerning Alberta Indians, Hutterites and Ukrainians: An Available Data Stereotype Validation Technique.* Edmonton: The University of Alberta, Department of Sociology, Ph.D. dissertation.

————. 1973. "Arriving at 'truth' by definition: The case of stereotype inaccuracy." *Social Problems* 20 (Spring): 431–447.

Mercer, J. R. 1965. "Social system perspective and clinical perspective: Frames of reference for understanding career patterns of persons labelled as mentally retarded." *Social Problems* 13 (Summer): 18–34.

Mischel, W. 1969. "Continuity and change in personality." *American Psychologist* 24 (November): 1012–1018.

Packer, H. L. 1968. *The Limits of the Criminal Sanction.* Stanford: Stanford University Press.

Plog, S. C., and R. B. Edgerton (Eds.) 1969. *Changing Perspectives in Mental Illness.* New York: Holt, Rinehart, and Winston, Inc.

Rice, S. A. 1928. *Quantitative Methods in Politics.* New York: Alfred A. Knopf, Inc.

Robins, L. N., and P. O'Neal. 1958. "Mortality, mobility, and crime." *American Sociological Review* 23 (April): 162–171.

Roff, M. 1961. "Childhood social interaction and young adult bad conduct." *Journal of Abnormal and Social Psychology* 63 (September): 333–337.

Schaefer, E. S., and N. Bayley. 1960. "Consistency of maternal behavior from infancy to preadolescence." *Journal of Abnormal and Social Psychology* 61 (July): 1–6.

Scheff, T. J. 1966. *Being Mentally Ill.* Chicago: Aldine.

Schur, E. M. 1971. *Labeling Deviant Behavior: Its Sociological Implications.* New York: Harper and Row, Publishers.

Scott, R. A. 1969. *The Making of Blind Men.* New York: Russell Sage.

Solhaug, M. L. 1971. "Accuracy of 'bad men' stereotypes: A comparison of auto-stereotyping by lawbreakers with stereotyping by more lawful others." Edmonton: The University of Alberta, Department of Sociology. M. A. thesis prospectus.

Sudnow, D. 1966. *Passing On.* Englewood Cliffs, N. J.: Prentice-Hall.

Tannenbaum, F. 1938. *Crime and the Community.* Boston: Ginn and Company.

Terry, R. M. 1967. "Discrimination in the handling of juvenile offenders by social-control agencies." *Journal of Research in Crime and Delinquency* 4 (July): 218–230.

Thomas, A., et al. 1970. "The origin of personality." *Scientific American* 223 (August): 102–109.

Turner, R. H. 1969. "The public perception of protest." *American Sociological Review* 34 (December): 815–831.

———. 1972. "Deviance avowal as neutralization of commitment." *Social Problems* 19 (Winter): 308–321.

Ward, R. H. 1971. "The labeling theory: A critical analysis." *Criminology* 9 (August–November): 268–290.

Witkin, H. 1965. "Psychological differentiation and forms of pathology." *Journal of Abnormal Psychology* 70 (October): 317–336.

Zax, M., et al. 1968. "Follow-up study of children identified early as emotionally disturbed." *Journal of Consulting and Clinical Psychology* 32 (August): 369–374.

Questions for Discussion

1. What is the difference between master and subordinate statuses, on the one hand, and master and auxiliary status traits, on the other? How do these apply to "deviants"?

2. Provide examples of primary and secondary deviance. How can the institutionalization of the "mentally retarded" produce secondary deviance?

3. Contrast the way in which social class affects the social reaction to "juvenile delinquency" as opposed to "mental retardation." What do you think the reasons are for this difference?

4. Do you agree with Nettler's evaluation of the labeling perspective? Why or why not? How applicable are Nettler's criticisms to Mercer's and Chambliss's articles?

Selected References

Becker, Howard S. *Outsiders: Studies in the Sociology of Deviance.* New York: Free Press, 1963.

A succinct statement of the labeling perspective, together with some empirical studies of jazz musicians, marijuana use, and social controls on marijuana.

Glassner, Barry. "Labeling Theory." In *The Sociology of Deviance,* ed. M. Michael Rosenberg, Robert A. Stebbins, and Allan Turowetz. New York: St. Martin's Press, 1982, pp. 71–89.

Since the emergence of the labeling perspective some twenty-five years ago, there has been widespread popular acceptance and considerable critical commentary. Though Becker and Lemert have urged that "labeling" be examined beyond its original applications, according to Glassner it has not been. He counsels that three aspects of labeling be studied: categorical, contextual, and potential labeling.

Gove, Walter R., ed. *The Labelling of Deviance.* New York: Sage, 1975.

A collection of papers in which experts refute the alleged ability of the labeling perspective to account for alcoholism, drug addiction, mental retardation, and mental illness.

Harris, Anthony R., and Gary D. Hill. "The Social Psychology of Deviance: Toward a Reconciliation with Social Structure." *Annual Review of Sociology* 8. Palo Alto, Calif.: Annual Reviews, 1982, pp. 161–86.

Summarizes some of the literature which faults labeling explanations of deviance and social problems.

Lemert, Edwin M. *Social Pathology: A Systematic Approach to the Theory of Sociopathic Behavior.* New York: McGraw-Hill, 1951.

An early, influential, and systematic theory that centers its attention on the social reactions to rule-breaking behavior. Clearly a book that was ahead of its time.

Link, Bruce G., Francis T. Cullen, Elmer Struening, Patrick E. Shrout, and Bruce P. Dohrenwend. "A Modified Labeling Theory Approach to Mental Disorders." *American Sociological Review* 54 (June 1989): 400–423.

An empirical study which supports Scheff's labeling theory of mental illness. Mental patients, after their release from the hospital, anticipated rejection and adopted a role to defend against stigma (secondary deviance).

Plummer, Ken. "Misunderstanding Labelling Perspectives." In *Deviant Interpretations,* ed. David Downes and Paul Rock. New York: Barnes & Noble, 1979, pp. 85–121.

Plummer says that "the critics drastically overstate their case if they believe that they can announce the 'death' of labeling theory." He refutes charges that labeling theory has limited application and that when tested is usually found to be empirically wrong.

Rubington, Earl, and Martin S. Weinberg, eds. *Deviance: The Interactionist Perspective.* 5th ed. New York: Macmillan, 1987.

Broadened the labeling perspective and coined the term "interactionist perspective." The editors have amassed some fifty-five articles and organized them according to their relevance for the labeling perspective.

Scheff, Thomas J. *Being Mentally Ill: A Sociological Theory.* Rev. ed. New York: Aldine de Gruyter, 1984.

The revised edition of this systematic explanation of mental illness by means of the labeling perspective includes the theory as first expounded in 1966, a discussion of the considerable debate it engendered among sociologists, and research since its first publication that lends support to the theory.

Schneider, Joseph W. "Social Problems Theory: The Constructionist View." *Annual Review of Sociology* 11. Palo Alto, Calif.: Annual Reviews, 1985, pp. 209–29.

Schneider outlines the social constructionist argument, reviews almost thirty papers published in the journal *Social Problems* that apply this perspective to a diversity of social problems, and notes strong and weak points of this approach.

Schur, Edwin M. *Labeling Deviant Behavior: Its Sociological Implications.* New York: Harper & Row, 1971.

Codifies a number of propositions on the development and application of deviant labels and on their personal, organizational, and social consequences.

Schur, Edwin M. *Labeling Women Deviant: Gender, Stigma, and Social Control.* New York: Random House, 1984.

Schur reviews a number of studies of gender and applies the labeling perspective to the social situations of women. Inequality between the genders establishes the conditions under which women come to be defined as deviant if they either fail to act as women are "expected to" or act "like men." He demonstrates how the basic concepts of the labeling perspective help to account for how men and women come to define certain women as deviant and the effects of those definitions on their self-concepts and life chances.

Scull, Andrew T. "Deviance and Social Control." In *Handbook of Sociology,* ed. Neil Smelser. Newbury Park, Calif.: Sage, 1988, pp. 667–93.

In this review article, Scull argues that the labeling perspective cannot account for the simultaneous presence of deviant behavior and the absence of its presumed effective cause, social control.

7 / CRITICAL PERSPECTIVE

All societies and their cultures experience change. As part of the culture, perspectives on social problems also change. As we have seen, a sense of crisis in a society affects thinkers who try to develop a comprehensive understanding of the society and its problems. And, in a similar fashion, a sense of crisis within the discipline of sociology fosters the development of new perspectives on social problems. Thus, the emergence of a new perspective generally signifies that current perspectives do not explain social problems in a whole or consistent manner. Such a situation led to the development of the critical perspective.

THE MAIN IDEA OF THE CRITICAL PERSPECTIVE

Patterns of values, statuses, and norms come to center around important societal concerns. For example, maintenance of order becomes the task of the political institution; replenishment of the population, the task of the family; "learning," the task of the educational institution; and producing and distributing goods and services, the task of the economic institution. All social institutions are interrelated and exercise influence on one another, but of them all, many believe that the economic institution exerts the greatest influence on people, their prospects, and their patterns of interaction with one another. And similarly, though people have numerous social statuses, their position in the economic institution is viewed as the most important.

From the point of view of Marxian thought, there are essentially two positions available in the economic institution—one in which people own or control economic enterprises, and one in which they labor primarily for the benefit of the former. Each of these classes develops life patterns that stem from its position in the economic enterprise. People come to learn class interests and values through association with others similarly situated in the economic institution. Classes become the key social units because, through the dynamics of relations between these classes, one can predict the kinds of social problems that will come into being. Central to the array of problems is class dominance and conflict. When members of one of these classes act on behalf of their own class interests, they enter into conflict with the other class, whose interests are diametrically opposed.

For example, the class that owns and controls economic enterprises exercises considerable control over the government. In consequence, it exerts greater influence on the laws the government makes. This class gets civil laws passed that are in accord with its economic interests. In addition, it helps to mold the criminal law. It directs attention to those people most likely to break certain laws that buttress capitalism and brings pressure on agencies of social control to see that these people are caught, tried, and punished for any infractions of the law. The ruling class also deflects attention from any rule-breakers within its ranks and shields them from exposure to enforcement. Thus, the class that owns and controls economic enterprises extends its influence into a number of other aspects of life. So it is that the critical perspective seeks to account for a host of social problems.

THE SOCIAL SOURCES OF THE CRITICAL PERSPECTIVE

Crises call into question the ability of older viewpoints to offer either understanding or remedial action. These are the kinds of social and cultural circumstances that gave rise to the critical perspective. The persistent crises of interrelated social problems generated doubts in the minds of some thinkers that any of the prevailing perspectives could offer a meaningful account for what seemed to be the problems of society. Facing the double crisis that confronts social policy and social thought, some thinkers created the critical perspective by uniting various perspectives with an earlier tradition of social thought. Theorists in Germany drew on idealist philosophy[1]; those in England, on radical politics; and those in the United States, on a combination of philosophy and political activism. The result has been several strands of thought on social problems that share a number of characteristics, though they go by different names. Under "critical perspective," we have grouped a number of viewpoints labeled by the theorists themselves or others as "critical theory," "critical criminology," "new criminology," "radical criminology," "radical sociology," and "neo-Marxism." While having a number of viewpoints in common, these approaches exhibit some differences. Thus, within the "critical perspective," there are thinkers who emphasize philosophy, those who emphasize political activism and the

---

1. A philosophy that considers the active contribution of the human mind in the formation of our knowledge of the world. Thus it provides a philosophical justification for taking the role of "culture" seriously.

need for social change, and those who focus on the perspective's explanatory potential.

What crises gave rise to these variants of the critical perspective? What were their sources in traditional social thought? And who were the thinkers who developed these versions of the critical perspective?

The critical perspective stems from the Marxist tradition. During his lifetime, Karl Marx (1818–1883) produced a host of works that do not easily lend themselves to classification. He wrote philosophy, social and political history, and a three-volume magnum opus on economics titled *Das Kapital* (*Capital* in English). He was both a theorist and a political activist for most of his life, devoting most of his energies to unseating the capitalists and bringing the working class to political power in Western Europe. His work had broad influence in the Western world during his lifetime. Since his death, his influence has widened and deepened to the point that it is now the basis of revolutionary political thought in Asia and the Third World. In addition, Marxist thought continues to influence the work of scholars in philosophy, economics, politics, and sociology.

As Marx and Engels argued in *The Communist Manifesto,* the history of all societies has been the history of class exploitation and struggle. First there was tribal society, then slavery, then feudalism, and then capitalism. The seeds of the new society are contained in the death of the old social forms. Just as the rising middle class overthrew feudalism, thereby ushering in capitalism, so in time will the proletariat (the working class) unite and overthrow the bourgeoise (the capitalists) and usher in socialism, which, in time, will give way to a classless society.

The capitalist economic system is based on market competition and the pursuit of self-interest. Thus, each enterprise seeks to produce the most at the least cost for the highest possible profit. As a result, the working class experiences such miseries as poverty, unemployment, shorter life expectancy, poor physical and mental health, alcoholism, and high rates of crime against persons, property, and public order. The only solution to these miseries is for the workers to unite and take control of the capitalist republic.

In Germany, early members of what became known as the Frankfurt School—for example, Theodore Adorno, Max Horkheimer, and Herbert Marcuse—extended and developed Marx's ideas in a number of directions. With the rise of Nazism, they fled Germany. Fascism in Europe, along with the failure of the Soviet Union to develop into a democratic socialist state, led members of the Frankfurt School to doubt that the working class could ever achieve the role that Marx had both planned and predicted for it. Just as psychoanalysis seeks to liberate its patients from the unconscious conflicts that entrap them, so the Frankfurt School sought to liberate and emancipate people by bringing cultural factors to the forefront of Marxian analysis. Thus the Frankfurt sociologists showed how the basic assumptions of capitalism pervade all aspects of people's lives. Their major thrust (which they developed in the United States) was and is to develop a comprehensive and detailed critique of the culture of advanced capitalism.

In Britain, the 1960s were a period of declining influence on the international scene, of the emergence of a high rate of unemployment, and of growth in the immigration of Pakistanis and blacks. A number of British sociologists saw a pattern of social problems that seemed to have become both interwoven and intractable; depressed industries, high inflation, poverty, racism, increasing rates of crime, delinquency, drug use, and the like.

A group of these sociologists met to assess the extent to which the available perspectives on social problems made sense and offered some practical solutions to these pressing social problems. Their deliberations produced these conclusions: current perspectives on social problems of whatever school seemed unable to account for the pattern of social problems; the Marxist tradition seemed to offer the most fruitful way of both looking at and solving the problems; and a detailed focus on the social problem of crime would provide the best example of this holistic perspective on social problems.

The upshot of their labors was an important book, published in 1972. *The New Criminology,* written by Ian Taylor, Michael Walton, and Jock Young, set itself two important tasks. The first was to review and analyze the existing array of sociological theories of crime. The second was the development of a new theory of crime that would present satisfactory explanations of the major aspects of crime as a social problem: the promulgation of criminal laws, their violation, and their enforcement. Taylor, Walton, and Young outlined, analyzed, and criticized a number of sociological theories, including the deviant behavior perspective and the labeling perspective. Then, in their last chapter, they outlined the questions on crime that an adequate theory must answer. While their last chapter does not present a new theory, the line of questions they ask and the answers they presume the perspective will find make it quite clear that they have developed a systematic Marxist argument on crime as a social problem. A subsequent collection of readings that they edited, *Critical Criminology,* contains some additional arguments. The implications of their point of view for description, analysis, explanation, and action come forth quite explicitly in their second book. As Britain enters the more advanced stages of capitalist society, crime rates will only increase. The only remedy, the authors say, is to change Great Britain into a socialist society. The authors claim that the reduction of social inequalities will correspondingly reduce crime rates drastically. Like their mentor, Karl Marx, the new criminologists believe that the proof of any way of looking at the world rests on the ability of that perspective to help change that world.

In the United States, the 1960s also became an extremely turbulent decade, one characterized by the assassination of political and civil-rights leaders, the beginning of protests against the Vietnam War, the civil-rights movement, riots, the white backlash and flight to the suburbs, and the rebirth of the feminist movement. The turbulence of the 1960s carried over into the 1970s, which saw the Watergate scandals, the winding down of the Vietnam War, economic recession, and the oil crisis. In the early 1970s, an American version of the critical perspective began to emerge. And, much as in Britain, a strand of this thought centered around the analysis of crime as a social problem.

The American version of the critical perspective grounded itself in the holistic orientation of Marx—that events in the history of any given society take place in specific social, economic, and political circumstances, and that these events generally are interrelated. Class conflict came to be seen as the cause of the many problems that appeared in different institutional contexts. Theorists who extended and developed a neo-Marxist view of social problems in the United States also argued that both the deviant behavior perspective and the labeling perspective had only limited explanatory potential compared with the broader and more systemic view that saw social problems as the inevitable outcome of the conflict between the owning-controlling class and the working class.

Two important writers who advanced and developed the American critical perspective evolved in their thought from a position of value conflict to the more systematic Marxist conception of class conflict. Both Richard Quinney and William J. Chambliss had already, by the late 1960s, contributed important works advancing a value conflict interpretation of social problems. By the early 1970s, each shifted and developed this perspective into its present critical form. For instance, Quinney's book *The Social Reality of Crime* located among a variety of different interest groups the power to define certain acts as criminal. In his later works, *Class, State, and Crime* and *Critique of Legal Order,* Quinney postulated that all crimes are a consequence of the capitalist society.

In 1964, Chambliss published a paper entitled "A Sociological Analysis of the Law of Vagrancy." In this paper, he showed how different interest groups, over time, came forward to define the crime of vagrancy as a way of pursuing or protecting their own interests. In essence, this work exemplified a value conflict approach to the social problem of vagrancy. In 1975, Chambliss published "The Political Economy of Crime," in which he demonstrated a basic assumption of the critical perspective about corruption.

A number of other sociologists have contributed to the critical perspective. They have added to the programmatic statement of the perspective, applied it to specific issues, or used it to point out the deficiencies of the other perspectives on social problems.

The most general criticism of the critical perspective has been that it is a political ideology, or a theory that, unlike most standard theories, does not specify the conditions under which it could be disproved. Regardless, the critical perspective continues to remain an important perspective on social problems because of its close links to the Marxist tradition and because it offers a broad historical view on how social problems come into being and how they can be reduced, if not eliminated, by concerted political action.

CHARACTERISTICS OF THE CRITICAL PERSPECTIVE

Holism, a key assumption of the critical perspective, requires that analysts examine the whole social system, rather than any of its specific parts. Social problems are interrelated with a number of events, changes, and pressures operating on all social institutions. The main elements of the critical perspective are as follows:

Definition.   A social problem is a situation that develops out of the exploitation of the working class.

Causes.   In the broadest sense, the form of social organization that capitalist society produces causes a wide range of specific social problems. With regard to the social problem of crime, it is the system of class domination that creates and sustains it. For example, capitalists sustain poverty and make and enforce rules in their own interests.

Conditions.   Important conditions of social problems are the extent and severity of class domination and conflict, working-class consciousness, and fluctuations in the business cycle. When domination and conflict are less visible or of lesser strength, if large segments of the working class are unaware of their common interests, and if there is an upturn in the business cycle, awareness of social problems will lag considerably behind their actual occurrence.

Consequences.   Though capitalist societies go through cyclic periods, social problems are proportional to advances in the stages of the development of capitalism. Thus, writers using critical perspective predict, for example, that crime rates will rise with advances in the development of capitalism.

Solutions.   Only political activism can resolve the consequences of the capitalist system. Either through reform or revolution, the working-class movement must struggle to achieve a classless society, thereby eliminating the host of social problems that are endemic in a social system based on social inequality.

SUMMARY AND CONCLUSION

Crises, turbulence, and upheaval seem to be common occurrences in modern, urban, industrial societies. These periods of crisis demand responses by members of society. These crises similarly reverberate within the discipline of sociology and affect prevailing perspectives on social problems. Thus, sociologists in Germany, Great Britain, and the United States found that crises that their particular societies were experiencing called into question the adequacy of the dominant social problems perspectives of the day.

In all three of these countries, a body of thought on social problems made its appearance under a variety of names. It developed into a profound critique of capitalist society and culture that sees social problems as endemic to capitalistic society. Thus, the essential causes of social problems reside in class dominance and conflict: the "haves" hold on to what they have and maintain what they have at the continued expense of the "have-nots." Class conflict results from the system of class domination that perpetuates social inequality. Ultimately, the rich get richer and the poor get poorer. The only solution to the assortment of social problems that are common to advanced capitalist societies is for the working class to win the class struggle and usher in true socialism, which will lead to a classless society.

CRIME AND THE DEVELOPMENT OF CAPITALISM

Richard Quinney

"Crime," says Quinney, "is inevitable under capitalist conditions." Capitalists own and control the production of work, law, and culture. The working class, by contrast, has nothing to sell save its own labor. This economic, political, and cultural inequality provides both the dynamics and the consequences of the capitalist system. The consequences only increase the need of the capitalist class to dominate and of the working class to adapt. The responses of both classes to the situation produce a variety of crimes. The capitalist class commits crimes of domination, government, and control that produce such social injuries as corruption, sexism, racism, and economic exploitation. The working class commits crimes of accommodation and resistance. The only solution to the expanding and increasing rate of crime, Quinney says, comes about when the working class shifts from individual crimes of accommodation to crimes of collective resistance. Such a consciousness forged in a manifest struggle between the classes will ultimately change the system from capitalist to socialist, thereby reducing, if not eliminating, the many kinds of crimes the capitalist system engenders.

The state . . . arose to protect and promote the interests of the dominant class, the class that owns and controls the means of production. The state exists as a device for controlling the exploited class, the class that labors, for the benefit of the ruling class. Modern civilization, as epitomized in capitalist societies, is founded on the exploitation of one class by another. Moreover, the capitalist state is oppressive not only because it supports the interests of the dominant class but also because it is responsible for the design of the whole system within which the capitalist ruling class dominates and the working class is dominated.[1] The capitalist system of production and exploitation is secured and reproduced by the capitalist state.

The coercive force of the state, embodied in law and legal repression, is the traditional means of maintaining the social and economic order. Contrary to conventional wisdom, law, instead of representing the community custom, is an instrument of the state that serves the interests of the developing capitalist class.[2] Law emerged with the rise of capitalism. As human labor became a commodity, human relations in general began to be the object of the commodity form. Human beings became subject to juridic regulation; the capitalist mode of production called forth its equivalent mode of regulation and control, the legal system.[3] And criminal law developed as the most appropriate form of control for capitalist society. Criminal law and legal repression continue to serve the interests of the capitalist class and the perpetuation of the capitalist system.

Through the legal system, then, the state forcefully protects its interests and those of the capitalist class. Crime control becomes the coercive means of checking threats to the existing social and economic order, threats that result from a system of oppression and exploitation.

Yet the coercive force of the state is but one means of maintaining the social and economic order. A more subtle reproductive mechanism of capitalist society is the perpetuation of the capitalist concept of reality, a nonviolent but equally repressive means of domination. As Alan Wolfe has shown, in the manipulation of consciousness the existing order is legitimated and secured:

> The most important reproductive mechanism which does not involve the use of state violence is consciousness-manipulation. The liberal state has an enormous amount of violence at its disposal, but it is often reluctant to use it. Violence may breed counter-violence, leading to instability. It may be far better to manipulate consciousness to such an extent that most people would never think of engaging in the kinds of action which could be repressed. The most perfectly repressive (though not violently so) capitalist system, in other words, would not be a police state, but the complete opposite, one in which there were no police because there was nothing to police, everyone having accepted the legitimacy of that society and all its daily consequences.[4]

Those who rule in capitalist society—with the assistance of the state—not only accumulate capital at the expense of those who work but impose their ideology as well. Oppression and exploitation are legitimized by the expropriation of consciousness; since labor is expropriated, consciousness must also be expropriated.[5] In fact, *legitimacy* of the capitalist order is maintained by controlling the consciousness of the population. A capitalist hegemony is established.

Thus, through its various reproductive mechanisms capitalism is able to maximize the possibility of control over citizens of the state. Ranging from control of production and distribution to manipulation of the mind, capitalism operates according to its own form of dictatorship. André Gorz writes:

> The dictatorship of capital is exercised not only on the production and distribution of wealth, but with equal force on the manner of producing, on the

model of consumption, and on the manner of consuming, the manner of working, thinking, living. As much as over the workers, the factories, and the state, this dictatorship rules over the society's vision of the future, its ideology, its priorities and goals, over the way in which people experience and learn about themselves, their potentials, their relations with other people and with the rest of the world. This dictatorship is economic, political, cultural and psychological at the same time: it is total.[6]

Although the capitalist state creates and manages the institutions of control (employing physical force *and* manipulation of consciousness), the basic contradictions of the capitalist order are such that this control is not absolute and, in the long run, is subject to defeat. Because of the contradictions of capitalism, the capitalist state is more weak than strong.[7] Eventually the capitalist state loses its legitimacy and no longer is able to perpetuate the ideology that capital accumulation for capitalists (at the expense of workers) is good for the nation or for human interests. The ability of the capitalist economic order to exist according to its own interests is eventually weakened.[8] The problem becomes especially acute in periods of economic crisis, periods that are unavoidable under capitalism.

In the course of reproducing the capitalist system, crimes are committed. One of the contradictions of capitalism is that some of its laws must be violated in order to secure the existing system.[9] The contradictions of capitalism produce their own sources of crime. Not only are these contradictions heightened during times of crisis, making for an increase in crimes of domination, but the nature of these crimes changes with the further development of capitalism.

The crimes of domination most characteristic of capitalist domination are those crimes that occur in the course of securing the existing economic order. These *crimes of economic domination* include the crimes committed by corporations, ranging from price fixing to pollution of the environment in order to protect and further capital accumulation. Also included are the economic crimes of individual businessmen and professionals.

Then there are the *crimes of government* committed by the elected and appointed officials of the capitalist state. The Watergate crimes, carried out to perpetuate a particular governmental administration, are the most publicized instances of these crimes. There are also those offenses committed by the government against persons and groups who would seemingly threaten national security. Included here are the crimes of warfare and the political assassination of foreign and domestic leaders.

Crimes of domination also occur in the course of state control. These are the *crimes of control*. They include the felonies and misdemeanors that law-enforcement agents, especially the police, carry out in the name of the law, usually against persons accused of other violations. Violence and brutality have become a recognized part of police work. In addition to these crimes of control, there are crimes of a more subtle nature in which agents of the law violate the civil liberties of citizens, as in the various forms of surveillance, the use of provocateurs, and the illegal denial of due process.

Finally, many *social injuries* committed by the capitalist class and the capitalist state are not usually defined as criminal in the legal codes of the state.[10] These systematic actions, involving the denial of basic human rights (resulting in sexism, racism, and economic exploitation), are an integral part of capitalism and are important to its survival.

Domination and repression are basic to class struggle in the development of capitalism. The capitalist class and the state protect and promote the capitalist order by controlling those who do not own the means of production. The labor supply and the conditions for labor must be secured. Crime control and crimes of domination are necessary features and natural products of a capitalist political economy.

ACCOMMODATION AND RESISTANCE

The contradictions of developing capitalism heighten the level of class struggle and thereby increase (1) the need to dominate by the capitalist class and (2) the need to accommodate and resist by the classes exploited by capitalism, particularly the working class. Most of the behavior in response to domination, including actions of the oppressed defined as criminal by the capitalist class, is a product of the capitalist system of production. . . .

[T]he class that does not own or control the means of production must adapt to the conditions of capitalism. Accommodation and resistance to the conditions of capitalism are basic to the class struggle. The argument here is that action by people who do not own and control the means of production, those who are exploited and oppressed, is largely an accommodation or resistance to the conditions produced by capitalist production. Thus, criminality among the oppressed classes is action (conscious or otherwise) in relation to the capitalist order of exploitation and oppression. Crime, with its many historical variations, is an integral part of class struggle in the development of capitalism. . . .

Many crimes of accommodation are of this . . . nature. Nevertheless, these actions occur within the context of capitalist oppression, stemming from the existing system of production. Much criminal behavior is of a parasitical nature, including burglary, robbery, drug dealing, and hustling of various sorts.[11] These are *predatory crimes*. The behavior, although pursued out of the need to survive, is a reproduction of the capitalist system. The crimes are nevertheless antagonistic to the capitalist order. Most police activity is directed against these crimes.

In addition to predatory crimes are *personal crimes*, which are usually directed against members of the same class. These are the conventional criminal acts of murder, assault, and rape. They are pursued by those who are already brutalized by the conditions of capitalism. These actions occur in immediate situations that are themselves the result of more basic accommodations to capitalism.

Aside from these lumpen crimes, actions are carried out, largely by the working class, that are in resistance to the capitalist system. These actions, sometimes directed against the work situation, are direct reflections of the alienation of labor—a struggle, conscious or unconscious, against the exploitation of the life and activity of the worker. For example, workers may engage in concrete political actions against their employers:

> On the assembly lines of the American automobile industry, this revolt extends as far as clandestine acts of sabotage against a product (the automobile body) which appears to the worker as the detestable materialization of the social uselessness and individual absurdity of his toil. Along the same lines is the less extreme and more complex example of miners fighting with admirable perseverance against the closing of the mines where they are exploited under inferior human and economic conditions—but who, individually, have no difficulty in recognizing that even if the coal they produced were not so bad and so expensive, their job, under the prevailing conditions, would still be abominable.[12]

Moreover, large numbers of workers under advanced capitalism become expendable. For the capitalist the problem becomes that of the kind and size of labor force necessary to maximize production and realize surplus value. The physical well-being and spiritual needs of the worker are not the concern; rather, capitalism requires an "industrial reserve army" that can be called into action when necessary and relieved when no longer needed—but that is always available. Marx observed in *Capital*:

> But if a surplus laboring population is a necessary product of accumulation or of the development of wealth on a capitalist basis, this surplus population becomes, conversely, the lever of capitalist accumulation, nay, a condition of existence of the capitalist mode of production. It forms a disposable industrial reserve army that belongs to capital quite as absolutely as if the latter had bred it at its own cost. Independently of the limits of the actual increase of population, it creates, for the changing needs of the self-expansion of capital, a mass of human material always ready for exploitation.[13]

Under these conditions, "the labor force consists of two parts, the employed and the unemployed, with a gray area in between, containing the part-time or sporadically employed. Furthermore, all these categories of workers and potential workers continuously expand or contract with technological change, the ups and downs of the business cycle, and the vagaries of the market, all inherent characteristics of capitalist production."[14] Many workers are further exploited by being relegated to the degradations and uncertainties of a reserve army of labor.

For the unemployed, as well as for those who are always uncertain about their employment, this life condition has its personal and social consequences. Basic human needs are thwarted when the life-giving activity of work is lost or curtailed. This form of alienation gives rise to a multiplicity of psychosocial maladjustments and psychic disorders.[15] In addition, unemployment means the loss of personal and family income. Choices, opportunities, and even life maintenance are jeopardized. For many people, the appropriate reaction consists not only of mental disturbance but also of outright acts of personal and social destruction.

Although the statistical evidence can never show conclusively the relation between unemployment and crime, largely because such statistics are politically constructed in the beginning to obscure the failings of a capitalist economy, there is sufficient observation to recognize the obvious fact that unemployment produces criminality. Crimes of economic gain increase whenever the jobless seek ways to maintain themselves and their families. Crimes of violence rise when the problems of life are further exacerbated by the loss of life-supporting activity. Anger and frustration at a world that punishes rather than supports produce their own forms of destruction. Permanent unemployment—and the acceptance of that condition—can result in a form of life where criminality is an appropriate and consistent response.

Hence, crime under capitalism has become a response to the conditions of life.[16] Nearly all crimes among the working class in capitalist society are actually a means of *survival*, an attempt to exist in a society where survival is not assured by other, collective means. Crime is inevitable under capitalist conditions. . . .

Class struggle involves a continuous war between two dialectically opposed interests: on one hand, capital accumulation for the benefit of a nonworking minority class that owns and controls the means of production and, on the other hand, control and ownership of production by those who actually labor. Since the capitalist state regulates this struggle, the institutions and laws of the social order are intended to assure the victory of the capitalist class over the working class. Yet the working class constantly struggles against the capitalist class, as shown in the long history of labor battles against the conditions of capitalist production.[17] The resistance continues as long as there is need for class struggle, that is, as long as capitalism exists.

With the instruments of force and coercion on the side of the capitalist class, much of the activity in the working-class struggle is defined as criminal. Indeed, according to the legal codes, whether in simply acting to relieve the injustices of capitalism or in taking action against the existence of class oppression, actions against the interests of the state are crimes. With an emerging consciousness that the state represses those who attempt to tip the scales in favor of the working class, working-class people engage in actions against the state and the capitalist class. This is crime that is politically conscious.

Crimes of accommodation and resistance thus range from unconscious reactions to exploitation, to conscious acts of survival within the capitalist system, to politically conscious acts of rebellion. These criminal actions, moreover, not only cover the range of meaning but actually evolve or progress from *unconscious reaction* to *political rebellion*. Finally, the crimes may eventually reach the ultimate stage of conscious political action—*revolt*. In revolt, criminal actions are not only against the system but are also an attempt to overthrow it.

The movement toward a society can occur only with political consciousness on the part of those oppressed by capitalist society. The alternative to capitalism cannot be willed into being but requires the conscious activity of those who seek new conditions of existence. Political consciousness develops in an awareness of the alienation suffered under capitalism. The contradiction of capitalism—the disparity between actuality and human possibility—makes large portions of the population ready to act in ways that will bring about a new existence. When people become conscious of the extent to which they are dehumanized under the capitalist mode of production, when people realize the source and nature of their alienation, they become active in a movement to build a new society. . . .

The only lasting solution to the crisis of capitalism is socialism. Under late, advanced capitalism, socialism will be achieved in the struggle of all people who are oppressed by the capitalist mode of production, namely, the workers and all elements of the surplus population. An alliance of the oppressed must take place.[18] Given the objective conditions of a crisis in advanced capitalism and the conditions for an alliance of the oppressed, a mass socialist movement can be formed. . . .

Notes

1. David A. Gold, Clarence Y. H. Lo, and Erik Olin Wright, "Recent Developments in Marxist Theories of the State," *Monthly Review* 27 (November 1975): 36–51.

2. Stanley Diamond, "The Rule of Law Versus the Order of Custom," *Social Research* 38 (Spring 1971): 42–72; and Michael Tigar, with the assistance of Madeleine Levy, *Law and the Rise of Capitalism* (New York: Monthly Review Press, 1977).

3. E. B. Pashukanis, "The General Theory of Law and Marxism," in *Soviet Legal Philosophy*, trans. and ed. Hugh W. Babb (Cambridge, Mass.: Harvard University Press, 1951), pp. 111–225; and Isaac D. Balbus, "Commodity Form and Legal Form: An Essay on the 'Relative Autonomy' of the Law," *Law and Society Review* 11 (Winter 1977): 571–88. Discussions of Pashukanis are found in C. J. Arthur, "Towards a Materialist Theory of Law," *Critique* 7 (Winter 1976–77): 31–46; and Steve Redhead, "The Discrete Charm of Bourgeois Law: A Note on Pashukanis," *Critique* 9 (Spring–Summer 1978): 113–20.

4. Alan Wolfe, "Political Repression and the Liberal State," *Monthly Review* 23 (December 1971): 20.

5. Alan Wolfe, "New Directions in the Marxist Theory of Politics," *Politics and Society* 4 (Winter 1974): 155–57.

6. André Gorz, *Strategy for Labor: A Radical Proposal,* tr. Martin A. Nicolaus and Victoria Oritz (Boston: Beacon, 1967), pp. 131–32.

7. Wolfe, "New Directions in the Marxist Theory of Politics," p. 155.

8. See Stanley Aronowitz, "Law, Breakdown of Order, and Revolution," in *Law Against the People: Essays to Demystify Law, Order and the Courts,* ed. Robert Lefcourt (New York: Random House, 1971), pp. 150–82; and John H. Schaar, "Legitimacy in the Modern State," in *Power and Community: Dissenting Essays in Political Science,* ed. Philip Green and Sanford Levinson (New York: Random House, 1970), pp. 276–327.

9. See Richard Quinney, *Criminology* (2nd ed.; Boston: Little, Brown, 1979), pp. 163–261.

10. Tony Platt, "Prospects for a Radical Criminology in the United States," *Crime and Social Justice* 1 (Spring–Summer 1974): 2–10; and Herman and Julia Schwendinger, "Defenders of Order or Guardians of Human Rights?" *Issues in Criminology* 5 (Summer 1970): 123–57.

11. Judah Hill, *Class Analysis: United States in the 1970's* (Emeryville, Calif.: Class Analysis, 1975), pp. 86–87.

12. Gorz, *Strategy for Labor,* pp. 57–58.

13. Karl Marx, *Capital,* vol. 1 (New York: International Publishers, 1967), p. 632.

14. Editors, "The Economic Crisis in Historical Perspective," *Monthly Review* 26 (June 1975): 2.

15. K. William Kapp, "Socio-Economic Effects of Law and High Employment," *Annals of the American Academy of Political and Social Science* 418 (March 1975): 60–71.

16. David M. Gordon, "Capitalism, Class, and Crime in America," *Crime and Delinquency* 19 (April 1973): 163–86.

17. Sidney Lens, *The Labor Wars: From the Molly Maguires to the Sitdowns* (New York: Doubleday, 1973); Jeremy Brecher, *Strike!* (Greenwich, Conn.: Fawcett, 1972); Samuel Yellin, *American Labor Struggles* (New York: Russell, 1936); and Richard O. Boyer and Herbert M. Morais, *Labor's Untold Story* (New York: Cameron Associates, 1955).

18. James O'Connor, *The Fiscal Crisis of the State* (New York: St. Martin's, 1973), pp. 221–56.

TOWARD A POLITICAL ECONOMY OF CRIME

William J. Chambliss

In this reading Chambliss shows that members of the dominant class break the criminal law but get punished for doing so much less frequently than do their criminal counterparts in the lower class. Chambliss describes such a situation in Ibados, Nigeria, and Seattle, Washington. He concludes that this study generally supports "the Marxian assertion that criminal acts which serve the interests of the ruling class will go unsanctioned while those that do not will be punished."

It is obviously fruitless to join the debate over whether or not contemporary theories of criminal etiology are adequate to the task. The advocates of "family background," "differential association," "cultural deprivation," "opportunity theory," and a host of other "theories" have debated the relative merits of their explanations *ad infinitum*. . . . I should like, however, to present a summary of data from a study of crime and criminal law which compares selected aspects of these phenomena in Nigeria and the United States. In so doing I hope to shed some light on the Marxian paradigm without pretending to resolve all the issues.

My data come from research in Seattle, Washington, and Ibadan, Nigeria. The research methods employed were mainly those of a participant observer. In Seattle the research spanned almost ten years (1962–1972), and in Ibadan the research took place during 1967–1968. In both cities the data were gathered through extensive interviewing of informants from all sides of criminal law—criminals, professional thieves, racketeers, prostitutes, government officials, police officers, businessmen and members of various social class levels in the community. Needless to say, the sampling was what sociologists have come to call (with more than a slight bit of irony) "convenience samples." Any other sampling procedure is simply impossible in the almost impenetrable world of crime and law enforcement into which we embarked.

Excerpted from William J. Chambliss, "Toward a Political Economy of Crime," *Theory and Society*, 2, Summer 1975, pp. 157–170. Reprinted by permission of Kluwen Academic Publishers. Copyright © 1975 by Martinus Nijhoff Publishers.

Nigeria and America both inherited British common law at the time of their independence. Independence came somewhat later for Nigeria than for America, but the legal systems inherited are very similar. As a result, both countries share much the same foundation in statues and common law principles. While differences exist, they are not, for our purposes, of great significance.

In both Nigeria and the United States, it is a crime punishable by imprisonment and a fine for any public official to accept a bribe, to solicit a bribe or to give special favors to a citizen for monetary considerations. It is also against the law in both countries to run gambling establishments, to engage in or solicit for prostitutes, to sell liquor that has not been inspected and stamped by a duly appointed agency of the government, to run a taxi service without a license, etc. And, of course, both nations share the more obvious restrictions on murder, theft, robbery, rape and the standard array of criminal offenses. In both countries there is striking similarity in the types of laws that do *not* and those that do get enforced.[1]

CRIME AND LAW ENFORCEMENT IN NIGERIA

In both Nigeria and the United States, many laws can be, and are, systematically violated with impunity by those who control the political and economic resources of the society. Particularly relevant are those laws that restrict such things as bribery, racketeering (especially gambling), prostitution, drug distribution and selling, usury and the whole range of criminal offenses committed by businessmen in the course of their businesses (white collar crimes).

In Nigeria the acceptance of bribes by government officials is blatantly public and virtually universal. When the vice president of a large research organization that was just getting established in Nigeria visited the head of Nigerian Customs, he was told by the Customs Director that "at the outset it is important that we both understand that the customs office is corrupt from the top to the bottom." Incoming American professors were usually asked by members of the faculty at the University if they would be willing to exchange their American dollars on the black market at a better exchange rate than banks would offer. In at least one instance the Nigerian professor making this request was doing so for the military governor of the state within which the university was located. Should the incoming American fail to meet a colleague who would wish to make an illegal transfer of funds, he would in all likelihood be approached by any number of other citizens in high places. For example, the vice president of the leading bank near the university would often approach American professors and ask if they would like to exchange their money through him personally, and thereby receive a better exchange rate than was possible if they dealt directly through the bank.

At the time of my study, tithes of this sort were paid at every level.

Businessmen desiring to establish businesses found their way blocked interminably by bureaucratic red tape until the proper amount of "dash" had been given to someone with the power to effect the result desired. Citizens riding buses were asked for cigarettes and small change by army soldiers who manned check points. The soldiers, in turn, had to pay a daily or weekly tithe to superior officers in order to be kept at this preferential assignment. At the border one could bring French wine, cigarettes and many other prohibited commodities into Nigeria, so long as prior arrangements had been made with the customs officers either in Lagos (the capital of the country) or at the check point itself. The prior arrangements included payment of a bribe.

As a result of bribes and payoffs, there flourished a large and highly profitable trade in a wide variety of vices. Prostitution was open and rampant in all of the large cities of Nigeria—it was especially well developed in those cities where commerce and industry brought large numbers of foreigners. Gambling establishments, located mainly in large European-style hotels, and managed incidentally by Italian visitors, catered to the moneyed set with a variety of games of chance competitive with Monte Carlo or Las Vegas. There was a large, illicit liquor trade (mostly a home-brewed gin-like drink), as well as a smaller but nevertheless profitable trade in drugs that received political and legal protection through payoffs to high-level officials.

In at least Ibadan and Lagos, gangs of professional thieves operated with impunity. These gangs of thieves were well organized and included the use of beggars and young children as cover for theft activities. The links to the police were sufficient to guarantee that suspects would be treated leniently—usually allowed to go with no charges being brought. In one instance an entire community within the city of Ibadan was threatened by thieves with total destruction. The events leading up to this are revealing. The community, which I shall call Lando, had been victimized by a gang of thieves who broke into homes and stole valuable goods. The elders of Lando hired four men to guard the community. When thieves came one evening the hired guards caught and killed three of them. The next day the Oba of the community was called on by two men from another part of the city. These men expressed grave concern that some of their compatriots had been killed in Lando. The Oba informed them that if any other thieves came to Lando they would be dealt with similarly. The thieves' representatives advised the Oba that if such a thing happened the thieves would burn the community to the ground. When the Oba said he would call the police, it was pointed out to him that the chief of police was the brother-in-law of one of the thieves. Ultimately an agreement was reached whereby the thieves agreed to stop stealing in Lando in return for the Oba's promise that the thieves could sell their stolen property in Lando on market day.

Ibadan is a very cosmopolitan city which lies in the Yoruba section of western Nigeria. Although dominated by the Yoruba, there are nonetheless a large number of Hausa, Ibo and other ethnic groups in the city. The Hausa who are strongly Muslim (while the Yoruba are roughly 50% Christian) occupy a ghetto within Ibadan which is almost exclusively Hausa. Despite the fact that the Hausa are an immigrant group where one might expect the crime rate to be high, there are very few Hausa arrested for crime. (See Table 1.) This is particularly impressive since there is general belief that the Hausa are responsible for some of the more efficient and effective groups of professional thieves in the area. The explanation for this apparently lies in the fact that the Hausa have a strong leadership which intervenes with payoffs and cash to government and police officials whenever a member of their community is in any difficulty.

Table 1. Arrest Rate for 1,000 Population, Ibadan, Nigeria 1967

Immigrant areas	Indigenous area	Hausa area
1.41	.61	.54

Payment of bribes to the police is usually possible whenever an arrest is likely. An incoming American who illegally photographed an airport was allowed to go (without even destroying his film), upon payment of $15.00 to the arresting officer. Six dollars was sufficient for the wife of an American professor to avoid arrest for reckless driving. A young son of a wealthy merchant was arrested on numerous occasions for being drunk, driving without a license, stealing and getting into fights. On every occasion the police returned him to the custody of his parents without charges being filed when the father paid the arresting officer (or the policeman on the desk) thirty to forty-five dollars.

Such practices are not atypical, but were instead the usual procedure. It was said, and research bears this out, that one with money could pay to be excused from any type or amount of crime.

Who, then, did get arrested? In general, those who lacked either the money or the political influence to "fix" a criminal charge. The most common youth arrest was for "street trading"—that is, selling items on the street. The second most frequent offense was "being away from home" or "sleeping out without protection." Among adults, "suspiciousness," public indecency, intoxication and having no visible means of support were the most common offenses. Although robbery, theft and burglary were common offenses (in a sample of 300 residents of Ibadan, 12.7% reported having been the victim of burglary), arrests for these offenses were much less frequent.

Anyone who has lived or traveled in foreign countries will not be surprised by these findings. What is usually not recognized, however, is that these same kinds of things characterize crime and criminal law enforcement in the United States (and possibly every other nation) as well.

CRIME AND LAW ENFORCEMENT IN SEATTLE

Seattle, like Ibadan, is a city of 1,000,000 people with its own police, government, and set of laws inherited from Great Britain. In Seattle, as in Ibadan, any type of vice can be found. It is only necessary to travel away from the middle- and upper-class suburbs that ring the city, and venture into the never-never land of skidrow derelicts, the Black ghetto or a few other pockets of rundown hotels, cafes and cabarets that are sprinkled along freeways and by the docks. Here there is prostitution, gambling, usury, drugs, pornography, bootleg liquor, bookmaking and pinball machines.

The most profitable of these are gambling and usury. Gambling ranges from bookmaking (at practically every street corner in the center of the city), to open poker games, bingo parlors, off-track betting, casinos, roulette and dice games (concentrated in a few locations and also floating out into the suburban country clubs and fraternal organizations), and innumerable two and five dollar stud-poker games scattered liberally throughout the city.

The most conspicuous card games take place from about ten in the morning (it varies slightly from one "fun house" to the next) until midnight. But there are a number of other twenty-four hour games that run constantly. In the more public games the limit ranges from one to five dollars for each bet; in the more select games that run twenty-four hours a day there is a "pot limit" or "no limit" rule. These games are reported to have betting as high as twenty and thirty thousand dollars. I have seen a bet made and called for a thousand dollars in one of these games. During this game, which was the highest stakes game I witnessed in the six years of the study, the police lieutenant in charge of the vice squad was called in to supervise the game—not, need I add, to break up the game or make any arrests, only to insure against violence.

Prostitution covers the usual range of ethnic groups, age, shape and size of female. It is also found in houses with madams as in New Orleans, on the street through pimps, or in suburban apartment buildings and hotels. Prices range from five dollars for a short time with a street walker to two hundred dollars for a night with a lady who has her own apartment (which she usually shares with her boyfriend, who is discreetly gone during business operations).

High interest loans are easy to arrange through stores that advertise "your signature is worth $5,000." It is really worth considerably more; it may, in fact, be worth your life. The interest rates vary from twenty per cent for three months to as high as one hundred per cent for varying periods. Repayment is demanded not through the courts, but through the help of "The Gaspipe Gant" who call on recalcitrant debtors and use physical force to bring about payment. The "interest only" repayment is the most popular alternative practiced by borrowers, and is preferred by the loan sharks as well. The longer repayment can be prolonged, the more advantageous it is to the loan agents.

Pinball machines are readily available throughout the city, and most of them pay off in cash. The gambling, prostitution, drug distribution, pornography, and usury (high interest loans) which flourish in the lower class center of the city do so with the compliance, encouragement and cooperation of the major political and law enforcement officials in the city. There is, in fact, a symbiotic relationship between the law enforcement-political organizations of the city and a group of *local* (as distinct from national) men who control the distribution of vices.

The payoffs and briberies in Seattle are complex. The simpler and more straightforward are those made by each gambling establishment. A restaurant or cabaret with card room attached had to pay around $200 each month to the police and $200 to the "syndicate." In reality these were two branches of the same group of men, but the payoffs were made separately. Anyone who refused these payments was harassed by fire inspectors, health inspectors, licensing difficulties and even physical violence from enforcers who worked for the crime cabal in the city. Similarly, places with pinball machines, pornography, bookmaking or prostitution had to pay regularly to the "Bagman" who collected a fee for the police.

Payoffs to policemen were also required of tow truck operators, cabaret owners and other businesses where police cooperation was necessary. Tow truck drivers carried with them a matchbox with $3.00 in it and, when asked for a light by the policeman who had called them to the scene of an accident, they gave him the matchbox with the $3.00 inside. Cabaret owners paid according to how large their business was. The police could extract payoffs because the laws were so worded as to make it virtually impossible to own a profitable cabaret without violating the law. For example, it was illegal to have an entertainer closer than 25 feet to the nearest customer. A cabaret, to comply with this ordinance, would have had to have a night club the size of a large ballroom, at which point the atmosphere would have been so sterile as to drive customers away, not to mention that such large spaces are exceedingly expensive in the downtown section of the city. Thus, the police could, if they chose to, close down a cabaret on a moment's notice. Payoffs were a necessary investment to assure that the police would not so choose.

The trade in licenses was notoriously corrupt. It was generally agreed by my informants that to get a tow truck license one had to pay a bribe of $10,000; a card room license was $25,000; taxicab licenses were unavailable, as were licenses for distributing pinball machines or juke boxes. These licenses had all been issued to members of the syndicate that controlled the rackets, and no outsiders were permitted in.

There were innumerable instances of payoffs to politicians and government officials for real estate deals, businesses and stock transactions. In each case the participants were a combination of local businessmen, racketeers, local politicians and government officials.

Interestingly, there is also a minority ghetto within Seattle where one might expect to find a high crime rate. In Seattle this is the Japanese-American section of the city.

It is widely believed that the Japanese-Americans have a very low propensity to crime. This is usually attributed to the family-centered orientation of the Japanese-American community. There is some evidence, however, that this perspective is largely a self-fulfilling prophecy.[2] Table 2 shows a comparison between the self-reported delinquency and arrest rates of Japanese-American youth for a selected year. The data suffer, of course, from problems inherent in such comparisons, but nonetheless, the point cannot be gainsaid that the actual crime rate among Japanese-American youth is considerably higher than the conventional view would suggest.

Table 2. Comparison of Arrests (for 1963) and Self-Reported Delinquency Involvement by Racial Groups[a]

Racial group	Per cent arrested	Per cent self-reporting high delinquency involvement[b]
White	11	53
Negro	36	52
Japanese	2	36

[a]Based on data from Richard H. Nagasawa, *Delinquency and Non-Delinquency: A Study of Status Problems and Perceived Opportunity*, unpublished M.A. thesis, University of Washington, 1965, p. 35.
[b]A self-reported delinquency scale was developed and the respondents were divided, so that 50 per cent of the sample was categorized as having high, and 50 per cent as having low delinquent involvement.

Thus we see that in both the Hausa area of Ibadan and the Japanese-American section of Seattle there is reason to suspect a reasonably high crime rate, but official statistics show an exceptionally low one. When discussing Hausa crime earlier, I attributed this fact to the payoffs made by Hausa leaders to the police and other government officials.

Somewhat the same sort of system prevails in Seattle as well, especially with regard to the rackets. Whereas prostitutes, pornography shops, gambling establishments, cabaret operators and tow truck operators must pay off individually to the police and the syndicate, the Japanese-American community did so *as a community*. The tithe was collected by a local businessman, and was paid to the police and the syndicate in a group sum. Individual prostitutes and vice racketeers might at times have to do special favors for a policeman or political figure, but by and large the payoffs were made collectively rather than individually.

This collective payoff was in large measure attributable to a common characteristic present in both the Hausa and the Japanese-American communities, namely, the heterogeneous social class nature of the community. Typically, wealthy or middle-class members of the lower-class white slum or the Black ghetto moved out of these areas as rapidly as their incomes permitted. So too with Yoruba, Ibo or other ethnic groups in Ibadan. But many, though certainly not all, upper- and middle-class Hausa in Ibadan, and Japanese-Americans in Seattle retained their residence in their respective communities. As a result, the enforcement of any law became more problematic for law enforcement agencies. Arrests made of any youth or adult always carried with it the possibility that the suspect would have a politically influential parent or friend. There was also the possibility that a payoff of some sort (including political patronage) would override the policeman's efforts. Since there was also the necessity to hide from the middle- and upper-class the extent to which the police closed their eyes to the rackets, it was then convenient to avoid having many police in the Hausa and Japanese-American community. The myth of these areas as "no crime" sections of the city was thus very convenient. By contrast, since only those members of the middle- and upper-class who were seeking vice would come to the skidrow area, or the Black ghetto, then the presence of the police was not problematic, and in fact helped to assure the "respectable" citizen that he could partake of his purient interests without fear of being the victim of robbery or violence.

As in Nigeria, all of this corruption, bribery and blatant violation of the law was taking place, while arrests were being made and people sent to jail or prison for other offenses. In Seattle over 70% of all arrests during the time of the study were for public drunkenness.[3] It was literally the case that the police were arresting drunks on one side of a building while on the other side a vast array of other offenses were being committed with police support and management.

What then are we to conclude from these data about the etiology of criminal behavior? For a start, the data show that criminal behavior by *any reasonable* definition is *not* concentrated in the lower classes. Thus, to the extent that a theory of the causes of criminal behavior depends on the assumption that there is a higher rate of criminality in the lower classes, to that extent, the theory is suspect. These data on Seattle and Ibadan link members of the ruling class, legal and political officials and racketeers in joint ventures which involve them actively and passively in criminal activities as part of their way of life.

This conclusion, ironically, is identical with Edwin Sutherland's only he came to this view from his study of corporation ("white-collar") crime. However, he then went on to propose an explanation for criminality which was essentially socio-psychological: Sutherland asked why some *individuals* became involved in criminal behavior while others did not. My contention is that this question is meaningless. Everyone commits crime. And many, many people whether they are poor, rich or middling are involved in a way of life that is criminal; and furthermore, no one, not even the professional thief or racketeer or corrupt politician commits *crime all the time*. To be sure, it may be politically useful to say that people become criminal through association with "criminal behavior patterns," and thereby remove the tendency to look at criminals as pathological. But such a view has little scientific value, since it asks the wrong questions. It asks for a psychological cause of what is by its very nature a socio-political event. Criminality is simply *not* something that people have or don't have; crime is not something some people do and others don't. Crime is a matter of who can pin the label on whom, and underlying this socio-political process is the structure of social relations determined by the political economy. It is to Sutherland's credit that he recognized this when, in 1924, he noted that:

> An understanding of the nature of Criminal law is necessary in order to secure an understanding of the nature of crime. A complete explanation of the origin and enforcement of laws would be, also, an explanation of the violation of laws.[4]

But Sutherland failed, unfortunately, to pursue the implications of his remarks. He chose instead to confront the prevailing functionalist perspective on crime with a less class-biased but nonetheless inevitably psychological explanation.

The argument that criminal acts, that is, acts which are a violation of criminal law, are more often committed by members of the lower classes is not tenable. Criminal acts are widely distributed throughout the social classes in capitalist societies. The rich, the ruling, the poor, the powerless and the working classes *all* engage in criminal activities on a regular basis. It is in the enforcement of the law that the lower classes are subject to the effects of ruling class domination over the legal system, and which results in the appearance of a concentration of criminal acts among the lower classes in the official records. In actual practice, however, class differences in rates of criminal activity are probably negligible. What difference there is would be a difference in the type of criminal act, not in the prevalence of criminality.

The argument that the control of the state by the ruling class would lead to a lower propensity for crime among the ruling classes fails to recognize two fundamental facts. First is the fact that many acts committed by lower classes and which it is in the interests of the ruling class to control (e.g., crimes of violence, bribery of public officials, and crimes of personal choice, such as drug use, alcoholism, driving while intoxicated, homosexuality, etc.) are just as likely—or at least very likely—to be as widespread among the upper classes as the lower classes. Thus, it is crucial that the ruling class be able to control the discretion of the law enforcement agencies in ways that provide them with immunity. For example, having a legal system encumbered with procedural rules which only the wealthy can afford to implement and which, if implemented, nearly guarantees immunity from prosecution, not to mention more direct control through bribes, coercion and the use of political influence.

The Marxian paradigm must also account for the fact that the law will also reflect conflict between members of the ruling class (or between members of the ruling class and the upper class "power elites" who manage the bureaucracies). So, for example, laws restricting the formation of trusts, misrepresentation in advertising, the necessity for obtaining licenses to engage in business practices are all laws which generally serve to reduce competition among the ruling classes and to concentrate capital in a few hands. However, the laws also apply universally, and therefore apply to the ruling class as well. Thus, when they break these laws they are committing criminal acts. Again, the enforcement practices obviate the effectiveness of the laws, and guarantee that the ruling class will rarely feel the sting of the laws, but their violation remains a fact with which we must reckon.

It can also be concluded from this comparative study of Ibadan and Seattle that law enforcement systems are *not* organized to *reduce crime* or to enforce the public morality. They are organized rather to *manage* crime by cooperating with the most criminal groups and enforcing laws against those whose crimes are minimal. In this way, by cooperating with criminal groups, law enforcement essentially produces more crime than would otherwise be the case. Crime is also produced by law enforcement practices through selecting and encouraging the perpetuation of criminal careers by promising profit and security to those criminals who engage in organized criminal activities from which the political, legal and business communities profit.

Thus, the data from this study generally support the Marxian assertion that criminal acts which serve the interests of the ruling class will go unsanctioned while those that do not will be punished. The data also support the hypothesis that criminal activity is a direct reflection of class position. Thus, the criminality of the lawyers, prosecuting attorneys, politicians, judges and policemen is uniquely suited to their own class position in the society. It grows out of the opportunities and strains that inhere in those positions just as surely as the drinking of the skidrow derelict, the violence of the ghetto resident, the drug use of the middle-class adolescent and the white-collar crimes of corporation executives reflect different socializing experiences. That each type of criminality stems from social-psychological conditioning is to say nothing unique about crime and criminality, but only to posit what would have to be a general theory of human psychology—something which places the task beyond the scope of criminology and which has also been notoriously unsuccessful.

The postulates in the paradigm that deal with expected differences between capitalist and socialist societies have not been tested by the data presented, because our data come from two capitalist societies. Crime statistics which might permit a comparison are so unreliable as to be useless to the task. A comparison between East and West Germany would be most enlightening in this regard, as would a comparison between Yugoslavia and Italy, Cuba and Trinidad, or China and India. I have the impression that such a series of comparisons would strongly support the Marxist hypothesis of crime rates being highest in capitalist societies.

SUMMARY AND CONCLUSION

As Gouldner and Friedrichs have recently pointed out, social science generally, and sociology in particular is in the throes of a "paradigm revolution."[5] Predictably, criminology is both a reflection of and a force behind this revolution.

The emerging paradigm in criminology is one which emphasizes social conflict—particularly conflicts of social-class interests and values. The paradigm which is being replaced is one where the primary emphasis was on consensus, and within which "deviance" or "crime" was viewed as an aberration shared by some minority. This group had failed to be properly socialized or adequately integrated into society or, more generally, had suffered from "social disorganization."

The shift in paradigm means more than simply a shift from explaining the same facts with new causal models. It means that we stretch our conceptual framework and look to different facets of social experience. Specifically, instead of resorting inevitably to the "normative system," to "culture" or to socio-psychological experiences of individuals, we look instead to the social relations created by the political and economic structure. Rather than treating "society" as a full-blown reality (reifying it into an entity with its own life), we seek to understand the present as a reflection of the economic and political history that has created the social relations which dominate the moment we have selected to study.

The shift means that crime becomes a rational response of some social classes to the realities of their lives. The state becomes an instrument of the ruling class, enforcing laws here but not there, according to the realities of political power and economic conditions.

There is much to be gained from this re-focusing of criminological and sociological inquiry. However, if the paradigmatic revolution is to be more than a mere fad, we must be able to show that the new paradigm is in fact superior to its predecessor. In this paper I have tried to develop the theoretical implications of a Marxian model of crime and criminal law, and to assess the merits of this paradigm by looking at some empirical data. The general conclusion is that the Marxian paradigm provides a long neglected but fruitful approach to the study of crime and criminal law.

Notes

1. Throughout the paper we rely on data from Ibadan and Seattle as a basis for discussing the patterns in both countries. This lead may disturb some, and if so, then the study may be considered as directly referring only to the two cities—with only a possible application more generally. From a variety of research studies and my own impressions, I am convinced that what is true of Ibadan and Seattle is only true of Nigeria and the United States, but whether or not this is the case should not affect the overall conclusions of this inquiry.

2. Richard H. Nagasawa, *Delinquency and Non-Delinquency: A Study of Status Problems and Perceived Opportunity,* Unpublished M. A. thesis, Seattle: University of Washington, 1965. See also William J. Chambliss and Richard H. Nagasawa, "On the Validity of Official Statistics," *Journal of Research in Crime and Delinquency,* January, 1969, pp. 71–77.

3. James P. Spradley, *You Owe Yourself a Drunk,* Boston: Little Brown and Co., 1970, p. 128.

4. Edwin H. Sutherland, *Criminology,* Philadelphia: J. P. Lippincott, 1924, p. 11.

5. Alvin W. Gouldner, *The Coming Crisis in Western Sociology,* New York: Basic Books, 1970; Robert W. Friedrichs, *A Sociology of Sociology,* New York: The Free Press, 1970. For a more general discussion of paradigm revolution in science, see Thomas S. Kuhn, *The Structure of Scientific Revolutions* (2nd edition), Chicago: University of Chicago Press, 1970.

REPRESSION AND CRIMINAL JUSTICE IN CAPITALIST AMERICA

Raymond J. Michalowski and Edward W. Bohlander

In this excerpt, the authors offer a critical perspective explanation of why most people believe that "crime" is a social problem. Formal agencies of social control apply legal sanctions against those who commit common crimes against property. Constantly learning about these sanctions, most people come to share the view that these actions are criminal, against mainstream cultural values, and social problems. It could not be otherwise, the

From Raymond J. Michalowski and Edward W. Bohlander, 1976, *Sociological Inquiry* 46: 95–106. By permission.

authors argue. The capitalist class controls the definition of crime. And capitalist class interests dictate that harms caused by the disadvantaged, more often than those inflicted by the advantaged, be seen as crimes.

In the U.S. the legal order serves the interests of the capitalist ruling class by (1) facilitating the pursuit of capitalist goals, (2) legitimizing the repression of the economically and politically disadvantaged classes which must exist to maintain a capitalist distribution of wealth and who threaten capitalist interests through criminal activity, and (3) creating and maintaining a definition of "crime" which guarantees the continued enjoyment of the first two benefits by the ruling class. Table 1 presents the effects of the capitalist legal order upon both the power-advantaged and the power-disadvantaged, and the overall contribution of these effects to the definition of crime. The following discussion examines each of these effects in greater detail.

SUBSTANTIVE LAW

Since the development of rational theories of jurisprudence, the justification for substantive criminal laws has been centered around the need to protect the conforming members of society from the "harmful" behaviors of deviants. Designing a social order within which the maximum number of individuals could enjoy freedom from the harmful acts of others has always been the ostensible reason for the creation of criminal codes. However, the specific definition of "harm" has always reflected the perceptions and interests of the ruling classes. In fact, Diamond (1971) argues convincingly that is the emergence of a ruling class with self-interests distinct from those of the society as ruled by custom which has occasioned the creation of legal states.

Substantive criminal law in the U.S. is characterized by a strong emphasis upon common-law crimes involving the perpetration of some harm upon one individual by another acting out of relatively immediate self-interest. Harms committed by individuals serving corporate interests and perpetrated upon either large segments of the society, or upon the society as a whole, are for all practical purposes omitted from our substantive criminal law.

The effects of this upon the power-advantaged group are two-fold. First, the high priority given common-law crimes insures that harms involving individual victims will be seen as attacks upon the state rather than the occasion for personal retribution. By identifying these conflicts as attacks upon the legal order, the state can appropriate to itself the sole right of capturing and punishing offenders (Schafer, 1968). This right defined by class fiat thereby insures the ruling classes "that monopoly of force which characterizes the mature state" (Diamond, 1971).

Table 1. Effects of the Capitalist Legal Order

Component	Effects upon the power-advantaged classes	Effects upon the power-disadvantaged classes	Effects upon perception of the crime problem
Substantive criminal law	a. Ensures a monopoly of force b. Excludes a majority of readily accessible harmful behavior (corporate crimes)	a. Includes all readily accessible harmful behaviors (common-law crimes)	a. Crime is seen primarily as common-law offenses
Formal sanctions	c. Qualitatively and quantitatively minimal for crimes most readily accessible	b. Qualitatively and quantitatively severe for crimes most readily accessible	b. Common-law offenses appear to be far more serious than corporate crimes
Procedural law	d. Have the best chance of avoiding prosecution e. Have the best chance of avoiding conviction	c. Have the worst chance of avoiding prosecution d. Have the worst chance of avoiding conviction	c. The majority of people prosecuted and convicted are members of the power-disadvantaged classes who have committed common-law crimes, giving the impression that the power-disadvantaged classes are the "dangerous" classes
Interpretive institutions	f. Devote little attention to crimes most readily accessible	e. Devote nearly all attention to crimes most readily accessible	
Discretionary actions	g. Further reduce likelihood of prosecution h. Further reduce likelihood of conviction	f. Further increase likelihood of prosecution g. Further increase likelihood of conviction	

Secondly, by de-emphasizing or not including harms resulting from the search for corporate profit, the substantive criminal law gives owners and managers a relatively free reign in the pursuit of capitalist goals. This distinction exists even where the harms caused in the search for corporate profit are more socially injurious than common-law offenses.

The law, for example, did not prohibit the Ford Motor Company from placing automobile gas tanks in such a position that there is a high risk of explosion in a rear-end collision. While such poor design costs approximately 5,000 lives per year, Ford reasoned that design changes were not warranted since their cost would exceed the "cost" of the lives lost. While individual murders causing one, or even several deaths are never overlooked by the criminal law, disregard for human life exhibited by major corporations is not legally defined as criminal behavior in capitalist America.

While the substantive criminal law de-emphasizes corporate crimes, it insures that nearly all of the socially harmful behaviors readily *accessible* to members of the power-disadvantaged classes are defined as "criminal" acts. Attempts to gain material advantage in some manner not authorized by the capitalist opportunity structure (property crimes), or acts which threaten the state monopoly of force (personal crimes), are given the greatest emphasis. This emphasis upon the harmful behavior most accessible to the disadvantaged gives the impression that the disadvantaged class is also the "dangerous" class, and diverts the conventional definition of crime away from the harmful behaviors of the ruling class.

FORMAL SANCTIONS

The statutorily prescribed sanctions for common-law crimes are generally far more severe than those attached to corporate crimes. This difference is both qualitative and quantitative.

The most common form of sanction prescribed for common-law crimes is incarceration, while for business-related offenses the most common form of penalty is a monetary fine. In the State of Ohio, for example, all of the acts listed under "offenses against property" are punishable by incarceration, while only forty percent of the offenses listed under the "pure food and drug law" can result in a deprivation of liberty. Furthermore, while nearly all of the property crimes are determined to be felony offenses punishable by prison sentences, ranging from one year to life, there is not a single violation of the pure food and drug law classified as a felony, and the maximum period of incarceration for any of these violations is 100 days. Generalized harms resulting from corporate crime when formally addressed by state are in the main handled through administrative or civil processes which seldom if ever result in individual loss of liberty and more often than not the penal sanction imposed is merely nominal.

Since common-law crimes are more readily accessible to members of the disadvantaged classes and corporate crimes more readily accessible to members of the ruling class, and since incarceration is a qualitatively more severe form of sanction than a nominal fine, it can be concluded that the sanctions applied to members of the power-disadvantaged group are quantitatively *and* qualitatively more severe than those applied to corporate criminals.

The penalties attached to crimes play a significant role in informing citizens of the seriousness of an offense. Since the penalties attached to corporate crimes are quantitatively less severe than those attached to common-law crimes, the sanction component of the criminal justice process emphasizes the "dangerous" nature of common-law offenses while presenting the harms perpetrated against large numbers of citizens by individuals serving corporate interests as minor offenses.

PROCEDURAL LAW

The procedural law component of the criminal justice process guarantees that the bulk of those individuals prosecuted and convicted will be members of the power-disadvantaged group. It serves the interests of the power-advantaged group by insuring that they have the least likelihood of being prosecuted, and, if prosecuted, the dominant class enjoys the maximum advantage in defending against the charges.

Procedural rules permit the arrest of common-law felons on the basis of probable cause, while violations of many laws governing corporate behavior require a complex sequence of complaint, show-cause orders, injunctions and violations of injunctions before criminal prosecutions result. Consider for a moment why is it *not* the case that burglars are given the opportunity to show cause why they should not be enjoined from burglarizing homes. Our procedural laws maximize the number of common-law offenders—who by the nature of the substantive law are generally members of the disadvantaged class—and minimize the number of corporate offenders who will ever face criminal proceedings following from the harms they cause.

Even in those unusual circumstances where criminal charges are indeed faced by the power-advantaged, procedural law creations such as money bail and the demand for legal counsel greatly improve the position of those from the power-advantaged group. The substantial body of literature on the effects of both pre-trial release through bail opportunity and public versus privately retained counsel on one's success in avoiding conviction serves as evidence of the procedural law in service of the power-advantaged.

INTERPRETIVE INSTITUTIONS

The interpretive institutions of the criminal justice process are the sub-systems of police, courts and corrections. The police sub-system is comprised of those agencies who must identify violations of law and bring the offenders before the court for prosecution. The organization of our policing efforts are directed toward controlling the common-law crimes of the power-disadvantaged. Few agencies exist to police the activities of corporate criminals, and where they do exist they are often drastically understaffed and underfunded. For example, it was recently reported that the Internal Revenue Service seldom conducts detailed audits of corporate tax returns since it generally lacks staff with sufficient expertise to understand the complexity of such returns (*Charlotte Observer,* April 14, 1974). Furthermore, many of the agencies designed to police corporate activities are staffed by representatives from the very agencies being policed. These representatives serve more a liaison capacity benefitting the corporate community than as unbiased agents of societal control. Yet, it is exceedingly unlikely that we would allow even "reformed" housebreakers to police other housebreakers.

Every city police defines its basic responsibility as the control of common-law crimes. Violations against consumers of the commonwealth, such as air and water pollution, are generally handled, if at all, by small regulatory agencies with little power and only minimal funding relative to the task at hand.

The courts and their related processes are clearly disadvantageous to those who are not members of the power-advantaged classes. The effects of the near-total breakdown of balance in our adversary system of prosecution are felt most heavily by those who cannot afford high-powered and equally high-priced legal counsel. The failure of those in political power to provide for a court system of sufficient size to handle even those criminal cases defined as serious, coupled with the overloading of court calendars with insignificant offenses of the poor, such as public intoxication and drug possession, gives criminal courts the squalid, overcrowded appearance which clearly identifies those prosecuted there as "undesirables."

The correctional sub-system exists almost entirely for the management and control of common criminals of the disadvantaged-class. Historically, offenders who have committed corporate crimes or political power crimes have seldom undergone the pains of imprisonment. On those few occasions when they have, as in the case of the criminals in the Nixon Administration, they have been sentenced to short terms in minimum security institutions.

These facts—that the police devote most of their attention to, that the courts generally convict, and that the prisons only punish common-law offenders—give further credence to the conventional impression that the "true" harms in society are common-law offenses and that the only harm-producers are members of the identifiable disadvantaged classes.

DISCRETIONARY ACTIONS

It is this component of the criminal justice process which most clearly demonstrates the repressive role of capitalist criminal justice. At every stage in the criminal justice process discretionary actions are taken which generally either benefit members of the power-advantaged group or which solidify and fix harmful effects on the politically and economically disadvantaged. The most prominent uses of this discretion are found in the decision to take into custody, the setting of bail, and the application of sentence. While these are the most well-established modes of repressive discretion, the potential for repression exists each time an actor in an interpretive institution decides upon a course of action.

The closer an individual is perceived as being to the locus of power—middle or upper status—the less likely he is of being arrested following an actual law violation; the less likely he will be denied release through excessive bail; and the less likely he will be subjected to incarceration as a penal sanction, as would be the risk of a member of the "dangerous" disadvantaged class.

The current efforts to adjust bail inequities reflect the entrenched nature of such discretionary biases. An individual's acceptability for release on recognizance is generally based upon his perceived social proximity to the powerful classes. An individual's geographic and job stability, the nature of his occupation and whether or not he owns property in the area are basic considerations in evaluating candidates for pre-trial release. On the basis of such "community stability" criteria, it is clear that the closer an individual's life-style conforms to one which is perceived as serving capitalist interests, the more likely he will be released on his own recognizance.

In the imposition and execution of sentence, similar discretionary favors are given members of the ruling class. That a presidential advisor could receive a sentence of six months for his part in the burglary of Daniel Ellsberg's psychiatrist's office, while disadvantaged "common offenders" spend years in prison for essentially the same offense is the archtype of discretionary repression.

REPRESSION AND CONSENSUS IN CAPITALIST AMERICA

While the interests of those with the power to make and enforce law receive immediate support from the criminal justice process, by far the greatest gain is through the power-advantaged class' control of the definition of crime.

Individuals learn the social meaning of actions through the responses those actions elicit from others. This learning can be either personal or imitative. At the personal level, we learn the meaning of our own behaviors through the consequences we experience as a result of those behaviors. At the level of imitative learning, the meaning of actions is acquired by observing the consequences experienced by others as a result of their actions (Bandura and Walters, 1963, p. 47).

The meaning of crime, like all other behaviors, is acquired through social learning, and for most individuals the social meaning of crime is acquired through imitative learning. The official responses—both dramatized and real—experienced by others for harmful acts prohibited by law provide a definition of crime. The understanding of what constitutes crime, the relative seriousness of various criminal acts and the established perception of who is "criminal" are based upon observations of the types of harmful acts prosecuted as criminal, the relative severity of the sanctions applied to these acts, and the types of individuals associated with these acts. Thus, those who control law making, establish penal sanctions, and administer justice also control the definition of crime.

While the substantive criminal law proscribes nearly all of those harmful acts accessible to the disadvantaged, it fails to include a large proportion in the harmful acts accessible only to members of the ruling class in search of corporate profits. This initial codification and dichotomous classification of harmful acts into criminal, and, by omissions non-criminal, sets the stage for a perception of crime which rests almost exclusively upon the common-law crimes of the power-disadvantaged.

Where harms committed in the service of capitalist goals are included in either the criminal law or in administrative regulatory codes, the penalties attached for violation are substantially less than those applied to common-law crimes. Persons socialized into a society where they observe that an individual can be deprived of his liberty for several years for breaking into a house, but will only pay a small fine for selling adulterated foods will *tend to assume that breaking into the house is the more serious of the two behaviors.*

The substantive laws and formal sanctions determine, for the most part, what behaviors we define as criminal and the relative seriousness we attach to these behaviors. The procedural laws, interpretive institutions and discretionary actions operate to guarantee that the bulk of individuals made accessible for social-observation and, to use Garfinkel's term, "public degradation" as convicted criminals, are members of the power-disadvantaged classes.

The procedural law makes an independent contribution to the definition of "criminal" by establishing a structure incomprehensible and problematic to negotiate successfully by those who are not economically and politically advantaged. The very procedures ostensibly designed to insure a balance in the adversary process between the individual and the state actually operate to give the disadvantaged an exceedingly poor chance of avoiding conviction.

The interpretive institutions, and the discretionary decisions made within them, are a result of the definition of crime created by the substantive and procedural laws and formal sanctions, while at the same time serving as contributors to the definition of the "crime problem." The laws and penalties concerning crime dictate that these agencies focus upon the apprehension and conviction of common-law offenders. Since common-law offenders have been conventionally defined as the most dangerous criminals, they become the least likely to benefit from police, courtroom, or "correctional" discretion. These factors further reinforce the perception that the true source of the crime problem is rooted in the relatively poor and powerless who commit common-law offenses, since citizen-observers see only that dimension of the crime problem wherein the poor and the powerless are convicted and punished for individual crimes against persons or property.

Members of the ruling class control the making of substantive and procedural laws, the statutory and discretionary determination of sentences, the character of interpretive institutions and both the detrimental and beneficial results of discretionary actions. Through all of this the powerful class shapes a definition of crime which supports their capitalist interests by insuring that the bulk of offenses from which individuals will acquire the meaning of crime bear no resemblance to the harmful acts of corporate profiteers, and that the majority of offenders—by the example of whom we learn to identify who is the criminal—bear no resemblance to members of the capitalist ruling class.

Given the nature of the law making and enforcing processes the fact that sub-groups in society would agree upon the relative seriousness of crimes is of little surprise. Each of these groups must derive its understanding of crime from the same basic pool of social responses to harmful acts. All members of society, regardless of sub-group membership, observe that the common-law crimes committed by the poor and the powerless are the most frequently prosecuted and most severely punished. Given this common universe of experience, it is unlikely that members of various subgroups would arrive at different evaluations of the seriousness of various crimes.

The existence of consensus, however, does not mean that the law serves the interests of all. The criminal justice process exists to insure the perpetuation of the established social order, and a primary method is through control of the definition of crime. Sub-groups tend to agree upon what is serious, not because this definition serves their own or society's interests but because it is difficult to understand a social creation such as crime outside of the social context in which it is presented.

Criminal justice in America serves the interests of the capitalist ruling class primarily through its creation of a consciousness which helps all believe that their interests are being served by a capitalist definition of "crime." Such consciousness manipulation preserves the "legitimacy" of the state and, unlike violent repression, does not run the risk of generating counter-violence.

References

Bandura, A. and Walters, R. 1963. *Social Learning and Personality Development.* N.Y.: Rinehart and Winston.

Diamond, S. 1971. "The Rule of Law Versus the Order of Customs," *Social Research* 38: 42–47.

Schafer, S. 1968. *The Victim and His Criminal.* N.Y.: Random House.

WOMEN: CASTE, CLASS, OR OPPRESSED SEX?

Evelyn Reed

Many people believe that the male domination of women rests ultimately on biology. The handicap of child-bearing functions is seen as the source of inequality between the sexes. But Reed argues that oppression of women derives from social not biological roots. During primitive communism, women were the equals of men, both performing similar productive roles in society. The advent of private property brought the institution of monogamy and changed the sexual division of labor, subsequent inequality, and oppression. The worth of women sank to its lowest point under capitalism. Women, however, should not be viewed as members of a caste or a class because they share with men the fact of class oppression. Emancipation of oppressed women will occur when they join with men to fight for the establishment of a socialist society.

The new stage in the struggle for women's liberation already stands on a higher ideological level than did the feminist movement of the last century.

Many of the participants today respect the Marxist analysis of capitalism and subscribe to Engels's classic explanation of the origins of women's oppression. It came about through the development of class society, founded upon the family, private property, and the state.

But there still remain considerable misunderstandings and misinterpretations of Marxist positions, which have led some women who consider themselves radicals or socialists to go off course and become theoretically disoriented. Influenced by the myth that women have always been handicapped by their childbearing functions, they tend to attribute the roots of women's oppression, at least in part, to biological sexual differences. In actuality its causes are exclusively historical and social in character.

Some of these theorists maintain that women constitute a special class or caste. Such definitions are not only alien to the views of Marxism but lead to the false conclusion that it is not the capitalist system but men who are the prime enemy of women. I propose to challenge this contention.

The findings of the Marxist method, which have laid the groundwork for explaining the genesis of woman's degradation, can be summed up in the following propositions:

First, women were not always the oppressed or "second" sex. Anthropology, or the study of prehistory, tells us the contrary. Throughout primitive society, which was the epoch of tribal collectivism, women were the equals of men and recognized by men as such.

Second, the downfall of women coincided with the breakup of the matriarchal clan commune and its replacement by class-divided society with its institutions of the patriarchal family, private property and state power.

The key factors which brought about this reversal in woman's social status came out of the transition from a hunting and food-gathering economy to a far higher mode of production based upon agriculture, stock raising and urban crafts. The primitive division of labor between the sexes was replaced by a more complex social division of labor. The greater efficiency of labor gave rise to a sizable surplus product, which led first to differentiations and then to deep-going divisions among the various segments of society.

By virtue of the directing roles played by men in large scale agriculture, irrigation and construction projects, as well as in stock raising, this surplus wealth was gradually appropriated by a hierarchy of men as their private property. This, in turn, required the institution of marriage and the family to fix the legal ownership and inheritance of a man's property. Through monogamous marriage the wife was brought under the complete control of her husband who was thereby assured of legitimate sons to inherit his wealth.

As men took over most of the activities of social production, and with the rise of the family institution, women became relegated to the home to serve their husbands and families. The state apparatus came into existence to fortify and legalize the institutions of private property, male dominion and the father-family, which later were sanctified by religion.

This, briefly, is the Marxist approach to the origins of woman's oppression. Her subordination did not come about through any biological deficiency as a sex. It was the result of the revolutionary social changes which destroyed the equalitarian society of the matriarchal gens or clan and replaced it with a patriarchal class society which, from its birth, was stamped with discriminations and inequalities of many kinds, including the inequality of the sexes. The growth of this inherently oppressive type of socioeconomic organization was responsible for the historic downfall of women.

But the downfall of women cannot be fully understood, nor can a correct social and political solution be worked out for their liberation, without seeing what happened at the same time to men. It is too often overlooked that the patriarchal class system which crushed the matriarchy and its communal social relations also shattered its male counterpart, the fratriarchy— or tribal brotherhood of men. Woman's overthrow went hand in hand with the subjugation of the mass of toiling men to the master class of men.

The import of these developments can be more clearly seen if we examine the basic character of the tribal structure which Morgan, Engels and others described as a system of "primitive communism." The clan commune was both a sisterhood of women and a brotherhood of men. The sisterhood of women, which was the essence of the matriarchy, denoted its collectivist character. The women worked together as a community of sisters: their social labors largely sustained the whole community. They also raised their children in common. An individual mother did not draw distinctions between her own and her clan sisters' progeny, and the children in turn regarded all the older sisters as their mutual mothers. In other words, communal production and communal possessions were accompanied by communal child-raising.

The male counterpart of this sisterhood was the brotherhood, which was molded in the same communal pattern as the sisterhood. Each clan or phratry of clans comprising the tribe was regarded as a "brotherhood" from the male standpoint just as it was viewed as a "sisterhood" or "motherhood" from the female standpoint. In this matriarchal-brotherhood the adults of both sexes not only produced the necessities of life together but also provided for and protected the children of the community. These features made the sisterhood and brotherhood a system of "primitive communism."

Thus, before the family that had the individual father standing at its head came into existence, the functions of fatherhood were a *social*, and not a *family* function of men. More than this, the earliest men who performed the services of fatherhood were not the mates or "husbands" of the clan sisters but rather their clan brothers. This was not simply because the processes of physiological paternity were unknown in ancient society. More decisively, this fact was irrelevant in a society founded upon collectivist relations of production and communal child-raising.

However odd it may seem to people today, who are so accustomed to the family form of child-raising, it was perfectly natural in the primitive commune for the clan brothers, or "mothers' brothers," to perform the paternal functions for their sisters' children that were later taken over by the individual father for his wife's children.

The first change in this sister-brother clan system came with the growing tendency for pairing couples, or "pairing families" as Morgan and Engels called them, to live together in the same community and household. However, this simple cohabitation did not substantially alter the former collectivist relations or the productive role of the women in the community. The sexual division of labor which had formerly been allotted between clan sisters and brothers became gradually transformed into a sexual division of labor between husbands and wives.

But so long as collectivist relations prevailed and women continued to participate in social production, the original equality between the sexes more or less persisted. The whole community continued to sustain the pairing units, just as each *individual member of these units made his and her contribution to the labor activities.*

Consequently, the pairing family, which appeared at the dawn of the family system, differed radically from the nuclear family of our times. In our ruthless[ly] competitive capitalist system every tiny family must sink or swim through its own efforts—it cannot count on assistance from outside sources. The wife is dependent upon the husband while the children must look to the parents for their subsistence, even if the wage earners who support them are stricken by unemployment, sickness or death. In the period of the pairing family, however, there was no such system of dependency upon "family economics" since the whole community took care of each individual's basic needs from the cradle to the grave.

This was the material basis for the absence, in the primitive commune, of those social oppressions and family antagonisms with which we are so familiar.

It is sometimes said or implied that male domination has always existed and that women have always been brutally treated by men. Contrariwise, it is also widely believed that the relations between the sexes in matriarchal society were merely the reverse of our own—with women dominating men. Neither of these propositions is borne out by the anthropological evidence.

It is not my intention to glorify the epoch of savagery nor advocate a romantic return to some past "golden age." An economy founded upon hunting and food gathering is the lowliest stage in human development, and its living conditions were rude, crude and harsh. Nevertheless, we must recognize that male and female relations in that kind of society were fundamentally different from ours.

Under the clan system of the sisterhood of women and the brotherhood of men there was no more possibility for one sex to dominate the other than there was for one class to exploit another. Women occupied the most eminent position because they were the chief producers of the necessities of life as well as the procreators of new life. But this did not make them the oppressors of men. Their communal society excluded class, racial or sexual tyranny.

As Engels pointed out, with the rise of private property, monogamous marriage and the patriarchal family, new social forces came into play in both society at large and the family setup which destroyed the rights exercised by earliest womankind. From simple cohabitation of pairing couples there arose the rigidly fixed, legal system of monogamous marriage. This brought the wife and children under the complete control of the husband and father who gave the family his name and determined their conditions of life and destiny.

Women, who had once lived and worked together as a community of sisters and raised their children in common, now became dispersed as wives of individual men serving their lords and masters in individual households. The former equalitarian sexual division of labor between the men and women of the commune gave way to a family division of labor in which the woman was more and more removed from social production to serve as a household drudge for husband, home and family. Thus women, once "governesses" of society, were degraded under the class formations to become the governess of a man's children and his chief housemaid.

This abasement of women has been a permanent feature of all three stages of class society, from slavery through feudalism to capitalism. So long as women led or participated in the productive work of the whole community, they commanded respect and esteem. But once they were dismembered into separate family units and occupied a servile position in home and family, they lost their prestige along with their influence and power.

Is it any wonder that such social changes should bring about intense and long-enduring antagonism between the sexes? As Engels says:

> Monogamy then does by no means enter history as a reconciliation of man and wife, and still less as the highest form of marriage. On the contrary, it enters as the subjugation of one sex by the other, as the proclamation of an antagonism between the sexes unknown in all preceding history. . . . The first class antagonism appearing in history coincides with the development of the antagonism of man and wife in monogamy, and the first class oppression with that of the female by the male sex (*Origin of the Family, Private Property, and the State*).

Here it is necessary to note a distinction between two degrees of women's oppression in monogamous family life under the system of private property. In the productive farm family of the preindustrial age, women held a higher status and were accorded more respect than they receive in the consumer family of our own city life, the nuclear family.

So long as agriculture and craft industry remained dominant in the economy, the farm family, which was a large or "extended" family, remained a viable productive unit. All its members had vital functions to perform according to sex and age. The women in the family helped cultivate the ground and engaged in home industries as well as bearing children, while the children and older folks produced their share according to ability.

This changed with the rise of industrial and monopoly capitalism and the nuclear family. Once masses of men were dispossessed from the land and small businesses to become wage earners in factories, they had nothing but their labor power to sell to the capitalist bosses for their means of subsistence. The wives of these wage earners, ousted from their former productive farm and homecraft labors, became utterly dependent upon their husbands for the support of themselves and their children. As men became dependent upon their bosses, the wives became more dependent upon their husbands.

By degrees, therefore, as women were stripped of their economic self-dependence, they fell ever lower in social esteem. At the beginning of class society they had been removed from *social* production and social leadership to become farm-family producers, working through their husbands for home and family. But with the displacement of the productive farm family by the nuclear family of industrial city life, they were driven from their last foothold on solid ground.

Women were then given two dismal alternatives. They could either seek a husband as provider and be penned up thereafter as housewives in city tenements or apartments to raise the next generation of wage slaves. Or the poorest and most unfortunate could go as marginal workers into the mills and factories (along with the children) and be sweated as the most downtrodden and underpaid section of the labor force.

Over the past generations women wage workers have conducted their own labor struggles or fought along with men for improvements in their wages and working conditions. But women as dependent housewives have had no such means of social struggle. They could only resort to complaints or wrangles with husband and children over the miseries of their lives. The friction between sexes became deeper and sharper with the abject dependency of women and their subservience to men.

Despite the hypocritical homage paid to womankind as the "sacred mother" and devoted homemaker, the *worth* of women sank to its lowest point under capitalism. Since housewives do not produce commodities for the market nor create any surplus value for the profiteers, they are not central to the operations of capitalism. Only three justifications for their existence remain under this system: as breeders, as household janitors, and as buyers of consumer goods for the family.

While wealthy women can hire servants to do the dull chores for them, poor women are riveted to an endless grind for their whole lives. Their condition of servitude is compounded when they are obliged to take an outside job to help sustain the family. Shouldering two responsibilities instead of one, they are the "doubly oppressed."

Even middle class housewives in the Western world, despite their economic advantages, are victimized by capitalism. The isolated, monotonous, trivial circumstances of their lives lead them to "living through" their children—a relationship which fosters many of the neuroses that afflict family life today. Seeking to allay their boredom, they can be played upon and preyed upon by the profiteers in the consumer goods fields. This exploitation of women as consumers is part and parcel of a system that grew up in the first place for the exploitation of men as producers.

The capitalists have ample reason for glorifying the nuclear family. Its petty household is a goldmine for all sorts of hucksters from real estate agents to the manufacturers of detergents and cosmetics. Just as automobiles are produced for individual use instead of developing adequate mass transportation, so the big corporations can make more money by selling small homes on private lots to be equipped with individual washing machines, refrigerators, and other such items. They find this more profitable than building large-scale housing at low rentals or developing community services and child-care centers.

In the second place, the isolation of women, each enclosed in a private home and tied to the same kitchen and nursery chores, hinders them from banding together and becoming a strong social force or a serious political threat to the Establishment.

What is the most instructive lesson to be drawn from this highly condensed survey of the long imprisonment of womankind in the home and family of class society—which stands in such marked contrast to their stronger, more independent position in preclass society? It shows that the inferior status of the female sex is not the result of women's biological makeup or the fact that they are the childbearers. Childbearing was no handicap in the primitive commune; it *became* a handicap, above all, in the nuclear family of our times. Poor women are torn apart by the conflicting obligations of taking care of their children at home while at the same time working outside to help sustain the family. Women, then, have been condemned to their oppressed status by the same social forces and relations which have brought about the oppression of one class by another, one race by another, and one nation by another. It is the capitalist system—the ultimate stage in the development of class society—which is the fundamental source of the degradation and oppression of women.

Some women in the liberation movement dispute these fundamental theses of Marxism. They say that the female sex represents a separate caste or class. . . . Let us examine these two theoretical positions and the conclusions that flow from them.

First, are women a caste? The caste hierarchy came first in history and was the prototype and predecessor of the class system. It arose after the breakup of the tribal commune with the emergence of the first marked differentiations of segments of society according to the new divisions of labor and social functions. Membership in a superior or inferior station was established by being born into that caste.

It is important to note, however, that the caste system was also inherently and at birth a class system. Furthermore, while the caste system reached its fullest development only in certain regions of the world, such as India, the class system evolved far beyond it to become a world system, which engulfed the caste system.

This can be clearly seen in India itself, where each of the four chief castes—the Brahmans or priests, the soldiers, the farmers and merchants, and the laborers, along with the "out-castes" or pariahs—had their appropriate places in an exploitative society. In India today, where the ancient caste system survives in decadent forms, capitalist relations and power prevail over all the inherited precapitalist institutions, including the caste relics.

However, those regions of the world which advanced fastest and farthest on the road to civilization bypassed or overleaped the caste system altogether. Western civilization, which started with ancient Greece and Rome, developed from slavery through feudalism to the maturest stage of class society, capitalism.

Neither in the caste system nor the class system—nor in their combinations—have women comprised a separate caste or class. Women themselves have been separated into the various castes and classes which make up these social formations.

The fact that women occupy an inferior status as a *sex* does not *ipso facto* make women either an inferior caste or class. Even in ancient India women belonged to different castes, just as they belong to different classes in contemporary capitalist society. In the one case their social status was determined by birth into a caste; in the other it is determined by their own or their husband's wealth. But the two can be fused—for women as for men. Both sexes can belong to a superior caste and possess superior wealth, power and status. . . .

Turning to the other position, it is even more incorrect to characterize women as a special "class." In Marxist sociology a class is defined in two interrelated ways: by the role it plays in the processes of production and by the stake it has in the ownership of property. Thus the capitalists are the major power in our society because they own the means of production and thereby control the state and direct the economy. The wage workers who create the wealth own nothing but their labor power, which they have to sell to the bosses to stay alive.

Where do women stand in relation to these polar class forces? They belong to all strata of the social pyramid. The few at the top are part of the plutocratic class; more among us belong to the middle class; most of us belong to the proletarian layers of the population. There is an enormous spread from the few wealthy women of the Rockefeller, Morgan and Ford families to the millions of poor women who subsist on welfare dole. *In short, women, like men, are a multiclass sex.*

This is not an attempt to divide women from one another but simply to recognize the actual divisions that exist. The notion that all women as a sex have more in common than do members of the same class with one another is false. Upper-class women are not simply bedmates of their wealthy husbands. As a rule they have more compelling ties which bind them together. They are economic, social and political bedmates, united in defense of private property, profiteering, militarism, racism—and the exploitation of other women.

To be sure, there can be individual exceptions to this rule, especially among young women today. We remember that Mrs. Frank Leslie, for example, left a $2 million bequest to further the cause of women's suffrage, and other upper-class women have devoted their means to secure civil rights for our sex. But it is quite another matter to expect any large number of wealthy women to endorse or support a revolutionary struggle which threatens their capitalist interests and privileges. Most of them scorn the liberation movement, saying openly or implicitly, "What do we need to be liberated from?" . . .

It is true that all forms of class society have been male-dominated and that men are trained from the cradle on to be chauvinistic. But it is not true that men as such represent the main enemy of women. This crosses out the multitudes of downtrodden, exploited men who are themselves oppressed by the main enemy of women, which is the capitalist system. These men likewise have a stake in the liberation struggle of the women; they can and will become our allies.

Although the struggle against male chauvinism is an essential part of the tasks that women must carry out through their liberation movement, it is incorrect to make that the central issue. This tends to conceal or overlook the role of the ruling powers who not only breed and benefit from all forms of discrimination and oppression but are also responsible for breeding and sustaining male chauvinism. Let us remember that male supremacy did not exist in the primitive commune, founded upon sisterhood and brotherhood. Sexism, like racism, has its roots in the private property system.

A false theoretical position easily leads to a false strategy in the struggle for women's liberation. Such is the case with a segment of the Redstockings who state in their *Manifesto* that "women are an oppressed *class.*" If all women compose a class then all men must form a counterclass—the oppressor class. What conclusion flows from this premise? That there are no men in the oppressed class? Where does this leave the millions of oppressed white working men who, like the oppressed blacks, Chicanos and other minorities, are exploited by the monopolists? Don't they have a central place in the struggle for social revolution? At what point and under what banner do these oppressed peoples of all races and both sexes join together for common action against their common enemy? To oppose women as a class against men as a class can only result in a diversion of the real class struggle. . . .

The underlying source of women's oppression, which is capitalism, cannot be abolished by women alone, not by a coalition of women drawn from all classes. It will require a worldwide struggle for socialism by the working masses, female and male alike, together with every other section of the oppressed, to overthrow the power of capitalism, which is central today in the United States.

In conclusion, we must ask, what are the connections between the struggle for women's liberation and the struggle for socialism?

First, even though the full goal of women's liberation cannot be achieved short of the socialist revolution, this does not mean that the struggle to secure reforms must be postponed until then. It is imperative for Marxist women to fight shoulder to shoulder with all our embattled sisters in organized actions for specific objectives from now on. This has been our policy ever since the new phase of the women's liberation movement surfaced a year or so ago, and even before.

The women's movement begins, like other movements for liberation, by putting forward elementary demands. These are: equal opportunities with men in education and jobs; equal pay for equal work; free abortions on demand; and child-care centers financed by the government but controlled by the community. Mobilizing women behind these issues not only gives us the possibility of securing some improvements but also exposes, curbs and modifies the worst aspects of our subordination in this society.

Second, why do women have to lead their own struggles for liberation, even though in the end the combined anticapitalist offensive of the whole working class will be required for the victory of the socialist revolution? The reason is that no segment of society which has been subjected to oppression, whether it consists of Third World people or of women, can delegate the leadership and promotion of its fight for freedom to other forces—even though other forces can act as its allies. . . .

The maxim of the Irish revolutionists—"who would be free themselves must strike the blow"—fully applies to the cause of women's liberation. Women must themselves strike the blows to gain their freedom. And this holds true after the anticapitalist revolution triumphs as well as before.

In the course of our struggle, and as part of it, we will reeducate men who have been brainwashed into believing that women are naturally the inferior sex due to some flaws in their biological makeup. Men will have to learn that, in the hierarchy of oppressions created by capitalism, their chauvinism and dominance is another weapon in the hands of the master class for maintaining its rule. The exploited worker, confronted by the even worse plight of his dependent housewife, cannot be complacent about it—he must be made to see the source of the oppressive power that has degraded them both.

Finally, to say that women form a separate caste or class must logically lead to extremely pessimistic conclusions with regard to the antagonism between the sexes in contrast with the revolutionary optimism of the Marxists. For unless the two sexes are to be totally separated, or the men liquidated, it would seem that they will have to remain forever at war with each other.

As Marxists we have a more realistic and hopeful message. We deny that a woman's inferiority was predestined by her biological makeup or has always existed. Far from being eternal, woman's subjugation and the bitter hostility between the sexes are no more than a few thousand years old. They were produced by the drastic social changes which brought the family, private property and the state into existence.

This view of history points up the necessity for a no less thoroughgoing revolution in socioeconomic relations to uproot the causes of inequality and achieve full emancipation for our sex. This is the purpose and promise of the socialist program, and this is what we are fighting for.

EVALUATING THE CRITICAL PERSPECTIVE

Marshall B. Clinard and Robert F. Meier

The critical perspective regards deviance as conflict, generally as a rational adjustment to the contradictions of the capitalist social and economic system. The strengths of the perspective, as Clinard and Meier point out, rest on its focusing attention on how political, economic, and social structures shape legal definitions of crime and deviance. They claim that its explanatory scheme has much more to say about how groups make rules and en-

Excerpt, pp. 90–93, from *Sociology of Deviant Behavior*, Sixth Edition, by Marshall B. Clinard and Robert F. Meier, copyright © 1985 by Holt, Rinehart and Winston, Inc., reprinted by permission of the publisher.

force them than about how individuals come to violate them. Similarly, the inverse relationship between power and punishment ("those who commit conventional crimes (generally lower-class citizens) are much more likely to be arrested, convicted, and sentenced to longer prison terms than those who commit white-collar and corporate crimes") adds validity to the critical perspective. Its weaknesses, they say, inhere in the fact that there are many more sources of conflict than political or economic ones, that laws benefit all classes (not just the ruling or powerful class) and do not cause criminal or deviant behavior by themselves, that few empirical studies support the claims of the critical perspective, and that the perspective makes more sense as an ideology than as a theory.

The conflict model has made an important contribution to the study of deviance. It has focused attention on the role of political, economic, and social structure in the definition of deviance, particularly through laws of the political state. Conflict theorists point out basic problems and contradictions of contemporary capitalism. They note that much crime is a reflection of societal values and not merely a violation of those values.[1] The basic issue is how values are translated into crimes and other rules, and it is on this point that conflict theory focuses. Several problems are inherent in the conflict view.

EXPLANATION OF RULES OR BEHAVIOR?

Conflict theory does little to inform us about the process by which a person comes to commit crimes or to develop deviance. It does raise pertinent questions about the origin of laws and norms, but it is essentially an explanation for the formation and enforcement of certain rules and laws.[2] To conflict theorists, the basic structure of a society, both economic and social, shapes the behavior of individuals and not socialization processes or peer-group and subcultural patterns.[3] When the conflict approach does deal with the individual, it assumes that deviance is a rational and purposive activity. Because the socialization process is ignored, deviance is assumed to be a rational process in which behavior is selected from available norms, values, and roles.[4]

OTHER SOURCES OF CONFLICT

The Marxist view is overly restricted to the relation of social class and economic power interests to norms regulating deviance and crime. Such norms are outgrowths of much broader conflicts of interest groups that include not only social class and economic interests, but other power conflicts based, for example, on religion, sex, age, occupation, race and ethnicity, and those attempting to regulate morality or to protect the environment.[5]

WHO BENEFITS?

Not all laws are necessarily devised by and operated for the advantage of one particular group. The conflict approach may be more applicable to those acts that generate disagreement about their deviant nature, such as political crime, prostitution, the use of certain drugs, and homosexuality, than to acts that reveal no such disagreement. In fact, it would appear that there is general consensus about both the illegal nature of the behavior and the seriousness of the act in the case of most acts presently defined in the United States as conventional or ordinary crime.[6] Laws against homicide, robbery, burglary, and assault benefit all members of society, regardless of economic position. Any statement that the elite alone benefit from such laws neglects the fact that most victims of these offenses are poor, lower-class urban residents and not members of any elite, however broadly defined. Although certainly the elite have more property to lose from theft or robbery, persons who actually lose the most are those who are the least able to afford it. If, on the other hand, one regards the operations of the criminal justice system, one sees considerable validity in the conflict perspective in the sense that those who commit conventional crimes (generally lower-class citizens) are much more likely to be arrested, convicted, and sentenced to longer prison terms than those who commit white-collar and corporate crimes.[7]

THE POWERFUL MAKE THE RULES EVERYWHERE

The assumption that powerful groups dictate the content of the criminal law, as well as other rule-making processes, and their enforcement for the protection of their own interests is too broad. All types of groups are involved in lawmaking, each with specific interests and concerns.[8] Powerful groups do have substantial input into the legal structure, but this is the case in any social system, whether capitalist, socialist, or communist. By penalizing those who violate it, the criminal law always defends the existing order and those holding power in it. It means little to say that the rules are made by those who have something to gain from those rules. This leaves unanswered important questions related to the characteristics of the "powerful," the process whereby some norms are made into law and others are not, the selective enforcement of those laws, and differences in lawmaking and enforcement processes in different economic and political systems.

LAW DOES NOT "CAUSE" BEHAVIOR

Although the conflict perspective points to the criminal law, supported by certain interest groups, as the ultimate cause of criminal behavior, it does not follow logically that the law is responsible for the behavior. In referring to the labeling perspective, which generates similar confusion with its emphasis on rule-making and deviance by interest groups, Edward Sagarin observes that "without schools, there would be no truancy; without marriage, there would be no divorce; without art, there would be no art forgeries; without death, there would be neither body-snatching nor necrophilia. Those are not causes; they are necessary conditions."[9] There would be no crime if there were no laws to prohibit some behavior, but the existence of a law is not sufficient to account for the behavior.

EMPIRICAL EVIDENCE

The empirical evidence supporting the conflict perspective tends to be broad and selective. General statements are made, but substantiating empirical evidence in terms of objective scientific evidence is often lacking, or existing contradictory evidence is omitted. Paul Friday has noted: "Conclusions of research on the social control agencies are used as theoretical support in addition to journalistic and 'muckraking' techniques drawing major conclusions from isolated case studies. The opinion of most conflict-oriented criminologists is that traditional 'scientific' methodology cannot be effectively used to uncover social structural inconsistencies."[10]

Few well-designed and operationalized research studies have been made of the conflict perspective; most, in fact, have been designed to support the ideology of this viewpoint by sometimes overlooking negative evidence. Here are three examples. First, most evidence has been taken from an analysis of capitalist U.S. society as a whole, with little recognition of variations by state or differences between the United States and many Western European countries. Second, while it is true that conventional criminal laws are directed primarily at the behavior of the lower class, this does not mean that social control agents such as the police are always repressive (they also stop family quarrels)[11] or that large corporations are not sanctioned for violations.[12] The penalties imposed by the government on businesses are not in any way proportionate to those imposed on lower-class criminals, but it must be recognized that even the enormous corporate power in this country is subject to the control of the state. Third, variations in sentencing of conventional offenders frequently seem to rest on factors other than class bias and the political power of elite groups.[13]

THEORY AS IDEOLOGY

The ultimate acceptance of the conflict view, particularly the Marxist view, depends only partially on the availability of a body of empirical evidence supporting the claim of the perspective. Perhaps more than any other approach to deviance, this theory has an ideological base that will either hasten or retard its acceptance, depending upon the observer's political and social viewpoint. Other sociological perspectives are not completely free of ideology, but the conflict theorists' emphasis on combining theory with practice in a socialist framework makes more obvious and explicit the political connotations of its explanatory scheme. The movement toward socialism is the end product of a fully developed conflict theory. As Richard Quinney summarized: "The underclass, the class that must remain oppressed for the triumph of the dominant economic class, will continue to be the object of crime control as long as the dominant class seeks to perpetuate itself; that is, as long as capitalism exists."[14] If the elimination of deviation and crime through the dissolution of capitalism and the transition to socialism is perceived to be too costly, however, the appeal of the conflict view diminishes considerably. It is not sufficient merely to analyze the conditions under which deviance develops; one must also be willing to change those conditions in a political sense. We are thus talking about someone who is not only committed to science as a means to discover the "real" world but someone who is also a political being committed to a political ideology, an ideology that, it is believed, can eradicate deviance. Thus appeal to scientific evidence leaves untouched the ideological component of conflict theory.[15]

Notes

1. Paul C. Friday, "Changing Theory and Research in Criminology," *International Journal of Criminology and Penology*, 5 (1977), pp. 159–170.

2. Ronald L. Akers, *Deviant Behavior: A Social Learning Perspective*, 2nd edition (Belmont, Calif.: Wadsworth, 1977), p. 29.

3. Alex Thio, "Class Bias in the Sociology of Deviance," *The American Sociologist*, 8 (1973), pp. 1–12.

4. See Alvin W. Gouldner, *The Two Marxisms: Contradictions and Anomalies in the Development of Theory* (New York: Seabury Press, 1980). On pp. 58–60 Gouldner distinguishes two forms of Marxist thought, one that emphasizes the rational aspects of human conduct, the other stressing the view that behavior follows lawlike patterns.

5. See John Horton, "The Rise of the Right: A Global View," *Crime and Social Justice* 15 (1981), pp. 7–17. In his first book on conflict and crime, Quinney adopted a much broader approach than social class, particularly in his discussion of the conflict of religious interests, Richard Quinney, *The Social Reality of Crime* (Boston: Little, Brown, 1970), pp. 37–39, 60–72.

6. See V. Lee Hamilton and Steve Rytina, "Social Consensus on Norms of Justice. Should the Punishment Fit the Crime?" *American Journal of Sociology*, 85 (1980), pp. 1117–1144, and Peter H. Rossi, Emily Waite, Christine E. Bose, and Richard

E. Berk, "The Seriousness of Crime: Normative Structure and Individual Differences," *American Sociological Review,* 39 (1974), pp. 224–237.

7. Jeffrey H. Reiman, *The Rich Get Richer and the Poor Get Prison: Ideology, Class, and Criminal Justice,* 2nd edition (New York: Wiley, 1984).

8. For a study examining the role of such groups see Richard A. Berk, Harold Brackman, and Selma Lesser, *A Measure of Justice: An Empirical Study of Changes in the California Penal Code, 1955–1971* (New York: Academic Press, 1977).

9. Edward Sagarin, *Deviance and Deviants* (New York: Holt, Rinehart and Winston, 1975), pp. 143–144.

10. Friday, p. 165.

11. See Otwin Marenin, "Parking Tickets and Class Repression: The Concept of Policing in Critical Theories of Criminal Law," *Contemporary Crises,* 6 (1982), pp. 241–266.

12. See Marshall B. Clinard and Peter C. Yeager, *Corporate Crime* (New York: Free Press, 1980).

13. This issue is debated, from each side, in Theodore G. Chiricos and Gordon P. Waldo, "Socioeconomic Status and Criminal Sentencing: An Empirical Assessment of a Conflict Proposition," *American Sociological Review,* 40 (1975), pp. 753–772, and Ivan Jankovic, "Social Class and Criminal Sentencing," *Crime and Social Justice,* 10 (1978), pp. 6–16.

14. Richard Quinney, *Critique of Legal Order* (Boston: Little, Brown, 1974), p. 16.

15. See, generally, Gouldner.

Questions for Discussion

1. Why is crime "inevitable under capitalist conditions"? For which social class(es)? What is the nature of these crimes? Is crime needed to solve the social problems produced by capitalism? What does Quinney think? What do you think?

2. Chambliss titles his article "Toward a Political Economy of Crime." What does this mean? Do you agree with Chambliss? Why or why not? How does his point of view enter into the article by Michalowski and Bohlander?

3. How can sexism be viewed as the result of capitalism? What other social problems can be seen this way?

4. Clinard and Meier outline the strengths and weaknesses of the critical perspective. Discuss these. What is your judgment: Do the strengths outweigh the weaknesses or the weaknesses, the strengths? Support your position.

Selected References

Anderson, Charles H. *Toward a New Sociology.* Rev. ed. Homewood, Ill.: Dorsey Press, 1974.
   An introductory sociology text based almost exclusively on the critical perspective. Anderson shows how many of the social problems in the United States derive from the social, cultural, and economic structure of contemporary corporate capitalism. He follows Marx in attributing most of these problems to alienation and sees the role of the sociologist as that of examining the causes and conditions of oppression and injustice, disseminating that information, and working for a more just and equitable society.

Antonio, Robert J. "The Origin, Development, and Contemporary Status of Critical Theory." *Sociological Quarterly* 24 (Summer 1983): 325–51.
   The rise of Stalinism in the Soviet Union and of fascism in Germany, and the failure of the proletariat to revolt in all modern urban-industrial-capitalist orders contributed to the emergence of the Frankfurt School. Most of the scholars who composed the Frankfurt School fled Germany for the United States, where they continued their extensive writings in a broad area that came to be known as "critical theory." Antonio traces the development and spread of this broad Marxist perspective in sociology. He closes with a brief note on a research project that combined data collection, explicit values on the part of the researchers, and the use of research for political purposes.

Balkan, Sheila, Ronald J. Berger, and Janet Schmidt. *Crime and Deviance in America: A Critical Approach.* Belmont, Calif.: Wadsworth, 1980.
   The authors examine crime and deviance from the critical perspective. They compare and contrast the crimes of the powerful with those of the powerless; they examine women as criminals and as victims; they analyze the political economy of mental illness; and they conclude by "blaming the system" rather than "blaming the victim." They say that if all social problems are rooted in capitalist society, then the solution to these problems will come about only through a transition from capitalism to democratic socialism.

Bernard, Thomas. "The Distinction Between Conflict and Radical Criminology." *Journal of Criminal Law and Criminology* 72 (Spring 1981): 362–79.
   As new perspectives on social problems come into being, there is the task of sorting them out and noting exactly where they fit in relation to the new as well as the earlier perspectives. In this piece, Bernard notes the similarities and the differences between two important viewpoints: conflict and radical criminology.

Greenberg, David F. "Delinquency and the Age Structure of Society." *Contemporary Crises* 1 (April 1977): 189–223.
   Contradictions in the political economy of capitalism produce rising rates of juvenile delinquency in advanced capitalist societies. Overproduction, exclusion of youth from the labor market (compulsory schooling, declining need for their labor) and teenagers' need for money combine to generate the social problem of juvenile delinquency.

Harring, Sidney L. *Policing a Class Society: The Experience of American Cities, 1865–1915.* New Brunswick, N.J.: Rutgers University Press, 1983.
   Through a number of case studies, principally of the Buffalo, Chicago, and Milwaukee police, Harring shows how members of the business class gained direct or indirect control of the police in these cities and used the police to repress the working class in one of two ways: by breaking strikes and preventing the formation

of labor unions, or by selectively enforcing laws prohibiting public drunkenness, vagrancy, gambling, and prostitution.

Inciardi, James A., ed. *Radical Criminology: The Coming Crises.* Beverly Hills, Calif.: Sage, 1980.

A collection of nineteen essays that outline radical criminology and offer arguments both for and against the development and acceptance of this perspective.

Kellner, Douglas. *Critical Theory, Marxism, and Modernity.* Baltimore: Johns Hopkins University, 1989.

A review and examination of the various intellectual sources of the critical perspective. Closes with suggestions for forming alliances with various contemporary social movements.

Liazos, Alexander. *People First: An Introduction to Social Problems.* Boston: Allyn and Bacon, 1982.

Liazos's thesis is that capitalism causes many problems in the United States, intensifies others, and makes it difficult to solve most. The social issues he deals with include social stratification, democracy, work, the professions, imperialism and hunger, communities, women, racism, the environment, crime, health, and education. He argues that socialism will solve many social problems.

Lilly, Robert J., Francis T. Cullen, and Richard A. Ball. *Criminological Theory: Contexts and Consequences.* London: Sage, 1990.

Devotes one chapter to an assessment of the contributions of critical criminology.

Melossi, Dario. "Overcoming the Crisis in Critical Criminology: Toward a Grounded Labeling Theory." *Criminology* 23 (May 1985): 193–208.

Melossi suggests that a synthesis of labeling theory with critical criminology will very likely improve the predictive power of the critical perspective.

Skolnick, Jerome H., and Elliott Currie. *Crisis in American Institutions.* 6th ed. Boston: Little Brown, 1985.

A popular text-reader on social problems, which reprints forty articles. A modified critical perspective collection.

Spitzer, Steven. "Toward a Marxian Theory of Deviance." *Social Problems* 22 (June 1975): 638–51.

Spitzer derives a set of propositions from Marxist theory that offer an explanation for increases in petty crimes and welfare problems in urban areas. The core of his argument rests on how the workings of the capitalist economy generate surplus labor, or what Marx called "the industrial reserve army."

Sykes, Gresham. "The Rise of Critical Criminology." *Journal of Criminal Law and Criminology* 65 (Spring 1974): 206–13.

A sympathetic appraisal of the conditions giving rise to the formulation of critical criminology and a prediction that the point of view is here to stay.

Taylor, Ian, Paul Walton, and Jock Young, eds. *Critical Criminology.* London: Routledge and Kegan Paul, 1975.

A collection of papers by three of the founders of critical criminology and a number of their followers.

Davis, Nanette J., and Clarice Stasz. *Social Control of Deviance: A Critical Perspective.* New York: McGraw-Hill, 1990.

The authors state that from the point of view of the critical perspective, political process is the central issue in deviance and control. This includes the importance of power in the creation of, organization of, and change in methods of control.

8 / SOCIAL CONSTRUCTIONISM

The turbulence of the 1960s and the early 1970s started to subside soon after the Vietnam War ended. Academics and their students returned to "business as usual." In terms of the dual mandate, the emphasis on the solution of social problems (which turmoil favors) became less salient and the development of sociology (which social tranquillity favors) became more of a focus. The social constructionist perspective became part of this change. It advanced a radical *subjectivist* perspective on the sociology of social problems.

THE LABELING PERSPECTIVE: THE CRITIQUE FROM OUTSIDE

Excluding the introductory course in sociology, the largest course in most sociology departments continues to be the course on social problems. As noted earlier in the book, since most of the students who take "Social Problems" are not majors in sociology, most colleges define it as a "service" course, and this important fact of academic life has played a role in the theory-research versus description-solution dilemma. To nonmajors, descriptions and solutions are more interesting than theories and research questions. Thus, textbook writers continue writing social problems texts in which detailed descriptions of social problems and their alleged objective conditions outweigh theoretical and research questions on how these situations came to be seen as social problems. As the reading of any one of the leading texts today will show, the best of them convey an enormous amount of information about a variety of social problems, teach sociology on the side, and still manage to remain silent on the development of sociological theory.

What set the groundwork for the theoretical breakthrough provided by social constructionism in the mid-seventies? Paradoxically, it all came about because of the success and the failure of the labeling perspective. First, we consider the "success," then, the "failure."

The "Success" of the Labeling Approach. All theories that have a lasting influence (e.g., Darwinism, Marxism, and Freudianism) ultimately get reduced to oversimplifications. In time, people need only repeat a key term to give the impression of both knowing and understanding the theory. That all of this happened with what came to be called "labeling theory" seems quite clear. A theory that said a good deal more about the sociology of deviance spread rapidly because of the apparent simplicity and neatness of its key concept, "labeling." This helped to produce its success.

The "Failure" of the Labeling Approach.   In Howard Becker's version of the labeling perspective, Edwin Sutherland's threefold classification of criminology still held sway: criminology is the study of the making, breaking, and enforcing of rules. Becker, in his book *Outsiders,*[1] says deviants are people who are labeled as such. There are three elements in this process: the making of labels, the application of labels, and the reaction to being labeled.

The sociological community ignored the making of labels and concentrated on who applied the labels to whom and how the people so labeled lived with these labels. Critiques, conceptual and empirical, centered on labeling's silence on etiology and on its central proposition that enforcement of rules increased deviant behavior, launched people on deviant careers, and engendered deviant subcultures.

Two different philosophies of social science governed the intellectual responses to the labeling perspective. The "objectivist" tradition, focusing on casual explanation, showed that labeling failed as a theory of deviant behavior on two counts: either no testable "hypotheses" could be deduced from its postulates or its "hypotheses" were refuted by the "facts." The "subjectivist" tradition, focusing more on how people came to understand their own and others' actions, concentrated on how people designated as social deviants coped with the problems of deviant roles and whether participation in deviant subcultures helped to solve those problems for them.[2] If objectivists relied heavily on official statistics and questionnaire data, subjectivists were more apt to gather their data through fieldwork.

While objectivists and subjectivists both examined, albeit with different research methods, the conditions under which deviant persons are made, they paid considerably less attention to its complementary question, namely, What are the conditions under which *alleged situations are made out to be deviant?* Furthermore, although the labeling perspective could just as easily be applied to social problems as to deviance, somehow both critical and sympathetic responses to the labeling perspective concentrated

---

1. Howard S. Becker, *Outsiders: Studies in the Sociology of Deviance* (New York: Free Press, 1963).

2. See Earl Rubington and Martin S. Weinberg, eds., *Deviance: The Interactionist Perspective,* 5th ed. (New York: Macmillan, 1987).

on the question of *labeling deviance* as opposed to *labeling social prob-lems.*

In arguing for a subjectivist orientation, Becker pointed out that the emergence and enforcement of a rule had its own natural history. He cited Sutherland's groundbreaking 1950 study which set forth the conditions un-der which sexual psychopath laws were passed. He then went on to apply a similar argument to how the Marijuana Tax Act came into being and what followed its passage.

Subsequent students of social problems applied this point of view to examining other laws. The great bulk of research, following the publication of *Outsiders,* as already noted, however, was on labeling deviants, not social problems, and the consequences of the labeling.

The debate between two sociologists, Walter Gove and Thomas Scheff, throughout the next decade, symbolized for many what might be called "the rise and fall of the labeling perspective." Scheff argued in his book *Being Mentally Ill,* which first appeared in 1966, that the single most important causal factor in mental illness was labeling.[3] Gove, in a series of publications, argued that disturbed behavior rather than social re-sponses to such behavior was the main cause of mental illness. Gove later convened a conference in 1975, the proceedings of which were later pub-lished as *The Labeling of Deviance.*[4] This book rejected the labeling per-spective with subsequent chapters refuting its application to mental retardation, drug addiction, mental illness, and alcoholism. Ronald Akers summed up the situation when he wrote as follows:

> The labeling perspective captured the imagination of researchers, theo-rists, and practitioners in the 1960s. It continued as a major but much less dominant theory in the 1970s. By the late 1970s, however, it was clear that labeling theory was in decline. It was criticized from several quarters for not being supported by research and was attacked by radicals for ideological impurity. It remains as a recognized and important ap-proach, always included in textbook discussions of theories of deviance. . . . But labeling theory does not generate the interest and research it once did.[5]

But observers of debates between these two schools of thought often remarked that here was a good example of people talking past one an-other. A clarification and a focus on the third subject of Becker's book—the study of the conditions under which situations are made out to be problems—became the province of the social constructionist perspective.

3. Thomas Scheff, *Being Mentally Ill: A Sociological Theory* (Chicago: Aldine de Gruyter, 1966).

4. Walter Gove, *The Labeling of Deviance: Evaluating a Perspective* (New York: Halsted Press, 1975).

5. Ronald L. Akers, *Deviant Behavior: A Social Learning Approach,* 3d ed. (Belmont, Cal.: Wadsworth, 1985), p. 32.

THE LABELING PERSPECTIVE: CRITIQUE FROM INSIDE

Adherents as well as opponents called aspects of the labeling perspective into question. The most significant criticism from adherents came from two important articles appearing in the journal *Social Problems* in 1973. These two papers, coauthored by John Kitsuse and Malcolm Spector, mark the birth of the *social constructionist perspective*.[6]

Kitsuse and Spector argued that sociologists had written about social problems for more than fifty years, but had yet to come forward with a real theory of social problems. A true sociology of social problems had yet to exist, they said.

In effect, Kitsuse and Spector went on to show that none of the perspectives treated in this book can answer the question, What truly makes a situation out to be a social problem in the first place? For instance, textbooks, particularly after Fuller and Myers's articles appeared, stated that a social problem consisted of a subjective as well as an objective condition. Yet none of them could answer the question as to why some situations got designated as a social problem while others did not. The authors simply took it for granted that everyone would concede that what they chose to include as social problems in their textbooks *were* social problems. This basis of inclusion, which either made the general public or the authors to be "judges" of social problems, only begged the question, How did this situation come to be defined as a social problem whereas another one did not?

Spector and Kitsuse noted that in the introduction to another of Becker's books, *Social Problems*,[7] Becker agreed with Fuller and Myers that social problems consisted of both an *objective condition* as well as a *subjective definition*. It is here that Kitsuse and Spector made their strongest and most critical point. Becker had said that social problems are what people think they are, but then he went on to presume that *there was such a situation as that which they were complaining about*. This is where Spector and Kitsuse parted company with all previous perspectives on social problems. Their argument really centers on the process by which people come to think of something as a "social problem" without any reference to an "objective condition." Unlike all the other perspectives, Spector and Kitsuse asked a different set of questions. What did some people say was a social problem? How did they go about making that situation into a "social problem"? What did other people do in response to this conceptuali-

---

6. John I. Kitsuse and Malcolm Spector, "Toward a Sociology of Social Problems: Social Conditions, Value Judgments, and Social Problems," *Social Problems* 20 (Spring 1973): 407–19; Malcolm Spector and John I. Kitsuse, "Social Problems: A Reformulation," *Social Problems* 21 (Fall 1973): 145–59

7. Howard S. Becker, *Social Problems: A Modern Approach* (New York: John Wiley, 1966).

zation? What were the consequences of the definition of that situation as a social problem? In a word, what Spector and Kitsuse had done was to subjectify more fully the labeling perspective.

CONSTRUCTIONISM'S RISE, DEVELOPMENT, AND CHANGE

Spector and Kitsuse are sympathetic critics of the labeling perspective. Spector wrote an important piece, "Legitimizing Homosexuality,"[8] which graphically demonstrates Becker's point that ultimately definitions of deviance are political (only groups with power can effectively label behavior as deviant and only pressure groups can muster enough power to redefine such behavior as acceptable). In addition, Spector served as editor of the journal *Social Problems* (1981–1984) and during that time published a number of important pieces in the new tradition of constructionism. Kitsuse and Spector's two 1973 articles in *Social Problems* set down the essentials of their sociology of social problems. They expanded these articles into chapters in their 1977 book *Constructing Social Problems,* which has since come to be the locus classicus of the perspective.[9]

Conrad and Schneider's *Deviance and Medicalization,* first published in 1980, linked labeling with constructionism and indicated that a new perspective was forming.[10] Joseph Schneider later joined with Kitsuse to edit a book entitled *Studies in the Sociology of Social Problems,* a collection of readings on social constructionism.[11] And to mark the emergence of this latest perspective on social problems, Schneider wrote an important chapter reviewing work in this new and developing approach in the *Annual Review of Sociology* in 1985.[12] In turn, Schneider went on to serve as editor of *Social Problems* (1987–1990). Like Spector before him, he encouraged work in constructionism and the journal published a number of theoretical, critical, and research papers on constructionism during his tenure. Still later, Kitsuse and Schneider sponsored a series of books on social problems. In addition to reissuing *Constructing Social Problems,* they also fostered a collection of constructionist papers on social problems edited by Joel Best titled *Images of Issues.*[13] Both this concentration and

---

8. Malcolm Spector, "Legitimizing Homosexuality," *Society* 14 (May 1977): 52–56.

9. Malcolm Spector and John I. Kitsuse, *Constructing Social Problems* (Menlo Park, Cal.: Cummings, 1977).

10. Paul Conrad and Joseph W. Schneider, *Deviance and Medicalization: From Badness to Sickness* (St. Louis: Mosby, 1980).

11. John Kitsuse and Joseph Schneider, *Studies in the Sociology of Social Problems* (Norwood, N.J.: Ablex, 1984).

12. Joseph W. Schneider, "Social Problems Theory: The Constructionist View," *Annual Review of Sociology* 11 (Palo Alto, Cal.: Annual Reviews, 1985): 209–29.

13. Joel Best, *Images of Issues: Typifying Contemporary Social Problems* (New York: Aldine de Gruyter, 1989).

dispersion of work in such a short period of time clearly demonstrated the arrival of a new perspective on social problems.

In that short time, Kitsuse and Spector had accomplished a number of things: they had synthesized the value-conflict and labeling perspectives; they had turned the field on its head by arguing that subjective definitions, not objective conditions, were the "source" of social problems and the proper object of study of those sociologists who sought to develop a sociological theory of social problems; they had pointed out the usefulness of "a natural history of social problems"; and they had stimulated a flood of studies that took quite seriously their radical definitional approach to the study of social problems.

CHARACTERISTICS OF THE CONSTRUCTIONIST PERSPECTIVE

To some degree, from a widened labeling perspective, Spector and Kitsuse argue that social problems are what people think they are. Objective conditions that may or may not exist and may in some ways give rise to the conception that a social problem exists are of no interest to them. Adopting a radically subjectivist position, they focus all attention on the problem-defining process, in who goes about defining a situation as a problem, what kind of a definition they formulate, how they present their arguments to others, how others respond to their complaints, and what the upshot of the interaction is between those who complain and those who respond.

Definition. The process itself whereby people define a condition, alleged or actual, as a social problem.

Cause. The problem-defining activities people engage in as they seek a redress of grievances.

Conditions. The process involving interaction between complainants, as initiators, and old or new agencies, as responders to their demands for redress.

Consequences. There are, hypothetically, four stages in the natural history of social problems (see the Randall and Short selection in the readings that follow), when examined from the point of view of social constructionism. But since these stages are hypothetical and contingent on such matters as clarity of definition, management and strategy of gaining and maintaining attention, the relative power of complainants, and the agencies from which they seek redress, only empirical research can offer tentative answers to the question of consequences.

Solutions.   The constructionist perspective is silent on the question of solutions, deeming this a matter to be settled by research on the life course of the defining process.

SUMMARY AND CONCLUSION

The 1960s saw the rise of the labeling perspective, a view that held that deviance is what people say it is. This point of view quickly caught on, and stimulated research, writing, and criticism. By the mid-1970s, however, numerous objectivist researchers questioned what they saw as the perspective's major proposition: that labeling either sustains or increases deviant behavior.

The mid-seventies saw the emergence of a radicalization of the labeling perspective, social constructionism, as an approach to the study of social problems. Radically subjective, constructionists argued that the true subject of the sociology of social problems lay in finding out how people arrived at a definition of a social problem, how they fashioned their complaints, claims, and demands into a process of defining activities, and who responded to these activities. As the 1980s came to a close, though, constructionism had already developed its own schools: those who would center all of their research efforts on the subjective definition of the problem (strict constructionists) and those who would include data on the objective conditions that provide the social context for such definitions (contextual constructionists). Perhaps most significant of all, social constructionism fostered more research in showing how problems became problems and less on telling how to solve them.

THE DEFINITION OF SOCIAL PROBLEMS

John I. Kitsuse and Malcolm Spector

In this excerpt, Kitsuse and Spector part company with the value-conflict perspective. Fuller and Myers, for example, said that social problems consisted of an objective condition and a subjective definition. By contrast, Spector and Kitsuse argue that the latter, the process *by which a situation gets* defined *as a social problem, is what the sociology of social problems should focus on. Peoples' beliefs about situations, what they complain about, the form their protest takes, and so forth, should constitute the sociological study of social problems rather than a study of the objective facts. People can protest because of a material interest (they are affected by the situation in some way) or because of a moral interest (though personally unaffected by the situation, they consider it morally wrong and feel "that something should be done about it"). There is also a natural history to social problems: if some interest groups are able to convince others that a problem exists, others fail.*

Definition, the work of interest groups, and whether or not people come to define the situation the way interest groups do, make up, for Spector and Kitsuse, the social problems process.

THE "VALUE-CONFLICT" POSITION

Fuller and Myers (1941) stress both the objective conditions and the subjective awareness of social problems. They view the objective conditions as not *sufficient* (but rather as only *necessary*) for the existence of a social problem. This leads them to be concerned equally with explaining the causes of the objective conditions and the process by which they become defined as social problems.[1]

Here their formulation becomes confused. They use values, value-judgments and value-conflicts in several ways, leading them, in our judg-

From John I. Kitsuse and Malcolm Spector, *Social Problems* 20:4 (Spring 1973), pp. 407–419. Reprinted by permission of The Society for the Study of Social Problems and the authors.

ment, to stray from the course they initiate in their definition of the field. Waller (1936) and Fuller and Myers use the concept of values in three senses. First, value-judgments lead people to denounce conditions as undesirable and repugnant to them and to define such conditions as social problems. This is the import of their statement that "value-judgments lead people to define conditions." Thus values are the key element in explaining the subjective elements of social problems.

. . . [I]n his attempt to *explain the objective condition* as well as its definition as a problem, Fuller (1938:419) invokes values again:

> Value-judgments themselves are in most instances a formal cause of the *condition* which is regarded as undesirable.

In their typologies of social problems, Fuller and Myers (1941a) classify problems as to whether *the causes of the conditions include* physical events, value-judgments, or moral ambiguity.

In a third usage, value-judgments "not only help to create the condition but prevent its solution" (1941a:29) as well:

> A value-scheme which prohibits frank discussion of sex problems in the home and school is a causal item in the existence of the condition, venereal disease. The same taboos which contribute to the causation of the condition frustrate public programs which are designed to eradicate it. Similarly, value-judgments which deny social acceptance to the mother of a child born out of wedlock, not only contribute causally to such conditions as abortions, infant mortality, and abandoned children, all of which are socially disapproved, but such value-judgments also obstruct efforts to solve the illegitimacy problem by impeding free discussion of it (1941a:26).

Here Fuller and Myers point out with irony that the very people (social workers, liberal statesmen, and assorted other "do-gooders" among whom they included sociologists) who invoke their humanitarian mores to define conditions as social problems, themselves subscribe to and support policies *based on those same mores*, that insure the persistence of the social condition without alleviation, amelioration, or eradication.

Without questioning the validity of these last two formulations, we believe that the Fuller and Myers attempt to explain both *the objective and subjective*° aspects of social problems deflects the thrust of their original statement. While they move away from the functionalist position that conditions in themselves are sufficient for the existence of social problems, they do not move to the position that *objective conditions*° are *not necessary*. To the extent that they attempt to explain the existence of the objective conditions themselves, their position comes close to the very social disorganization formulation of which they are so critical (see especially Fuller, 1939). This is particularly clear in their statement that values both cause

°Italics added.

the condition and inhibit its solution, and in Waller's position that conflicts *in and between the mores themselves* produce social problems, with the implication that different values or mores, acting independently, may interfere with each other or work at cross purposes. To the extent that values, rather than individuals or groups of people, are seen as the active agents in the society, the formulation becomes elliptical, reified, and abstracted.

Thus, their attempt to explain both the existence of the objective conditions and the process by which some condition, real or imaginary, becomes defined as a problem introduces an ambiguity into their position on just what the role of values is in the production of social problems. The result is that values seem to be the active forces everywhere: in producing the condition, in leading people to define the condition as a problem, and finally, in inhibiting a solution. We interpret this ambiguity as a hedge against the charge of subjectivism, solipsism and worse. The logic of their formulation, however, does not require a statement of position on the question of whether or not an objective condition "in fact" exists. Becker (1966: 6) in his re-statement of the value-conflict view acknowledges that group definitions of social problems *usually do* have reference to some empirically verifiable social conditions. Groups do not typically get upset over "nothing." Our position is that one need not assume nor explain the existence of this *objective*° condition; indeed, to do so would deflect attention from investigation of the definitional process. The definition *may* be accompanied by empirically verifiable claims about the scale, intensity, distribution, and effects of the imputed social conditions; but it *may not* and theoretically it *need not* . . .

SOCIAL PROBLEMS AS PROCESS

Our analysis . . . leads us to propose that the explanation of the "subjective element" of social problems—the process by which members of groups or societies define a putative condition as a problem—is the distinctive subject matter of the sociology of social problems. Thus, we define social problems as *the activities of groups making assertions of grievances and claims with respect to some putative conditions.* The *emergence* of a social problem, then, is contingent on the organization of group activities with reference to defining some putative condition as a problem, and asserting the need for eradicating, ameliorating, or otherwise changing the condition. The central problem for a theory of social problems, so defined, is to account for the *emergence and maintenance of claim-making and responding activities.* Such a theory should comprehend the activities of any group making claims

°Italics added.

on others for ameliorative action, material remuneration, alleviation of social, political, legal, economic disadvantage or other consideration.

The existence of social problems depends on the continued existence of groups or agencies that define some condition as a problem and attempt to do something about it. To ask what are the effective causes of social problems, or what keeps social problems activities going, is to ask what keeps these various groups going.

Fuller and Myers, in answer to this question, saw the causes of social problems in value-judgments and value-conflicts that lead members of a society to call attention to conditions that they find offensive. Values may lead some groups to become indignant about some condition and call for its change. This is the force behind humanitarian reformers, crusaders, and do-gooders.

However, not all social problems activities spring from this sort of "disinterested" principled activity. Humanitarian crusaders by definition set out to improve the lot of more disadvantaged others. They are not, themselves, victims of the conditions they set out to ameliorate. When those who complain are themselves the victims of the conditions, we will call them an "interest group." Interest may be defined as real and material advantages or stakes in the outcome of a given line of activity. Interest groups are those who have something to gain or lose, not just as everyone else would be affected but over and above the way everyone in a society would be affected by a given change in law or policy.

Groups defining conditions as social problems then, may be kept going by interests or values, or any mixture or combination of them. Some of the interesting varieties might include the following:

1. Value groups may find that as they raise a condition as a social problem, they gain as allies other groups who have a vested interest in their position. Similarly, they may be opposed by groups who have a vested interest in the *status quo*.

2. Interest groups may find that the dialogue of public debate must take place in terms of values or ideals. Thus, in order to present its claims effectively, or argue its position, it must acquire a set of values that legitimate their claim.

3. A given protest group may find a convenient overlap between their interests and their values. That is, the things they want to ask for are just those things that are easily justified and legitimated.

4. Alternatively, a group may find itself cross-pressured when their interest requires them to sacrifice or ignore some strongly felt value, or their values require them to work against their own best interests—the liberal position on school busing may be an example of this.

5. To the extent that a disinterested value-oriented group is successful

in their activity, they may develop various interests to protect organizations, careers, reputations, etc. They may face a crisis of the "routinization of disinterest" when they become vulnerable to the charge of being interested and self-serving rather than humanitarian.

In the preceding . . . we have attempted to define a subject matter for the study of social problems in a clear and unambiguous manner amenable to empirical investigation. It remains now to justify the addition of this new conceptual category "social problems" by contrasting it to previously used or related and overlapping categories. We have suggested that previous treatments of social problems failed to distinguish their own subject matter from such related fields as social pathology, social disorganization, value-conflicts, and deviant behavior. As we have indicated, our approach has little (or nothing) in common with social pathology or disorganization formulations of social problems. We begin our analysis with the activities of individuals and groups in a society, not with a formulation about what any society must do or have for its survival, nor with any idea about whether protest activities are good (functional) or bad (dysfunctional) for its maintenance. Nor does our approach share the concerns of the study of deviant behavior conceived as the analysis of the etiology of certain acts or behaviors that violate norms or result in official responses to these acts. Such a conception forms a fundamentally different subject matter from our sociology of social problems. We are interested in the activities of making claims, and the response to these claims *as claims*. Deviant acts are not usually taken to be claims nor does the response to them typify them as claims. However, when claims and grievances are responded to *as deviance*, then these processes would be subject matter for investigation within our formulation (cf. Horowitz and Liebowitz: 1968).

The approach we take does, however, contain an affinity with some developments in the so-called labelling perspective on deviance. It shares an interest in the process by which a phenomenon (an act or a condition) comes to be defined in a specific way. It shares also an insistence that acts or conditions may be intelligibly studied only with difficulty or not at all if such definitional processes are ignored. Further, some studies within the labelling formulation provide examples of the initial processes that we take to be the bases of the phenomena we wish to identify as social problems. Becker's (1963) discussion of moral entrepreneurship and of the development of the marijuana tax act exemplify this theoretical articulation (see also Cook: 1969 and Dickson: 1968).

In addition to these several social problems categories, our formulation invites comparison to the study of social movements and to the study of interest groups. Indeed, our definition of social problems could be interpreted to include the whole of "political sociology." This, however, is not our intention. Specifically, the rise of political parties or revolutionary groups whose aim is to take control of social institutions falls at the margins of our definition, although they comprise the core of the study of social movements and political sociology. For the most part, groups that create social problems do so by making demands on existing institutions, not by trying to form institutions themselves. They share a concern to "get someone to do something" about the putative conditions. Such groups, of course, may transform themselves into genuine political parties if they fail to gain satisfaction from the existing regime. In doing so, however, their specific "social problems" are likely to be lost or transformed by intra- and inter-organizational political processes and concerns. By proposing these analytic distinctions, we wish to provide for the investigation of organized protests and social movements that do not conform to the models of political parties or revolutionary movements and thus tend to be ignored by political sociologists.

Finally, our formulation bears a similarity to the so-called "group approach" to politics exemplified in the classic formulations of Bentley (1908) and Truman (1951). It will, however, be instructive to contrast Truman's definition of interest group with our distinction between interest groups and "dis-interested" or value-oriented groups. Truman (1951:33–4) defines interest groups as

> any group, that, on the basis of one or more shared attitudes, makes certain claims upon other groups in the society for the establishment, maintenance or enhancement of forms of behavior that are implied by the shared attitudes. These shared attitudes (deal with) what is needed or wanted in a given situation, observable as demands or claims upon other groups in the society. The shared attitudes, moreover, constitute the interests.

Truman's definition is much broader than our own conception and would include both interested and dis-interested groups. In our formulation, an interest may be defined as any social arrangement upon which some individuals or groups claim to depend, rely, use, or need in the conduct of their daily activities. The scope of this definition is intentionally broad; it is meant to suggest that almost any aspect or object in social life may become the focal point for social problems activity. *Not all groups that enter the social problems arena, however, do so to defend some interest.** Similarly, not all activities of interest groups lead to the emergence of social problems.

As Truman (1951:38) points out, many interest groups are highly altruistic, supporting causes in which they have no vested interest. Although the vocabulary of motives in contemporary society leaves little room for altruism and self-sacrifice as explanations of conduct, we recognize that individuals and groups may be moved by moral indignation and outrage to demand

*Italics added.

that "something be done." Thus, our approach modifies Truman's conception of interest groups to recognize differences between those affected by the condition and those participating in the social problems enterprise for other reasons.

CONCLUSION

. . . [Prior] approaches [to social problems] harbor crucial ambiguities as to the distinctive nature of the phenomenon of social problems and the kind of theory one would have to develop to account for it.

We have presented a definition of social problems drawn from our analysis of the functionalist and value-conflict approaches [which also consider "objective" conditions as relevant to sociology]. It proposes that the explanation of the "subjective elements" of social problems—the process by which some groups successfully define a condition as a problem within their society—is the distinctive task of the sociology of social problems.

We believe the theoretical approach to this subject matter contains three elements. One is a theory of interests, for many of the groups that participate in the process of definition do so in order to pursue or protect their own social, political, economic, and other interests. A second element is a theory of moral indignation, for some groups attempt to define a condition as a social problem because it offends their sense of values; it seems wrong to them that the condition exists at all. The third element is a theory of natural history, because we conceive social problems not as static conditions or instantaneous events, but rather as a sequence of activities that may move through different stages.[2] These different stages may be characterized by different casts of characters, different kinds of activities, different dilemmas, and call for different kinds of analysis. Furthermore, the development of social problems through these stages may be marked by critical contingencies that impede or facilitate it.

Notes

1. It should be noted that Merton pays lip service also to the dual nature of social problems: "Social problems are not subjective states of mind; they are also objective states of affairs" (1971:788). However, his discussion of manifest and latent problems indicates quite clearly that the objective state of affairs takes precedence over subjective states of mind in the definition of social problems.

2. Blumer (1971) has recently proposed a five-stage career model of social problems that begins to address this question.

References

Becker, Howard S. 1963. *Outsiders: Studies in the Sociology of Deviance.* New York: Free Press.

———. 1966. *Social Problems: A Modern Approach.* New York: John Wiley.

Bentley, Arthur F. 1908. *The Process of Government: A Study of Social Pressures.* Bloomington, Indiana: The Principia Press.

Blumer, Herbert. 1971. "Social problems as collective behavior." *Social Problems* 18 (Winter): 298–306.

Cook, Shirley. 1969. "Canadian narcotics legislation, 1908–1923: A conflict model interpretation." *The Canadian Review of Sociology and Anthropology,* 6 (February): 36–47.

Dickson, Donald T. 1968. "Bureaucracy and morality: An organizational perspective on a moral crusade." *Social Problems* 16 (Fall): 143–157.

Fuller, Richard. 1938. "The problem of teaching social problems." *American Journal of Sociology* 44: 415–435.

———. 1939. "Social problems," pp. 3–59 in Robert E. Park (ed.), *An Outline of the Principles of Sociology.* New York: Barnes and Noble.

———, and Richard Myers. 1941a. "Some aspects of a theory of social problems." *American Sociological Review* 6 (February): 24–32.

———. 1941b. "The natural history of a social problem." *American Sociological Review* 6 (June): 320–328.

Horowitz, Irving Louis, and Martin Liebowitz. 1968. "Social deviance and political marginality: Toward a redefinition of the relation between sociology and politics." *Social Problems* 15 (Winter): 280–296.

Merton, Robert K., and Robert A. Nisbet. 1971. *Contemporary Social Problems.* Revised. New York: Harcourt, Brace and World.

Truman, David B. 1951. *The Governmental Process.* New York: Alfred Knopf.

Waller, Willard. 1936. "Social problems and the mores." *American Sociological Review* 1 (December): 922–934.

MEDIA AND THE SOCIAL CONSTRUCTION OF RISK

Robert A. Stallings

Two conditions for the emergence of a social problem, according to the Spector-Kitsuse model, are defining a situation as a problem and getting organizational action on that definition.

Stallings examines the risk-defining role newspapers play in the process. His study of newspaper reports on the collapse of a New York Thruway bridge which killed ten people establishes two points: how news reports create interpretations of causes and proposed solutions to a social problem in the making, and how risks of patterned bridge collapses failed to gain acceptance as a bona fide social problem. Coverage in the New York Times, *for example, went from detailed coverage of the incident to reports of risks of bridge collapses in New York State to risks of a pattern of future collapses in the United States as a whole.*

The risk of future bridge collapses, however, failed to gain acceptance as a social problem. The newspaper reports found many rather than one cause of risk of collapse. Since the responsibilities for these risks were dispersed widely over a number of relatively weak organizations, none was able to collectively muster sufficient resources to press successfully claims that bridge safety was a serious public problem.

. . . Most of the time people ignore the risks in everyday life. However, when the taken-for-granted outcomes of routine activities fail to occur—a commercial airliner crashes rather than landing safely, the earth trembles violently rather than imperceptibly, a highway bridge collapses rather than conveying vehicles safely from one bank to another—risk and safety often become matters of public discussion and remedial public policy making (Meltsner 1978; May 1985; for an exception to this sequence, see Schoenfeld, Meier, and Griffin 1979). Forces that seemed benign, under control, or nonexistent appear to be malicious, unchecked, and omnipresent in the aftermath of such dramatic events.

From *Social Problems* 37:1 (February 1990), pp. 80–95. Reprinted by permission of The Society for the Study of Social Problems.

We turn to people with special insight into the hidden forces behind these events to help us better cope with the risks that we now suddenly recognize. Although a few of us may have direct contact with specialists, most of us rely on news organizations to bring the experts to us. We watch, listen, and read about the likely causes of the unsettling event and hope to be reassured about the absence of future harm. In other words, the reality of risk for most of us exists mainly in images created by others. These images "keynote" our collective attempt to make sense out of the world, including its risks, by helping to structure the lines along which initial discussions proceed.

Discourse about risk consists of two interrelated processes (see Lazarsfeld, Berelson, and Gaudet 1944; Katz 1957; Van den Ban 1964): personal conversations about risk, and media discourse about risk. Whether rejected, accepted, or modified, comments by expert risk definers contained in news accounts serve as points of departure for personal conversations. Risk-related comments therefore constitute a source of raw material for public discourse on risk. Such comments are public descriptions of a putative condition (Spector and Kitsuse 1977) that other experts and opinion leaders may challenge, that ordinary people may converse and disagree about, and that governmental officials may comment on. They usually identify a cause of the putative condition and imply a course of action, though not necessarily in that order (Hewitt and Hall 1973).

Whatever their awareness of what people are saying in their personal conversations, risk definers drawn into media discourse are keenly aware of each other's public statements and positions. Gans (1979:291), for instance, observed that ". . . elected and appointed officials are, by all odds, the most intensely interested news audience." Many corporations also designate employees to monitor, collect, or summarize news accounts that involve or affect them. In addition, corporations and politicians sometimes commission survey research ("polls") on relevant markets or constituencies. Put differently, while people in the news often have only piecemeal glimpses of the reactions of their audience, they have a much clearer picture of the range of statements that others present to that audience.

Media discourse is only part of public discourse in the aftermath of a dramatic event. However, it is an important source of raw material for both media organizations and private conversations (Fishman 1978; Gans 1979). . . . One such recent event was the collapse of a bridge.

THE DRAMATIC EVENT AND ITS COVERAGE IN THE NEWS

At 10:45 a.m. Sunday, 5 April 1987, four cars and a tractor trailer fell 80 feet from a disintegrating interstate highway bridge into Schoharie Creek in upstate New York 40 miles northwest of Albany. All were travelling on the Thomas E. Dewey Thruway (I-90) when a shifting pylon dropped three of the five spans of the 540-foot bridge, and the vehicles, into the flood-swollen creek below. Nine bodies ultimately were recovered, with a tenth victim still missing but presumed drowned.

Here I examine accounts of the Schoharie Creek bridge collapse published in the national edition of the *New York Times*. Coverage of the collapse began in the *Times* on the morning after the incident, Monday, 6 April 1987, and continued off-and-on throughout the summer. Two major story lines developed. One focused on the bridge collapse, its causes, and who was responsible. The other portrayed unsafe bridges as an emerging public problem symbolized by this incident.

PATTERNS OF CAUSATION IN NEWS ACCOUNTS

News accounts of both the Schoharie Creek bridge collapse and the nation's bridge problem published in the *New York Times* contain two distinctly different views of causation. One depicts the causes of collapses and other deficiencies as acts of nature. The other sees causation in terms of human agency.

The Schoharie Creek Bridge Collapse

Natural causes. News accounts identify several elements of the natural environment as potential causes of the Schoharie Creek bridge collapse. Most attributed the collapse to the cumulative effects of heavy rains and flooding on the foundation of the bridge supports. Federal highway officials, for example, said that flooding contributed to "scouring," a term referring to the fact that rapidly flowing water had gouged out the earth and gravel upon which the bridge's concrete footings rested. As these footings dropped deeper into the eroding creek bed, the steel pylons they supported eventually pulled away from the roadway overhead. Sections of the concrete and steel bridge subsequently tumbled into the creek. The *Times* provided a diagram of the bridge with its key components labeled, for example, "Footing," "Pylon," etc. (Boorstin 1987).

Human agency. Several human agents soon appeared in accounts of the collapse. These are individuals and organizations whose actions or inaction seemingly implicated them in the bridge collapse. Early accounts laid causal responsibility at the feet of New York State officials.[1] Investigative reporters for the *Times* suggested that the Schoharie Creek bridge had not been properly inspected. The improper inspection theme quickly grew to include several points. Some were matters about which experts disagreed. None were described in the *Times* as illegal or as anything but irregular. Most appear to a sociologist to be normal compromises and adjustments in everyday work routines. Their status as potential causes of the collapse emerged only in hindsight.

A major element of the improper inspection theme was that at the time of the most recent scheduled inspection of the bridge in April 1986, neither the footings nor the creek bed under them were directly examined. The inspector then gave the bridge a rating of five on a seven-point scale, a rating described as meaning "minor deterioration and is functioning as designed." The inspector gave the footings a rating of nine, however, meaning that their condition was "unknown but not necessarily dangerous." New York Thruway Authority officials explained that the footings could not be directly inspected because the water level in the creek was too high at the time. (The Schoharie Creek bridge was one of 861 bridges in the State of New York maintained by the Thruway Authority, an independent public authority established in 1950.) They pointed out that three subsequent "informal" inspections (a term never defined or clarified) during the summer of 1986 found the footings to be in good condition.

The improper inspection theme soon encompassed still other aspects of the inspection process. First, the Thruway Authority performed no follow-up tests for scouring. State law requires such tests whenever bridge footings can not be directly inspected. Second, the inspector who conducted the follow-up informal inspections made no written record of them. Third, the inspector's supervisor failed to sign the April 1986 inspection report. Finally, the April inspection occurred 31 months after the previous one, not two years afterward as required by federal regulation. Again, none of these actions seem sinister or especially unusual, but reporters searching for causes in the aftermath of the collapse held them up to a different and brighter light.

Three new aspects of the impropriety issue emerged in subsequent accounts. Reporters questioned why the State of New York allowed the Thruway Authority to use one-person inspector "teams" on its interstate highway bridges whereas the state's transportation department, which has jurisdiction over all state bridges not part of the interstate highway system, routinely used two-person inspection teams. Reporters wondered why the Thruway Authority allowed the Schoharie Creek bridge to be inspected by an individual who was not a licensed professional engineer. They also asked why the Thruway Authority did not rotate bridge inspectors, noting that the same person conducted the two most recent inspections of the bridge (i.e., in 1983 and 1986).

Other aspects of human agency appeared as various investigations of the bridge collapse got underway. Thruway Authority officials pointed out that Schoharie Creek was narrowed during original construction despite warnings by the state's engineers that to do so might endanger the bridge in the event of flooding. Reporters commented that this would mean that design flaws rather than faulty maintenance and inspection were a cause of the collapse. The Thruway Authority's former chief engineer also re-called the dispute over narrowing the creek bed in his testimony at the National Transportation Safety Board (NTSB) hearings in July 1987. Other engineers testified that the Thruway Authority ignored recommendations ten years before the collapse to add reinforcing rocks (known as "riprap") around the footings to protect against scouring. The failure to again add riprap when the bridge underwent major reconstruction in 1981 became a focus of the NTSB's investigation. Thruway Authority representatives continued to point in the other direction, citing faulty and hurried construction in 1954 that resulted in no steel rods being used to secure the footings to their concrete piers. The question of why no one warned the Thruway Authority about flooding in Schoharie Creek and elsewhere on 4–5 April also came up.

The Condition of the Nation's Bridges as a Public Problem.   In the course of their investigative reporting on the bridge collapse in New York State, *Times* reporters uncovered a Federal Highway Administration (FHA) report on deficient bridges in all fifty states. A second story line quickly emerged, this one concerning an apparent nationwide problem with unsafe bridges. An article filed from Kansas City four days after the collapse focused on another interstate highway bridge in the St. Louis area whose steel pins holding girders in place had sheared, dropping the roadway surface three inches.[2] A Missouri highway department crew performing unrelated work in the vicinity at the time immediately closed the bridge, averting any injuries. The *Times* article began by declaring that there were "indication[s] that the problem of deteriorating highway bridges reaches far beyond any one state" (Robbins 1987:1).

A lengthy article the following Sunday (Tolchin 1987) further documented the extent of the national bridge problem. The article quotes extensively from a report prepared by a private consulting firm. The consultants found that there were approximately 150 bridge collapses annually in the United States, mostly in rural areas, resulting in an average of 12 fatalities each year. This article also described five other bridge collapses during the first four months of 1987, three in Missouri (the leading deficient-bridge state), one in Pennsylvania, and one in California.

Natural causes.   In these and subsequent articles, experts quoted by *Times'* reporters identified several natural forces as among the many causes of the nation's bridge problem. One account listed the age of a majority of the nation's bridges as a major factor contributing to their precarious condition. Another account identified climate as a factor and cited the interaction of age and climate as one reason the problem was more extensive in the Northeastern United States. Other candidates in this category included normal vehicle usage as well as the interaction of age and usage.

Human agency. As in accounts of the Schoharie Creek bridge collapse, news sources associated several aspects of human agency with this newly discovered problem involving the nation's bridges. Unlike the references to specific individuals and agencies in accounts of the Schoharie Creek bridge collapse, accounts of human agency in the case of the nation's bridge problem feature stereotypes of actors personifying underlying social forces.

The article on the near-collapse of the bridge near St. Louis introduced in the role of fool (Klapp 1949)—as in "penny wise, pound foolish"—the "voter/taxpayer" as the personification of what is often referred to as the taxpayer revolt or the fiscal limitation movement. " 'The country is not spending enough money on maintenance' " proclaimed a civil engineer (Robbins 1987). Other highway and engineering experts commented that Missouri's ranking as the nation's leader in the number of deficient bridges resulted from a lack of funds for maintenance and repair in that state. The article reveals that Missouri ranked seventh in the nation in the number of miles of highways but fiftieth in revenue spent to maintain them.[3]

Federal "bureaucrats" soon became a villain in accounts of the nation's bridge problem. One agency to which this label was applied was the FHA— the agency with the deficient bridge list. The *Times* (Stuart 1987) reported that two days after the Schoharie Creek bridge collapse the FHA proposed several regulatory changes regarding interstate highway bridges. Among them was a proposal to relax mandatory biennial inspections. The FHA argued this would give states greater flexibility. Rather than automatic inspection at fixed intervals, scarce state resources could be better used to conduct more frequent inspections of deficient bridges if sound bridges could be inspected less frequently. Unfortunately for the FHA, the *Times* observed that this was the second time around for this proposal. A similar proposal to eliminate mandatory two-year inspections in 1984 was withdrawn because it, too, came on the heels of a bridge collapse on the Connecticut Turnpike (Stuart 1987).

Representatives of claims-making groups criticized the revived FHA proposal. A spokesperson for the Center for Highway Safety (a "consumer advocacy group" in the words of the *Times*) argued that highway bridge inspections should be more rather than less frequent. Representatives of the American Association of State Highway and Transportation Officials expressed divided opinions on the proposed regulatory changes. The *Times* described as a positive aspect of the FHA proposal a call for all interstate highway bridge inspectors to be licensed by the National Society for Professional Engineers.

The label "politicians" identifies another set of human agents appearing in news accounts after the Schoharie Creek bridge collapse. Here the trail led by implication to both the White House and the Congress. The *Times* reported that the NTSB in 1987 had only 12 highway investigators and that the agency had investigated only five bridge collapses in its entire 20-year history. Highway investigators at the NTSB concentrated on school bus crashes, serious commercial bus accidents, and hazardous chemical spills. Under the Reagan administration, the *Times* noted, the NTSB shrank from 400 to 320 employees and the FHA from 4,200 to 3,400. It reminded readers that Congress passed a highway bill in early 1987 authorizing $8.15 billion for bridge rehabilitation, overriding a veto by the president to do so.

Another human agent appearing in the *Times* is the "trucker." An engineer cited as the second most frequent cause of bridge collapses "someone trying to move an overload of unprecedented magnitude" across a bridge (Tolchin 1987). (He identified washed-out supports as the leading cause of bridge collapses.) Another highway expert pointed out that bridges normally did not collapse under the weight of an overload itself. Weakened structures typically collapsed later, meaning that those at risk from excessive loads were innocent motorists rather than the offending truckers. Law enforcement officials interviewed in both Missouri and New York State admitted that load restrictions were difficult to enforce and were frequently violated. A background article describes another bridge collapse in New York State in 1986 whose probable cause was an overloaded truck hauling a large crane (Stuart 1987).

News accounts of the safety of bridges, in short, contain numerous proposed causes for both the collapse of the I-90 bridge and for the condition of bridges nationwide. What began as an account of a "simple" but tragic accident resulting from an act of nature soon became an account of the various ways that human beings contributed to the incident. The stockpile of potential causes grew and changed as news accounts moved from a focus on responsibility for the collapse of the Dewey Thruway bridge to responsibility for the deficient condition of bridges in the State of New York and finally to responsibility for the condition of bridges across the entire nation. Accounts published in the *Times* presented news audiences with an evolving description of a public problem and with several proposed causes to explain it.

PATTERNS OF CAUSATION ABSENT FROM NEWS ACCOUNTS

Identifying causes that are *absent* from accounts of the bridge collapse and of the public problem of bridges is more difficult than describing those that are present. It is important analytically to do so, however, and an excellent precedent exists in the social problems literature: Gusfield's (1981: 45–47) description of how causation in the drinking-driving problem became attached to drivers rather than to highways, motor vehicles, or other factors.

A first step is to classify proposed causes according to the social institution with which they are associated. For example, causes appearing in these accounts in the *Times* deal with *secular* rather than religious forces. Apart from an eyewitness interviewed at the scene who was quoted in the first article as saying that the Schoharie Creek bridge collapse was "the work of God" (Uhlig 1987), accounts contain no comments by experts who sought to explain the collapse as "the work of Satan" or "the will of God" (cf. Lofland 1981:193–203).

The absence of still other causes that could have but did not enter this media discourse come into view. No news source identifies market forces as a potential cause either of the collapse or of the bridge problem. An implicit reference to economic activity appeared when highway experts cited overloaded trucks as a major cause of bridge failures and deterioration, but there was no explicit link established between economic conditions in the trucking industry, production pressures that might lead to overloading vehicles, and the condition of bridges. Nor did anyone make a causal connection between the condition of bridges and such economic variables as the state of the American economy, the value of the dollar on foreign currency markets, industrial competition from other nations, or the price of crude oil.

Also absent were accounts framing the situation as a *partisan political* matter. Although a *Times* reporter implied as much in reviewing reductions in force at the FHA and NTSB during the Reagan administration and in recalling the president's veto of a highway appropriations bill, none of the attributed news sources make an explicit case for any of the following as causes of the problem with bridges: increasing the nation's defense capability at the expense of infrastructure maintenance; balancing the federal budget (the reporter's description of staff reductions at NTSB and FHA did not portray these as deficit-reduction trade-offs); reducing the scope of federal regulatory activity (although an obvious tie-in could have been made with the FHA's proposal to drop mandatory two-year inspections); or shifting fiscal responsibility for various activities from the federal government to the states.

Absent also are any accounts containing a sociological perspective on bridge problems and collapses. For example, there was no *organizational* or *interorganizational* perspective presented to explain the failure of bridges. Such a perspective might have treated the so-called inspection improprieties differently, for example as the everyday compromises and trade-offs of work organizations.[4] No account quotes any news source who described the bridge problem in particular or infrastructure decay in general as an inevitable by-product of *class struggle* in advanced capitalist nations like the United States (cf. Castells 1978; O'Connor 1973). Nor did anyone cite as a factor contributing to the nation's problems with its bridges the unintended consequences of *life style* involving patterns of work and leisure and the modes of transportation sustaining them. (Life style was a theme in the public policy debate just a decade earlier during the so-called energy crisis of the 1970s.) . . .

SELECTION OF NEWS SOURCES AND SELECTIVE PATTERNS OF CAUSATION

With an array of potential causes to choose from, why do some rather than others enter into media discourse? I suggest that an answer lies in the relationship between journalists such as those at the *New York Times* and their news sources.

Journalists simultaneously create and perpetuate an image of reality when they assemble news products. The use and perpetuation of a frame (Goffman 1974:10–13) is inevitable in selecting, re-creating, and presenting events as news. This frame is grounded in an existing view of a world-taken-for-granted (Berger and Luckmann 1966)—for journalists working in the "prestige press," a largely upper-middle class, urban, white, male world-taken-for-granted (Gans 1979:68–69, 208–11). Both reality creation and re-ality perpetuation occur when journalists select news sources. The organizational, occupational, and disciplinary points of view of those sources, transformed by reporters and editors into sentences, paragraphs, and headlines, present an account of how the world works in terms of risk and safety.

Put simply, the selection of an image of risk—including patterns of causation—takes place in the selection of news sources. There were no Marxist explanations of falling bridges as the by-product of advanced cap-italism because there were no Marxist sources identified or quoted in the *Times*. Similarly, there were no organizational, cultural, and economic pat-terns of causation because the sources used in preparing these news ac-counts did not include sociologists, anthropologists, and economists.

How and why are some individuals rather than others selected as news sources? Selection may be understood as an organizational process rather than as the separate (and idiosyncratic) decisions of individual journalists. That is, a variety of cultural, structural, and technological variables char-acterizing the media as work organizations (Tuchman 1978; Gans 1979) influences the selection of sources. This examination of what news accounts contained and what they did not contain suggests (but cannot confirm) some of these influences. For example, like most members of the educated middle class, journalists in the prestige press see stories involving the haz-ardousness of the built environment as secular matters having scientific content. Hence, reporters framed accounts of the Schoharie Creek bridge collapse and of the nation's collapsing and deficient bridges in a civil en-gineering context. They quoted scientists and engineers rather than reli-gious leaders, seers, prophets, and medicine men. Had an engineer stated that the collapse of bridges was the work of the devil, it is unlikely that in 1987 the *New York Times* would run a headline such as "Collapsing Bridges Seen as Work of Satan, According to Safety Expert."

Journalists' preconceived notions of organizational domain (Thompson 1967) are another selection criterion. That is, sources used in preparing news products usually hold jobs in organizations that journalists link to the issues. Some are with organizations "owning" the incident or problem in the sense of political responsibility (Gusfield 1981:13–16). In the Schoharie Creek bridge collapse these included inspectors from the New York Thruway Authority, emergency service and rescue personnel, and officials of the FHA and the NTSB. Other organizations have a stake in the issue as a result of previous claims-making activity. These include social movement organizations, labor unions, and professional associations. Examples in the present case were the Missouri Motor Truck Association, the Road Information Program, the American Association of State Highway and Transportation Officials, and the Center for Highway Safety.

When several organizations can claim equal stakes in the problem, journalists' views of organizational prestige are important in selecting news sources. This is often the case when journalists seek experts from universities. Other things being equal, news sources who contribute to accounts are more likely to be affiliated with elite research universities (Stanford, MIT, the California Institute of Technology, for instance) than with liberal arts colleges or community colleges.

Exceptions to the association between organizational prestige and experts' participation in media discourse often stem from geographic location. That is, journalists are more likely to select news sources from organizations that are easily accessible (Gans 1979:124–25; Molotch and Lester 1975: 255–58). Less prestigious organizations may produce expert sources because the logic of reporting suggests that location gives them special insight. For example, the *Times* reporter preparing the article on the interstate highway bridge closure near St. Louis probably contacted members of the engineering faculty at the University of Missouri because he assumed that they would be uniquely qualified to comment on bridge conditions in that state.

Other dynamics surrounding media organizations influence the inclusion and exclusion of news sources—and hence of the points of view they represent—as participants in media discourse about risk. Several factors increase the likelihood that corporate and governmental officials, for example, will contribute to news accounts. The need for novelty and an attempt to avoid saturation over time (Hilgartner and Bosk 1988:62–64; Gans 1979:167–71) produces a shift away from victims and eyewitnesses as news sources toward members of special commissions and investigative bodies. The specialized resources of governments and corporations provide deadline-conscious reporters with usable materials (Nelkin 1987:128–31; Friedman 1981; Gans 1979:121–22, 128–31). Finally, legal advisers to media organizations prefer news sources who reduce the probability of libel suits (Shapiro 1989).

CHARACTERISTICS OF "WINNING" ACCOUNTS

Media discourse following a dramatic event such as an airliner crash or a bridge collapse can contain many different characterizations of risk and its causes. Some will drop by the wayside as the story unfolds, but others will persist and gain acceptance. What distinguishes "winning" accounts—in particular, those dealing with cause-and-effect—from the rest? A completely satisfactory answer to this question is beyond the scope of this paper, but news accounts examined here do suggest two features of accounts that persist in the public arena. First, successful accounts tend to identify the dramatic (but single) event as part of a *pattern* encompassing other similar events. Second, they usually propose a *causal explanation* of this pattern that satisfactorily subsumes all known cases to date.

Placing the Dramatic Event in Context: Pattern Construction.   An isolated incident and a series of like events are quite different in terms of the logic required to make them sensible. The isolated incident is easier to dismiss (and to disown) as simply an aberration, an exception, or a result of improbable circumstances that are unlikely to be duplicated. A pattern, on the other hand, implies regularities; repeated occurrences are difficult to dismiss as chance (Gusfield 1981:82).

Any link among events is not an inherent property of the events themselves. One event is similar to another when people recognize only their common properties while forgiving their differences. In other words, a pattern exists when someone successfully creates a link among events that others might see as unique. A corollary is that the treatment in media discourse of events as unique may also be the result of hard work by claimsmakers. Maintaining the singularity of an incident can be an important aspect of what Gusfield (1981:12–13) calls disownership. News accounts following the accident at Three Mile Island, Pennsylvania, in 1979, for example, contained examples of industry and federal officials insisting that this incident was unique and should not be considered part of a pattern of nuclear reactor incidents indicating an inherent lack of safety in the production of nuclear energy (President's Commission on the Accident at Three Mile Island 1979).

Journalists, aided by their news sources, facilitate the creation of such patterns in the public arena. Fishman (1978) describes how the emergence of a news theme ("crimes against the elderly") combined with police reports of incidents involving elderly victims to produce a crime wave in New York City. Following the Schoharie Creek bridge collapse, investigative reporters for the *New York Times* disclosed previous bridge failures, some involving the interstate highway system. The FHA's list of the nation's deficient bridges provided a steady supply of incidents (Fishman 1978:538). Headlines such as "Another Bridge Falls Near Thruway Collapse" (*New York Times* 1987) and "Near Collapse of Missouri Bridge Points Up Extent of Repair Needs" (Robbins 1987) transformed the I-90 bridge collapse from an isolated event—possibly a chance occurrence—into one more example of the hazardous condition of the nation's highway system.

Pattern construction viewed as a collective phenomenon is analogous to the retrospective construction of deviant identities at the interpersonal level. After a "normal" individual is publicly linked to some bizarre behavior, acquaintances often recall and reinterpret previous quirks and eccentricities that seem consistent with this new identity (Kitsuse 1962:253). Such retrospective interpretation increases the plausibility of the newly acquired deviant label. Claims-making groups in existence at the time of a dramatic event perform an analogous function in media discourse about risk. Their spokespersons contribute to pattern construction when they place the incident alongside previous events that were also of concern.

To say that news organizations such as the *New York Times* or claims-making groups such as the Center for Highway Safety "created" a pattern (i.e., the series of interstate highway bridge incidents) and placed the Schoharie Creek bridge collapse within it is not to say that either caused the bridge to collapse or fabricated reports of other collapses. However, the decision to treat the several collapses as linked, and in the case of the *Times* to seek out news sources who could explain how and why they were linked, is an organizational decision, not something that is a self-evident attribute of these events.

Competing for Causal Supremacy.   Establishing the plausibility of a connection among events begs the question of *why* the events are connected. A "winning" account that accomplishes the construction of a pattern also offers a credible explanation for that pattern consistent with the "facts" publicly available at the time. The ability to compete for causal supremacy varies as a function of journalists' and their sources' abilities to do several things.

First, they must establish a criterion by which dramatic events—past and present—appear to be similar. An event could be characterized by any number of attributes. Once selected, the classifying criterion for judging similarity and difference limits the range of both proposed causes and possible solutions. For example, the earliest accounts of the Schoharie Creek bridge collapse used the State of New York as a distinguishing criterion. If several bridge collapses had in common their location within this state, then accounts suggesting a causal relationship between the condition of bridges and some attribute of the state (its administrative agencies, its political leadership, its public expenditure patterns, its climate, its economic base, its trucking industry, its geography, etc.) would have been highly competitive in the public arena. However, the state's bridges were not the responsibility of a single agency; the state of Missouri seemed to have even worse problems; different contractors built the several failed and deficient bridges across the country; the nation's bridges are exposed to different climatic conditions; and so forth. The criterion of similarity quickly became the interstate highway system, and the search for causes shifted to the federal government along with the states.

Second, the logic used by journalists and their sources to identify a prior common condition as the cause of a series of events resembles what John Stuart Mill called the First Canon or the *Method of Agreement* ([1843] 1919:253–66). (In contrast, the physical and social sciences employ Mill's Third Canon, the *Joint Method of Agreement and Difference,* i.e., the logic of controlled experimentation.) Not all of the nation's collapsed and deteriorating bridges could be explained by flooding, controversial inspection practices, short-cuts by contractors, or overloaded trucks. What they all had in common—both those that failed as well as those listed as deficient—was the fact that, according to many highway experts, insufficient money was being spent for their maintenance and rehabilitation.

Using the method of agreement to identify a condition common to all cases judged to be similar is one reason that winning accounts depicting cause-and-effect are overwhelmingly *monocausal* (cf. Gusfield 1981:72–74). Early accounts may imply that many interrelated factors explain the pattern (e.g., the aging process, climatic conditions, weight-restriction violators, and inadequate maintenance), but later accounts tend to converge on a single factor emerging as *the* cause. Not everyone need agree on the same factor; opposing sides may promote differing, contradictory, or conflicting causes, but opposing accounts will likely contain monocausal rather than multivariate explanations.

Monocausal explanations also gain favor over multicausal ones because they suit the needs of contributors to media discourse. For example, focusing on a single cause concentrates responsibility, thus simplifying the process of disownership. Simple explanations simplify the writing of news copy for audiences assumed to have little tolerance for complexity (Nelkin 1987:124–28). Also, monocausal accounts consume less of the limited space in the news media than do those containing complex, multicausal explanations.

Third, winning causal accounts (in this culture, at least) tend to identify individuals as causal agents rather than physical or social forces (see also Gusfield 1981:36–45; Gans 1979:8). Nature seldom operates without at least some assistance from human agents (e.g., Spector and Kitsuse 1977: 46–47). Even when they note the presence of natural forces, journalists and their sources often point to acts of omission that could have prevented matters from deteriorating to the point of catastrophe (Perrow 1984 makes a similar point in his discussion of "operator error"): Yes, flood waters may have been the immediate cause of the shifting footing that tossed sections of the overpass into the creek, but why weren't the bridge footings properly inspected in 1986? Why wasn't riprap added when the bridge was over-hauled in 1981? Why was the creek bed narrowed despite engineers' warn-ings that this could make footings vulnerable during floods?

Which individuals do winning accounts identify? Cultural tool kits (Swidler 1986) offer a long list of potential villains and fools (Klapp 1962), but journalists generally favor individuals at the top of politically responsible governmental hierarchies (see Gans 1979:62–68). Practicing a trickle-up principle, journalists continually seek out "smoking guns." While a person at the bottom of some organization (such as a bridge inspector) may be the specific individual who did or did not do something, journalists and mem-bers of some claims-making groups assign responsibility for the incident to individuals at the top because it happened "during their watch." As the story of the Schoharie Creek bridge collapse unfolded, the search for per-sons responsible shifted: (1) from the Thruway Authority; (2) to the State of New York when that state's second-place ranking among the fifty states in the number of deficient bridges became known; (3) to the federal gov-ernment when the problem seemed to be nationwide in scope.

Public officials, in contrast to journalists, generally favor the opposite strategy (Ross and Staines 1972; Drabek and Quarantelli 1967). Since they tend to be either elected officials or top administrative heads, their public descriptions of causal responsibility reflect the principle of the "least pow-erful irresponsible individual" (see also Gusfield 1981:43–45). In other words, the actions of the agency (e.g., the Thruway Authority) and its pol-icies were correct; the unfortunate situation developed because certain (less powerful) individuals acted irresponsibly. In the Schoharie Creek bridge collapse, an inspector and his supervisor should have acted differently; pre-vious administrations did not exercise sufficient oversight when the bridge was built; and so on.

Since media discourse is an open and fluid process, new events may undermine a winning account at any time. For example, a subsequent in-cident may be characterized by some new feature not fitting the classifying scheme used to establish event similarity. Journalists and their sources may re-examine previous events to see if there is some other feature they all seem to share.[5] Identification of a new common element may then shift responsibility onto a new set of actors, thereby implying a different solution.

RISK, DRAMATIC EVENTS, AND PUBLIC PROBLEMS

Central to the sociology of risk is the assumption that the status of events, activities, and conditions as either risky or safe is not self-evident. "Data" for assessing risk do not exist independently of human observation nor do they interpret themselves. It is easy for us to assume that the world is safe and that many risks are non-existent, however, because the stock market does not fall 1,000 points every session, airliners rarely fail to arrive safely at their destinations, and the earth seldom shakes violently enough to topple buildings (see also Turner, Nigg, and Paz 1986:88–114). Only in specialized arenas such as conferences, professional journals, and legislative committee hearings is one likely to find regular discussions of a more risky world. Claims-makers for other issues dominate public arenas such as network television news broadcasts, tabloids at the checkout stands of supermarkets, and private conversations—each with its own limited "carrying capacity" (Hilgartner and Bosk 1988).

A dramatic event gives different claims-makers and risk definers access to these larger public arenas. This statement is easily misunderstood, because events are dramatic only when people use them to dramatize (Molotch and Lester 1975:102). News organizations bring us into contact with people who, in telling us about an event, invite us to see greater risks than we thought we knew, a world less safe than we assumed. Journalists bring these spokespersons and these points of view into media discourse when they decide how news accounts should be framed and which sources can assist with such framing. Policy makers (or more accurately, members of their staffs) also influence selection when they invite experts to testify at the public hearings covered by reporters.

The sociological significance of these selection processes is that popular beliefs about risk and safety cannot be studied simply as individual cognitive processes, as the term "risk perception" implies. Focusing solely on the recipient of news accounts ignores the effect of organizational decisions (such as those affecting the access of risk definers to media discourse) on the social construction of risk. Furthermore, rather than blaming the media for distorted, alarmist, and unnecessarily convoluted reporting, a sociological view of media discourse on risk suggests that any contradictions, alarm, and complexity in news accounts reflect by and large what journalists hear from various claims-makers, stakeholders, and other expert news sources.

This paper deals with one type of risk in its earliest phase as a public policy issue. Only through successful claims-making will the condition of the nation's bridges and highways become a public problem (Spector and Kitsuse 1977; Mauss 1975; Blumer 1971). Between the summer of 1987 and the winter of 1990, the bridge issue did not fare well in competition with fully developed problems such as AIDS, the war on drugs, and the environment. It remained an "unconstructed" social problem (Best and Horiuchi 1985:495). This analysis of news accounts suggests part of the reason why. The media discourse of 1987 contained accounts of bridges as a *public safety issue*. Claims-makers included primarily social movement organizations concerned with consumer (i.e., highway) safety and politically weak government transportation agencies. These claims-making groups lacked the resources (e.g., widespread, sustained public support) to move the condition of bridges as a safety issue the full length of the public-problem process.

However, scattered news reports in late 1989 suggest that a different contingent of claims-making groups is taking over the issue of the condition of bridges and highways. These accounts frame the issue not as one of safety but as an *economic issue*. In a front-page article in the *Wall Street Journal* (Yoo 1989:Al) titled "As Highways Decay, Their State Becomes Drag on the Economy," a representative of the Federal Reserve Bank of Chicago identified highway deterioration as "a root cause of the decline of American competitiveness." Whether the resources of groups such as the Highway Users Federation, the American Trucking Associations, and businesses depending heavily on highway transportation will be sufficient to successfully define the condition of bridges and highways as a public problem remains to be seen. Whatever the outcome, media discourse will continue to be a major source of raw material for public discussion.

Notes

1. See Gusfield (1981:10–16) for distinctions among problem ownership, causal responsibility, and political responsibility.

2. Investigative reporting took place in Missouri apparently as a reflection of that state's top ranking among the fifty states on the FHA's list of deficient bridges.

3. With lack of money proposed as the cause of Missouri's problems, the *Times* noted that three weeks after the bolt-shearing incident voters approved a statewide referendum to raise the gasoline sales tax four cents per gallon. This action also increased the flow of federal matching funds to the state for highway and bridge maintenance.

4. I am indebted to Lee Clarke for calling my attention to this point.

5. The ascendance of a successful explanation of cause and effect also influences how journalists depict these subsequent events. Events whose features seem sufficiently unlike those making up the pattern are likely to be dismissed as random or unrelated incidents rather than treated as disconfirming evidence. Illustrative of this hypothesis is the way in which frequent on-ground near collisions between two commercial airliners remained unconnected to the problem of safe air travel that in 1987–88 was already defined by both journalists and federal aviation officials as one caused by general aviation pilots.

References

Berger, Peter L., and Thomas Luckmann. 1966. The Social Construction of Reality. Garden City, N.Y.: Doubleday.

Best, Joel, and Gerald T. Horiuchi. 1985. "The razor blade in the apple: the social construction of urban legends." Social Problems 32:488–99.

Blumer, Herbert. 1971. "Social problems as collective behavior." Social Problems 18:298–306.

Boorstin, Robert O. 1987. "U.S. theory is that bases of thruway bridge shifted." New York Times 9 April:13, national edition.

Castells, Manuel. 1987. City, Class and Power. London: Macmillan.

Drabek, Thomas E., and E. L. Quarantelli. 1967. "Scapegoats, villains, and disasters." Trans-actions 4:12–17.

Fishman, Mark. 1978. "Crime waves as ideology." Social Problems 25:531–43.

Friedman, Sharon M. 1981. "Blueprint for breakdown: Three Mile Island and the media before the accident." Journal of Communication 31:116–28.

Gans, Herbert J. 1979. Deciding What's News. New York: Random House.

Goffman, Erving. 1974. Frame Analysis: An Essay on the Organization of Experience. New York: Harper and Row.

Gusfield, Joseph R. 1981. The Culture of Public Problems: Drinking, Driving and the Symbolic Order. Chicago: University of Chicago Press.

Hewitt, John P., and Peter M. Hall. 1973. "Social problems, problematic situations, and quasi-theories." American Sociological Review 38:367–74.

Hilgartner, Stephen, and Charles L. Bosk. 1988. "The rise and fall of social problems: a public arenas model." American Journal of Sociology 94:53–78.

Katz, Elihu. 1957. "The two-step flow of communication: an up-to-date report on an hypothesis." Public Opinion Quarterly 21:61–78.

Kitsuse, John I. 1962. "Societal reaction to deviant behavior: problems of theory and method." Social Problems 9:247–56.

Klapp, Orrin E. 1949. "The fool as a social type." American Journal of Sociology 55:6–11.

―――. 1962. Heroes, Villains, and Fools: The Changing American Character. Englewood Cliffs, N.J.: Prentice-Hall.

Lazarsfeld, Paul F., Bernard Berelson, and Hazel Gaudet. 1944. The People's Choice. New York: Duell, Sloan, and Pearce.

Lofland, John. 1981. Doomsday Cult: A Study of Conversion, Proselytization, and Maintenance of Faith. Enlarged edition. New York: Irvington.

May, Peter J. 1985. Catastrophes: Federal Disaster Relief Policy and Politics. Westport, Conn.: Greenwood Press.

Mauss, Armand L. 1975. Social Problems as Social Movements. Philadelphia: Lippincott.

Meltsner, Arnold J. 1978. "Public support for seismic safety: where is it in California?" Mass Emergencies 3:167–84.

Mill, John Stuart. [1843] System of Logic. Book III. London: Longmans, Green, and Company. 1919.

Molotch, Harvey, and Marilyn Lester. 1975. "Accidental news: the great oil spill as local occurrence and national event." American Journal of Sociology 81:235–60.

Nelkin, Dorothy. 1987. Selling Science: How the Press Covers Science and Technology. New York: W. H. Freeman.

New York Times. 1987. "Another bridge falls near thruway collapse." 13 April: 15, national edition.

O'Connor, James R. 1973. The Fiscal Crisis of the State. New York: St. Martin's.

Perrow, Charles. 1984. Normal Accidents: Living With High-Risk Technologies. New York: Basic Books.

President's Commission on the Accident at Three Mile Island. 1979. The Need for Change: The Legacy of TMI. Washington, D.C.: U.S. Government Printing Office.

Robbins, William. 1987. "Near collapse of Missouri bridge points up extent of repair needs." New York Times 9 April: 1, national edition.

Ross, Robert, and Graham L. Staines. 1972. "The politics of analyzing social problems." Social Problems. 20:18–40.

Schoenfeld, A. Clay, Robert F. Meier, and Robert J. Griffin. 1979. "Constructing a social problem: the press and the environment." Social Problems 27:38–61.

Shapiro, Susan P. 1989. "Libel lawyers as risk counselors: pre-publication and pre-broadcast review and the social construction of news." Paper presented at the annual meetings of the American Sociological Association.

Spector, Malcolm, and John I. Kitsuse. 1977. Constructing Social Problems. Menlo Park, Calif.: Cummings.

Swidler, Ann. 1986. "Culture in action: symbols and strategies." American Sociological Review 51:273–86.

Stuart, Reginald. 1987. "Highway agency would end two-year inspections of bridges." New York Times 10 April:1, national edition.

Thompson, James D. 1967. Organizations in Action: Social Science Bases of Administrative Theory. New York: McGraw-Hill.

Tolchin, Martin. 1987. "$50 billion needed for bridge repair, Congress is told by federal agency." New York Times 12 April: 13, national edition.

Tuchman, Gaye. 1978. Making News: A Study in the Construction of Reality. New York: Free Press.

Turner, Ralph H., Joanne M. Nigg, and Denise Heller Paz. 1986. Waiting for Disaster: Earthquake Watch in California. Berkeley: University of California Press.

Uhlig, Mark A. 1987. "At least 10 may have died in fall of New York thruway bridge." New York Times 8 April:14.

Van den Ban, A. W. 1964. "A revision of the two-step flow of communication hypothesis." Gazette 10:237–49.

Yoo, John. 1989. "As highways decay, their state becomes drag on the economy." Wall Street Journal 30 August:A1.

WOMEN IN TOXIC WORK ENVIRONMENTS

Donna M. Randall
James F. Short, Jr.

Spector and Kitsuse argue that the emergence and development of a social problem is a political process. They postulate four stages in this process: creating an issue, gaining official recognition of it, becoming dissatisfied with the established procedures of handling such issues, and rejecting them and attempting to replace them with one's own measures. Randall and Short's study of the Bunker Hill controversy shows that, unless groups gather sufficient resources at all stages of the process, the problem may remain in abeyance. Twenty-five women, excluded from working in a lead smelter, made vigorous claims about discrimination and were successful in calling attention to their plight and creating an issue. The women's claims, however, failed to reach the next three stages which Spector and Kitsuse constitute as the natural history of a social problem. In sequence, the union to which the women belonged, the state employment commission, and the Occupational Safety and Health Administration all lacked sufficient power and resources to carry the problem through each of the projected stages to the successful conclusion of Spector and Kitsuse's cycle. Randall and Short conclude that further research on the stages of social problems needs to focus on the power and resources that agencies can bring to the claims-making process. Because neither union, employment commission, nor the Occupational Safety and Health Administration had sufficient power, the process ceased at the stage of official recognition.

The relative importance of objective conditions and related social construc-tions in social problem development continues to be debated.[1] It is gen-erally agreed that, while all such problems are based in identifiable conditions, conditions per se are insufficient to explain the emergence and persistence of social problems. "Natural history"[2] models, beginning with Fuller and Myers (1941), have attempted to identify the general stages through which social problems develop. More recently, social construction-

From *Social Problems* 30/4 (April 1983). Copyright © 1983 by the Society for the Study of Social Problems. Reprinted by permission of the publisher.

ist models stress the importance to social problem development of the activities of claims-making groups[3] in defining conditions as offensive and seeking to remedy those situations, and the responses of others to these activities. The latter models are more sensitive than earlier ones to the influence of political processes on the development of social problems.

Spector and Kitsuse (1977) note that the identification and development of a social problem is negotiated through a process that is fundamentally political. Successful definition of a social problem requires creation of a public issue and official recognition. Once achieved, however, official recognition may or may not result in satisfactory measures (according to the claimants) to deal with the problem. If dissatisfied, the claims-making group may or may not reach the point of rejecting established procedures and pursuing alternatives.

Major political variables critical to social problem development are: (1) the use by a claims-making group of an ideology to make the complaint more forceful; (2) the ability to recognize the appropriate parties to complain to; and (3) the ability to marshal enough power to press claims (Spector and Kitsuse, 1977:141). By focusing on the latter of these political variables—the ability of claims-making groups to marshal power—this paper elaborates the Spector and Kitsuse model. Power is the ability to modify the attitudes or behavior of another; it requires both access to relevant resources and the ability to use these resources. As Gamson (1968: 94) notes, resources "when properly applied in sufficient quantities, will change the probability of the outcome of a decision. They must be controlled by the influencer and capable of being brought to bear on the authorities in interaction with them."

Power resources are many and varied; they include money, access to media, organizational factors such as commitment and unity of purpose (Olsen, 1978:37), the numbers of adherents to a cause, as well as their status, material possessions, knowledge, expertise, skill, and legitimacy of both individuals and organizations. Many resources have the potential to become power resources; the relative power of a particular resource in any situation depends on the extent to which that resource will aid a claims-making group in carrying out various tasks. Power resources thus arise from the context of action.

While Spector and Kitsuse recognize power as one of the political variables influencing social problem development, they do not systematically explore its role in that process. . . . [They have a] four-stage natural history model [that] can be made more useful by explicit consideration of power resources available to parties, including government agencies, in each stage of social problem development. The effectiveness of claims-making groups and those to whom complaints are made is highly dependent on control over relevant resources.

Spector and Kitsuse do not explore the role of *government* in the construction of social problems. Yet, government agencies often are powerful claims-making groups. In this paper we first theoretically examine the resources useful to claims-making groups in *each of the four stages of Spector and Kitsuse's model.*[*] Then we apply our revised model to a case study of the problems of women who work in toxic environments. This particular case represents the convergence of two social problems: discrimination against women in hiring, and the risks of employment in hazardous work environments.

Our case study is based upon personal and telephone interviews with government agency officials, corporate management at the Bunker Hill mining company in Kellogg, Idaho, United Steelworkers of America local and international officials, male and female employees of the Bunker Hill Company who were not affected by the exclusionary policy, and female workers of the company who were affected by the policy. We conducted most of the interviews in the spring and summer of 1981. Additional data were obtained through archival research, a mail survey of private groups and organizations concerned with the employment of women in toxic workplaces, and a request for information filed under the Freedom of Information Act.[4]

A POWER RESOURCE MODEL OF SOCIAL PROBLEM DEVELOPMENT

Stage One: Social Problem Definition and Issue Creation.   Following Spector and Kitsuse, in the first stage of social problem development, a group asserts the existence of a condition, identifies the condition as undesirable and problematic, and seeks to publicize these assertions, to stimulate controversy, and to create a public issue[5] over the condition. A group may perceive a condition to be undesirable because of a substantial change in the estimate of risk, in personal or social acceptance of risk, or in the management of risk (Lowrance, 1976:102). For example, public estimates of risk regarding cyclamates changed when controversial evidence was introduced in the late 1960s about the potential health risks associated with such chemicals. The U.S. government ban on the use of cyclamates was the result of this new evidence (Lowrance, 1976:102). In this case, scientific evidence concerning the risk to health of the consumption of cyclamates proved conclusive. The use of cyclamates ceased to be part of the social problem of public health when the condition defined as problematic by a prestigious claims-making group—the scientific community—was "solved" in a manner acceptable to that group. The soft beverage industry—the

[*]Italics added.

major "victims" of this solution—quickly adopted new ingredients for their diet beverages.

Scientific evidence does not always produce such results, however; nor are all claims by groups seeking to change conditions successfully resolved by the discovery and presentation of new information. Whereas a claims-making group seeks to increase public awareness of a condition defined as undesirable and to create a public issue, opposing groups committed to maintaining the status quo may seek to limit public awareness of the condition, or to define the condition in terms acceptable to the public.

Many public resources can be useful to claims-making groups (and to those in opposition) at this stage of social problem development. Three in particular were critical for the case study we discuss below: access to the media, support from other groups, and government activity.

1) *Access to the media:* The media possess the ability to define news, and they may express and dramatize claims. By allocating personnel, time, space, resources, and attention to certain activities but not others, the media determine what events will be news (Gans, 1979). The image of a claims-making group portrayed in the media can also influence the development of a social problem by attracting (or repelling) potential recruits (Spector and Kitsuse, 1977:21). Thus, groups vie for media coverage and seek to influence the content of news relevant to claims in dispute.

2) *Support from other groups:* Claims-making groups often turn to other groups for support in their efforts to convert problematic conditions into public issues. Coalition formation enlarges the scope of conflict by attracting more adherents. There is an inherent risk in entering into coalitions, however. The more participants involved in a controversy, the more difficult it is for the original claims-making group to maintain "control" over the social problem (Ross and Staines, 1972:26). Other issues than that of the original claims-making group may become of greater concern to the coalition (Spector and Kitsuse, 1977:145).

3) *Government activity:* A claims-making group may also call upon the government to prevent its claim from being suppressed by opposing groups.

> The government is a great engine for expanding the scale of conflict. Its work is aided and abetted by a host of public and private agencies and organizations designed to exploit every rift in the private world (Schattschneider, 1960: 13).

A powerful government can be of great use to claims-making groups by providing an arena for the discussion of issues, publicizing claims, and protecting conflicting groups against retaliation (Schattschneider, 1960:17). Government—its constituent bodies and agencies—often is a powerful interest group since the interests of government may be served by transforming certain social problems into public issues. Attention may be diverted from other problems; an official or agency may gain recognition, support, and resources by calling attention to a problematic condition and by intervention aimed at changing that condition. The self-interest of government agencies in creating public issues has led Beck (1978:359) to claim that "the appearance of a problem may not signify a difficulty in need of a solution, but an 'organized' solution in search of a difficulty to treat."

Stage Two: Official Recognition of the Problem.

Once a claims-making group has been successful in attracting public attention, the typical career of a social problem, according to Spector and Kitsuse, moves toward official recognition of the problem. The claims-making group seeks to convince an official agency to recognize the legitimacy of the claim, to obtain an official investigation of the claim, to have a remedy proposed that is favorable to the group's interests, and to have an agency designated to handle the claim.

Official recognition is enhanced by access to financial resources, by the ability to attract and to organize supporters, and by the effectiveness of information and communication skills designed to convince others of the legitimacy of claims. By employing financial resources, and/or organizing boycotts, demonstrations, threats, mass media campaigns, and by attempting to exert influence through highly placed officials, a group may be able to force agency recognition (Spector and Kitsuse, 1977:148). Agency recognition need not always be forced, however. Government agencies and professions are also interest groups, as the history of the welfare state demonstrates (Hagan and Leon, 1977). An agency may recognize the legitimacy of the claim because officials believe that the claim is properly within the jurisdiction of the agency (it is part of the job description) or that the agency will benefit by recognizing the claim.

Once the legitimacy of the claim has been recognized, the claims-making group typically seeks an official investigation into the claim. At this point, the group will likely be asked to document its claims. The greater the empirical support for its claims, the more success the claims-making group will have in legitimizing its claims. As Douglas and Wildavsky (1982: 80) observe, however, "[knowledge] of danger is necessarily partial and limited: judgements of risk and safety *must be* selected as much on the basis of what is valued as on the basis of what is known." And, as Manis (1976:42) notes:

> Modern science is inherently political. The tools, techniques and facilities of research are increasingly expensive. As a consequence, the activities of pure and applied science are guided by those who hold the purse-strings. Though knowledge is a basis of power, so too political and economic power control the search for knowledge.

Once investigation into a social problem begins, therefore, the initiating group may begin to lose control over the claim. Investigation may in fact be designed to "cool" an issue, as has often been observed. Other opinions on the issue may be sought in addition to that of the claims-making group; those individuals conducting the investigation may become the "new" experts on the social problem (Spector and Kitsuse, 1977:149). More organized groups will be more successful in maintaining control after an investigation has occurred; those less organized may not have this ability.

Once official investigation into the claim has occurred, the claims-making group seeks resolution of the social problem. Resolution typically is a complex bargaining process between opposing groups, a process characterized by "compromises, concessions, tradeoffs, deference to influence, response to power, and judgments of what may be workable" (Blumer 1971:304). Resolution can range from passive acknowledgement to active attempts by an institution to handle the problem (Spector and Kitsuse, 1977:148). "Final" resolution will reflect the distribution of power assets.

At the end of the second stage, a social problem is typically at its career peak: an agency has recognized the problem, thus officially conferring legitimacy on it, and other groups may have joined in the conflict in supporting the initial claims-making group. The social problem may be "solved" at this point. Yet, government response may be perceived unsatisfactory. Here again power resources are critical, and the social problem may enter into a third stage of development.

Stage Three: Group Dissatisfaction with Established Procedures.
Procedures established to deal with a problem may prove unsatisfactory for a variety of reasons. When they do so, a variety of responses are possible. Groups with larger memberships and the ability to discipline and to organize their members will be better equipped to express their dissatisfaction with the established procedures. More powerful groups will be able to renegotiate procedures, to reform existing practices, to have high level administrators dismissed, or to have a new, more specialized, institution established (Spector and Kitsuse, 1977:152). Those with fewer resources will be unable to influence the procedures established for dealing with the imputed conditions, to change the bureaucratic handling of complaints, or to generate sympathy for their complaints. Such groups are likely to have little confidence in the agency and its procedures; eventually, they may view the agency's operation with cynicism, resignation, and despair.

Stage Four: Rejection of Established Procedures.
Dissatisfaction with official response may lead a claims-making group to seek alternate solutions to their claims. Again, success is highly dependent upon access to resources. The group must be able to discipline and to organize effectively its members and to maintain its leaders. An established agency may seek to co-opt the group's members, to drain off its leadership, or to discredit its leaders (Spector and Kitsuse, 1977). Therefore, whether a dissatisfied group has

sufficient resources, discipline, and organization will determine the success of further efforts to address their claims.

APPLICATION OF THE MODEL: THE BUNKER HILL CONTROVERSY

For decades, claims-making groups have asserted the existence of, and have sought to remedy, hazardous work environments and discrimination against women. These two social problems converge in the form of exclusionary employment policies which prohibit fertile female employees from working around industrial chemicals believed to be toxic.

The Bunker Hill Company is a mining concern which, until its closure in 1981, operated a zinc refinery, fertilizer plant, and lead smelter in Kellogg, Idaho. After many years of independent operation, the company became a subsidiary of Gulf Resources and Chemical Corporation in 1968. In 1982, after Gulf Resources had closed all Bunker Hill production operations, a group of North Idaho investors purchased the company, with avowed plans to re-open operations when market conditions warranted.

Historically, women were not allowed to work in the lead smelter except for a brief time during the Second World War, when male employees were in short supply. After the war the women gradually quit these jobs for a variety of reasons. In 1972, Bunker Hill once again opened high-paying production jobs in the smelter and the zinc plant to women, this time in response to pressure from the federal Equal Employment Opportunity Commission (EEOC) (Tate, 1981:78). Between 1972 and 1975 approximately 45 women were hired as production workers. Thirty were placed in the lead smelter and 15 in the zinc plant. Both locations involved exposure to lead, since zinc contains some lead and zinc smelting can produce lead poisoning.

In April 1975, corporate management, fearful of possible damage to the unborn children of female workers exposed to lead—and possible lawsuits against the company—enacted an "exclusionary policy" which prohibited fertile women from working around lead. The policy explicitly required that women who wished to work in lead exposure areas of the company be sterilized. A letter from a physician was required as proof of sterilization. Those who failed to do so would be transferred from the lead smelter and the zinc plant and reassigned to "safe" work areas. Corporate management informed the women that a battery plant in the United States had enacted a similar exclusionary policy and that no government action had been taken against that company.

After being informed of the new corporate policy, the 29 women who were assigned at the time to the lead smelter and zinc plant were reassigned to the mine yard (maintenance) crew. They were told to report to the mine yard supervisor for work the next day. The women were then assigned "make-work" jobs: they picked up gum wrappers, dusted shelves in the warehouses, and posted signs on the plant grounds.

The Bunker Hill women affected by the policy were undecided about what to do about the policy. Six of the women interviewed had undergone sterilization before the policy was enacted, for diverse reasons unrelated to exposure to lead. For these women, the choice of action was obvious: they simply obtained a letter from their physicians attesting to their operations and returned to their former jobs shortly afterwards.

Other women underwent sterilization in order to return to their former jobs. The precise number of women who sought sterilization is disputed and cannot now be determined with certainty. A representative from the EEOC interviewed 25 women in 1978 and concluded that none of the affected women underwent sterilization in order to be allowed to return to a previous job.[6] However, in 1980, a physician sent by the federal Occupational Safety and Health Administration (OSHA) determined that "at least three women obtained sterilization procedures within the next two or three months with physician letters solely to be allowed by the company to return to their former jobs."[7]

The policy generated considerable opposition from a variety of sources: the Bunker Hill women, their union, equal opportunity agencies at both state and federal levels, and the OSHA. Each of these groups identified the policy as offensive and, in varying degrees, sought to eliminate the corporate practice. Despite opposition, however, the company continued to enforce the policy without major modifications.

WOMEN AS CLAIMANTS

Stage One: Social Problem Definition and Issue Creation. Several of the Bunker Hill women sought support for their claims-making activities from other sources, notably the government and the media. First, however, the women attempted to obtain support in their struggle against the company by turning to their union local. However, the local of the United Steelworkers of America (USWA) did not possess enough resources (personnel, medical expertise, and technological information) to be of much help to the women. The local consisted of 14 officers, only two of whom (the president and financial secretary) were full-time employees. The local had no medical evidence to prove that lead could harm male as well as female reproductive systems, though this was widely believed to be the case. The only medical evidence known to the union came exclusively from the physician on contract to Bunker Hill. In addition, the local did not strongly back the women because it could not envision a technological solution to the dilemma. Local union officials believed that it was impossible to clean up the workplace to the point where it would be safe for fertile women. Therefore, the local was not a powerful ally for the women.

The women then turned to the headquarters of the union for support. The USWA represented 1.4 million workers in the United States and Canada (U.S. Congress: House, 1976:439), including workers in many lead smelters and refineries. Through handling numerous complaints from workers about lead and researching lead's medical effects, the USWA had become familiar with health problems caused by lead. Yet, even with such resources, the USWA appeared unwilling to challenge Bunker Hill's policy. As a union representative explained, the USWA had conflicting interests in the controversy. While it wanted to represent the women, it did not want to discourage the company from hiring women. The Bunker Hill Company had only hired women since 1972 and, at the time of the conflict, was the only smelter in the United States doing so. If the union protested too strongly, the company might have closed off the plant to fertile and non-fertile women alike.

The USWA was reluctant to use its resources in the conflict for another reason: it might lose a suit against Bunker Hill. The USWA had no specific policy on corporate exclusionary practices. The union believed a successful challenge of the Bunker Hill policy would be difficult. As a consequence, the resources of the USWA were not available to the Bunker Hill women.

Denied effective union support, the women sought government support in problem definition and issue creation. On the advice of the union local, the women filed complaints with the Idaho Human Rights Commission and the EEOC soon after the policy was announced. The women did not receive an immediate response from these agencies and felt frustrated.

While many of the Bunker Hill women perceived the controversy to be a discrimination issue, the women did not seek support from feminist groups. None of the Bunker Hill women interviewed belonged to or supported such groups. Indeed, many of the women adamantly denied any contact with or receiving any information from women's groups.

Throughout the developing controversy the women sought access to the media in order to draw public attention to their complaints. Here they were more successful. The media perceived the drama in the controversy, and therefore its news value. A powerful corporation was "coercing" women to be sterilized in order to keep their jobs. From the day the "exclusionary policy" was announced, the controversy was covered extensively in the Washington state and Idaho newspapers (*Coeur d'Alene Press*, 1975: 3; *Spokane Daily Chronicle*, 1975:5; Tate, 1975:1).

The ensuing publicity was not well received by Bunker Hill officials. The company did not want to defend its policy in public, believing the policy to be an internal matter. Officials were confident of their right to enforce and maintain the policy. Media attention succeeded, where other efforts had failed, to move the controversy into the public arena. The women's complaints progressed to Stage Two in a social problem career: official recognition.

Stage Two: Official Recognition of the Problem. Media attention to
the plight of the women eventually culminated in official recognition by
two government agencies—the Idaho Human Rights Commission (IHRC)
in the fall of 1975, and the EEOC in the winter of 1976. The IHRC was
the first official body to recognize the sex discrimination complaints of the
women. Subsequent to the IHRC's investigation, the agency developed a
memorandum of understanding to be signed by the company and the
women. The memorandum stated that the company's removal of all fertile
women from lead exposure areas was justified and reasonable, but that
female employees must be reimbursed for any wage differences between
the employee's former position and the interim work assignment in the
mine yard crew.[8]

The IHRC's efforts at negotiation failed: company executives reportedly
refused to sign the agreement.[9] The IHRC was virtually powerless; it had
no official policy on corporate exclusionary practices, it had no investigative
subpoena power, and it had limited resources as a state agency.

The EEOC officially recognized the legitimacy of the complaints filed
by 18 of the women four months after the IHRC had attempted to negotiate with Bunker Hill. Under a work-sharing agreement between the agencies, the EEOC began its investigation only after the IHRC finished its
own and submitted findings to the EEOC. The 18 women at Bunker Hill
who had filed a complaint with the EEOC were then asked to participate
in an official investigation by the EEOC. With an official investigation underway and their claims the object of official attention, the dissatisfied
women enjoyed their "finest hour."

The women lost control over the course of their complaints after
EEOC's two-week investigation was completed in February 1976. They
were no longer responsible for defining the nature of their complaints, their
role having been relegated to providing information to the EEOC. The
agency took the claims-making activity from the women and negotiated a
settlement with the company without any of the women present.

The settlement reached by the EEOC and the company reflected both
gains and losses for the women. The women were asked to concede that
lead could have a negative effect on their health and to recognize that they
could no longer be allowed to work around lead. In return, they would be
reimbursed for losses in wages; guaranteed their current jobs as long as
they could perform the work; promised that the controversy would not
affect their future employment; and transferred out of temporary assign-
ments on the mine yard crew to other "safe" work areas.

The terms of the resolution to the controversy reflected the conflicting
groups' access to needed resources. The women had virtually no power:
the EEOC had taken over their claims and they were excluded from the
negotiation process; as a group, they were torn by dissension as to the
appropriate resolution to their claims. As one woman explained, all the

women who were affected by the policy "hung tight" in complaining about the corporate policy and in trying to get the policy abolished. The group's solidarity weakened once the EEOC's investigation occurred, however. Some of the women wanted the corporate exclusionary policy to be revoked so that they could resume their jobs in the smelter and zinc plant. Others were not as demanding; they simply wanted to get out of the mine yard crew. In the end, the settlement only satisfied the second group. Yet, all of the women agreed to sign the settlement during the month following its development.

For their part, the EEOC forced Bunker Hill to negotiate, but the agency lacked the power to change the company's exclusionary policy. The EEOC did not have an official policy on corporate exclusionary practices nor did it have another critical resource—strong sanctions to accompany the threat of a discrimination suit. From Bunker Hill's perspective, an employment discrimination charge was preferable to a possible damages lawsuit. Dennis Brendel, the company's vice president of environmental affairs, explained: "Bunker Hill is willing to be criticized for not employing some women—but not for causing birth defects" (Anderson, 1980:B3). Without an official position on exclusionary policies and sufficient sanctions to accompany its threats, the EEOC could only negotiate a monetary settlement between the women and Bunker Hill. The company, as a consequence, signed the agreement and was able to maintain its policy.

Stage Three: Group Dissatisfaction with Established Procedures.
The EEOC's negotiated remedy left many of the women dissatisfied. While the agency gave legitimacy to their complaints, their demands remained unsatisfied. Without an official position on exclusionary policies, the EEOC could not institutionalize and routinize the handling of the complaint. Similar complaints in the future would have to be negotiated on a case-by-case basis. The complaints wanted a clearcut policy decision by the EEOC on exclusionary policies, but they didn't get it. The women felt that the EEOC really did not want to get involved with the issue of exclusionary policies and was only making a symbolic response to their complaints. All that was accomplished was a negotiated settlement with the company. The problem of exclusionary policies remained unresolved. As one woman we interviewed observed, "The sterilization issue was a vague question and the EEOC answered it in a vague way."

In addition, some women were upset at the outcome of negotiation because they felt they had been "pushed" into the settlement. Company officials, perceiving the strength of their position, informed the women that they would agree to the settlement only if all 18 women would sign the agreement. Almost all of the women readily agreed. One woman explained: "The question was settled when $1,000 bills were flashed in the faces of the women." However, a couple of the women did not want to accept the settlement and resisted doing so for some time. One of these women said she agreed to sign in the end because she felt "pressured" by the other women.

Thus, the EEOC's attempts to resolve the controversy failed to satisfy the demands of the complainants. The women, as a claims-making group, were unable to discipline and organize their members. They could neither force the company to renegotiate the settlement nor influence the EEOC handling of future exclusionary matters. The resolution of their claim left many of the women extremely cynical about the EEOC's and the federal government's interests in exclusionary policies.

Stage Four: Rejection of Established Procedures. The Bunker Hill women, while cynical and disillusioned with the EEOC's response, had limited financial resources and they were torn by dissension. At this point their claims-making activities came to an end.

THE OCCUPATIONAL SAFETY AND HEALTH ADMINISTRATION AS CLAIMANT

Initiation of Claims-Making Activities. In April 1980, four years after Bunker Hill's exclusionary policy had been officially "resolved" by the EEOC, another claims-making group, the Occupational Safety and Health Administration (OSHA) joined in the controversy. Even though the OSHA had been aware of Bunker Hill's exclusionary policy for years,[10] the agency only became actively interested in the policy in 1980, following establishment of a new lead standard in 1978. The new standard dealt with reproductive hazards in the workplace (U.S. Department of Labor, 1978). This standard limited the amount of lead workers could be exposed to and protected workers through a provision known as "medical removal protection." Under this provision, male or female workers who were in risk of health damage or who were pregnant or planning pregnancies were allowed to be temporarily reassigned to safer parts of a plant while retaining full salary and seniority.

The American Cyanamid Corporation of Willow Island, Virginia, was the first object of the OSHA's attention. In October 1979, the OSHA cited American Cyanamid (*Secretary of Labor v. American Cyanamid Co.*, 1980) for the maintenance of a "fetus protection" policy (U.S. Department of Labor, 1979a). While the case was under review by the Occupational Safety and Health Review Commission (OSHRC), a quasi-judicial review board, the OSHA cited the Bunker Hill Company in 1980 for a similar violation (U.S. Department of Labor, 1980).

Bunker Hill also had a history of noncompliance with OSHA regulations, and the agency may have perceived the controversy to be an excellent opportunity to exert regulatory control over the company.[11] Bunker Hill had long been at odds with the OSHA and the Environmental Protection Agency (EPA) for violating regulations on permissible lead levels in the workplace and the environment.[12]

The OSHA's initial efforts as a claims-making group were to allege the existence of an undesirable condition, to claim jurisdiction over the matter, to conduct an investigation into the issue, and to set forth proposals for reform. The OSHA did not have a specific standard on exclusionary policies, so it relied on the general duty clause of the Occupational Safety and Health Act of 1970[13] as a basis for the violation. Under this clause, employers are required "to provide employment and a place of employment free from recognized hazards causing or likely to cause death or serious physical harm."[14] The OSHA's proposed remedy for the alleged condition was immediate withdrawal of the policy and a $10,000 fine.

OSHA's Claims Publicized. Having defined the Bunker Hill situation as undesirable, the OSHA's claims-making efforts then turned toward publicizing the claims, stimulating a controversy over the matter, and turning the alleged condition into a public issue. A single resource—access to the media—was used to achieve these goals. Access to the press was not difficult. While any individual or group can be a source for news, highly placed social actors often have greater access to the media. Gans (1979:119) observes that while news sources can be located anywhere:

> . . . in practice, their recruitment and their access to journalists reflect the hierarchies of nation and society. The president of the United States has instantaneous access to all news media whenever he wants it; the powerless must resort to civil disturbances to obtain it.

Gans (1979:282) also notes that highly placed news sources are easily and quickly available, reliable and productive, and often the most efficient sources of news.

On September 11, 1980, the OSHA issued a three-page press release detailing the charges against Bunker Hill and explaining the technical terms in the citation. The names of two press agents, with office and home phone numbers, were made available by the OSHA to answer any questions. In the following months, a number of OSHA officials, including the local OSHA area office director, an industrial hygienist, a medical officer, and lawyers for regional litigation, were available to make statements to the press about exclusionary policies. The OSHA was able to supply a sensational story to the press. The exclusionary policy received much media attention, and the OSHA's claims were widely publicized in such papers as the *Wall Street Journal* (Schlender, 1980) and the *New York Times* (Severo, 1980).

Bunker Hill's Reaction. Bunker Hill lacked the necessary resources to prevent the issue from reemerging in the media. Company use of the media was hampered by the fact that the company was taken by surprise by the citation—no response was prepared in advance—and by the imposition of a "gag" order (a court order barring publicity of the law suit) by a federal judge which prevented the company from influencing the content and amount of news pertinent to the exclusionary policy. In March 1980, Judge McNichols, a federal district court judge in Boise, Idaho, ordered all parties to a law suit involving the lead poisoning of Kellogg school children not to speak to the press (*Yoss v. Bunker Hill Co.*, 1977). As a defendant in the law suit, Bunker Hill was prevented from discussing any issue related to the health effects of lead. The company could not defend its position on its exclusionary policy until the law suit was settled.

On September 19, 1980, Bunker Hill formally contested the charges in a one-sentence letter to the OSHA. With Bunker Hill's adamant denial of wrongdoing, the case was scheduled to be heard before a judge on the OSHRC.

OSHA Seeks a Mandate and Remedies.

Once the OSHA had cited Bunker Hill, the agency's claim of an official mandate for responsibility over exclusionary policies became the major issue in the controversy. On one hand, the USWA was strongly behind the OSHA's involvement in exclusionary policies. The union resented having been left out of negotiations between the EEOC and the company. While the USWA did not actively seek OSHA intervention, it was eager to have the controversy reopened. On the other hand, private citizens, including many Bunker Hill employees, Bunker Hill officials, and some within the OSHA, questioned the appropriateness of the agency's involvement. The question of the legitimacy of the OSHA's jurisdiction in exclusionary policy matters was left to the courts to decide.

While the OSHA was awaiting a court ruling on its involvement with exclusionary policies, the agency sought to negotiate an informal settlement with Bunker Hill. However, the company, sensing the agency's weak position, refused to negotiate. Stellman (1977:185) described the powerlessness of the agency:

> Unfortunately, the progress of OSHA has been slow and its guarantees for safety and health not met. The penalties for violations are minimal, generally averaging less than $30 per violation. The anti-discrimination clause is poorly enforced, and OSHA's initiative in enforcing the act is usually barely noticeable. A major part of the problem has been that two Administrations during which OSHA came into existence were dedicated to its destruction. In fact, former President Gerald Ford had vowed to "throw OSHA into the ocean." This attitude, of course, makes it difficult for the OSHA staff to perform its functions.

Lacking the power to force Bunker Hill to negotiate, and with its legal standing in the controversy questioned, the OSHA's efforts to negotiate with Bunker Hill failed. As with the issue of its legal standing, the issue of a suitable remedy was left for the courts to decide.

In late spring of 1981, the OSHRC reviewed the case on exclusionary policies involving American Cyanamid. The commission ruled that the OSHA did not have a legitimate right to investigate exclusionary policies (*Secretary of Labor v. American Cyanamid Co.*, 1980). The similarity between the American Cyanamid case and the Bunker Hill case was evident to OSHA officials and, shortly thereafter, the citation against Bunker Hill was dropped. The OSHA had lacked two critical power resources: an official mandate from the courts (crucial for obtaining jurisdiction over the policies) and political support under the current federal administration. The OSHA's claims-making activities came to an end. The issue of the exclusionary policy at Bunker Hill had, once again, been settled in favor of the company.

DISCUSSION

An analysis of the Bunker Hill controversy presents an opportunity to assess social constructionist models of social problem development. The case suggests that the *power resources available to government agencies*° are critical to the outcome of their intervention efforts. The IHRC could not legally force Bunker Hill to negotiate, lacked investigative subpoena power, had not developed an official policy on corporate exclusionary practices, and had limited financial resources as a state agency. As a consequence, the IHRC had minimal impact on the development of the Bunker Hill controversy.

Like the IHRC, the EEOC lacked an official position on corporate exclusionary policies and effective bargaining power. The agency did not have strong sanctions at its disposal to accompany threats of a discrimination suit. With its limited resources, all the EEOC could do was negotiate a monetary settlement between the women and Bunker Hill. Many of the claims-making women did not perceive this settlement as favorable to their best interests.

The OSHA possessed more resources than either the IHRC or the EEOC and was able to have greater influence over the development of the controversy. Interpreting Bunker Hill's exclusionary policy as a violation of its newly promulgated lead standard, the OSHA was able to grant legitimacy to its own claims, to initiate an investigation into its own assertions, to propose its own remedies for alleged violations, and to claim that subject matter of the controversy properly fell within its own jurisdiction. The OSHA was thus able to carry out certain activities that other groups could accomplish only later in the claims-making process. In addition, as an of-

°Italics added.

ficial agency, the OSHA had greater access to the media than most claims-making groups and, as a result, could more readily publicize its claims, create a controversy, and turn matters into public issues. Yet, the OSHA's claims-making efforts failed because the agency lacked two key resources to ensure success: an official mandate from the courts and political support.

In broad outline, the sequence of events predicted by the Spector and Kitsuse model is supported. Modifications are required, however, when government agencies act as claimants. The model was unable to predict the sequence of events when the OSHA acted as claimant. This difficulty extends to other controversies in which official agencies act as claimant. For example, in applying the Spector and Kitsuse framework to the problem of teenage drinking, Chauncey discovered that the involvement of government agencies critically influences social problem development. A problem may first be recognized by an agency and then publicized by that agency in an effort to gain public support for its activities. In an analysis of the National Institute on Alcohol Abuse and Alcoholism's claims-making activities in the area of teenage drinking, Chauncey (1980:47) observes:

> In this role as *actor* or *creator*, government agencies will be shown as dependent upon other interest groups and the public at large for the legitimation of their efforts. . . . The possibility that social problems may be *created* in government towers and legitimated in public squares will be added to the more familiar likelihood that some problems are also created in squares and legitimated in towers.

The controversy at Bunker Hill with the OSHA as a claimant appears to follow a similar course—first creation, then legitimation. Legitimation proved insufficient to sustain the agency's position when the court suit failed and the then-current federal administration did not pursue the issue.

Official agencies have assumed active roles in the creation of other social problems, as well. Gusfield (1975) maintains that the National Institute of Alcohol Abuse and Alcoholism also took "possession" of the problem of drinking and driving, and gave both focus and location to the issue within the larger set of alcohol-related problems. Becker (1963) demonstrates the responsibility of the Treasury Department's Bureau of Narcotics for producing public awareness of the "marijuana problem." The agency coordinated efforts with other enforcement agencies; it approached Congress with a draft of the Marijuana Tax Act and requested its passage; and it actively campaigned for the problem to be placed within its jurisdiction. Nuehring and Markle (1974) and Markle and Troyer (1979) have described the Public Health Service's (PHS) active involvement in anti-smoking activities. In addition to the Public Health Service, the Civil Aeronautics Board, the Federal Trade Commission, and the Interstate Commerce Commission have adopted a strong anti-smoking stance by issuing coercive and stringent rulings. Nuehring and Markle (1974) speculate that the PHS' involvement stems from internal organizational needs for basic survival, role identification, and behavior based upon the exertion of power. Chauncey notes that government agencies have helped publicize a number of other social problems and policies aimed at their solution or amelioration: for example, the war on poverty, sickle cell anemia, water pollution, cancer, missile gaps, domestic subversion, and the military industrial complex (1980:47).

We are now in a position to suggest how the theoretical model we set forth earlier should be modified in order to account for government involvement in the construction of social problems. *Government agencies*° commonly assume the role of claims-making groups. When they do so, the sequence of events for the first two stages of the model *are reversed:*°

Stage One: Creation of Social Problems
A government agency may assert the existence of a condition, define the condition as undesirable, assert the legitimacy of its claims, investigate those claims, and propose a remedy for the perceived undesirable condition.
Stage Two: Legitimation of Social Problems
By publicizing its claims, a government agency may seek to create controversy over those claims, and to generate public support for its position. The agency must also establish the legitimacy of its mandate regarding both claims and solutions which are favorable to its interest.

Only the first two stages of the convergence of the problems of equal opportunity for women and exposure to toxic work environments can be traced from our data. Objectively, these conditions remain, but their status as a social problem is ambiguous. We think it likely that they will reemerge, perhaps in other forms as the broader class of toxic work environments continues to be discovered, discussed, and responded to. The OSHA's failure to be more effective in the developmental stages of the Bunker Hill controversy is but one possible scenario in the involvement of government in social problem development.

The involvement of government agencies in claims-making activities complicates the course of social problem development. In our case study, the OSHA was *both* claimant and the official agency responding to claims. The court decision against the agency in the American Cyanamid case signalled the OSHA's failure in its claims-making efforts. Further efforts were effectively stalled by an unsympathetic federal administration. It appears that when an official agency acts alone as claimant, it must be very sure of success, or that further support will be forthcoming from appropriate administration sources. Lacking such support, failure at the second stage may foreclose further claims-making activities, though new information, a

°Italics added.

stronger "case," or a more favorable political climate may permit or encourage such activities in the future.

SUMMARY

*We have refined Spector and Kitsuse's four-stage model of social problem
development by giving explicit consideration to resources needed by claims-
making groups within each stage of development.* ° The refined model predicts that groups with greater access to needed resources will be able to
create a public issue over a condition alleged to be undesirable, to obtain
official recognition for their complaints, to resolve favorably their complaints about the agency's handling of the complaint, and to reject and to
replace, if desired, agencies designated to handle the complaints. The refined model is a useful guide for viewing the development of a fairly complex controversy involving a number of social actors and a variety of issues.
By applying the model to the Bunker Hill controversy, we are able to move
beyond description and to view the dynamics of the development process.
    *The pattern of events we observed at Bunker Hill, with the female em-
ployees as claimants, conformed to the theoretical model. It was not as
successful in accounting for the sequence of events that took place when an
official agency acted as claimant. In effect, the order of the first and second
stages was reversed*° when the OSHA served as claimant. By definition,
the agency was able to grant official recognition of the social problem.
Public support was then sought, along with legitimation and sanctioning
power through the courts. Failure at this stage led to the withdrawal of the
agency from further claims-making activities.

    The need for more detailed analyses of social problem development is
clear. While attention to the power resources of conflicting groups contributes to our understanding of the career of the Bunker Hill controversy, the
precise role of those resources in other social problems remains problematic.

    While this particular chapter of the Bunker Hill controversy is closed,
the larger social problem of women in toxic work environments has not
been resolved. Lead is not the only toxic substance which threatens reproductive damage. Fertile workers are also being exposed to benzene, beryl-
lium, mercury, vinyl chloride, and ionizing radiation. Despite the apparent
hazards associated with working with such substances, women are increasingly seeking employment in toxic work environments under the protection
of the equal employment opportunity laws, increasingly being exposed to
toxic substances, and increasingly assuming risks of reproductive damage.

    Recognizing the health hazards presented by toxic substances, industrial
firms are beginning to implement exclusionary policies. While such policies

°Italics added.

are designed to protect fertile females from possible fetal damage, they significantly curtail job opportunities for women. Hricko (1978:400) estimates that if women of childbearing age are not allowed to work where there is lead exposure, almost two of every three female applicants for an estimated 1.3 million jobs would be turned away.

Exclusionary policies and toxic work environments will likely become major social issues in the future. As in the Bunker Hill controversy, the outcome of social problem development over such issues will depend upon the resources—technical, financial, and political—available to participants in the controversies. The importance of better theories and documentation of these processes is clear.

Notes

1. Since approximately 1920, the issue of whether social problems were *inherently* social problems (an "objectivist" orientation) or arose from the activities of claims-making groups (a "subjectivist" orientation) has been the subject of a major debate. This issue is discussed at length by Spector and Kitsuse (1977), who clearly favor the "subjectivist" orientation to social problems.

2. The term "natural history" originated with Fuller and Myers (1941) and was used to describe the temporal development of social problems. It was probably best defined by Park (1955:36): "Natural history, in fact, is nothing more nor less than an account of an evolutionary process—a process by which not the individual but the type evolves."

3. Following customary usage, we employ the phrase "claims-making groups" to refer to individuals (and groups) participating in organizations and social movements involved in social problem development. No particular form or type of group is implied by this image.

4. Freedom of Information Act 5 U.S.C. Section 552.

5. Whereas a social problem consists of a group's claim to an undesirable condition, a public issue reflects the agreement of others to that claim.

6. Information obtained from a request filed under the Freedom of Information Act, 5 U.S.C. 552.

7. Obtained under the Freedom of Information Act, 5 U.S.C. 552.

8. Obtained under the Freedom of Information Act, 5 U.S.C. 552.

9. Corporate executive, July 15, 1981: personal interview.

10. For instance, in 1976 during Congressional Oversight Hearings on the Occupational Safety and Health Act, the controversy at Bunker Hill was discussed (U.S. Congress: House, 1976:386). The controversy was again mentioned in 1979 at a Department of Labor seminar on occupational diseases (U.S. Department of Labor, 1979b:188).

11. Corporate executive, July 21, 1981: personal interview.

12. Union official, September 2, 1981: personal interview.

13. Sections 5 (a)(1) of the Occupational Safety and Health Act, 29 U.S.C. 651–678 (1976).

14. 29 U.S.C. 654(a)(1)(1976).

References

Anderson, Steven. 1980. "Bunker Hill: Sterilization not required." Idaho Statesman (Boise), September 17:sec. B, pp. 1, 3.

Beck, Bernard. 1978. "The politics of speaking in the name of society." Social Problems 25(4): 353–360.

Becker, Howard S. 1963. Outsiders: Studies in the Sociology of Deviance. New York: Free Press.

Blumer, Herbert. 1971. "Social problems as collective behavior." Social Problems 18(3): 298–306.

Chauncey, Robert L. 1980. "New careers for moral entrepreneurs: Teenage drinking." Journal of Drug Issues 10(1): 48–70.

Coeur d'Alene Press (Idaho). 1975. "Females transferred." April 17:3.

Douglas, Mary, and Aaron Wildavsky. 1982. Risk and Culture: An Essay on the Selection of Technological and Environmental Dangers. Berkeley: University of California Press.

Fuller, Richard C., and Richard R. Myers. 1941. "The natural history of a social problem." American Sociological Review 6(3): 320–328.

Gamson, William A. 1968. Power and Discontent. Homewood, Illinois: Dorsey Press.

Gans, Herbert J. 1979. Deciding What's News: A Study of CBS Evening News, NBC Nightly News, Newsweek, and Time. New York: Vintage Books.

Gusfield, Joseph R. 1975. "Categories of ownership and responsibility in social issues: Alcohol abuse and automobile use." Journal of Drug Issues 5(4): 285–304.

Hagan, John, and Jeffrey Leon. 1977. "Rediscovering delinquency: Social history, political ideology, and the sociology of law." American Sociological Review 42(4): 587–598.

Hricko, Andrea. 1978. "Social policy considerations of occupational health standards: The example of lead and reproductive effects." Preventive Medicine 7:394–406.

Lowrance, William W. 1976. Of Acceptable Risk: Science and the Determination of Safety. Los Altos, California: William Kaufmann.

Manis, Jerome. 1976. Analyzing Social Problems. New York: Praeger Publishers.

Markle, Gerald E., and Ronald J. Troyer. 1979. "Smoke gets in your eyes: Cigarette smoking as deviant behavior." Social Problems 26(5): 611–625.

Nuehring, Elaine, and Gerald E. Markle. 1974. "Nicotine and norms: The re-emergence of a deviant behavior." Social Problems 21(4): 513–526.

Olsen, Marvin E. 1978. The Process of Social Organization: Power in Society. New York: Praeger.

Park, Robert Ezra. 1955. Society: The Collected Papers of Robert Ezra Park, Volume 3. Glencoe, Illinois: Free Press.

Ross, Robert, and Graham Staines. 1972. "The politics of analyzing social problems." Social Problems 20(1): 18–40.

Schattschneider, E. E. 1960. The Semisovereign People: A Realist's View of Democracy in America. New York: Holt, Rinehart and Winston.

Schlender, Brenton R. 1980. "Sterilization is main issue in OSHA suits." Wall Street Journal, December 9:25.

Severo, Richard. 1980. "Should firms screen the workplace or the worker?" New York Times, September 24:E22.

Spector, Malcolm, and John I. Kitsuse. 1977. Constructing Social Problems. Menlo Park, California: Cummings.

Spokane Daily Chronicle (Washington). 1975. "Thirty moved from smelter." April 17:5.

Stellman, Jeanne. 1977. Women's Work, Women's Health. New York: Pantheon Books.

Tate, Cassandra. 1975. "Women shifted from Bunker Hill smelter jobs." Morning Tribune (Lewiston, Idaho). April 17:A1.

———. 1981. "American dilemma of jobs, health in an Idaho town." Smithsonian 12(6):74–83.

U.S. Congress: House of Representatives. 1976. Statement of George Becker, Safety and Health Representative, United Steelworkers of America. House Committee on Education and Labor, Subcommittee on Manpower, Compensation, and Health and Safety. 94th Congress, 2nd Session, Part 2. Washington, D.C.: U.S. Government Printing Office.

U.S. Department of Labor. 1978. "Occupational exposure to lead." Federal Register 43(220), November 14:52952–53014.

———. 1979a Citation and Notification of Penalty (Issued to the American Cyanamid Company), October 9.

———. 1979b Lost in the Workplace: Is There an Occupational Disease Epidemic? Proceedings from a Seminar for the News Media, Washington, D.C., September 13–14. Washington, D.C.: U.S. Government Printing Office.

———. 1980. Citation and Notification of Penalty (Issued to the Bunker Hill Company), September 11.

Cases Cited

Secretary of Labor v. American Cyanamid Co., OSHRC Docket No. 79-5762 (July 15, 1980).

Yoss v. Bunker Hill Co., U.S. District Court for the State of Idaho, Civil 77-2030 (June 2, 1977).

DEBATES ABOUT CONSTRUCTIONISM

Joel Best

Best examines criticisms of constructionism, types of constructionists, and practical as well as theoretical uses to which constructionism may be put. Hostile critics say it makes no sense to ignore "objective conditions" which constitute the core of social problems and that constructionists ignore the harms and suffering social problems cause. Sympathetic critics answer that years of studying the objective aspects of problems have yet to alleviate suffering let alone produce a genuine sociological theory of social problems; furthermore, if no one points to the harms, the situation remains undefined as a social problem.

Still other sympathetic critics argue that constructionists either make assumptions about objective conditions or worse, believe they know when objective conditions have changed or not. If so, they are unable to fulfill the constructionist imperative which requires information on the beliefs of the people involved in the social problems process rather than the beliefs of sociologists.

As a result, two schools of thought have emerged within the developing constructionist tradition: strict social constructionists, those who only study the claims-making process, and contextual constructionists, who take into account what is known about objective conditions. Best says people who want to solve problems would do well to study the successful claims-making of others.

The constructionist approach to studying social problems emerged from some sociologists' dissatisfaction with the dominant, objectivist stance. Constructionists argued that defining social problems in terms of objective conditions within society had two key flaws: it ignored the fact that identifying a social condition as a social problem required subjective judgment; and, *by labeling conditions with little in common as social problems, objectivism*

*could not serve as a foundation for more general theories of social prob-
lems.*°

In contrast, constructionists define social problems in terms of claims-
making; they focus on the subjective judgments (claims that X is a social
problem) that the objectivists slighted.[1] And the constructionist approach
offers a basis for developing new theories—about claims, claims-makers,
claims-making cycles, and social policy formation, among other topics.

The constructionist approach is relatively new, and it remains controversial. Critics attack constructionism from several sides: some sociologists
defend objectivism and criticize the constructionist stance, or they argue
that objectivism and constructionism can be easily reconciled; others warn
that constructionism is inherently inconsistent, that its theoretical assumptions are contradictory; while, even among sociologists who see themselves
as working within the constructionist tradition, there are disagreements
about what sorts of analysis ought to be called "constructionist."

CONSTRUCTIONISM'S CRITICS: ATTACKS FROM OUTSIDE

Constructionism offers a dramatic break from the traditional objectivist
approach to studying social problems. Even the term "social problem" has
a different meaning when constructionists use it. Still, some sociologists
who remain more-or-less committed to the objectivist perspective deny that
constructionism represents a genuinely different approach. They argue that
objectivism and constructionism are merely "two sides of the same coin,"
and that the two theoretical perspectives can be easily reconciled.

Most often, these efforts to minimize the differences between objectivism and constructionism only give lip service to constructionist concerns.
For instance, in many textbooks, definitions of social problems mention the
role of subjective judgments in identifying the problems, but constructionist
issues receive no further attention in these books. Such treatments mis-
understand the nature of constructionism, which involves more than ac-
knowledging that definitions of social problems are subjective. By defining
social problems in terms of claims-making, constructionists set a new
agenda for those who would study social problems; their research addresses
a distinct set of questions about the nature of claims, those who make
claims, and so on. Thus, a traditional, objectivist approach to homelessness
might focus on measuring the size of the homeless population, learning
why some people become homeless, or otherwise exploring homelessness
as a social condition, while a constructionist analysis would ask whose claims
brought homelessness to public attention, how those claims typified the
homeless, how the public and policymakers responded to the claims, and
so on. Because the two perspectives define social problems differently and

°Italics added.

focus on different issues, it is no small matter to reconcile objectivism and constructionism in a single, integrated theory.

Other objectivist critics acknowledge that constructionism has a unique approach—one they deplore. They argue that constructionists' focus on claims-making ignores a far more important subject: the harmful social conditions which are the "real" social problems. The constructionist response is twofold: (1) there is nothing wrong with studying social conditions, but decades of objectivist research on social conditions have failed to lay a foundation for general theories of social problems; and (2) it is important to remember that we only recognize social conditions as "really" harmful because someone made persuasive claims to that effect. Again, objectivism and constructionism ask different questions; the relative value of the two sets of questions depends upon what we want to know.

However, the most influential critique of constructionism comes, not from objectivists, but from two sociologists, writing from a subjectivist stance, who charge that constructionists base their analysis on hidden, objectivist assumptions. Steve Woolgar and Dorothy Pawluch (1985a) argue that constructionism is internally inconsistent. They note that, while constructionists identify their focus as subjective judgments or claims, constructionist analyses usually assume a knowledge of objective social conditions. Thus, a standard constructionist explanation might proceed: although social condition X remained unchanged, X became defined as a social problem when people began making claims about it. Woolgar and Pawluch point to the (often unstated) assumption that X was unchanged. Constructionists are careful to identify claims about *putative* conditions as the proper subject for social problems analysis, implying that the nature of the social conditions is irrelevant (and perhaps unknowable); yet they typically assume that they know the actual status of the social condition (as an unchanging phenomenon). For Woolgar and Pawluch (1985a:216), this contradiction is at the core of constructionism: "The successful [constructionist] social problems explanation depends on making problematic the truth status of certain states of affairs selected for analysis and explanation, while backgrounding or minimizing the possibility that the same problems apply to assumptions upon which the analysis depends." Woolgar and Pawluch call this selective attention to objective conditions "ontological gerrymandering."

THE DEBATE WITHIN CONSTRUCTIONISM

Woolgar and Pawluch's critique launched a lively debate among those who saw themselves as constructionists (Gusfield, 1985; Hazelrigg, 1985, 1986; Pfohl, 1985; Schneider, 1985b; Woolgar and Pawluch, 1985b). At issue were the analytic assumptions at the perspective's foundation. What assumptions about the objective social world are appropriate? Should all such

assumptions be avoided, or are some acceptable? What are the consequences of making different assumptions? Constructionists gave different
answers to such questions.

At one extreme are those who might be called *strict constructionists*,
who argue that social problems analysts should avoid making assumptions
about objective reality. In their view, constructionists should examine the
perspectives of claims-makers, policymakers, and other members of society.
The actual social conditions are irrelevant; what matters is what the members say about those conditions. Strict constructionists focus on claims-
making; they do not presume to judge the accuracy of the members' claims.

In fact, because they adopt a phenomenological perspective, strict constructionists question the analyst's ability to make judgments about social
conditions. Phenomenological sociology argues that all we know about the
world is a social construction. This includes the claims that members make
about social issues, but it also includes the analyses that constructionist
sociologists write about claims-making. In this view, the sociologist is not
specially privileged; he or she is just another actor trying to make sense of
the surrounding world. A sociologist who makes statements about social
conditions is simply another claims-maker, one more participant in the
claims-making process. Strict constructionists, then, find little attraction in
reconciling constructionist and objectivist theories, since they view the
members' claims, rather than the validity of those claims, as the subject
matter for the study of social problems. On the other hand, strict constructionists find considerable merit in Woolgar and Pawluch's critique, and they
strive to avoid making (even implicit) assumptions about objective reality.

At the other extreme are those sociologists who treat constructionism
as a synonym for *debunking*. The constructionist stance draws a basic distinction between social conditions and members' claims about those conditions; claims are about putative conditions which may or may not exist.
Sociologists who want to draw attention to mistaken or distorted claims
sometimes describe those claims as "socially constructed." This usage
equates social construction with error, and ignores the way that all claims—
and all other human knowledge—are socially constructed. Debunking assumes that the analyst knows the actual nature of objective reality.
Debunking is the crudest form of constructionism. In fact, strict constructionists would argue that debunking should not be considered a form of
constructionism, that it is objectivist sociology, since the debunker's focus
is the actual nature of social conditions, rather than the claims-making process.

Is there a middle ground between the phenomenological and debunking versions of constructionism? The former seems to constrain the analyst,
who must avoid all assumptions about social conditions, while the latter
loses sight of claims-making as the focus for social problems analysis.

In fact, much—perhaps most—constructionist research seems to fall between these extremes, into what might be called *contextual constructionism*.[2] Contextual analysts remain focused on the claims-making process, yet they acknowledge making some assumptions about social conditions— precisely the sort of assumptions Woolgar and Pawluch warn against. But contextual analysts argue that such assumptions locate claims-making within its social context. For some researchable questions, this context may be unimportant: studies of claims-making rhetoric need not concern themselves with the accuracy of claims or the actual nature of the social conditions about which claims are made. But knowledge about social conditions may help explain why particular claims emerge when they do.

Suppose we study a campaign against "increasing crime in the streets." What might account for those claims? A strict constructionist might note the claims-makers' references to higher crime rates or rising fear of crime. But the strict constructionist would view these references as part of the claims, without making any assumptions that there were really increases in crime or the fear of crime. In contrast, a contextual constructionist might look at official crime statistics or polls measuring the fear of crime—even if the claims-makers never referred to statistics or polls. Suppose, for instance, that claims-makers campaigned against increasing crime at a time when there was no increase in the crime rate. A contextual constructionist might well choose to make something of the discrepancy between the claims and other information about social conditions.

Here, we can see a key difference between strict and contextual constructionists. Obviously, any assertion about social conditions is a social construction. A claim that crime (or the fear of crime) is increasing is just that—a claim. But calling a statement a claim does not discredit it. Contextual constructionists argue that any claim can be evaluated. It may be based on various sorts of evidence, such as official criminal justice statistics or public opinion polls, which are, in turn, social constructions—products of the organizational practices of police departments, polling firms, and so on. Strict constructionists often argue that one set of claims (e.g., statistics about rising crime) cannot be used to explain other claims (e.g., claims-making about "crime in the streets"). But contextual constructionists assume that they can know—with reasonable confidence—about social conditions. They acknowledge the socially constructed nature of crime rates and other information about social conditions, but they assume that such information can be used to (imperfectly) describe the context within which claims-making occurs.

For strict constructionists, such assumptions move the analyst in the direction of objectivism. They note an analyst cannot judge claims without presuming to know more than the claims-makers. Strict constructionists question the basis for this presumption. If all knowledge is socially constructed, how can the contextual analyst claim special, superior understanding of social conditions?

Contextual constructionists incorporate knowledge about social conditions in several ways. In addition to using social conditions to explain the emergence of claims, an analyst may refer to social conditions in explaining why some claims receive attention or shape social policy. Or contrasting claims with information about the social conditions which the claims describe may reveal that claims-makers have used dramatic, atypical examples or inflated statistics.

Contextual constructionism is evident in several chapters in this book [*Images of Issues*] which characterize claims as inaccurate, distorted, or exaggerated. For instance, Best concludes that claims-makers offered inflated statistics for the number of children abducted by strangers; Albert contrasts claims about the dramatic growth of heterosexually transmitted AIDS with official records showing little change in the proportions of homosexuals and drug users among new AIDS cases; Scritchfield uses fertility statistics to discredit claims about an infertility epidemic; and Reinarman and Levine argue that surveys showing little change in self-reported drug use challenge claims about rapidly expanding cocaine use. These chapters (as well as others) use official statistics to assess claims—one of the most common ways contextual constructionists incorporate knowledge about social conditions into their arguments.

Note that analysts can handle official statistics in different ways. In debunking, for instance, one simply accepts the official figures as true, accurate representations of reality—an approach which seems more objectivist than constructionist. But a contextual constructionist views official statistics as social constructions, and is more likely to ask why claims-makers ignore them. Why, when federal surveys found no increase in self-reported drug use, did federal officials mount a campaign against a crack epidemic? Here, the analyst uses official statistics, not to describe actual social conditions, but to assess claims-makers' choices. Did the anti-crack crusaders somehow not know about the surveys of self-reported drug use, or did they choose to ignore the surveys' findings and, if so, why? Treating official statistics as accurate measures of social conditions may move an analyst outside the constructionist tradition, but the error in treating official statistics as claims in their own right is less obvious.

In practice, it may be impossible for an analyst to avoid making (sometimes implicit) statements about social conditions: these claims were made by those claims-makers; those claims-makers have these interests and concerns; changes in the larger society made people more (or less) receptive to the claims; and so on. Even the chapters in this book [*Images of Issues*] which seem to adopt the strict constructionists' narrow focus on claims incorporate knowledge about social conditions. Thus, Baumann suggests that applied social scientists' interest in elder abuse reflects, in part, opportunities for funding for research and intervention, as well as their success in earlier campaigns against other forms of family violence; Gray explains claims-making about popular music as a reflection of larger political and social debates; Troyer argues that the religious and fiscal concerns of some Republican Congressional leaders helped discourage a return to federal pro-tobacco policies; and Loseke warns that the standard typification of wife abuse provides a poor guideline for police encountering family violence. Even though these analysts focus closely on the content of claims, their interpretations depend upon knowledge of social conditions.

Strict constructionism advocates a sort of analytic purity, in which the analyst makes no presumptions about actual social conditions. Yet, in practice, background assumptions about social conditions would seem to play a part in any analysis of claims-making. This is, of course, what Woolgar and Pawluch (1985a) warned against. But it is not clear that the strict constructionist' goal of an analysis free of assumptions about objective conditions is possible. Certainly, contextual constructionist would argue that the strict constructionist stance limits the kinds of questions an analyst can ask.

USING THE CONSTRUCTIONIST PERSPECTIVE

The debates over the theoretical underpinnings of constructionism may give the impression that this is a dry, academic, ivory-tower perspective of little practical value. It would be a shame to end on that note. Once understood, the constructionist perspective can be useful, both for would-be claims-maker and would-be social problems analysts.

Constructionism as a Guide to Making Claims.   Relatively few people achieve national recognition as claims-makers—invited to testify before Congress, photographed for newsmagazines, and interviewed on the evening network news. But not all claims-making occurs in the national arena. Claims-making also takes place in state capitols and city halls, in communities and neighborhoods, at workplaces, and on college campuses—wherever people try to draw attention to what they think are troublesome conditions.

Constructionist research offers valuable lessons for would-be claims-makers. Claims-makers face practical obstacles: they must attract attention, enlist support, and shape policy. Constructionist research shows how other claims-makers have dealt with these obstacles. In a sense, constructionist case studies present guidelines for what works (and what does not), and under which circumstances. Studying sociologists' analyses of successful and unsuccessful claims-making can help would-be claims-makers plan their own campaigns.

Applying Constructionism to New Topics.   While insights from constructionist research can be used to help design new claims-making campaigns, constructionism remains most useful as an analytic tool.

Constructionism is a stance, an orientation, a perspective we can apply to better understand the world around us.

We live in a world where claims-making has become routine. The front page of a typical morning newspaper probably features three or four examples of claims-making. Claims account for large shares of the material presented in newsmagazines, on news broadcasts, before Congressional hearings, on radio and television talk shows, and so on. Usually these claims highlight fresh aspects of familiar social problems—say, a report that researchers have identified another cancer-causing substance. Less often, the claims-makers say they have discovered a brand new problem.

While the media offer a steady supply of contemporary claims, it is also easy to identify historical examples of claims-making. American history, for instance, features campaigns for the abolition of slavery, women's suffrage, temperance, and so on. While more often described as political or social movements, these were, obviously, instances of claims-making.

Whether contemporary or historical, claims can be studied by adopting the constructionist perspective.[3] This requires focusing on the claims themselves, the claims-makers, and the claims-making process.

Claims. The first task in constructionist analysis is to locate examples of the claims being made. The sources for claims vary, depending upon how and when the claims were made, the claims-makers' credentials, and so on, but standard sources include: (1) press coverage—both printed (newspaper and newsmagazine articles) and broadcast (evening network news, "60 Minutes"); (2) scholarly and professional books and periodical articles; (3) popular treatments—trade books, articles in general-interest magazines, or talk shows; (4) testimony before Congressional hearings; (5) pamphlets, flyers, handouts, and other ephemeral materials; (6) public opinion polls; and (7) interviews with claims-makers.

Sometimes it is possible to trace the shifting level of interest in a social problem by measuring the frequency with which a particular type of claim is made. For instance, Albert showed that the number of popular magazine articles about AIDS rose and fell as the disease went through a series of typifications. Sociologists often use indexes to the mass media (e.g., the *Reader's Guide to Periodical Literature*, the *New York Times Index*, or the *Television News Index and Abstracts*) to measure changing levels of media coverage.

Once a set of claims has been located, their content can be analyzed. Several questions become important: What is being said about the problem? How is the problem being typified? What is the rhetoric of claims-making—how are claims presented so as to persuade their audiences?

Claims-Makers. A second focus for analysis is claims-makers. To begin, the claims-makers must be identified. Who actually makes the claims? Whom (if anyone besides themselves) do the claims-makers say they represent? Are the claims-makers leaders or representatives of particular or-ganizations, social movements, professions, or interest groups? With whom are they allied or linked through previous contacts? Are they experienced claims-makers, or novices? Do they reflect a particular ideology? What are their interests—in the issue they raise, in the policies they are promoting, and in the success of the campaign? How does the fact that these are the people making the claims shape the claims which get made?

The Claims-Making Process. Claims evoke varying responses. Some claims are ignored—the claims-makers choose not to pursue their cam-paign and the matter is quickly forgotten. Occasional claims-makers have dramatic success stories: people listen to the claims, and quickly respond by adopting whatever policies the claims-makers recommend. Most often, of course, campaigns have mixed success: only prolonged claims-making produces results; or the claims-makers manage to organize an active social movement, but have difficulty changing social policy; or it becomes nec-essary to mount a cycle of campaigns, each leading to small policy changes. Obviously, claims-making processes are complex, and a good deal of com-parative research will be needed before they can be understood. Some basic questions about any claims-making campaign might include: Whom did the claims-makers address? Were other claims-makers presenting rival claims? What concerns and interests did the claims-makers' audience bring to the issue, and how did those concerns or interests shape the audience's re-sponse to the claims? How did the nature of the claims or the identity of the claims-makers affect the audience's response?

In addressing the various questions raised by constructionists, it is im-portant to remain focused on claims-making, to avoid being distracted by the social conditions about which claims are being made. This does not necessarily mean that conditions cannot figure into the analysis (although strict constructionist analysis requires that the analyst avoid presuming to have special knowledge about them). Certainly, conditions should never become the focal point. Strict constructionists are likely to ask how claims-makers perceive conditions, or how they describe those conditions. Con-textual constructionists may also ask whether it is likely that claims-makers have misrepresented or inaccurately described the conditions, or how con-ditions may account for claims or the reaction to them.

In short, constructionism has become a useful, active research tradi-tion—one which holds the promise of general theories of social problems.

Notes

1. Spector and Kitsuse's (1977) *Constructing Social Problems* and an earlier article by Herbert Blumer (1971) have been the most influential theoretical statements of

the constructionist perspective. Other key documents include Schneider and Kitsuse's (1984) collection of original constructionist essays, and Schneider's (1985a) review article (which lists many early case studies). Of course, many other studies of the social construction of particular social problems have appeared in the meantime.

The constructionist approach to social problems is related to recent intellectual movements in other disciplines, including philosophy, anthropology, communications, literary analysis, and political science. Variously called semiotics, symbolic anthropology, deconstructionism, or constructionism, these movements share a concern with understanding how people assign meaning to their worlds. It is useful to compare studies of social problems construction with work from political science (Edelman, 1988), anthropology (Geertz, 1973), or popular culture studies (Radway, 1984).

2. The split between strict constructionism and contextual constructionism is visible, even in the perspective's central theoretical statements. *Constructing Social Problems* (Spector and Kitsuse, 1977) takes a strict constructionist position, while Blumer (1971) and Gusfield (cf. 1985) reveal the contextual constructionists' willingness to make assumptions about objective social conditions.

3. Spector and Kitsuse (1977:159–71) offer a number of practical suggestions for would-be analysts.

References

Blumer, Herbert. 1971. "Social Problems as Collective Behavior." *Social Problems* 18:298–306.

Edelman, Murray. 1988. *Constructing the Political Spectacle.* Chicago: University of Chicago Press.

Geertz, Clifford. 1973. *The Interpretation of Cultures.* New York: Basic Books.

Gusfield, Joseph R. 1985. "Theories and Hobgoblins." *SSSP Newsletter* 17 (Fall): 16–18.

Hazelrigg, Lawrence E. 1985. "Were It Not for Words." *Social Problems* 32:234–37.

———. 1986. "Is There a Choice Between 'Constructionism' and 'Objectivism'?" *Social Problems* 33 (October/December): S1–S13.

Pfohl, Stephen. 1985. "Toward a Sociological Deconstruction of Social Problems." *Social Problems* 32:228–32.

Radway, Janice A. 1984. *Reading the Romance.* Chapel Hill: University of North Carolina Press.

Schneider, Joseph W. 1985a "Social Problems Theory: The Constructionist View." *Annual Review of Sociology* 11:209–29.

———. 1985b "Defining the Definitional Perspective on Social Problems." *Social Problems* 32:232–34.

Schneider, Joseph W., and John I. Kitsuse (eds.). 1984. *Studies in the Sociology of Social Problems.* Norwood, NJ: Ablex.

Spector, Malcolm, and John I. Kitsuse. 1977. *Constructing Social Problems.* Menlo Park, CA: Cummings.

Woolgar, Steve, and Dorothy Pawluch. 1985a "Ontological Gerrymandering: The Anatomy of Social Problem Explanations." *Social Problems* 32:214–27.

———. 1985b "How Shall We Move Beyond Constructivism?" *Social Problems* 33: 159–62.

Questions for Discussion

1. In what way is Kitsuse and Spector's approach to the study of social problems different from that of Fuller and Myers? How is it different from the focus of labeling theory? Do you think these differences are important ones? If yes, in what ways? If not, why not?

2. According to Randall and Short, what is the most important variable in the development of social problems? What forms can this variable take?

3. What does Stallings delineate as the two processes involved in the social construction of risk? Who influences the construction of risk and how do they do so? Following the Schoharie Creek bridge incident, how was the risk and danger of other possible collapsing bridges constructed?

4. What is the social constructionist critique of the objectivist stance? What are the critiques of the constructionist approach? What is your position in this debate?

Selected References

Best, Joel. *Threatened Children.* Chicago: University of Chicago Press, 1990.
    A social constructionist account of how people, groups, and media came to create varieties of child abuse as a social problem.

Best, Joel, ed. *Images of Issues: Typifying Contemporary Social Problems.* New York: Aldine de Gruyter, 1989.
    This collection examines thirteen social problems from the constructionist perspective. Contains Best's useful distinction of strict and contextual constructionists.

Conrad, Peter. "Medicalization and Social Control." *Annual Review of Sociology* 18. Palo Alto, Calif.: Annual Reviews, 1992, pp. 209–32.
    A review and analysis of publications since 1980 which bear on the role of medical specialists in the construction of social problems.

Conrad, Peter, and Joseph W. Schneider. *Deviance and Medicalization: From Badness to Sickness.* Philadelphia: Temple University Press, 1992. Expanded Edition with a new afterword by the authors.
    The authors show how alcoholism, child abuse, delinquency, drug addiction, homosexuality, hyperkinesis, and mental illness have been redefined over time by

relabeling crimes, habits, or sins as illnesses. An important work in the history of sociological perspectives on social problems. Conrad and Schneider's book helped develop the social constructionist perspective.

Holstein, James A., and Gale Miller, eds. *Perspectives on Social Problems,* vol. 1. Greenwich, Conn.: JAI. Press, 1989.
   Fifteen papers that deal with different aspects of constructionism.

Holstein, James A., and Gale Miller, eds. *Reconsidering Social Constructionism: Debates in Social Problems Theory.* New York: Aldine de Gruyter, 1993.
   In this wide-ranging collection of original articles, Holstein and Miller have assembled views supporting as well as attacking social constructionism. They have also included a number of pieces applying this perspective to a variety of social problems.

Jenkins, Philip. *Intimate Enemies: Moral Panics in Contemporary Great Britain.* Hawthorne, N.Y.: Aldine de Gruyter, 1992.
   Jenkins applies the constructionist perspective to moral panics of the 1980s. He shows how activists, groups, media, and government combine to create social problems of serial killers, child abuse, and satanism.

Kirk, Stuart A., and Herb Kutchins. *The Selling of DSM: The Rhetoric of Scientific Psychiatry.* Hawthorne, N.Y.: Aldine de Gruyter, 1992.
   The authors show how the development of a "scientific" classification of mental disorders resolved on paper the problem of uncertainty in diagnosis. Government, mental health professions, and insurance companies quickly adopted DSM-III.

Miller, Gale, and James A. Holstein, eds. *Constructionist Controversies: Issues in Social Problems Theory.* Hawthorne, N.Y.: Aldine de Gruyter, 1993.
   A collection of papers extending, applying, and criticizing the perspective of social constructionism.

Schneider, Joseph W. "Social Problems Theory: The Constructionist View." *Annual Review of Sociology* 11. Palo Alto, Calif.: Annual Reviews, 1985, pp. 209–29.
   Schneider outlines the social constructionist argument, reviews almost thirty papers published in the journal *Social Problems* that apply this perspective to a diversity of social problems, and notes strong and weak points of this approach.

Schneider, Joseph W., and John I. Kitsuse. *Studies in the Sociology of Social Problems.* Norwood, N.J.: Ablex, 1984.
   A collection of eight papers that deal with various aspects of the constructionist perspective.

III / THE PROSPECTS

9/A SOCIOLOGICAL REVIEW OF THE PERSPECTIVES

The purpose of this book has been to show the different ways in which American sociologists have viewed social problems from the early twentieth century until the present. In this chapter, we would like to review briefly the central themes of the perspectives, their relative strengths and weaknesses, and how they represent different ways of resolving the dual mandate. (The "dual mandate," it will be recalled, refers to sociology's dual goals of solving social problems and of developing sociology as a discipline.)

THE SEVEN PERSPECTIVES: A RAPID REVIEW

The study of social problems is entangled as much with changes in American society as with the development of American sociology. A rapid review of the perspectives illustrates the point. (See Table 1.)

1. Social Pathology. In the early years of American sociology, an optimistic spirit gripped its founders. Committed to a broad social philosophy, they saw their task as the demonstration of how society could grow to fulfill a scheme of natural law and progress. These sociologists became social reformers, and as they focused on the social problems of the day, their work was infused with moral indignation. They formulated this indignation in terms of a medical model, regarding one set of social problems as the work of persons who were "sick"—that is, defective, delinquent, or dependent." At the same time, these early sociologists were also morally indignant at those who occupied command posts in business, industry, and government, attributing many of their actions to vice, greed, corruption, and power.

Today, a revised version of the pathology perspective shows even more concern with institutional arrangements. The moral indignation remains, but now it is the society and its institutions, rather than nonconformity, that modern social pathologists regard as "sick." At the same time, they continue to advocate the moral education of the individuals involved as the solution to such problems.

Table 1. Prime Periods of the Perspectives

Period 1: Establishing a base (1905 to 1918)	Period 2: Forming a scientific policy (1918 to 1935)	Period 3: Integrating theory, research, and application (1935 to 1954)	Period 4: Cultivating specialties (1954 to 1970)	Period 5: Reemergence of macro theory (1970 on)
Social pathology	Social disorganization	Value conflict	Deviant behavior	Critical
			Labeling	Social constructionism

2. Social Disorganization. In the second phase of American sociology, reformism began to give way to a conception of the sociologist as a scientist building a new academic discipline. Sociologists in this period directed their efforts toward devising concepts, developing theories, and producing empirical research rather than making moral, philosophical, or critical pronouncements. Thomas and Znaniecki, for example, argued that sociology must follow in the footsteps of other, more developed, sciences by staking out a special subject matter. In an effort to develop sociology along these lines, sociologists of this period focused on social rules rather than persons in their study of social problems. In so doing, they fashioned the social disorganization perspective, attributing a large variety of problems to a breakdown in tradition, a conflict between rules, or an absence or inadequacy of rules.

3. Value Conflict. During the third period of American sociology, most sociologists continued to argue for the development of sociological theory. Nonetheless, a relatively small band of sociologists began to argue against pursuing the development of sociology as a value-free science. Instead, they advocated working for the benefit of society. As this critical band examined social problems, most of them came to feel that such problems are inevitable because people cannot agree on social policies. And usually the reason people disagree is not because they do not know the rules, but because they hold different values or pursue their own interests. Given the turmoil of the Great Depression and World War II, the value conflict perspective made sense. Whereas the social disorganization perspective encouraged sociologists to remain aloof from struggles within the society, the value conflict position encouraged them to integrate theory, research, and application, and to espouse values and take sides on social issues.

4. Deviant Behavior. Early in the fourth period of American sociology, the deviant behavior perspective came into being. Building on the social disorganization perspective, it continued sociology's orientation as, first and foremost, a science. It assumed that the sociologist's job is testing the implications of theory, rather than solving society's numerous problems. Although people have since drawn on the deviant behavior perspective in efforts to solve problems of crime and delinquency, sociologists in this tradition studied social problems primarily because they had relevance for sociological theory. In the course of specialization, however, these sociologists restricted their attention almost exclusively to the study of deviant behavior, defined as a violation of normative expectations. Thus, this influential perspective on social problems concentrated attention on the causes of deviance, on deviant behavior systems, and on social control.

5. Labeling. Late in the fourth period of American sociology, the labeling perspective arose, in large part from questions left unanswered by the deviant behavior perspective. For example: How do people and situations come to be defined as problematic or deviant? With what effects? And how are some people able to avoid being so labeled even though they may have done something "deviant"? Thus, while the deviant behavior perspective defines social problems as objective violations of normative expectations, the labeling perspective sees social problems as being whatever people say they are (that is, as subjectively constructed). Like the deviant behavior perspective, the labeling perspective is specialized, focusing primarily on social definitions of and reactions to social problems, with little interest in other facets of social problems.

6. Critical Perspective. The political nature of the turbulence in the 1970s led to a focus on social problems as created by the ruling class. This focus carried over into sociology. Some sociologists in this period began to ask whether any of the existing perspectives explained the plethora of social problems being identified or suggested workable solutions for them. Others thought that the perspectives neglected the theoretical in their concern for the socially problematic. Thus, adopting a broader, macro, more holistic view, some writers began to look at how various social problems are related to the political-economic structure of society. Drawing on the numerous and complex strands of the European Marxist tradition, they directed their attention to class relations. Individuals, differently situated with respect to the economic market, came to share interests and values. Their effort to maintain, protect, and further these interests makes for the class struggle, which Marx saw as both the basic source of social problems and, ultimately, their solution.

7. Social Constructionism. Despite years of studying social problems, sociologists have yet to develop a theory of social problems. Spector and Kitsuse said their colleagues failed because either they accepted commonsense definitions of social problems ("what everybody knows") or they as "experts" decided what alleged situations were social problems. Their criticism gave rise to the constructionist perspective. Numerous situations have existed where objective conditions were present, but a subjective definition of a "social problem" was absent. These circumstances gave rise to the constructionists' question, What do people have to do to make an alleged situation a "social problem"? Spector and Kitsuse's answer: people have to work at it. In their words, some people have to come forward and "make claims." Thus, social problems are a social process, they have a natural history, and unless all of the conditions, necessary and sufficient are present, the problem does not "come into being." The necessary condition is the subjective definition while the sufficient condition consists of the actions other people take in response to the "claims-makers' " definition of the situation.

Thus each of seven perspectives has its own emphasis. The social pathology perspective focuses on *persons;* the social disorganization perspective stresses *rules;* the value-conflict perspective looks at *values and interests;* the deviant behavior perspective emphasizes *roles;* the labeling perspective examines *social reactions;* the critical perspective focuses on *class relations;* and the constructionist perspective concentrates on the *claims-making process.*

In addition, each perspective implies its own causal chain by which these elements (persons, rules, values and interests, roles, social reactions, class relations, and claims-making) are linked. For example, both the deviant behavior and the labeling perspectives deal with deviant roles and social reactions. In the deviant behavior perspective, however, deviant roles *precipitate* social reactions, while the labeling perspective regards deviant roles as *consequences of social reactions.* Similarly, in the value-conflict perspective, *values and interests produce roles;* in the critical perspectives *roles produce values and interests.* And, lastly, in the social constructionist perspective *social reactions produce values and interests.*

APPLICABILITY

Each perspective has been more powerful in dealing with some types of problems than others, and each seems more likely to be employed in some cases than in others. In this section, we briefly consider the relative strengths and weaknesses of the perspectives.

When notions about the person as an immoral or dehumanized entity are strongly held, the pathology perspective finds fertile ground. Instances of destructiveness to oneself or others are examples.[1] Unless there are

1. See, for example, Viola W. Bernard, Perry Ottenberg, and Fritz Redl, "Dehumanization: A Composite Psychological Defense in Relation to Modern War," in *Behavioral Sciences and*

clearcut and unambiguous indicators of the "pathological" elements, however, such an analysis is likely to embody merely the analyst's personal prejudice.

The social disorganization approach works best when it is restricted to studying the organization of specific social units and the effects of rapid change on such units.[2] For instance, it is a powerful tool for understanding the disorganizing effects of advancing technology on particular towns (for example, "Hilltown"). The social disorganization approach has been faulted, however, for its failure to provide objective indicators of social disorganization and, in the absence of such indicators, for using abstract concepts to conceal implicit value judgments.

The value conflict approach has proved particularly useful where issues are sharply defined by polarization and conflict between groups. The history of Prohibition is a good example.[3] Where the conflicting values or interests of opposing groups cannot be clearly identified, however, this perspective is not as applicable.

Deviant behavior analysis has had and can be expected to have continued popularity in the study of deviance. Interestingly enough, the strengths of the labeling perspective are precisely the weaknesses of the deviant behavior approach, and vice versa. Where clearly defined and uniformly supported norms are involved, the deviant behavior perspective is relatively straightforward and useful. But where agreement on norms is lacking, and where norms do not have strong social support, the labeling perspective makes a special contribution by focusing on the situational contingencies and consequences of labeling.[4] Thus, while the social processes surrounding such crimes as armed robbery and burglary are likely to be studied more from the perspective of deviant behavior, the social processes surrounding "crimes without victims," such as marijuana use and abortion, are more likely to be studied from the labeling perspective. And when social inequality can be seen to underlie a large-scale problem, the holistic critical perspective may define the problem as the typically expected consequence of capitalist society and culture.

The mass media of communication (popular magazines, newspapers, professional journals) highlight social problems that are likely sources for

Human Survival, ed. Milton Schwebel (Palo Alto, Calif.: Science and Behavior Books, 1965), pp. 64–82.

2. See, for example, Robert K. Merton and Robert Nisbet, eds., *Contemporary Social Problems: An Introduction to the Sociology of Deviant Behavior and Social Disorganization,* 3rd ed. (New York: Harcourt Brace Jovanovich, 1971).

3. See Joseph R. Gusfield, *Symbolic Crusade: Status Politics and the American Temperance Movement* (Urbana: University of Illinois Press, 1969).

4. The affinity of labeling theorists for socially ambiguous subject matter is not theoretically necessary. This focus does, however, dramatize the imputational process. See Prudence Rains, "Imputations of Deviance: A Retrospective Essay on the Labeling Perspective," *Social Problems* 23 (October 1975): 1–11.

constructionist analyses. The media afford numerous opportunities for students to focus on makers of claims, the content of those claims, and the audience. And, perhaps most important of all, they provide the data for exploring in detail the natural history of social problems.

The type of social problem, however, is not the only factor that influences which perspective a sociologist will employ. In the next section, we speculate about some of the other factors involved in the selection of perspectives.

THE DUAL MANDATE AND SOCIOLOGICAL PERSPECTIVES

As we see it, the major point of tension for sociologists studying social problems lies in the dual mandate—that is, to solve social problems as well as to develop sociology as a discipline. In responding to this dual mandate, sociologists adopt four predominant roles. Although sociologists may switch roles during the course of their careers or combine all four roles at once, one of the four roles is usually dominant in the work of any particular sociologist. And along with that dominant role goes a preference for one perspective on social problems over another.

The four roles are theorist, researcher, applier, and critic. Both theorists and researchers focus on developing sociology as a discipline. Theorists develop a network of interrelated propositions that they hope will ultimately explain a vast array of seemingly unrelated events. The social disorganization perspective, for example, contains the nucleus of a theory advanced to explain a broad assortment of social problems. And the labeling perspective has elaborated the theoretical framework of symbolic interactionism.[5]

Researchers, however, seek empirical data. They may derive a set of testable hypotheses from a given sociological theory in order to support or disprove it by means of empirical research. The growing body of studies based on the deviant behavior and labeling perspectives reflects the work of researchers.

For appliers and critics, sociology should work primarily on behalf of society. Appliers draw on the implications of a given sociological theory in order to propose solutions for specific social problems. The deviant behavior perspective has been particularly popular among appliers, and numerous rehabilitation programs have been fashioned along these lines— for example, for juvenile delinquents or drug addicts.[6] The labeling perspective has also proved to be useful in this regard. More and more people

5. See, for example, Earl Rubington and Martin S. Weinberg, eds., *Deviance: The Interactionist Perspective,* 5th ed. (New York: Macmillan, 1987).

6. Opportunity theory was applied in President Lyndon Johnson's War on Poverty and in the New York community-action agency called Mobilization for Youth. For the source of these

have become aware of the negative consequences of labeling various "crimes without victims," and with this increased awareness there has been a trend toward decriminalization.[7] Abortion has been legalized; some states have changed their laws regarding marijuana use; and so on.[8]

Critics tend to protest against the status quo and to seek broader changes in the structure of society (the most extreme being revolution). Since the work of Karl Marx has been the major theoretical inspiration for most critics of society, they tend to draw most heavily from the critical perspective. Prior to the 1970s, though, the critics tended to draw on the value conflict perspective or the reviving social pathology perspective.

In responding to the dual mandate, sociologists also adopt different stances in teaching social problems courses. In the late 1960s and early 1970s, for example, students clamored for greater "relevance" in their college courses. Thus, many sociologists began to give more attention in their teaching to the concrete problems of society than they had in the past and to assume the role of applier or critic in their teaching. This demand was short-lived, however, and today most sociologists have returned in their teaching to a study of the work of theorists and researchers and to the development of knowledge in the discipline.

It is impossible to predict what the future holds. Nonetheless, the interaction between sociology and society promises to continue. As such, it will probably influence sociological perspectives on social problems for some time to come.

Questions for Discussion

1. Now that you are familiar with all of the perspectives, which one(s) do you prefer for analyzing social problems? Why? Does the usefulness of each perspective depend on which particular social problem you are trying to analyze? If so, how? If not, why not?

programs, see Richard A. Cloward and Lloyd E. Ohlin, *Delinquency and Opportunity: A Theory of Delinquent Gangs* (New York: Free Press, 1960). For an application of sociological theory to the rehabilitation of juvenile delinquents, see Lamar T. Empey and Jerome Rabow, "The Provo Experiment in Delinquency Rehabilitation," *American Sociological Review* 26 (October 1961): 679–95. For an application to the rehabilitation of drug addicts, see Rita Volkman Johnson and Donald R. Cressey, "Differential Association and the Rehabilitation of Drug Addicts," *American Journal of Sociology* 69 (September 1963): 129–42.

7. See, for example, Rubington's study of responses to the repeal of the public drunkenness statute in Massachusetts: Earl Rubington, "Top and Bottom: How Police Administrators and Public Inebriates View Decriminalization," *Journal of Drug Issues* 5 (Fall 1975): 412–25.

8. For an example of this approach to juvenile delinquency, see Edwin M. Schur, *Radical Nonintervention: Rethinking the Delinquency Problem* (Englewood Cliffs, N.J.: Prentice-Hall, 1973).

2. Consider some social problem currently discussed in the mass media or among your acquaintances. Which of the perspectives is reflected in the way the problem is conceptualized by each of the following: you, your parents, experts on the subject, journalists, legislators, the people directly involved in the problem, churches, people of different ages, people of different classes? What might account for differences in the perspectives of these groups?

3. To what extent do the perspectives overlap? Can any of the perspectives be seen as, to some degree, subsuming any of the others? Why or why not?

4. Using a social problem that interests you, analyze it from each of the perspectives. What are the major differences among your analyses? Now provide an eclectic analysis, using elements from a number of the perspectives.

Selected References

Blumer, Herbert. "Social Problems as Collective Behavior." *Social Problems* 18 (Winter 1971): 298–306.

A useful theoretical article that combines the value conflict and the labeling perspectives and treats social problems as aspects of social movements.

Downes, David, and Paul Rock. *Understanding Deviance: A Guide to the Sociology of Crime and Rule Breaking.* New York: Oxford University Press, 1982.

A systematic exposition and critique of social disorganization, deviant behavior, labeling, and critical perspectives that draws heavily on British and American theorists and researchers.

Hilgartner, Stephen, and Charles L. Bosk, "The Rise and Fall of Social Problems: A Public Arenas Model." *American Journal of Sociology* 94 (July 1988): 53–78.

Accepts the Spector and Kitsuse approach to the study of social problems. It goes on to establish a systematic method for establishing the conditions under which some situations attain social problem status whereas others do not.

Horton, John. "Order and Conflict Theories of Social Problems." *American Journal of Sociology* 31 (May 1966): 701–13.

Horton makes a number of points about the conditions under which sociological perspectives on social problems emerge and the ways in which sociologists construct definitions, causes, conditions, consequences, and solutions of social problems. He argues that definitions of social problems ultimately rest on assumptions about values and that radical and more liberal sociologists are more apt to construct value conflict perspectives, whereas less liberal and more conservative sociologists are more apt to construct deviant behavior perspectives.

Horton, John, Gerald R. Leslie, and Richard F. Larson. *The Sociology of Social Problems.* 9th ed. Englewood Cliffs, N.J.: Prentice-Hall, 1987.

This textbook on social problems has remained in print much longer than any other. Its longevity may rest on the fact that it examines a changing variety of social problems over the years from three perspectives: social disorganization, value conflict, and deviant behavior.

Julian, Joseph, and William Kornblum. *Social Problems.* 5th ed. Englewood Cliffs, N.J.: Prentice-Hall, 1986.

A leading text that examines a number of social problems through a variety of perspectives and concludes each chapter with suggestions on social policy.

Liska, Allen E. *Perspectives on Deviance.* Englewood Cliffs, N.J.: Prentice-Hall, 1981.

A text that systematically examines social disorganization, deviant behavior, labeling, and critical perspectives according to four headings: concepts, empirical support, critique, and implications for policy.

Mauss, Armand L. *Social Problems as Social Movements.* Philadelphia: Lippincott, 1975.

A textbook with a genuinely new approach to social problems. Blending the value conflict perspective with the labeling perspective, Mauss analyzes social problems as a special kind of social movement.

Merton, Robert K., and Robert Nisbet. *Contemporary Social Problems.* 3rd ed. New York: Harcourt Brace Jovanovich, 1971.

A highly influential textbook that examines social problems from both the deviant behavior and the social disorganization perspectives.

Orcutt, James D. *Analyzing Deviance.* Homewood, Ill.: Dorsey Press, 1983.

Orcutt classifies deviance in four ways, discusses how the various perspectives we described can fit into these categories, and then presents illustrations of how researchers have applied these conceptions to particular cases.

Peyrot, Mark. "Cycles of Social Problem Development: The Case of Drug Abuse." *Sociological Quarterly* 25 (Winter 1984): 83–96.

Shows how, over time, different definitions of drug abuse as a social problem came into being.

Pfohl, Stephen J. *Images of Deviance and Social Control: A Sociological History.* New York: McGraw-Hill, 1985.

This "text about texts" considers how sociologists and others have looked at social problems over time. Pfohl provides a detailed treatment of the perspectives we discussed.

Rose, Arnold M. "Theory for the Study of Social Problems." *Social Problems* 4 (January 1957): 189–99.

A stimulating attempt to reconcile conflict and disorganization theories as a means of both studying and solving social problems.

Rubington, Earl, Martin S. Weinberg, and Sue Kiefer Hammersmith, eds. *The Solution of Social Problems: Five Perspectives.* 2nd ed. New York: Oxford University Press, 1981.

A text-reader on the application of the first five sociological perspectives to the solution of social problems.